SEDUCED BY SECRETS

More fascinating than fiction, *Seduced by Secrets* takes the reader inside the real world of one of the most effective and feared spy agencies in history. The book reveals, for the first time, the secret technical methods and sources of the Stasi (East German Ministry for State Security) as it stole secrets from abroad and developed gadgets at home, employing universal, highly guarded techniques often used by other spy and security agencies.

Seduced by Secrets draws on secret files from the Stasi archives, including CIA-acquired material, interviews and friendships, court documents, and unusual visits to spy sites, including "breaking into" a prison, to demonstrate that the Stasi overestimated the power of secrets to solve problems and created an insular spy culture more intent on securing its power than protecting national security. It re-creates the Stasi's secret world of technology through biographies of agents, defectors, and officers and by visualizing James Bond–like techniques and gadgets.

In this highly original book, Kristie Macrakis adds a new dimension to our understanding of the East German Ministry for State Security by bringing the topic into the realm of espionage history and exiting politically charged commentary.

Kristie Macrakis is a professor of the history of science at Michigan State University. She received her Ph.D. in the history of science from Harvard University in 1989 and then spent a postdoctoral year in Berlin, Germany. She is the author of numerous books and articles on science and politics in modern Germany, including *Surviving the Swastika* (1993) and *Science under Socialism* (1999). She has received grants and fellowships from the National Science Foundation, the Fulbright Commission, the Humboldt Foundation, and the Institute for Advanced Study, Princeton.

Seduced by Secrets

Inside the Stasi's Spy-Tech World

KRISTIE MACRAKIS

CAMBRIDGE
UNIVERSITY PRESS

CAMBRIDGE UNIVERSITY PRESS
Cambridge, New York, Melbourne, Madrid, Cape Town, Singapore, São Paulo, Delhi

Cambridge University Press
32 Avenue of the Americas, New York, NY 10013-2473, USA

www.cambridge.org
Information on this title: www.cambridge.org/9780521887472

First published 2008

Printed in the United States of America

A catalog record for this publication is available from the British Library.

Library of Congress Cataloging in Publication Data

Macrakis, Kristie.
Seduced by secrets : inside the Stasi's spy-tech world / Kristie Macrakis.
p. cm.
Includes bibliographical references and index.
ISBN 978-0-521-88747-2 (hardback)
1. Intelligence service – Technological innovations – Germany (East)
2. Espionage, East German. 3. Germany (East). Ministerium für Staatssicherheit
I. Title.
UB271.G35M33 2008
327.1243′1009045 – dc22 2007028470

ISBN 978-0-521-88747-2 hardback

In Memory of Michael Macrakis (2001), Irene Chryss (2003),
and Charlie Macrakis (2005)

– all good spirits who passed away as this book
was being written

Contents

Contents

List of Photographs, Charts, and Table

CHARTS

TABLE

Abbreviations and Organizations

APN — Foreign Intelligence Service (*Aussenpolitische Nachrichtendienst*), founded in 1951, transformed into the HV A in 1956

BKA — Federal Criminal Office (*Bundeskriminalamt*)

BND — West German intelligence agency (*Bundesnachrichtendienst*)

BStU — Federal Commissioner for the Records of the State Security Service of the Former German Democratic Republic (*Der Bundesbeauftragter für die Unterlagen des Staatssicherheitsdienstes der ehemaligen Deutschen Demokratischen Republik*)

BfV — Federal Office for the Protection of the Constitution (*Bundesamt für Verfassungsschutz*)

CoCom — The Coordinating Committee for East-West Trade

DEC — Digital Equipment Corporation

E/*Einsatz* — The technical deployment department (*Einsatz* means "deployment")

FRG — Federal Republic of Germany

GDR — German Democratic Republic

HV A — Foreign intelligence arm of the Ministry for State Security (*Hauptverwaltung Aufklärung*)

IM — Unofficial staff member – either an agent or an informant (*Inoffizieller Mitarbeiter*)

KfS — Committee for State Security, Soviet Union (*Komitee für Staatssicherheit*)

KGB — Committee for State Security, Soviet Union (*Komitet Gosudarstvennoi Bezopasnosti*)

KoKo — Commercial Coordination Unit in the East German Ministry for Foreign Trade (*Bereich Kommerzielle Koordinierung*)

KTI   Criminal Technical Institute (*Kriminaltechnisches Institut*)
MfS   Ministry for State Security (*Ministerium für Staatssicherheit*)
NSA   National Security Agency, United States
OibE   Officers on a special mission (undercover officers) (*Offiziere im besonderem Einsatz*)
OTS   Technical Operations Sector (*Operativ-Technischer Sektor*)
SED   East German Communist Party (*Sozialistische Einheitspartei Deutschland*)
SIGINT   Signals intelligence
SIRA   System for Information, Research and Evaluation
SWT   Sector for Science and Technology in the HV A (*Sektor Wissenschaft und Technik*)
TBKs   Dead letter boxes or dead drops (*tote Briefkasten*)
VEB   Socialist companies (*Volkseigenebetrieb*)

Preface

What do you think spies are: priests, saints and martyrs? They are a squalid procession of vain fools, traitors too, yes; pansies, sadists and drunkards, people who play cowboys and Indians to brighten their rotten lives. Do you think they sit like monks in London balancing the rights and wrongs?

John le Carré, *The Spy Who Came in from the Cold*, 1963

This book grew out of my personal experiences living in divided Berlin during the mid-1980s. I was not a spy, but rather a Wall-hopper, student, and observer. Although I had read several John le Carré and Len Deighton novels that took place in the spy capital, Berlin, and even knew one of the Cold War's most celebrated spies – Adolf Henning Frucht, a Central Intelligence Agency (CIA) spy who was caught by the Stasi and then traded ten years later at the famous spy bridge, the Glienicke Brücke – I had no special interest in the subject. After returning to Berlin on the eve of unification in 1990 and witnessing the constant fire of revelations about the East German secret police, I could not believe all the secret activity that had taken place behind the scenes of the drab and banal black-and-white world I had experienced in communist East Berlin.

The first layer of secrecy I began to peel away at in a professional capacity was the history of science in East Germany. That quickly led to research on espionage and technology transfer and to a mysterious defector. Pretty soon I was hooked – I read every book on espionage history, started writing about it, and began teaching general courses on espionage during the Cold War. But to truly understand the spy world, I needed to get to know the spies – the agents, informants, case officers, technicians, defectors, and leaders – and that process involved total immersion in the spy world, including extensive interviews, site visits, and friendships on both sides of the Atlantic.

The fall of the Berlin Wall in 1989 created an unprecedented opportunity for historians to examine the files of a defunct intelligence and secret police organization. Yet the organization with the cumbersome name developed to house these files – the Federal Commissioner for the Records of the State Security Service of the Former German Democratic Republic (*Der Bundesbeauftragter für die Unterlagen des Staatssicherheitsdienstes der ehemaligen Deutschen Demokratischen Republik* [hereafter BStU]) – was not intended primarily for historians, but rather for the victims of state security, for retribution and restitution, and for political and educational purposes.[1] Unlike others, I wanted to use these files to reveal the secret methods and sources of a spy and security agency as they related to technology – to write about espionage history.

The major research for this book took place during a Fulbright Year in Berlin, 1998–99. I spent most of that year poring over thousands of files secured by the Citizen's Movement, supplemented with interviews and visits to spy sites. As I read the files, I quickly learned that the Ministry for State Security's function was much more differentiated than the revelations that had peppered the newspapers for a decade portrayed. It was not just an octopus strangling dissent with its repressive tentacles, but also a spy agency respected by former adversaries such as the CIA.

Curiously, it was only after the fall of the Berlin Wall that the pejorative term "Stasi" became widely associated with the East German Ministry for State Security. Before that, it was often referred to as "State Security," "the Ministry for State Security," or "MfS" in the press or in books (although it was apparently used in East Germany in the vernacular). In America, the *New York Times*, our newspaper of record, did not use the term "Stasi" until after 1989. I use both the term "Stasi" and "MfS" in this book; "Stasi" is more widely known but "MfS," as an acronym for the organization's proper name, is a more neutral term.

Writing about secrets is not easy. They are hidden and jealously guarded. They have to be patiently excavated like artifacts at an archeological dig. Underneath the outside layer – the Berlin I experienced – I found an enormous secret world with its own spy culture. Most of the papers from internal security were intact, but foreign intelligence inadvertently only left the bones behind – the names, code names, and material delivered but not the files. In 1998 the BStU managed to decode a massive database forgotten on reel-to-reel magnetic tape, and it was only at the tail end of my research in 2006 that sensitive microfilms acquired by the CIA were released after their return to the Germans. Putting flesh on those bones required reading trial documents from court cases and interviewing the officers and agents themselves. Most of the spy artifacts – the spy cameras, containers, and communication and listening devices – had been destroyed, and I had to hunt them down at exhibits, private collections, and the Western Federal Criminal Office (like our Federal Bureau of Investigation [FBI]).

Seduced by Secrets is pitched at a general audience as well as specialists in history and intelligence professionals. Readers interested in learning more about spying will find the style accessible, and specialists will appreciate the prodigious archival research. Surprisingly, a large portion of the material in the files was deadly dull. Since history is not an argument, but rather a selection of material, I have attempted to bring to life the more interesting episodes surrounding technology. As the title suggests, I have a point to make but illustrate it by weaving analysis into biographies and narrative. Most chapters begin with a description of a person or place. Like Barbara Tuchman, I believe biography provides a prism of history.[2]

Some readers may find the "you are there" approach a bit unconventional, as I occasionally include site visits in the text (anthropologists call similar activities "ethnography"). Although I make no moral commentary about what I witness, I do not remove myself from the scene. The author is your tour guide as we visit a prison inmate, the criminal evidence collection unit, the campus of the technical services division (and the restaurant where they ate), and a dog trainer. Fifty years from now, historians will not be able to conduct such activities.

Are there lessons to learn from this episode in Cold War history in which those in power overestimated the ability of intelligence and security to solve a nation's problems? The early twenty-first century has been a period dominated by the War on Terror. The United States of America has lost its innocence and secured previously open borders. Spying has become a dominant tool in fighting that war, and we as a nation have placed more faith in the power of technological espionage than any country in the world. Perhaps it is time to rethink our strategy.

Acknowledgments

This book could not have been written without the support of numerous people and organizations. Because it is based on thousands of files from the Ministry of State Security, the staff at the Federal Commissioner for the Files of the Former East German Ministry for State Security (BStU) needs to be singled out for their help and support in retrieving and preparing the files. When I arrived in Berlin during my sabbatical year in the fall of 1998, Wolfgang Borkmann was assigned to me as the staff member responsible for my application. We both never imagined that we would be working together for many years beyond the Fulbright year; I returned annually in the summer to retrieve more information. He not only prepared the files for viewing, but, with the absence of finding aids, he had to develop orders based on my areas of interest. It was a pleasure working together, and I am very grateful for his hard work. Heide-Marie Beidokat was also wonderful in helping me to prepare several articles before I began the book. I am grateful to Marianne Birthler, the Federal Commissioner of the BStU, for facilitating access to the *Rosenholz* files in 2005–2006.

The BStU is more than a repository for files. After it opened in 1992, it became the home for a national conversation about the recent past. Over the years, I too took part in these discussions. Thanks to Georg Herbstritt and Helmut Müller-Engbers for inviting me to speak at the 2003 BStU-sponsored conference in Berlin on the work of the Stasi in the West. I am pleased that they were both supportive of my intelligence history approach to studying the HV A, the MfS's (Ministry for State Security) foreign department. Unfortunately, their announced studies on the *Rosenholz* files had not yet been published as this book was going to press.

Numerous former officers and agents of the Ministry for State Security, the Soviet Committee for State Security (KGB), West German intelligence, and the CIA granted interviews and talked to me informally about their work. I am especially grateful to them for providing me insight into their world. Whereas most would like to remain anonymous, I can thank several high-profile people here. Peter Fischer was the first defector I met, and he helped me understand the life of someone on the run. I am grateful that he shared his biography with me and for his interest in the book. It was a treat interviewing the legendary spy chief Markus Wolf several times. I am only sorry that he passed away before this book was published, as I would have liked him to read my version of the history. I would also like to thank my co-conspirator for helping me gain access to a prison inmate.

Museums and criminal evidence collection departments in Germany and America allowed me to view and photograph Stasi artifacts housed at their collections. I am particularly grateful to Helmut Regenhardt and H. Keith Melton. Regenhardt showed me artifacts from the Federal Criminal Police Office's criminal evidence collection, and Keith Melton invited me to visit his fascinating private museum housing spy technology artifacts from all over the world. Thanks also to the Federal German Supreme Court for allowing me to read court documents about science agents.

This book could not have been written without the generous support of the Fulbright Commission and the National Science Foundation (SES 9811494). During later stages, the Humboldt Foundation provided me with a renewal of an earlier fellowship during one summer, and I was awarded several internal grants by my university that provided time to make headway on the writing.

Several friends, colleagues, and students read portions of the manuscript or the initial proposal. I was touched when Dr. Lily Macrakis read the whole manuscript during a summer vacation week in 2006 and encouraged me to hand it in to the Press. I am grateful to Jerry Livingston for his expert reading of two chapters. Tricia Jenkins, Mark Nock, Adam Sanborn, Ryan Sweeder, and Don Laguire each read one chapter and provided helpful feedback. Laurent Dubois and Robin Fleming read the proposal and offered constructive comments. I am especially grateful to two anonymous readers from Cambridge University Press. Their positive feedback and useful suggestions helped shape the final version of the book. I was very pleased when Dr. Charles Molhoek agreed to prepare another terrific index for me. During early stages of the research, Bernhard Priesemuth was helpful and a pleasure to talk to. It was enjoyable exploring Stasi sites with David Crawford.

At Cambridge University Press I am grateful for Lewis Bateman's interest in my work and to Eric Crahan, my editor, for his enthusiasm about the book project and good communication skills. Laura Wilmot did a thorough copyediting job.

Finally, this book is dedicated to three supportive good spirits who passed away as this book was being written: Michael Macrakis (2001), Irene Chryss (2003), and Charlie Macrakis (2005).

Introduction

Seduced by Secrets takes a radically different approach to the history of the East German Ministry for State Security (MfS/Stasi) by bringing the story into the realm of intelligence history and distancing itself from politically charged commentary. By examining the interplay between secrecy and technology at one of the most effective and feared spy agencies and secret police in the world, we can also do what all spy agencies fear: reveal the Stasi's secret spy-tech methods and sources.

Despite the little-known fact that almost half of all its agents planted in the West were stealing scientific and technical secrets and that more than eight thousand staff members at headquarters worked on providing James Bond–like technology to support espionage and security, the Stasi is primarily associated with the omnipresent informer. The general public already knows that husbands spied on wives and children on parents and that East Germany was probably the most spied-upon country in world history.

What the general public does not know is that technology was at the heart of the KGB's (Soviet Committee for State Security) and the Stasi's spying operations against the United States and the West. Whereas the Soviet's foreign intelligence operations have been extensively documented, books on the Stasi continue to emphasize solely the internal repressive arm, yet they too operated like the KGB abroad.

Not only did the MfS steal technology from abroad, they also created some of the spy world's most inventive technological gadgets at home. These activities were two sides of the same coin. Nothing is more secret than identities of agents, and the methods spy agencies use to obtain and communicate secrets. It is precisely these secret techniques that have fascinated the millions of readers of spy stories. Whether they are reading Ian Fleming or John le Carré, readers are mesmerized by the techniques unveiled: the subminiature spy cameras, secret writing, servicing of dead letter drops, running agents, turning agents into double agents, honey traps, surveillance, and a host of other elements of the secret spy world.

What readers often miss by the time the entertainment comes to an end is the purpose the agent hero had in risking his life for the government.[1] In John le Carré's great work of spy literature, *The Spy Who Came in from the Cold*, the drama becomes a great game of spy-versus-spy. Even though James Bond was often trying to keep Western nuclear weapons or code machines from the evil East, the effect the spy films and novels have is to portray the dazzling techniques as ends in themselves.

With the end of East Germany came the dissolution of the Stasi and access to, and preservation of, most of its top-secret files. This was an opportunity to examine the extent to which the real spy world resembled the fictionalized account. Even though we owe a great deal of thanks to the dissidents and the citizens' movement for preserving those files, they did not read them as historians once they were available. Seventeen years after the fall of the Berlin Wall is the right time for historians to investigate the Ministry for State Security's secret operations at home and abroad in the neglected but enormously important area of science and technology.

Ever since the industrial revolution, backward nations seeking to catch up to and surpass their rivals have used industrial and military espionage as a silent weapon. In the twentieth century the Soviet Union stunned the West when they stole America's atomic bomb secrets. During the Cold War, the KGB and the East German equivalent, the Stasi, assaulted the West with an army of secret agents targeting our companies and defense contractors. Recent cases flooding newspapers about Chinese industrial and defense spying against America document the persistence of this quest and the need for historical perspective.

Recent books have begun to document the United States' use of sophisticated technical means like spy planes, satellites, and submarines to gather intelligence during the Cold War. Technical intelligence is usually associated with the American style of espionage; the East Bloc's style tended to favor human spies. The East also incorporated technology into their tools for spies but used it as a complementary, not solo, technique. Because the West underestimated the East's successful use of technology in intercepting and listening to radio messages, for example, this gave the East a surprise weapon.

The Stasi had an effective collection outfit, but the ultimate success of scientific-technical intelligence lies in its integration into the host country. This is where the espionage faltered. It was not just the weak economy that led to failures; *Seduced by Secrets* shows that the Stasi became so caught up in the great game of espionage that it lost sight of its initial goals. Even when the goals were achieved, the daily activities of the spy world – the running of agents, catching spies, tracking enemies of the state, and making spy gadgets, to name just a few – led to the emergence of an insular spy culture more intent on securing its power than protecting national security.

Born during the Cold War division of Germany, the Stasi developed in the image of the KGB with a German personality. In the chaos of the occupation period, 1945–49, the KGB staked an outpost in Berlin-Karlshorst and conducted internal and external operations from the Soviet-occupied territory of East German soil. Meanwhile, communist Germans set up fledgling political police and information structures.

It was not until 8 February 1950, when the German Democratic Republic (GDR) became a sovereign state, that the German police structures from the occupation, such as the K-5 criminal police and the administration for the protection of the economy, developed into the Ministry for State Security. A year later, the foreign ministry set up the Foreign Political Intelligence Service, and thirty-year-old Markus Wolf took over the helm in September 1953. At the beginning, then, foreign intelligence was separate from internal security and the secret police, but both worked closely with Soviet advisors.

Two major events in 1953 – a defection to the West from foreign intelligence in April and the worker's uprising in June – reshaped the German structures, goals, and manpower. In 1956 foreign intelligence moved to the Ministry for State Security's compound in Lichtenberg and became a part of Minister Erich Mielke's empire. Unlike U.S. intelligence, the Stasi combined the roles of the CIA and the FBI/police under one roof.

The close association between foreign intelligence and domestic security is reflected in the organization of *Seduced by Secrets*. Foreign operations make up Part I (High-Tech) and spy gadgetry and counterintelligence are represented in Part II (Spy-Tech) – in other words, first we look at the people and then their techniques.

Whereas other books on intelligence history are sometimes organized around the directorates of a single spy agency, they are usually seen as discrete entities. Further, a similar book on the United States would not include the functions of the FBI because it is separate in geography, organization, and function from the CIA. Because this is a general book about technology at the Ministry for State Security, it includes both their espionage aspirations to acquire the best Western technology as well as the spy technology they attempted to create themselves. Frequently these activities were related; sometimes they were not. While seeking magical solutions to the country's problems by stealing technology, spies used the spy-tech gadgetry featured in Part II. But because foreign intelligence, counterintelligence, and internal security were under one roof, some of the spy technology was primarily used internally for tracking or surveillance.

The book opens in the 1950s with the case of Agent Gorbachev, as he provides a window onto the early years of scientific-technical espionage before it was professionalized into the Sector for Science and Technology. Although the sector's history consisted of more bureaucracy than Bond, it was still punctuated by deaths, kidnappings, and defections as its members stole scientific secrets from the West. Despite massive attempts at maintaining secrecy, a dazzling defector in 1979 and the CIA in 1992 managed to obtain material that helped expose their agent networks. The colorful James Bond–like life of the defector Werner Stiller illustrates how such a crisis squanders energy on the spy-versus-spy game.

A surprising number of Americans worked for the Stasi in computing and electronic eavesdropping. Their two most important sources were Americans who volunteered while they were stationed in West Berlin. Contrasting biographies of "Paul" and "Kid" – who both ended up in Fort Leavenworth Maximum Security Prison – sketch out the spy lives of two of the most damaging and important Stasi Cold War spies.

Computer espionage was the main technological target during the last decade of East Germany's existence, and the final chapter in the high-tech portion of the book tests the success of the espionage outfit and its sources as outlined in the earlier chapters.

Operations and spies need tools to carry out their trade. The second half of the book unveils the secrets of those tantalizing techniques the science spies used – the eyes, ears, and even noses. The invisible is made visible; the concealed is no longer hidden. The opening chapter on the history of the James Bond–like "Q" lab illustrates the Stasi's under-one-roof principle – the Technical Operations Sector (OTS) serviced both foreign intelligence and internal security and counterintelligence.

Spy buffs frustrated by secrecy surrounding invisible ink formulas and methods will finally be able to read about authentic secret writing formulas and how spies used them. They can even follow us into the laboratory as we reproduce them. Standard-issue spy equipment was imbedded in imaginatively conceived concealments, such as cameras in deer statues; the Stasi's big electronic ear was larger than anyone imagined.

Eavesdropping operations were so extensive that they covered counterintelligence, internal repression, and intelligence operations abroad (including Cuba) within one huge bureaucratic roof that was still part of the Ministry for State Security.

Fans of fictional portrayals like *CSI* (*Crime Scene Investigation*), or mystery novels, will be particularly interested in how the Stasi modified and applied criminalistic techniques like radioactive spy dust or smell science to their own work.

This book tells the story of how a spy and security agency was seduced by the power of technological secrets to solve intelligence and national problems, and, conversely, how it overestimated the power of stolen technology from the West to boost its own technological capacities. By doing so it challenges the myth of an effective spy agency. By the time of the fall of the Berlin Wall, the system had become so bankrupt that the spy-tech props of the cloak-and-dagger world had increasingly been brought or bought from the West. Other writers have covered the Stasi's repressive arm – its structures and function as the handmaiden of the state – and other topics such as the churches, the media, and politics.[2] *Seduced by Secrets* concentrates on the spy game, on its methods and sources and on its technology.

PART ONE

HIGH-TECH

I

Agent Gorbachev

It is September 1961, a few weeks after the building of the Berlin Wall on 13 August. A man of medium build, with slicked-back dark blond hair and a bit of a paunch, gets off the West Berlin subway at *Friedrichstrasse*, the location of the main border crossing to East Berlin. The cheap fluorescent lights give his face a greenish pallor as he navigates the maze-like underground passages and walks up to the cubicles of the East German border guards. Attracting the attention of one of the officers, he asks to be arrested.

Agent Gorbachev has crossed the border many times over the three years that he has been passing secret documents to East Germany. But he has never done it quite like this. The newly constructed Wall has made it more difficult to get into East Berlin. Gorbachev is worried because he has not heard a word from his East German case officer since the Wall went up, and he needs money.

Around midnight, Major Erich Pape, the case officer, finally arrives at the train station. He reassures Gorbachev that the reason for the silence was to protect him. Gorbachev suggests another meeting to pass on more material he has collected. Pape reluctantly agrees, but warns that further meetings will have to wait until the situation stabilizes. Later, in his notes on their midnight rendezvous beneath the streets of Berlin, Pape writes that Gorbachev was slightly drunk: He had needed a few drinks to gain the courage to make the journey. As he filed his notes in Agent Gorbachev's dossier, Major Pape surely never dreamed that they would one day become public record.[1] The Ministry for State Security (MfS) was good at keeping secrets.

But in the aftermath of the fall of the Berlin Wall in November 1989, much of the Stasi's vast archive of secrets – containing more than a hundred miles of files and 35 million index cards – has become available for scholars and ordinary citizens to peruse.

Agent Gorbachev – actually a West German physicist named Hans Rehder, who worked at Telefunken and AEG, roughly the West German counterpart of Westinghouse – was one of the Stasi's most prized sources. He sold industrial and technical secrets to the Stasi for twenty-eight years without getting caught. He would remain unknown today if not for a bureaucratic quirk. The Stasi's foreign arm, the super-secret HV A (*Hauptverwaltung Aufklärung*), managed to destroy most of its records before the opening of the archives. But Gorbachev happened to fall under the Stasi's domestic intelligence, or "counterintelligence," unit, by far the largest branch of the Stasi, and most domestic intelligence material was not destroyed. Thus Gorbachev's file, unlike those of many similar agents, was spared the paper shredder and is now a unique window into the workings of scientific and technical espionage during the Cold War.

Agent Gorbachev was far from unique in other ways. Thousands of respectable Western scientists, engineers, and businessmen, including Americans, worked for the Soviet Committee for State Security (KGB) and Eastern Bloc intelligence agencies during the Cold War, tools of organizations that knew exactly how to turn ordinary human weakness to their own ends.

Gorbachev's case can also provide us insight into industrial espionage even as it is practiced today. Since the end of the Cold War there has been an increase in state-sponsored and orchestrated economic and scientific espionage. The CIA was urged to conduct espionage for North American companies during the 1990s, and the National Security Agency (NSA) drew fire from the European Parliament, which alleged that Operation Echelon, a worldwide system used by the NSA to intercept foreign communications, was used for economic and scientific espionage.[2]

Countries such as Japan have proved to be far more capable of turning secrets into products than East Germany ever was. During the early twenty-first century massive Chinese industrial and defense spying against America, reminiscent of the Soviet's Cold War assault, produced considerable anxiety among counterintelligence officials and at companies.

THE MAKING OF A SPY

One thing seems certain: Hans Rehder never planned to be a spy for the communists. He did not have a particular ideological inclination toward communism. Born in 1912, he had joined Hitler's National Socialist Party in 1931 – more likely out of conviction than of necessity, because it was at that time a minority party – and presumably received plenty of anti-communist indoctrination.

Shortly after World War II ended, in 1946–47, the Soviets tried to deport scientists to the Soviet Union, and Americans tried to recruit them to spy for America. In 1946, the U.S. Army's Counterintelligence Corps (CIC) tried to recruit Rehder with the threat that his de-Nazification process would be negative if he did not cooperate. After several hard interrogations, Rehder claims to have had no more contact with them after 1947.[3]

He had never set foot in East Germany before 1957, when he made his initial contact with Stasi agents. From their point of view, however, there was nothing accidental about Rehder's recruitment. As early as 1955, Ernst Wollweber, the first MfS chief, directed staff to work in the West by penetrating West German companies and collecting scientific, technical, and military material to integrate into the economy. In 1956 the governmental Central Committee of the Communist Party amplified this request directly "to support our economy and our research and development installations with all available resources." Later that year, in another top-secret document, MfS chief Erich Mielke detailed the following objective: "The Ministry for State Security has the goal of acquiring, in steadily increasing volume, scientific-technical information and documents from West Germany and other capitalist countries."[4]

Toward this end, staff members created an overview of all major West German companies, in the form of object files, and its officers began systematic recruitment of leading personnel. The MfS had already established a network of domestic informants (called "unofficial staff members," or IMs) and often used these to recruit Westerners through business contacts.[5]

Rehder had been consulting for the (East German) Ministry for Machine Building for several years. An informant code-named "Simon," who worked at an East Berlin company that made radio receivers, struck up an acquaintanceship with Rehder and found out that he was deeply in debt. With a wife and four children to support, Rehder, even in his position as department head for small transmitters at Telefunken, was having a hard time making ends meet. Simon passed the information on to his case officers, who set up a meeting with Rehder at the Hotel Adria. At that meeting, Rehder said he was "ready, inasmuch as he could reconcile it with his conscience, to keep them abreast of the newest developments…

against an appropriate payment." His first payment was five hundred West German marks.[6]

For his first two years as a spy, Rehder did not know he was selling secrets to the MfS, believing he was selling them to representatives of the Ministry for Machine Building. Stasi agents had been using a cover story. Cover stories or "false-flag" operations – when intelligence officers tell a potential agent that they come from another country – were often employed when there was a sense that the potential recruit was hostile toward communist countries. It was not until January 1959 that Rehder's case officers, including Major Pape, apparently revealed to Rehder who they were. The files contain no description of Rehder's reaction to this news; he simply continued, apparently with great eagerness, to pass on company secrets for money. Perhaps the best clue that the Stasi had him in their pocket had come a few weeks earlier, when Gorbachev bragged that he had made an imprint of the key to the company archive. "With this key," he told the officers, "I am in the position to access all company secrets."[7]

The spy agency quickly became Rehder's personal line of credit without repayment or interest. By 1959 Rehder was considered so important that he received a salary of four hundred marks a month, in addition to lump-sum payments for document delivery. During the 1960s, he would receive between four hundred and six hundred marks at each meeting in which technical documents were delivered. In the course of his cooperation, Rehder and his family moved several times and received seven thousand marks for moving expenses. For the Stasi, it was a bargain: Within their first year of meetings in East Berlin, Gorbachev had passed on an estimated 1 million West German marks worth of technical documents; by 1961 that figure rose to 4–5 million West marks.[8]

On the long list of human weaknesses that intelligence agencies have used to enlist new agents, greed has always been one of the most effective. Aldrich Ames, the U.S.'s most notorious traitor, carried out secret files from his CIA office and delivered them to the KGB in garbage bags in exchange for millions of dollars. Klaus Kuron, West Germany's head of counterintelligence, offered to spy for East Germany out of professional frustration and to help pay for his children's education. Many West Germans spied for money; others spied for ideological reasons, for love, or for adventure. It was more common for West German citizens to spy for money than it was for domestic East German informants, who did it more often for ideological reasons or to advance their careers.

Code names were usually assigned to, or chosen by, an agent to protect his or her identity and often referred to characteristics of the agent. For

1. Wodka Gorbatschow. Rehder's code name, "Gorbachev," probably derived from Wodka Gorbatschow (shown here with a martini glass and a Stasi badge from the author's collection), a Berlin vodka manufactured since the 1920s. Gorbachev's case officers wrote that he enjoyed drinking alcohol and occasionally showed up drunk at meetings. (Randy Mascharka)

example, a scientist's code name might contain the word "researcher." Sometimes the code name would be just another German name, say, "Hans Bauer." Rehder received his code name, "Gorbachev," from the cases officers in 1958, even before he officially became an agent.[9] Of course, the future Soviet leader named Gorbachev was at this point unknown, even in Russia. Although no direct explanation for the name is given in the file, a clue may come from the evidence that Rehder liked to drink. Early in his relationship with MfS officers, he would suggest going out for a drink or buying a bottle of sec. He arrived at the *Friedrichstrasse* border crossing drunk at least several times. Perhaps most tellingly, he died of cirrhosis of the liver.

Before the Wall came down, the vodka brand "Wodka Gorbatschow" was regularly available in East Berlin foreign-currency stores. According to the label, the vodka had been manufactured in Berlin since the end of the tsarist period and had been a "favorite drink among Berlin's Russian colony since the beginning of the 1920s." So it is not difficult to surmise how this agent earned his code name.

BUILDING TRUST

Going out for a drink was only one of many ways that the Stasi attempted to get into an agent's good graces. If Gorbachev wanted a vacation in East Germany, they could arrange it for him – for free. In 1958, Gorbachev expressed an interest in vacationing on the Baltic Sea with his wife, Martha. The MfS financed a three-week vacation, arranged for hotel rooms, and provided them with false identity cards in the names of Hans and Maria Schreiber.[10]

On other occasions, the MfS invited Gorbachev and his wife, who selected the code name "Maria," to all-day social meetings in safe houses. To the Rehders, this may have seemed like generosity, but the meetings had a specific purpose: to "build trust" and to tie the agent further to the spy agency. By the fall of 1960, "Maria" had been recruited to assist with the espionage work. The couple was invited to spend a day at a guesthouse in an East Berlin suburb, Grünau. They were served breakfast, lunch, dinner, and coffee. At this meeting they received a twelve-piece set of Meissner porcelain, just one of many gifts that officers presented to Gorbachev over the years.[11]

On several occasions, Gorbachev brought gifts for his case officers. One officer told him that he could not accept gifts, and Gorbachev became upset and angry.[12] Although gift giving for the Stasi officers was part of the job, to Gorbachev it was a token of appreciation and friendship. Surely, the rejection of a gift underlined for him that the relationship was pure business.

In September 1964, the Rehders spent a couple of days visiting several factories, oil refineries, and the socialist city Eisenhüttenstadt. The trip also included a boat ride on the river Spree and meals. The "goal of this trip," reported Major Pape, was to "strengthen the trust of the agents in our state" and to show them the economic progress and building up of the German Democratic Republic.[13]

The case officer–agent relationship was always a complicated and ambiguous one. To some agents, the officer became a father confessor, a psychiatrist, or a close friend. Gorbachev typically met with his case officers once every two weeks before the Wall was built, and about once a month afterwards, and these meetings usually lasted four to six hours.

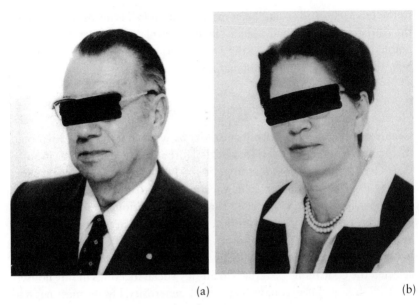

(a)   (b)

2. Hans and Martha Rehder. Hans Rehder (a) was a West German physicist who
worked at Telefunken and AEG. He was one of the Stasi's most prized agents from
1957 until his death in 1985. His wife, Martha (b), was recruited as a courier after
she learned of his spy activity and took active part in passing on technical secrets.
(BStU)

Although the details of personal conversations are sketchy, some sort of
relationship developed over these long hours. In spite of the Stasi's pro-
fessionalism, the friendship must at times have gone both ways. Agent
"Schöbel," who was sent by Gorbahev's last case officer, Erich Lehmann,
often remarked on how lively and charming Gorbachev's wife was, and
he paid her a visit after Gorbachev died in 1985.[14]

A final way in which the Stasi built trust was to bestow medals and honors on its agents. For obvious reasons, the agent was not allowed to take
these tokens of recognition home. Shortly before he retired, Gorbachev
asked to see his various medals.[15] In the West, as far as we know, he was
just another corporate manager. In the East, he was (secretly) a hero of
the state, the owner of a gold medal awarded by order of Colonel-General
Erich Mielke himself.

By socializing with Gorbachev, showering him with largesse, and presenting the East German view of politics (which made up a large part of
every meeting), the Stasi apparently convinced Gorbachev that there was
nothing wrong with what he was doing. Perhaps there is nothing more
chilling than to see the ease of the process by which the hesitant Hans

Rehder of 1957, still struggling with his conscience, was transformed into the confident Agent Gorbachev of 1959, bragging about his pirated company key.

TRADECRAFT

He may have been a purveyor of new technology, but Agent Gorbachev used less gadgetry in his spy craft than one would expect. He never even used a radio transmitter or receiver to communicate with his case officers, even though he was an expert ham radio operator who had trained Nazi security agents in radio communications. Instead, future meetings were usually arranged at the meetings themselves, or by telephone. After the Wall went up, a more complicated system was used whereby Gorbachev would write the time of the next meeting in a cigarette pack and throw it out of the train every Wednesday at 7:05 p.m. Gorbachev also was never trained in any other operational techniques, such as invisible ink or photography, until very late, when he learned microdot photography. In this respect, he differed greatly from East Germans who were groomed to become agents in the West. Gorbachev generally carried documents across the border in his normal briefcase (not one with secret compartments). For a brief period before the Wall went up, his wife transported undeveloped film hidden in a container – in her case a shopping bag outfitted with a secret compartment. Gorbachev was given a different container for transporting material and hiding film at home, but he preferred simply to bring the original documents over the border and bring them back to the office the next day.

Given the lack of disguise in his movements, it may seem surprising that Gorbachev never came close to being caught. "Western counterintelligence could have easily caused considerable damage by concentrating more forces at the *Friedrichstrasse* train station," says Werner Stiller, the most important officer from the foreign intelligence division (HV A) ever to defect to the West during the Cold War. A Western counterintelligence officer with whom I have spoken agrees with Stiller's assessment, but notes that the very high volume of traffic at a metropolitan subway stop made it difficult to track people even when they were leaving briefcases in train station lockers.[16]

On one occasion, Gorbachev's case officers thought that he was in danger of being exposed. In August 1962, an officer from the evaluation department, Walter Thräne, fled to West Germany with his girlfriend, raising the possibility that the identity of East German agents would be revealed to Western intelligence.

In preparation for such an event, the Stasi had already instructed Gorbachev and other agents on a procedure to be followed in which a third person conveyed a warning. The stranger would give the agent a badge showing the Russian gunboat *Aurora*, attached to a pin of the Eiffel Tower, and tell him, "I found this in front of your door; is it yours?" If the agent answered "Yes," then the stranger would report the news. After the building of the Wall, the badge signaled more serious news: It meant "extreme danger, get out of town immediately."[17]

A few days after Thräne disappeared, an agent code-named "Angel" showed up at the Rehders' door with the *Aurora* badge. Around midnight, the couple made their way to *Friedrichstrasse*, where they were picked up by the Stasi and brought to a safe house. There, Stasi officers informed them of the situation and their belief that Thräne knew where Gorbachev worked, and perhaps what his real name was. Gorbachev was unfazed by the possible danger, pointing out that there were many other physicists at AEG, and that because of his position he would not be immediately arrested.[18]

The case officer urged Gorbachev and his wife to move to East Berlin for safety and promised that all their material belongings would be replaced. However, the couple declined to take such a life-altering step on such short notice. Instead, after a quick review of what to do in case of trouble, they returned home via *Friedrichstrasse* at 3:00 in the morning.[19]

In the end, Gorbachev's *sangfroid* turned out to be justified. Thräne was not a real defector; he had left East Berlin for personal and professional reasons. His marriage was on the rocks, and he had recently been demoted from his position as acting head of a division for evaluation to a rank-and-file informant job. Nevertheless, the Stasi did not want to take the risk of having Thräne remain at large in West Germany. They kidnapped him and brought him back to East Germany, where they interrogated him and sentenced him to many years in prison.

GORBACHEV'S HAUL

Gorbachev was the most important Western agent employed by the operational unit for the "protection of the economy," known as Department XVIII, and provided the lion's share of all scientific and technical material collected there. The reason for this bureaucratic anomaly was that the precursor department (Department III – renamed and reorganized in 1964) for protecting the economy had been responsible for company espionage in the West as well as economic security. Some of Department III's agents were transferred to HV A, but Gorbachev was not.[20] He was recruited during a time of bureaucratic flux before foreign intelligence and domestic security/counterintelligence merged under the common roof of the Ministry for State Security.

Of course, most scientific and technical espionage was the responsibility of another division of the Stasi, the HV A's Sector for Science and Technology. This was the group from which Werner Stiller defected in 1979, and also the group to which all Gorbachev's documents were referred for evaluation.

Gorbachev provided the Stasi with blueprints, plans, scientific documents, and some prototypes from two leading West German firms. Between 1957 and 1959 he worked at Telefunken as head of the Department for Small Transmitters and passed on material related to radios and transmitters. After that, he headed up the Department of Automation at AEG until his retirement in 1977. He had the key to the company archive both times.

The MfS had a systematic method for collection and evaluation based on the state's economic plan. Industrial representatives could give the MfS a wish list of plans or hardware needed, and it would attempt to acquire the material. The evaluation department played the important role of intermediary between industry and agent. Not only did it funnel the industry wish lists to its agents, keeping in mind the country's economic needs and each agent's capabilities, but it also analyzed each item collected by the agents, "neutralized" them (in MfS lingo) so that the source would not be known, and passed the information back to industry or to research institutes. Agents could also bring unsolicited material if they thought it would be of interest, but this material was separated from the requested material.

Gorbachev delivered an unusually copious amount of material. The height of his cooperation seems to have been from the late 1950s to the early 1970s. In 1960, the year before the Wall was built, a case officer reported that Gorbachev delivered 505 documents. This seems to have been his record; in most years, unless meetings ceased for operational reasons, he averaged about 200. In 1968 he contributed 202 of the 289 documents acquired by Department XVIII. As he approached retirement in 1977, Gorbachev's deliveries dropped significantly. In the 1980s he was still working for the MfS, but instead of passing on secret documents, he was intercepting Western intelligence's radio messages and finding out their broadcast frequencies.[21]

The material Gorbachev delivered received high marks. In the Stasi's meticulously organized system, the evaluation department graded every piece of material on a scale of I to V, with I being the highest rating: "very valuable." The grades also served as a means of valuing the information; in the mid-1970s, an evaluation of I meant that the document or object had a minimum value of 150,000 West German marks. In other words, this was the amount in hard currency the German Democratic Republic (GDR) would have had to spend to develop or buy the product itself. Gorbachev's deliveries received many IIIs, some IIs, and an occasional I – a fairly typical pattern for a good agent.[22]

The most highly rated material that Gorbachev delivered was related to, as one might expect, the areas of military technology and the computer industry. In the mid-1960s, West Germany began producing a new tank, the Leopard 1, which, among other things, could be "sealed off" from nuclear radiation. In 1968, Gorbachev acquired and passed on an overview of the construction of the Leopard 1, including the operation and maintenance manual. Erich Mielke personally delivered this material to the Soviet Union.[23]

In 1972 Gorbachev passed on a report from AEG about product planning for small computers. The material included the complete information for two AEG computers and matched an order put in by industry. The evaluator gave this material the top grade because he found "such strategic documents of great value for the data processing industry."[24]

A large part of Gorbachev's material – on average, one-third – was passed on to the Soviet Union's liaison officer within the HV A's evaluation department. In 1967, for example, the Soviet Union received the most material from the topic of electronic data processing and process control (eighty-five items). Because Gorbachev's area of expertise after 1960 was automation, it is not surprising that the Soviets also received forty-six items relating to automation in nuclear power plants and machine presses.[25]

Probably the most interesting documents for the Soviet Union were the eight items related to military technology, including six on the Leopard's fire-control computer, which controlled the gun direction. Throughout the 1960s, Gorbachev enthusiastically provided material relating to AEG's work for the North Atlantic Treaty Organization (NATO) and the German Army on the control of torpedoes.[26] He occasionally provided other types of intelligence. In 1958, Gorbachev told his case officers that America was building a radar transmitter in Turkey to keep track of the Soviet missile program – information that was immediately passed on to the Soviets.[27]

Occasionally Gorbachev's work required him to receive additional scientific training. A particular focus of East Germany's economic espionage, from the late 1950s on, was the semiconductor industry. The GDR felt that it was behind the West in this area and sought to pull itself out of this backwardness by acquiring both company secrets and embargoed goods. Their program, conducted jointly with the Soviet Union, culminated in the duplication of the IBM 360 computer. To educate Gorbachev in this new industry, his case officers invited him to a several-day visit at the semiconductor factory in Frankfurt an der Oder in 1961.[28] Thereafter he provided valuable material relating to components for semiconductor research. Later chapters will explore to what extent agents' scientific material from the West helped East German science. But other agents surely shared Gorbachev's telling statement to his case officer: "I'm giving you the best technology available, why can't you use it?"[29]

Gorbachev's espionage may not have helped East Germany as much as it could have. Still, his work, and those of others, should not be dismissed as a harmless game. Western companies lost millions of dollars of business that they could have done with the East Bloc because the GDR and Soviet Union were able to acquire the same goods through espionage. The military secrets, such as the design of the Leopard tank, could have been used against the West had the balance of power ever changed and the Cold War turned hot. Finally, and paradoxically, every document that was smuggled from the West weakened true scientific innovation in East Germany by maintaining its dependence on the West.

Agent Gorbachev was just one of thousands of Westerners who spied for the Stasi and KGB. After the fall of the Berlin Wall, West German prosecutors investigated 7,099 officers and agents; by 1999 they had convicted only 253 West Germans and 23 East Germans of espionage.[30] Agent Gorbachev was not one of these; he died in 1985, five years before German reunification.

2

Stealing Secrets

White-haired, patrician, and proletarian, Heinrich Weiberg was a legend among foreign intelligence staff members and leaders. Until he retired, he rode his bicycle into work at the imposing, grey-stoned *Normannenstrasse* complex of buildings making up Stasi headquarters. He rarely joined the other major generals at their special dining room for lunch; instead, he preferred grabbing a sausage at the courtyard fast food kiosk, the *Imbiss*.[1] He was the founder and leader of the department for stealing scientific secrets from the West, the Sector for Science and Technology (SWT).

Weiberg started working for the Ministry for State Security (MfS) in Berlin in 1951, a year that marked the beginning of a decade of spy-city status for the divided metropolis; it became a breeding ground for spies. Recruitment of agents was rampant on both sides, with the United States, France, and Britain exploiting their perch as occupying powers in the western sectors of an island city that lay in the waters of a communist-run eastern zone of Germany. Likewise, the Soviets used their status in East Berlin and East Germany as a frontline for the emerging espionage wars. The Berlin tunnel was completed by the CIA and British intelligence in 1954 and was exposed eleven months later by the East Germans and Soviets. Hundreds of secret agents were caught and tried in Berlin. Officials were defecting both ways, to the East and to the West. There were many druggings and kidnappings, and, in 1955 alone, the "executioner's axe fell nine times . . . on anti-reds . . . labeled as agents, saboteurs and spies."[2] In the shadows of this intrigue, Weiberg set up a fledgling spy apparatus that traded in cloaks and daggers for business suits and briefcases.

By the middle of the 1950s, Weiberg and his staff developed an efficient pipeline for transferring scientific secrets from Western company safes and military installations into the laps of scientists and engineers working in East Bloc socialist companies. The pipeline began with East German scientists, who gave the sector their wish list for items from the West, and ended in the safes of targeted Western companies and defense contractors.

Like other founding fathers of the MfS, including Markus Wolf, Heinrich Weiberg had spent time in the Soviet Union before returning to East Germany in 1949. Unlike his colleagues who had been part of the prewar communist underground, he had served in the German *Wehrmacht* and was in Soviet captivity from 1940 to 1949. While in the Soviet Union, his only political experience was bicycling with the Red Sports Movement.

Born in Berlin in 1911, Weiberg studied chemistry and on his return to East Germany briefly worked at a sulfuric acid factory before taking on administrative functions at the Ministry for Heavy Industry. After joining the Stasi in 1951, he held leadership positions until his retirement in 1972. He met regularly with Markus Wolf, who thought of him as a "thorough academic" because he lectured to him like a professor on scientific topics such as the fast-breeder reactor.[3]

The Soviet Union played a crucial role in establishing scientific-technical intelligence in East Germany. Not only had Weiberg spent time in the Soviet Union, but Soviet advisers were on hand from Karlshorst, the Soviet compound in Berlin where the Committee for State Security (KGB) had its largest installation in all of the East Bloc, in the country of their most loyal East Bloc friends. The Soviet Union had, and Russia still has, an "acquisition organ" – Directorate T – very similar in nature to the Sector for Science and Technology, and they have a long tradition of stealing U.S. and Western technology through espionage. One of the greatest thefts in twentieth-century history was their acquisition of the United States' plans for building an atomic bomb.

Before foreign intelligence moved to the now infamous headquarters at *Normannenstrasse* in Berlin-Lichtenberg, they worked under deep cover in a lovely villa located at the outskirts of Berlin, using the name "Institute for Economic Research." Markus Wolf was asked to lead foreign intelligence when he was only thirty years old. During one of the service's first meetings in 1953, Weiberg complained that he only had four staff members and desperately needed scientific-technical personnel. Wolf was supportive and urged the Cadre Department to help Weiberg find qualified staff.[4]

One of the Stasi's earliest defectors, Gotthold Kraus, came from the institute and blew its cover in the West. The so-called Vulcan Affair in April 1953 was the first major event that allowed Western intelligence to learn about East German foreign intelligence and its elusive chief, "Mischa" Wolf.[5] This crisis, along with the workers' uprising later that year in June, caused an organizational re-shuffling. The ministry was degraded to a secretariat, and the Institute for Economic Research moved to *Normannenstrasse*. By 1956, the two organizations merged under the roof of the Ministry of State Security, and the institute became Department XV, then known as "main administration A," the well-known HV A.

Kraus handed West German counterintelligence the names of thirty-eight people, listed in a card file. The federal prosecutor later determined that only a handful of these people were agents for the MfS; the others were interesting people they had targeted for future recruitment. West German counterintelligence had caught an early glimpse into East German spy activities against West German businessmen and companies, and this glimpse disrupted East German operations.[6]

Weiberg's department for stealing scientific-technical secrets from the West developed from a relatively small unit – made up of only thirty-five staff members – that analyzed Western companies and recruited agents in the 1950s into the highly bureaucratized, successful Sector for Science and Technology in 1989, with its four hundred staff members and thousands of spies and support staff. The expansion of the Sector for Science and Technology, so renamed in 1971, reflected the importance of science and technology for the East Bloc and the unbridled expansion of the MfS. The sector's success and the importance of scientific-technical espionage is also reflected in the fact that by 1989 40 percent of all HV A agents worked there.[7]

State-sponsored and centrally organized, scientific-technical intelligence was a special feature of East Bloc intelligence. Whereas in the West, industrial espionage during the Cold War usually occurred from company to company, in the East it was directed and steered by the Ministry for State Security. With their orders coming from the Communist Party, which glorified the "scientific-technical revolution," the Stasi was truly the party's sword and shield, as their emblem pictures. The East aspired to not only "catch up to the West," but to surpass it scientifically. The grim reality, though, was that the country was mired in backwardness. As a former intelligence officer graphically put it, the goal of the espionage enterprise was to "make gold out of shit."[8]

Espionage opportunities were easily facilitated in West Germany, with whom East Germany shared a common language and culture. Unlike East Germany, by the 1960s and 1970s West Germany had achieved international standards in science and technology, and this knowledge and equipment had the potential to strengthen East Germany's crumbling scientific and economic edifice, or so hoped the East German regime. Some knowledge could be legally exchanged between East and West, but much technology could not be legally imported or transferred to the East Bloc due to embargo and industrial restrictions. Secrecy prevented internal company information and military science and technology from becoming a free-flowing information exchange. As a result, espionage agencies created scientific-technical intelligence units to meet the county's needs in a growing global technological community.

The trade embargo was one more obstacle East Germany had to overcome to achieve its scientific-technical goals. The West forbade the export of dual-use technology that could be used for both civilian and military purposes. The embargo was enforced through the Coordinating Committee for East-West Trade (CoCom), which developed lists of forbidden technology.[9] From the Western point of view, its technology could be turned against the West; from the Eastern point of view, the technology, especially that of computers, was essential to its survival. Whereas Western commentators have called the committee a "toothless watchdog," an East German high-tech smuggler has described it as "visibly paralyzing the dynamic of the economy in East Germany."[10]

HISTORY OF THE SWT

Robert Rompe, a leading East German physicist, played a pivotal role in the relationship between the KGB and the Stasi during the 1950s, especially in the area of applied physics. Although not an officer like Weiberg, his activity and expertise helped the fledgling sector develop a network of agents in the West. Rompe had already worked for the KGB in the Soviet Union and forged a personal connection between the scientific community, especially the Physical Society, and the MfS.[11] Rompe's industrial espionage activities date back to the Third Reich period. In an interrogation by the Central Committee because of alleged connections to Noel Fields, Rompe admitted to being engaged in "illegal activity before and after his entry (1932) in the [German Communist] Party." During that time he gathered "material on new work in the Berlin electrical industry. It was called BB [Betriebs-Berichterstattung – 'company reporting'] . . . later [he] worked at Osram [a Berlin electrical company]."[12]

Rompe was useful and important to the MfS for both strategic questions and personnel issues. Strategically, he worked together with Weiberg, a close friend, on how to build up the area, and, on the personnel level, he decided who to cultivate and recruit. Because of his towering position in a country as small as the German Democratic Republic (GDR) he exerted an enormous influence on training and placing students. Rompe soon became one of the sector's most valuable agents and was personally handled by Colonel Willi Neumann, deputy head of the sector.[13]

The most direct connection between the sector and the KGB was the Soviet liaison officer stationed in Berlin-Karlshorst, the Soviet's largest intelligence installation outside of the Soviet Union, who received information from the sector, often in the form of lists of the kinds of material collected called "accompanying material list."

Given the favorable conditions for espionage in divided Germany, the industrious character of the German people, and the undivided loyalty of East Germany to its Soviet masters, it is not surprising that, of all the East Bloc countries, the SWT contributed the lion's share of scientific, industrial, and military secrets to the Soviet Union.

During the fifties, both the KGB and Wolf's foreign intelligence department hid thousands of agents in the enormous flow of refugees to the West – there were some 3 million before the Berlin Wall was built in 1961. Among the agent refugees were a number of illegals – agents living abroad with new identities and biographies. Initially, the KGB trained a number of their own illegals – officers who had learned German and were assigned a false identity – but later they also trained East Germans. The highly secret illegals were then deployed in America or West Germany.[14]

The 1950s were the golden years of agent recruitment, especially at West German universities and especially with "migration agents." Migration agents were like illegals, but they often used their real name when they migrated west. East Bloc agencies thought in the long term: a student sympathetic to the regime could be steered in the right direction and then placed in a desired institution by an effective case officer after the student's degree was completed.

While the Soviet Union forged old and new contacts in East Germany, the Stasi started to build networks to work in West German companies and began to establish methods of evaluation. During the mid to late 1950s, espionage concentrated on the chemical industry, although atomic physics began to emerge as a strong focus.[15]

In 1956 Heinrich Weiberg's Department V, which was made up of about twenty staff members, was created for scientific-technical intelligence in the newly founded HV A.[16] Gradually areas of operations numbered 1, 2, and 3 emerged, covering the topics of physics and chemistry, computers, and space and military technology, respectively. Weiberg concentrated on developing operations abroad but not on scientific evaluation of the value of the material gathered through espionage. His officers went to school for political training, to learn how to run agents and to master communication methods. It was hard enough finding politically qualified candidates. As a result, during the early years Weiberg's group rarely had training in science or technology.

A Technology Transfer Switchboard

By contrast, the working group for scientific-technical evaluation created in 1956 employed many scientifically trained staff, who evaluated the material Weiberg's group hauled in from the West. This group began its work a few years after Weiberg but was an independent working group and serviced a number of other departments, including the department for economic espionage, which handled Agent Gorbachev.

The MfS had already installed personnel for "cadre and security questions" at the Office for Technology and the Office for Atomic Research and Technology in February 1956 in order to "prevent enemy elements from penetrating important companies and to keep state secrets." Four months later, in June 1956, the scientific-technical evaluation unit was created. This unit worked together with the one in the Office for Technology.[17]

The evaluation department became one of the most important and enduring units for passing on scientific and technical information from the field to scientists and industry. It was here that the collection of material was coordinated and evaluated. Strict secrecy reigned when it came to protecting the sources' identities. During the mid-fifties, the evaluation unit was central to scientific espionage and emerged as a technology transfer switchboard between industry and scientists, on the one hand, and the acquisition departments, on the other.

The working group's creation reflected the mandate set up during the Third Party Conference to attain an international level in all areas of the economy; the East German Communist Party (SED) thought quick developments in science and technology would help to achieve this goal. The party's slogan was "Modernization, Mechanization, Automation," and it foresaw a new industrial revolution resulting from nuclear energy, heavy industry, and the further development of technical progress. The Ministry for State Security supported the party's goals and greatly increased the volume of scientific-technical information and documents available to East German scientists and industry. Paul Bilke was appointed director of the group.[18]

Unlike his colleagues in operations, Bilke, who was born in Altenburg in 1928, had studied engineering at the Zwickau engineering school. A serious-looking man who could pass as an academic, Bilke joined the unit for economic and company espionage in 1953 before becoming head of evaluation in 1956. Bilke reportedly had an authoritarian style and browbeat his subordinates. By 1962 he had developed a strong group of sixteen staff members.[19]

Bilke's first crisis occurred on 11 August 1962, when his deputy, Walter Thräne, fled to West Berlin with his new girlfriend. Alarm bells went off at headquarters because everyone assumed he defected and planned on providing top-secret information to Western intelligence. Bilke's staff investigated what secret knowledge Thräne could have betrayed to the West, planned a conference to evaluate "deficiencies and weaknesses in political-operational work and in the education of staff members," and analyzed Thräne's personal and work history. Perhaps most chilling were the "operational measures" to find and retrieve the perceived traitor in order to sentence him to death.[20]

Like Bilke, Thräne had joined the evaluation group in 1956. Born on 23 July 1926 in Southeast Germany, he taught biology before entering the ministry in 1955 at the age of twenty-nine and, because of family pressure, had had the requisite party membership since 1946. His new position pressured him to become more politically engaged while attending the party school for Marxism-Leninism; he even earned some medals. As a valued member of the group, the evaluation unit praised him for helping to save industry a million West German marks. That he was highly regarded is reflected in his appointment as deputy director of the group in 1958. Success did not come without a price, however. His wife began to complain about his long hours and overtime as Bilke's deputy. His marriage was soon on the rocks, and he began to look elsewhere for female companionship. During business trips together Bilke brought him to dances where they met women, which often led to "intimate relations."[21]

By 1962, Thräne began to go to dances on his own. In January of that year he met a women twenty years younger at a dance in *Chemnitzerhof* and started an affair that broke his marriage and career. He left his wife after fifteen years of marriage. His work suffered. He began to disobey sacrosanct secrecy regulations and brought his girlfriend to meetings with an agent in Leipzig.[22]

His superiors quickly heard of the affair and applied its "ten laws of socialist morals and ethics." It may seem paradoxical that officers trained to lie and dupe the enemy had an entirely different code of ethics applied to their behavior at the workplace, but State Security considered the marriage vows between men and women sacred. If they discovered that a married employee was having an affair the suspect was called into the supervisor's office to have "a chat." Thräne had such a discussion and was told to bring his family affairs "into order." Instead, his life and health spiraled downward.[23]

Thräne was quickly demoted from his leadership position at the evaluation group to a rank-and-file informant for the "White Fleet" recreational boats on the rivers in Berlin. He hated the job. Two weeks later he fled to the West with his girlfriend through the *Friedrichstrasse* border. He simply asked the MfS border guard on duty how he could smuggle an agent into the West. The guard provided him with the appropriate paperwork, he boarded the subway with his girlfriend, and after a few subway stops was in West Berlin.

Thräne had no intention of supplying intelligence information to Western spy agencies. Instead he sought out one of his agents for help. This agent knew another, more sinister, informant, Arthur Tyroller, who reported the escape to Berlin headquarters. As a result, Thräne and his girlfriend were lured to Austria with the promise of work through an operation called "Action Boxer." They were then drugged, kidnapped, and returned to East Germany by five state security agents.[24]

The interrogators did not believe Thräne when he denied having contact with Western intelligence while in the West. They bellowed at him: "Your claims are improbable. Name the Western secret services with whom you came in contact after you fled!" He admitted to fleeing to the West, and because he worked for an intelligence agency that made him a traitor, but he never told anyone secrets from work.[25]

Thräne's motives had been personal, but still he described his growing disillusionment and the ideological contradictions he observed while working with West German agents. He marveled at the quality of the goods they stole from the West and the inability of the East to turn the results into products. He noted embezzlement at the office that occurred when they received Western goods like radios that were taken from post office packages from the West. The evaluation group soon gained a reputation as a "philosophers club" in which everyone had grown disillusioned with their work and the section head, Paul Bilke. Thräne did not like taking orders from him and would have liked to return to his work as a schoolteacher.

Thräne was initially sentenced to death but the ministry gave him a lighter sentence of fifteens years, even though there was no trial. His girlfriend received four years for "fleeing the republic." She was released from prison in 1966, and two years later Thräne's kidnapping became headline news in the West. Alfred Tyroller, his wife, and the driver were sentenced to four years in prison for the kidnapping. A few years later, in 1972, Thräne was released from prison early as part of a general amnesty. Internal security tried to turn him into an informant but he refused. Instead he spent the rest of his days in the grimy industrial town of Eisenhüttenstadt working in public transportation as a bus driver and administrator.[26] After the fall of the Wall he reported that he had been in solitary confinement for ten years.

The Thräne crisis led to a restructuring of the evaluation group. It merged with Weiberg's operations in 1962, establishing a unique unit within foreign intelligence such that the scientific-technical departments had their own evaluation department (renamed Department V) instead of sharing with the others. With this restructuring Bilke was demoted to deputy director but headed up evaluation again in 1971 with the founding of the Sector for Science and Technology. Harry Hermann succeeded him in 1976.[27] By 1989 the evaluation department, with its 113 staff members, was larger than each of the operation's departments.

Unlike traditional Western espionage, the evaluation of material was centrally organized and situated, and the needs of industry were funneled through the evaluation unit. All scientific-technical material collected by operational units was sent to the evaluators for an estimate of its value.

The first priority was to collect all material – including prototypes, blueprints, scientific papers, and so on – available in the area of science and technology, "neutralize" it so that the source would not be apparent, and pass it on to industry or research institutes. Every precaution was taken to protect the sources from being exposed as secret agents and thus prosecuted. Documents often had "strict source protection" written in block letters at the top. The group was organized to match the economic foci of industry and scientific developments in the GDR and to respond to the army's need for equipment.[28]

The staff members of the evaluation unit, who were all expected to be knowledgeable about science and technology, had constant contact with the relevant ministries. This account was supposed to contribute effectively to industry using the material collected by the spies, and industry was encouraged to provide "concrete tips" on further material to collect. In order to help with "systematic operational work," agents were recruited from the ranks of the "technical intelligentsia" to help with the evaluation of the material.[29]

Evaluators were also recruited from the ranks of scientists and engineers, who officially did not know they were evaluating stolen material, because it had been "neutralized." The material evaluated was usually passed on from the mediating ministries to the scientists and industry. To facilitate this transfer, the Stasi planted personnel at the governmental Ministry for Science and Technology, which was not part of the MfS like the SWT, and passed the information on to scientists so that they would not know it was acquired through espionage.[30]

Each staff member was required to keep up with the literature, to attend relevant lectures, and to keep abreast of scientists' research plans. This knowledge base then helped the evaluation unit create assignments for the agents, who passed on the material to the operational units through their case officers. Theoretically, the evaluation group had an overview of all the operational units' potential to procure scientific and technological material, although later on there was much greater compartmentalization.[31]

After receiving the material, the staff members of the evaluation unit had to provide the operational department with an "estimation of the value of the material." Each document received a grade ranging from "I," the highest, to "V," the lowest. In the mid-seventies an "I" meant the document or instrument had a minimum value of 150,000 West German marks – that is, if the GDR were to develop the research or buy the product itself, it would have to pay that amount in hard currency. At the regional office in Leipzig, the science division drew in 32 percent of all information for that office, and half of the information received marks of I or II.[32]

Because it was relatively easy for the sector to quantify the worth of the information and material collected, it was considered to be one of the most successful units in foreign intelligence. Reportedly the material it collected strengthened the economy by an order of 150 million hard currency marks, whereas the investment had only been 2.5 million marks. During the early eighties, an average of three thousand pieces of information had been acquired for 1.2 million Deutsche marks (the official West German currency, also known as DM) and 400,000 East German marks, while the economic usefulness for the country had been about 300 million East German marks.[33] Although the East saved on research and development costs, it never attained the "world stature" status it craved; instead it was merely struggling to keep up.

Occasionally foreign intelligence proposed its own projects that were not always in the party's plans or counterintelligence's wishes. One particularly noteworthy case was the polyurethane project. The sector had gathered information on, and the blueprints for, this plastic from one of

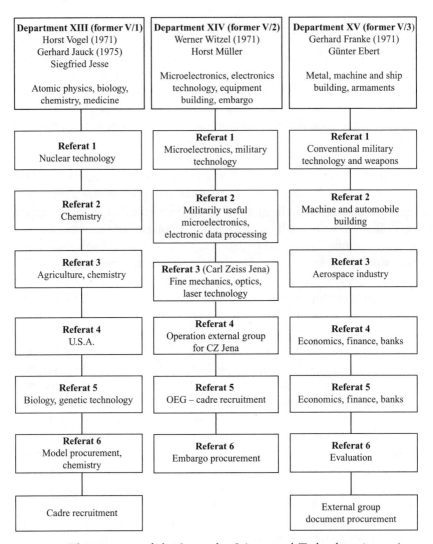

CHART 1. The structure of the Sector for Science and Technology (operations unit).

the successor firms to I.G. Farben, with the intention of using the Western information to build its own polyurethane factory. Markus Wolf and his staff were enthused about the advent of plastics; for them it was "a wonder material," as Wolf recalled many years afterwards. The party leadership, however, was not interested, and it took some persuasion and exploitation of "human weakness" to convince them of its importance. Apparently, the MfS bought Walter Ulbricht, then head of state, a plastic

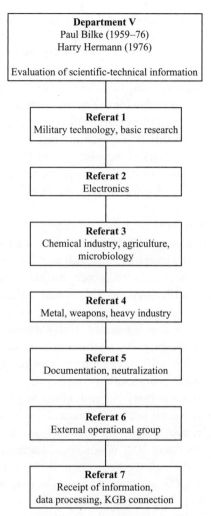

CHART 2. The structure of the Sector for Science and Technology (evaluation unit).

couch on the occasion of his birthday! And this gift convinced them the project was worth pursuing.

MORE BUREAUCRACY THAN BOND: ORGANIZATION OF THE SWT

The spy bureaucracy's staff members developed dossiers on agents, wrote reports, and shuffled paper from the in tray to the out tray, but the boredom was punctuated by the trappings of the secret world – case-officer meetings in exotic locales, ideological pep talks at the safe houses, secret communication methods, and the exchange of secrets for money.

1971 saw a change in leadership and style for East Germany. The avuncular Walter Ulbricht was replaced with the stiff Erich Honecker as head of state. It is not surprising that the security service expanded, since Honecker had been responsible for overseeing state security in the central committee. Like Ulbricht, Honecker glorified science and technology and promoted the advancement of "key technologies" such as microelectronics. The seventies saw a marked increase in East Bloc scientific-technical espionage. This expansion of espionage efforts reflected the importance of science and technology for the Warsaw pact's efforts at modernization and defense preparedness.

In a move that was more bureaucracy than James Bond, in July 1971 the science and technology unit underwent a major reorganization, and Department V increased its stature and staff as it became the independent Sector for Scientific-Technical Intelligence (*Aufklärung*), with three operational departments: XIII, XIV, and XV, as well as the one devoted solely to evaluation: V.

Weiberg was now head of the sector, and Wilhelm "Willi" Neumann was his deputy. Like Weiberg, Neumann was born in Berlin in the teens of the twentieth century (1913), came from a working class family, had spent time interned in Czechoslovakia (1945–48), and, most importantly, had joined the Communist Party in 1949. Horst Vogel, who later became synonymous with the sector because he assumed its directorship in 1975, was head of Department XIII, Werner Witzel head of XIV, and Gerhard Franke head of Department XV. When Vogel assumed leadership of the whole sector, Gerhard Jauck succeeded him in Department XIII.[34]

By the end of the GDR there were approximately five hundred SWT staff members.[35] There had been considerable expansion from the some thirty-five officers in the fifties to the five hundred in the 1970s and 1980s. The operational arm consisted of approximately 188 to 197 staff members, including officers, drivers, data entry personnel, and secretaries. The 1970s and 1980s saw the greatest number of new recruits. The younger generation had a higher number of staff members with scientific, technical, or economic backgrounds. Many had the American equivalent of a college education (a *Diplom*), and nineteen staff members had the equivalent of a Ph.D. Even though the three operational departments primarily dealt with recruiting and running agents, they still organized their work around the various scientific disciplines.

Department XIII (formerly Area V/1) was responsible for both basic and applied research in atomic physics, chemistry, medicine, biology, genetic technology, and agriculture.[36] Before the Wall fell, the West knew more about this department than any other because of Werner Stiller's 1979 defection. He provided details of the operations in the area of atomic physics and technology. He exposed key agents at the Karlsruhe Nuclear Research Center and at IBM and showed how his unit infiltrated institutions like the Physical Society in East Germany and the Karlsruhe Center; the secret information collected from Karlsruhe was passed on directly to the Soviet Union. Not only did the Soviet Union desire to know whether West Germany was building nuclear weapons, but the information was also useful for its nuclear power industry.

A subdepartment for American operations was established after the 1973 opening of the GDR embassy in the United States. In reality, most contacts were West Germans who had some kind of association with the United States. In 1989 the U.S. unit only had two West German sources – "Wolga" and "Traeger," five prospective agents, four recruiters, an investigator agent, and one with a cover address. It is not clear if they had any sources that were U.S. citizens or non-German foreign nationals.

Department XIV (formerly Area V/2) worked primarily in the area of computers both for military and civilian use. The department worked closely with the company Carl Zeiss Jena in computers, optics, and laser research. In an interview with the author, Markus Wolf called Jena "a child of the HV A." The cooperation between internal security's economic counterespionage unit (XVIII) and Jena exists to make the claim believable. The sector strongly supported the firm Carl Zeiss Jena after the Politburo Resolution in 1983 to build Jena into a center of excellence. The foreign department provided Carl Zeiss Jena with embargoed laser technology from the United States and strongly supported the secret military technology project 016 – a "cooperative" project with the Soviet Union to manufacture an infrared guided missile for ships.[37]

More telling is the fact that the computer espionage unit opened a "branch office" with its own evaluation unit at Carl Zeiss Jena in 1962 in order to directly service the company with information and material. Zeiss Jena was probably the most successful and internationally known company in East Germany and was especially known for its excellence in optics. The Stasi recognized Jena's old tradition of scientific excellence and the favorable "operational preconditions" created by the community of scientists affiliated with the university, institutes, and big companies.[38]

Department XV (formerly Area V/3) found a place in the espionage hall of fame through its success at acquiring Western military technology through its penetration of West Germany's most important defense contractor, *Messerschmidt-Bölkow-Blohm* (MBB). The Bavarian company

3. The author and Markus Wolf during an interview at a Berlin café. (Kristie Macrakis)

became a gushing fountain for the KGB's unquenchable thirst for top-secret rocket science and military technology information. One of the SWT's most applied departments, Department XV's other targets included banks and banking, space and aviation, and machine and vehicle building. Seemingly less successful was its involvement in economic espionage in banks and other economic institutes, though several undercover case officers seemed to have achieved a coup when they pilfered some information from Dresdner Bank in the 1980s.

There were at least half a dozen agents caught during and after the Cold War who worked at MBB, and one can only imagine whether there were any left undetected or who worked solely for the KGB. Several of the MfS agents acquired the complete set of blueprints for West Germany's tank "Leopard 2" and fighter plane "Tornado." The military technology was passed on to the Soviet Union.

The three operational units and the evaluation unit were at the core of the Sector for Science and Technology, but the sector also maintained several modestly named "working groups" that had managed to recruit quite a large number of agents by the 1980s. Working Group 1 was one of the most secretive units and was responsible for establishing legal and illegal residencies abroad. It prepared scientists for foreign service in the GDR's trade missions or, later, embassies, and worked with other East German citizens abroad, such as students or technicians. It was so secret that its unofficial staff members were not included in the comprehensive statistical files left behind as part of the CIA-acquired *Rosenholz* files. Nominally headed by Jauck, a young electronics engineer, Achim Lehe, took over in 1988 after serving as an officer there since 1975.[39]

About half of the officers in the residency group were also "officers on a special mission"; their case officers were colleagues from the group. Special mission officers were deep cover agents who actually held jobs in foreign countries in other areas of life, like the Ministry of Trade or Ministry of Science. Between 1972 and 1989, the residency hauled in more than 21,000 pieces of information, almost half of which came from the science attachés in Washington, DC.[40]

Because East Germany was not able to establish embassies abroad until 1972 due to the Hallstein Doctrine, their spy agencies were late in establishing legal residencies. Whether legal – through an embassy – or illegal – by sending "illegals" into enemy territory with new biographies – the foreign department did manage to extend its tentacles to many parts of the globe, including the United States. In his memoirs, HV A chief Markus Wolf writes, "Our main espionage efforts on American territory were devoted to expanding our knowledge of its science and technology," yet he claims failure in this endeavor because of blanket FBI surveillance and avoids referring to any specific cases from the sciences.[41]

The identities of two highly productive Washington, DC, agents were kept secret for many years, and anyone who stumbled across their code names – "Koren" and "Froebel" – speculated that they were treasonous Americans. Instead, these two stars turned out to be deep cover officers who were the science and technology counselors at the East German embassy in Washington, DC. Konrad Grote worked at the embassy between 1980 and 1985 and was ostensibly from the Ministry for Science and Technology. Hans-Joachim Zabel succeeded him and stayed until the fall of the Berlin Wall in 1989.[42]

Konrad Grote had a long career as a deep cover officer. He received a college degree in chemistry and became an agent in 1964. He was on the staff of the East German trade mission in London from 1969 until 1973, when he joined the Ministry for Science and Technology. That same year he was sent to Vienna as a member of the Ministry of Science and Technology working at the International Institute for Applied Systems Analysis, a

nongovernmental East-West think tank for science, where he stayed until
1976. It was during his time there that he became a full-time officer at the
Sector for Science and Technology in 1974, but spent the rest of his career
under deep cover. After his time in Washington, DC, Grote returned
home to the Ministry for Science and Technology, where he became head
of the Department for Capitalist Industrial Nations in 1988.[43]

During his five-year stint in Washington posing as the science coun-
selor, Grote passed on more than four thousand pieces of open source
material to the MfS. Despite the lack of secret material, Grote's haul predominantly received grades of II and III, with the overwhelming majority
receiving IIIs. The material he gathered was typical for science attachés
and provided an overview of science and technology in the United States
with a focus on defense-related issues and computing. He collected much
of this information while attending conferences and symposia. Samples
of the material include items like a report from Stanford on recognizing
chemical weapons material, one from the University of Southern California on using computer image analysis in the military, and many others
from the Department of Defense on general matters like how to conduct
foreign military sales.[44]

Like Grote, Zabel originally joined the MfS in Halle and worked at the
Ministry for Science and Technology, and, like Grote, he delivered a copious amount of material while he was in Washington – more than five thousand pieces of wide-ranging open source material. Unlike Grote, he never
finished high school and joined the Stasi in 1962 after a lively party career
as secretary for the Free German Youth. When he left Halle in 1980 for
Berlin he immediately became a deep cover officer in Washington, DC.[45]

Both Grote and Zabel worked in the United States during the decade of
the caught spy; this made their work very difficult because of the constant
FBI surveillance. During the 1980s about sixty spies in America who
worked for the Soviet Union and other East Bloc countries were caught,
in part, because of Ronald Reagan's clampdown on illegal technology
transfer and offensive against the "Evil Empire" and, in part, because
there had been an increase in spying. Among those spies caught were
several East Germans, including the controversial Alfred Zehe, a physicist
who reportedly bought classified material. His American lawyer saw this
case as a classic entrapment operation: an undercover naval intelligence
officer was sent to Embassy Row peddling outdated secret documents
on submarine sonar detection technology as bait. Zehe was arrested in
1983 and pleaded guilty in 1985, but was quickly exchanged – along

with three other East Bloc spies in America – for twenty-five spies from the communist side at the infamous spy-trading bridge in Berlin – the Glienicke Bridge.[46]

Back in Germany, however, the HV A had better luck, especially in recruiting American military men who lived in their own backyard. The three most successful American science spies lived in Germany and delivered sensitive material on electronic warfare: "Kid" (Jeffrey Carney), "Paul" (James Hall), and "Optik" (still unknown).

Considering that Working Group 3 for military technology ran at least eleven active sources in West Germany by 1989 and maintained six recruiters, it is puzzling that it was only considered a working group. Founded in 1978, its existence demonstrates the importance of defense-related information in the 1980s, especially information officially banned by the embargo. Its successes included two German sources working at the U.S. Army in Augsburg ("Hannes" – Michael Schoab, an officer – and "Acker" – Richard Krohe, a repairman), several sources in leadership positions in computer hardware, and the fact that it had more contact people – seventeen – in 1989 than any other department.[47]

Working Group 4 developed data-processing techniques and projects, and Working Group 5, headed by Stiller's former boss, Christian Streubel, was responsible for "using official contacts" in the area of science and technology, which included evaluating reports received from the travel cadre. Together all three working groups maintained about sixty staff members.

The new bureaucratic structures for scientific-technical espionage and the transformation of several departments into a sector in 1971 reflected an expansion of interest in science and technology and followed on the heels of the founding of Directorate T in 1967 in the Soviet Union. The status lift was also a reward for the scientific-technical successes of the 1960s. Whereas, during the 1950s, foreign intelligence sent hundreds of "migration" agents to the West in the stream of refugees, after the building of the Wall, the new challenge was to recruit Westerners as spies. And recruit they did. By 1989 at least thirty West German sources and backup staff recruited in the 1960s were still active in the West, and this was only a fraction of the initial recruitments.[48]

The increase of spying in West Germany in the late sixties did not go unnoticed by Western counterintelligence. As a result, West Germany began to be called the "world's busiest espionage center." The epicenter of this spying had shifted from the Berlin metropolis to the sleepy capitol on the Rhine – Bonn, West Germany – the inspiration for John le Carré's *A Small Town in Germany*. The capitol was reportedly "swarming with foreign agents," primarily from East Germany, the Soviet Union, and Czechoslovakia. Western officials had pieced together bits of information in a mosaic, but surmised that, with a concentration of NATO troops and arms in the center of Europe, Germany had become a "treasure chest for Eastern agents seeking military and scientific secrets."[49] That counterintelligence might be on the rampage scared some scientists – presumably spies – enough to return to the Eastern Bloc.

Guns not Butter

Whereas Weiberg spent the early sixties overseeing the growth of the sector and incorporating other industrial espionage units into his fiefdom, by the late sixties, there was greater emphasis placed on collecting information on military technology. During the late 1960s Erich Mielke directed Weiberg to increase the acquisition of prototypes, models, and documentation in military technology, including conventional weapons, airplanes and missiles, military electronics, ABC weapons, anti-weapons, and military vehicles.[50]

The HV A instructed all departments to gather information about military policies and plans from the United States, NATO, the Federal Republic of Germany (FRG), and China. Leaders specifically targeted armaments research and production in the United States and other NATO countries and "the development and production of new strategic weapons and weapons systems."[51] Two turning points occurred that sparked interest in military intelligence collection – one in 1969, in the aftermath of the Prague Spring, and another in 1984, in the wake of the Soviet's RYAN program, which sought to neutralize what they thought was a U.S.-planned nuclear strike.

1969 saw a major increase in staff for the sector, as thirty-four new positions were created. There was a reorganization so that collection in military technology was separated from tasks for the economy, with renewed emphasis placed on the collection of prototypes in military technology.[52]

Military strategy and acquiring information on military technology were of much greater importance than has been portrayed by defectors, leaders, and journalists, who often characterized the espionage as traditional industrial espionage. Between 1969 and 1989 the HV A general evaluation department VII received 7,293 pieces of information from the military technology unit (XV) – more than the other departments combined. Erich Mielke emphasized to Markus Wolf the importance of military technology, and Wolf's subordinates itemized the type of technology to look for.[53]

The MfS's acquisition of military technology greatly aided the Soviet Union, which had suppliers of information from all the East Bloc satellites. The United States grew especially concerned about the Soviets' acquisition of military technology in the 1980s and took active measures to put a stop to it. In fact, a white paper lists several hundred examples of "Soviet Military Equipment and Weapons Benefiting From Western Technology and Products," including tanks, missile technology, communications, radar, and microelectronics.[54]

By the late sixties, military and scientific-technical espionage were about equal in importance and effort expended. Typically, most of the military espionage was passed on to "friends" – the Soviet Union – and sometimes to the East German Army.[55]

In the first half of 1971 alone the sector acquired sixteen military-related items, including information on the successor to the *Starfighter*, the *Phantom*; information on the "enemy's" estimation of Warsaw Pact weapons systems; and documentation for NATO's communication system, as well as information from West Germany's leading companies on data processing. West German work on the fast breeder reactor fascinated Weiberg and was a high-priority target, as was the plutonium production of West German "imperialism."[56]

Some of the spy work seemingly involved regular business practice or traditional economic espionage. In 1971 the GDR's foreign trade ministry saved 15 million (it is not clear whether this is East German marks or DM) on the price of an atomic power plant because of material acquired on world market price comparisons. In addition, the Minister's Council used documents acquired to negotiate the price of gas and oil transportation through pipelines.[57]

Of course, the division's primary focus was the acquisition of scientific-technical plans, blueprints, documentation, and prototypes from the West for use by East German scientists or industry that matched the GDR's glorious five-year plans for the economy. It is not surprising that in the sixties and early seventies they collected information on polyester (to clothe the East German population), polyurethane (the plastic wonder material), and the fast breeder. By the early 1970s there was already strong interest in components for the computer industry such as solid-state circuits and other electronic instruments for data processing. Surprisingly, the division also acquired an ion implanter in 1971 – the sort of hardware item usually reserved for the shady commercial trader Alexander Schalck during the eighties. It was farsighted to have an interest in these huge, heavy, expensive machines, which were used to manufacture computer components. Weiberg thought it was a "real" but not "realized" way to manufacture computer components.[58]

The value of items was often represented as the amount of research and development costs saved as a result of espionage. During the first half of 1971, the ministries for chemistry, electronics, and machine building saved 26,333,000 marks (East German) for a total of fifty-seven institutes. Chemistry was still a major priority, and its ministry oversaw the most institutes (thirty-five), but the Ministry for Electronics saved 14,861,000 marks at its seventeen institutes.[59]

Professionalization and Crisis

Unlike the founding generation, by the early seventies more staff members had university training in science or technology than not. Whereas Weiberg had a scientific background, Neumann, his deputy, had worked as an offset printer before entering the MfS in 1952. During the seventies there was a drive to recruit officers with B.A.'s or M.A.'s (the *Diplom*) or even Ph.D.'s. Before this drive, the atomic physics unit, for example, consisted of a book printer, a guard, a wood engineer, a long-time security man from internal security, a Marxist-Leninist graduate, and a mechanical engineer.[60]

The Stasi usually recruited stalwart communists or, later, people from workers' or farmers' families. Constant selection criteria throughout the GDR period were SED membership and Free German Youth (*Freie Deutsche Jugend* or FDJ) membership. This was all part of the GDR's "affirmative action" program.

Horst Vogel, who became the leader of the sector in 1975 and influenced its direction and development a great deal, did not initially have training in science or technology but later went on to receive a degree in engineering. Born in Saxony in 1931, Vogel came from a working-class background. He first learned a trade as a locksmith and then attended university between 1952 and 1955 without earning a degree. His ambition was to become a teacher, before a kind, white-haired gentleman approached him to join the spy agency, which he did on 1 March 1955. He was twenty-four years old. He attended the HV A school during the academic year 1955–56 primarily for political education and some spy tradecraft. He returned to the university – the Technical University of Chemistry in Leuna-Merseburg – between 1 May 1968 and 31 August 1970, where he studied chemical economics and received a *Diplom* in engineering. This gave him the working papers to become an administrator. He became subdepartment head in the operations unit and quickly rose in the ranks after that, becoming deputy director of the whole HV A in 1987. His former subordinate and defector, Werner Stiller, has characterized him as an "espionage man in heart and soul" and a leader, but he also viewed him as intimidating. The mere mention of the turncoat's name used to make Vogel turn red in the face with anger: "No one wants to talk to him ... he's a miserable figure."[61]

Vogel used to live with other MfS generals and leaders in a villa near a lake in the exclusive section of northern Berlin called Obersee. After the Wall fell he moved to a socialist apartment building in the center of East Berlin. Although the living room had a nice view of the city, the apartment was a demotion, nothing like what he had when he was in power and donned a general's uniform. In the early post-Wall period he acted like a defeated general whose country has been occupied: "They [the West Germans] have our archive."[62]

The seventies was a productive decade for the Sector for Science and Technology, and it quickly gained the reputation of being the most effective foreign intelligence unit. Leaders hired new and better-educated staff members, and case officers recruited top agents, established productive residencies, and in general expanded the science and technology area significantly. But the decade also witnessed some serious setbacks for Markus Wolf and his associates. The West Germans launched "Operation Registration" – a methodical examination of suspect identification papers deposited at the registration offices. In the decade 1972–82, this operation yielded about two hundred MfS illegals that were living under assumed names in the West. In 1974, Günter Guillaume, aid to West German chancellor Willy Brandt and the spy who brought down his chancellorship, was exposed, bringing about one of the most celebrated spy cases of the Cold War. Only two years later the husband-and-wife team Lothar and Renate Lutz were arrested in 1976 for passing on super-secret defense information, which led to the arrest of sixteen other East German spies. West German counterintelligence was on the warpath. By the late seventies, the notorious Romeo method – whereby a man seduces a woman with access to secrets – was also uncovered. Whereas half a dozen secretaries in Bonn governmental offices were victims of this technique, it does not

appear to have been successful as a recruiting method in science and technology, probably because most sources were men.[63]

Rather than scaring spies away from the profession, the Günter Guillaume scandal inspired a West German, Wolfgang Rudolf ("Herzog") to
volunteer in 1974. He traveled to East Berlin and presented himself to the
porter at the doors of the Stasi headquarters near the Magdelena Street
subway stop and offered himself as an agent. The case officer was suspicious that the West German was a plant and undertook a thorough
background check. "Herzog" became one of the science division's most
productive agents, providing secret information from his employer, High
Temperature Reactor Building (HRB), for fifteen years. At his trial in
1994, he claimed he wanted to "make a contribution to securing the balance of power between East and West and to contribute to peace."[64]

Another 1970s success story was the establishment of one of the most
productive illegal residencies in the sector's history. Activities at the residency began with Horst Müller's recruitment of Rudi Wein, an Austrian
businessman sympathetic to communism. Horst Müller was a tall, slim,
friendly, dark-haired man who could easily be mistaken for a diplomat
rather than a spy. After all, he had spent five years behind diplomatic cover
at the GDR embassy in Berne, Switzerland. The Wein recruitment was just
one in a series of successes for Müller, including obtaining the plans for
nylon in the 1950s that led to his promotion to the head of the computer
division and acting director of the SWT in the 1980s. Gradually as more
and more agents were added, Vienna became a GDR-intelligence colony.
Front firms were established with strong connections to the GDR; many of
them banked in Switzerland and Vienna. The majority of the information
passed on to these front firms originated in Silicon Valley in America.[65]

Rudi Wein was allegedly a friend of the shady businessman Udo
Proksch, who was implicated in the sinking of the ship *Lucona* in the
Indian Ocean. Together, Wein and Proksch set up a high-technology firm
called Kibolac. By the end of the 1960s Kibolac had successful business
and trade contracts with East Germany. Many other firms involved in illegal technology transfer were also set up, including Rudolf Sacher Inc. and
Lylac.[66]

In the winter of 1968, Rudi Wein, Rudolf Sacher, and Karl-Heinz
Pneudl, a physicist, traveled to East Germany to meet with alleged business partners. A man calling himself Horst Winkler greeted them and
introduced himself as a staff member at the Ministry for Science and
Technology, a common cover for SWT officers. Winkler was in reality

Horst Müller. He received them warmly and arranged their hotel accommodations, visa procurement, and business appointments. At the time, they did not know they were dealing with intelligence professionals.[67]

In 1968 Wein, Sacher, and Pneudl received a patent from the East German patent office for an electronically controlled heating system modeled after a West German prototype. For this work the Kibolac firm received a fee of 1.2 million shillings. By 1971, a formal contract was signed in East Berlin between Rudi Wein (in the presence of his lawyer, Karl Zerner) and the heads of the SWT, Horst Vogel (cover name Horst Knorring) and Willi Neumann (cover name Willi Peter).[68]

When Müller took a posting at the East German embassy in Berne, Switzerland, under the cover of the first diplomatic secretary in 1972, Dr. Peter Bertag, head of the American unit, replaced him at the Vienna Residency.

When Stiller defected in January 1979, he blew the cover for the Vienna Residency. Stiller was not involved in running the residency, but he learned about it by reading Peter Bertag's – his officemate – files upside down across the desk.[69]

Although the HV A suffered setbacks during the seventies, its prized science unit was thriving. It came as a great surprise when first lieutenant Werner Stiller defected. He brought secret documents and a vast knowledge of the history, structure, organization, and operations of his atomic secrets department, as well as a general knowledge of the sector and of foreign intelligence operations. Until this point Western intelligence knew very little about the sector, though they had seen an increase in economic espionage during the 1970s. Stiller's defection was a real coup for West German intelligence; they celebrated it for many years after. Not only did Stiller's betrayal of his own agents lead to their arrests, but it provided the West Germans with clues to pursue other agents planted in West German companies and research institutes. Within months seventeen agents had been arrested. The Stiller defection also called renewed attention to the extent to which East Germany had penetrated West German institutions for science and technology as well as governmental agencies.

Compartmentalization was increased, departments reorganized, and Stiller's immediate superior, Christian Streubel, was placed under surveillance because Mielke thought the West German intelligence agency (*Bundesnachrichtendienst* or BND) might try to recruit him.

It seemed like Stiller's defection was infectious when Werner Teske, a captain from the SWT's economic unit, was imprisoned for allegedly committing espionage on 11 September 1980. Investigators found a copious amount of secret departmental material in his washing machine. In fact, Teske was not a copycat case, because he had been collecting material since 1976 and had planned to defect as early as 1978. However, he decided against it, because he could not bring his wife with him.[70]

The Ministry for State Security had approached Teske about becoming a full-time case officer when he was completing his Ph.D. at the Humboldt University in economics in 1969; he had already served the SWT as an instructor for two years. Although initially reluctant to give up his scholarly life at the university, he started working at the MfS the day after he defended his thesis on using statistical methods in budgets for the "state organs." Teske had planned to complete his *Habilitation* (a second dissertation) in order to become a professor and had previously never thought about working for foreign intelligence. When he was recruited, SWT officers promised he would be able publish his thesis and pursue the *Habilitation*, but a year later, in 1970, they reneged on their promise.[71]

After the novelty of working for a spy agency wore off, Teske grew nostalgic for life at the university, where he had the freedom to set his own hours, working at home if he wished. Whereas he had loved his work at the university, he grew discontent with his professional spy life. He told the interrogators investigating the case after his arrest: "On 31 August 1969 my activity at the university ended." It was a place that "brought me great joy," a place where "I was recognized," a place "where I was important and respected," and a place "where my opinions meant something."[72] Teske never understood why the MfS recruited a scholar with a Ph.D. (he was one of nineteen Ph.D.'s in the division) because his scholarly work had nothing to do with his spy life and felt that they had "destroyed" his professional goals. He told interrogators that he did not especially like making new contacts, a crucial skill for case officers. The defection was to be his revenge. The military-like organization, taking orders from superiors, and pushing papers at the office conflicted with his expectations and with his previous bucolic academic life. As his professional life spiraled downward, he drank an increasingly large amount of alcohol to numb his unhappiness.

On the surface, Teske appeared to be a successful case officer. He ostensibly ran fifteen Western agents – whom he called "patriots" – and had recruited seven GDR backup staff. In reality, many of his agents were no longer active or were not strategically placed. Interrogators focused on the four inactive agents, including "Ford." One extremely productive agent Teske ran was "Jack," a civil servant at the Ministry of the Interior in Köln.

"Jack" was apparently recruited with a false-flag operation in which the recruiter claims to work for a friendly spy agency. He could win a prize for the copious amount of material he passed on – more than two thousand pieces of quality information from 1973 to 1989.[73]

Although Teske consistently received bonuses and medals throughout the 1970s, his work began to deteriorate in 1976, and he was disciplined in 1978 for his behavior, which included dishonesty, deceiving his bosses, using work time for personal time, and drinking. The same problems resurfaced again in August 1980, and Teske was dismissed, because he again used work time for personal activities and lied to his bosses when they questioned him. An investigation began, which led to more serious accusations, including fabricating a report about a new contact and embezzlement. His bosses found that he had embezzled more than 40,000 marks – half East marks, half West German marks – by skimming money from his agents and instructors and falsifying receipts and other paperwork. He used the money at intershops to buy Western chocolate, coffee, clothes, and luxury items not available in the East and gave them to his family as presents on holidays. When the ministry searched his apartment they found thousands of pages of secretly filmed files on his agents and notes and copies of directives in the laundry room.[74]

Lengthy interrogations lasting more than half a year followed Teske's imprisonment on 11 September 1980. Not only did the court desire a confession, but interrogators also probed Teske to discover his motivation for committing treason.[75]

Most of the taped interrogations were conducted in a cool and professional manner. Teske was polite and forthcoming in his answers. He volunteered everything he knew and all information on his motivation, the chronology of his deeds, and the material he took. His admission that his intention to defect was premeditated was used against him in the final verdict. When an interrogator asked what he planned on doing once in the West, Teske replied that he wanted to work as a scholar doing research at one of the West German "East Research Institutes." At this point the interrogator lost his temper and bellowed at Teske, telling him that this so-called research was "enemy activity" directed against the GDR, that the East Institutes were controlled by Western secret services, and that he would be working with other East German traitors.[76]

After Stiller's defection and the MfS's inability to retrieve him to carry out the death sentence, the state seethed with institutional anger. Even though Teske never actually contacted Western spy agencies or fled to the West, he was sentenced to death for an especially serious case of espionage and for his intention to flee the country. His defense attorney's meek attempt at reducing the sentence fell on deaf ears. The harsh sentence was not meted out to set an example to other officers, as the trial was a secret military tribunal. On 26 June 1981 he was shot in the back of his neck, Soviet-style, at a Leipzig prison.[77] He paid the price for Stiller's success. He was the last spy to be executed before the state abolished the death penalty in 1987.

After the Stiller defection, collection decreased in his unit, but increased in the areas of computing and military technology during the last decade of the MfS's existence. The eighties were also the decade of the caught spy and the period when Ronald Reagan launched his aggressive attack against the Soviet Union and its minions. During the early 1980s, another hurdle was placed in front of the East Bloc when the CIA began "Operation Exodus" in an attempt to reduce the flow of illegal imports to all East Bloc countries. As one intelligence officer put it, "it became increasingly difficult to bypass the embargo." As a result, Horst Vogel set up a new group in 1987 to increase efforts at bypassing the embargo.[78]

THE OTHER PIPELINES

The SWT was not the only pipeline for facilitating the flow of Western scientific-technical and military secrets to the East. Counterintelligence – through its economic unit – also ran a number of agents in the West. The Ministry for Foreign Trade was another secret channel that worked semi-legally and legally in the West. They had a division euphemistically called "commercial coordination" or KoKo, headed by Alexander Schalck-Golodkowski, the shadowy figure whose corpulent build belied his indulgence in Western culinary pleasures.

Schalck's activities ranged from gun-running to trade in antiquities to illegal technology transfer. He had a close working relationship with the HV A and its leaders, Markus Wolf and Werner Großmann. The HV A and KoKo cooperated primarily in economic and scientific-technical espionage. He provided them with laundered funding and shared business contacts in the West and helped camouflage important activities, primarily through dummy front companies. KoKo was generous, supplying some 400 million West German marks in cash between 1987 and 1990.[79]

Two of the important dummy front companies included Interport, an industrial representative, and Intertechna, GmbH (which is an abbreviation for *Gesellschafter mit Beschränkter Haftung*, a category of capitalistic company that uses its own capital to cover its investments; usually not found in communist countries). They were founded on the initiative of the SWT in 1965 and 1969, respectively, but were bureaucratically placed under KoKo and located in East Berlin. The bureaucratic organization was complicated. The MfS did not legally own Intertechna because it belonged evenly to VEB (*Volkseigenebetrieb*, the term for East German socialist firms) Kombinat Zentronik Sömmerda, VEB Kombinat Robotron, and the KoKo firm Interver International Representative, GmbH. Horst Müller, head of the computer division (XIV), managed the personnel issues and business activity. In reality, this company was a pure import outfit used to acquire key technologies and microelectronics for the MfS and GDR industry. West German business partners included IBM Roece Inc., Vienna, and Siemens.[80]

By contrast, Interport was a pure HV A firm and was officially involved in the buying and selling of old-timers, but its real activity was the acquisition of prototypes and technologies from modern agricultural equipment to microelectronics. Robotron was its chief beneficiary. Because Interport had no official foreign trade rights, it was officially a KoKo firm Intrac.[81]

Whereas KoKo concentrated on acquiring equipment, especially computers, during the fifties, sixties, and early seventies, the SWT was engaged in typical espionage work – stealing blueprints, plans, scientific information, and so on, via agents scattered throughout the West. With the launching of the Microelectronics Program in 1977, the SWT established a special unit for importing embargoed goods, and it used front companies in Switzerland and Austria in order to transfer technology to the GDR through a "Western" company.

The SWT also performed a broader array of functions, such as surveying science and technology in West Germany through an analysis of institutions and their personnel. By definition, the task of scientific-technical intelligence included the "acquisition and analysis of the scientific-technical achievements of the enemy." The rationale for collecting information on Western nuclear weaponry and military technology was to anticipate the "surprise moment."[82]

Drama worthy of spy novels – the defections, the kidnappings, the deaths, and the money laundering – peppered the bureaucratic and operational routine of the Sector for Science and Technology. This often led leaders to lose sight of their initial goal of boosting East Germany's sagging economy through scientific-technical espionage.

AFTER THE FALL

After the fall of the Berlin Wall in November 1989, chaos reigned at Stasi headquarters. Leaders worked on developing a successor organization

called the Office for National Security in which foreign intelligence and
domestic security were no longer under one roof. It was not until unification was announced in March 1990 that the future of the Stasi as a
non-entity was clear. The Round Table – the government-sponsored group
responsible for making decisions about security issues and intelligence –
gave the HV A permission to destroy its files with the justification that
all countries have foreign intelligence and that the public is not permitted access to those secret files. Most of the files were case files on agents,
but a vast amount of directives and internal personnel files were officially
destroyed at the *Hohenschönhausen* campus in northern Berlin.

Western spy agencies pounced on the files and leaders like vultures. West
German counterintelligence and the criminal police approached officers
and offered immunity from legal prosecution in exchange for information
on important agents. As a former officer put it: "The West Germans came
first in a threatening and disrespectful way, then the CIA came with their
bags of money and respect for our work."[83] The CIA was most aggressive
in trying to turn leaders like Markus Wolf and Jürgen Rogalla, the head
of the U.S. department, offering upwards of a million dollars in exchange
for the really important agents and information on the KGB. In 1990 the
CIA also managed to acquire the HV A's crown jewels – the complete
microfilmed card catalogue of all their agents![84]

Only a small fraction of SWT officers willingly provided information to
West German security officials. One of these was Frank Weigelt, deputy
head of Department XV's *Referat* 3 for military technology. He defected
to West German counterintelligence, known as the *Bundesamt für Verfassungsschutz* or Federal Office for the Protection of the Constitution (BfV)
in April 1990. With his information, Western intelligence expanded its
knowledge of the SWT and could collect all his agents as well as information that led to their arrest.

Weigelt claims that his motivation for providing Western intelligence
with information was his fear that the KGB was going to take over many of
the top agents. The prime example he used was that of Dieter Feuerstein, a
West German engineer who worked at MBB, the military manufacturing
firm. Feuerstein had already expressed an interest in continuing his work
for the KGB in 1989, and in March 1990 SWT leaders prepared to pass
on their prized agent. Feuerstein, on the other hand, argues that Weigelt
set up a trap meeting on the streets of Berlin in May – after he switched
sides – in which he attempted to shuttle him into a waiting KGB car.[85]

Feuerstein was not the only Western national agent willing to work for
the KGB after the fall of the Berlin Wall. About 3.8 percent (19 out of

500) of agents investigated by West German prosecutors were asked by the MfS if they would continue to work with the KGB. At least four agents, including Feuerstein, agreed. Another West German who worked for the MBB – "Tom" – was initially recruited by the MfS's Karl-Marx-Stadt regional office in 1983 and was passed on to the KGB as a direct agent one year later and run under a false-flag operation, as his handler was an MfS officer. He began to work for the KGB again in 1995, was unmasked in 1997, and was brought to trial in 1999.[86]

Vladimir Putin, later president of Russia, was the KGB resident in Dresden between 1984 and 1990 and recruited foreigners and East Germans to work for the KGB under unofficial cover. Klaus Zuchold, a MfS technical officer in Dresden, met Putin in 1985 and by January 1990 Putin recruited Zuchold, asking him to be a sleeper agent while gathering information on politicians, businessmen, and scientists and telling him in the process about East German agents he had recruited. This relationship did not last long, as Zuchold reported Putin to West German counterintelligence officials in December 1990, blowing his spy network.[87]

Putin made friends with other MfS officers when he was in Germany who later became important and influential figures in Russia. One of his best friends was Mathias Warnig, a former SWT officer from the Department for Rocket Science and Technology (XV/3), who became the head of Dresdner Bank's Russian division. Warnig joined the MfS in 1975, when he was twenty years old, and a year later started studying at the Economic College in Berlin, receiving the equivalent of a college degree with a major in economics in 1981. In 1985, the same year Putin went to Dresden, Warnig was assigned to the group to establish residencies in the West (Working Group 1). This was a new development, and Warnig was trained and then sent to Düsseldorf in 1988 to recruit new agents. He became acting head of the SWT's Department XV/3 in 1989 and was sent to Dresden in October to cooperate with the KGB.[88]

After enrolling for management training at Dresdner Bank, Warnig was hired at their Berlin offices in March 1990. He reportedly told officials there that he had worked for the Ministry for Economics, the cover he used during Cold War times, because he knew that volunteering a Stasi biography at the time was professional suicide. He was sent to St. Petersburg in 1991 to open a new operation and by 2002 had become head of Dresdner Bank's Russian division.[89]

Cases like Feuerstein, Putin, Zuchold, and Warnig demonstrate that Western intelligence's fears that the Soviets would turn Germany into a recruiting ground and hub for espionage were well-founded, especially during the immediate post-Wall period. The playing field became increasingly treacherous for agents, however, after the *Rosenholz* files were returned to Germany in 1993. Nevertheless, Western counterintelligence continued to ferret out new cases of Soviet espionage into the 1990s. One of their chief targets after the Cold War continued to be scientific-technical intelligence.

Periodically, German and American newspapers carried alarmist headlines reporting on the activities of the Russian foreign intelligence at German firms. In 1999 there was a flare-up, and the *Berlin Morgenpost* reported that German industry should be on the lookout for Russian spies. In early 2005 magazines reported that Germany and America were "crawling with Russian spies." There were reportedly 130 Russian spies working undercover in Germany, targeting companies and scientific research institutes as well as political parties and the army. This prompted *Time* magazine to use the title of the old Cold War film *The Russians Are Coming* to characterize the onslaught.[90]

3

Hero, Traitor, Playboy, Spy

Peter Fischer enjoyed his new life at the campus of Washington University in St. Louis, where he was studying for an MBA. As an older student of thirty-four, he appreciated the student life of studying, reading, and meeting pretty girls. It was exciting unlocking the secrets of the stock market and by the time he finished his degree in 1983 he would become a "Master of the Universe," one of those stock market gurus.

People on campus who knew him thought of him as different because of his strong German accent and the fact that he had fled the communist East, where he had been a physicist at a fiber institute in Magdeburg, East Germany. He did not learn English until the summer before he started classes in 1981. He used to brag that he made 65 percent on the English section of the GMAT (Graduate Management Admission Test) after a semester of studying English and that he knew all the words in the dictionary. There was no question that he was a very intelligent man with an "amazing memory."[1] He had recently grown a mustache and his blond hair had become shaggy, framing his warm brown eyes. Handsome and affable, he had a muscular, athletic build and usually wore T-shirts and jeans and looked like most of the other American college students.

Although he adapted fairly quickly to life in America and made friends easily, he was often homesick and drove the five hundred miles to Chicago to watch Lufthansa planes take off.[2] He was totally cut off from friends and family in Germany. It had to be that way. He tried to suppress thoughts of the past and tapped into his adventurous streak for diversion. He took flying lessons and had other hobbies, such as windsurfing, scuba diving, hiking, skiing, and adventure sports like skydiving.

After completing his degree in 1983, Peter Fischer secured a job at the prestigious, private stock brokerage firm Goldman Sachs. During Goldman's summer training session in New York, he met a young, warm

New Yorker with Mafia connections. During their first date at Harry's Bar on Wall Street, he told her he loved her and wanted to marry her. They got married in August and flew to London, where he worked for Goldman's as a fixed income salesman; he then became head of continental sales in Europe and DM trading.[3] He made a six-figure salary and millions for the company. He had come a long way since his modest upbringing in the communist East.

As he sat on his balcony at his apartment in St. Louis in the summer of 1981, he began to reflect on his life and what brought him here. Why not write a book, he thought? Most of the students had lived ordinary lives: they had grown up in the suburbs and planned on attending college, getting a job, and getting married. His life was different. His real name was not Peter Fischer, he never worked in Magdeburg, and he did not exactly flee the communist East as he described. He wished he could tell people about his past, but he could not. The biography was created to protect him. Any slip of the tongue, wrongly placed trust, could threaten his life. He would write about his experiences, leaving out the part about his new identity and the biography supplied to him by the CIA's resettlement center. The West German intelligence agency (BND) had actually encouraged him to do it soon after he arrived in West Germany on 18 January 1979; they would later edit the manuscript.

WERNER STILLER

Peter Fischer was in fact Werner Stiller. He had been a case officer in the Ministry for State Security's Sector for Science and Technology for seven years. When he was finishing his physics degree at the Karl Marx University in Leipzig, local recruiters spotted, observed, and recruited him into the department for stealing nuclear secrets from the West. At the time, he outwardly displayed a conformist attitude toward the East German communist system. He has been an active member of the Free German Youth (*Freie Deutsche Jugend* or FDJ) from the time he was fourteen years old and held several leadership positions, including secretary; he joined the East German Communist Party (SED) in October 1968.[4]

Stiller was born out of wedlock on 24 August 1947 in the small town of Wesmar, near the highly industrial and grimy town of Merseburg, Leuna. His mother's husband was a prisoner of war, and in his absence she started an affair with Stiller's father, a blacksmith, who died when Stiller was seventeen. According to Fischer, they did not have a close relationship: "He wasn't a fine man, he even killed someone." His mother brought him up with his two older sisters. A high school teacher recognized some science talent in Stiller and suggested he go to the university and study physics. Although he had ability, he did not always apply himself and ended up with a grade of 2 (like a B in America) by the time he graduated and wrote a physics masters thesis on "Electron Spin Resonance Spectroscopy (ESR) – Research on Free Radicals in Fluid and Gel Phases."[5]

To make ends meet he also worked as a waiter during college. After a brief marriage to a high school friend ("In order to get an apartment. In the apartment one finds that you're not compatible."), he met a pretty young Hungarian woman, Erzsebet, while waiting tables at the Leipzig trade fair. After a passionate affair and many of Stiller's monthly visits to Hungary, the two got married in July 1970 and settled in Berlin in 1971, the site of his new job. He truly loved her, and liberal Hungary also offered a connection to the West. At first he worked at the Physical Society as an informant by day and as an agent at the ministry by night. During this time he learned some tradecraft, such as initiation of personal contacts, surveillance techniques, and servicing a dead letter drop. After a series of tests, he joined the ministry full-time in 1972 as a lieutenant. Even then he was known as someone who had a weakness for women, and he reportedly told a co-worker that there should be more of them to decorate the Physical Society.[6]

At first he felt uncomfortable at the Physical Society because he had to negotiate with the more senior scientists as equal partners. He quickly overcame these problems, and his physics expertise allowed him to understand their work. In the presence of academics he made "his opinion on the leading role of the working class and judgment on West German imperialism clear." According to this enlistment recommendation, "the candidate has a strong class point of view and solid political knowledge which he knows how to use . . . he has proven himself to be politically reliable, ready for deployment and a disciplined comrade, who has promise." The report also praised his character: "The candidate is an open, flexible, intelligent, multi-interested comrade who integrates himself well into the collective."[7]

After a semester at the ministry's introductory political course, which he passed with flying colors, he spent the early years of the job getting to know the sector's personalities and the agents run by the nuclear physics section. By working there he discovered how closely the ministry worked with German Democratic Republic (GDR) physicists. Robert Rompe, the doyen of East German physicists, helped establish many contacts, and his students were often recruited as agents. When Stiller was hired, in 1972, there was a new drive to recruit college-educated scientists into the newly expanding sector.[8]

All MfS (Ministry for State Security) evaluations describe Stiller as a politically active and an ideologically committed worker. He had promise, even though his work was sometimes criticized as superficial and he was urged to curb his "exuberant impulsiveness." In 1976 he was promoted to first lieutenant, placed in the cadre reserve for a position as acting *referat* head, and awarded a National People's Army Medal in bronze for his "rich ideas" in operational work and willingness to take risks. In addition to his good work in running inherited agents, he had recruited his first West German agent, a professor.[9]

WORKING AT THE SECTOR FOR SCIENCE AND TECHNOLOGY

Although Stiller met the apocryphal founding head of the sector, Heinrich Weiberg, when he came on board in 1972, the newly promoted Horst Vogel was his boss. At the time, he was a man with a presence. Stiller found him intimidating and noted his strong intelligence-related intuitions about people: "he was an intelligence officer in heart and soul."[10] But his immediate boss in the physics section was a man who reminded him of a jailhouse convict, with his gleaming, front gold tooth: Christian Streubel.

Streubel initiated Stiller into the spy world by handing him files of former and current agents to educate him on the operations of the unit. This was an interesting beginning to the job, and he learned about recruitment, human weaknesses, and how the MfS worked. When Streubel handed him the file on "Garden," he remarked that this was the big atom spy. Harald Gottfried (known as "Gärtner," or "Garden" in English) was one of those so-called agents of the future thrown into the stream of émigrés to West Germany in the 1950s – a classic HV A (foreign intelligence arm of the Ministry for State Security) migration agent. During the early years, these agents were more highly prized than recruited West Germans. Resettling an agent was a long process requiring much patience.

Stiller spent most of his time as a case officer recruiting and running domestic and Western agents. A typical workday for Stiller at the office consisted of taking the subway to *Magdelenastrasse*, getting off with the other stream of MfS employees, flashing his MfS ID at the gate to MfS headquarters, and taking the elevator to his thirteenth-floor office. Once at the office, Stiller reviewed his files, determining what was expected for work at the office and what was needed to run his agents to meet the department's goals. The buildings were structured around a courtyard, and the HV A occupied one of the newer buildings constructed in the 1970s, immediately on the right of the official entrance.

Compared to high-security spy agencies like the BND and the CIA, the MfS seemed primitive in the way it guarded its secrets. Although it had barbed wire on some of the surrounding walls and some security cameras, it was not especially high-tech. The buildings were a mix of Berliner old-style grey, cavernous structures and newer GDR socialist high-rise buildings characterized by their typical plastic flooring. There were a few safes in departments, and most case officers put their files in an office cabinet at the end of the day. Even Erich Mielke's office was modest for a major East Bloc security chief, with its plastic, toy-like red phone and flimsy-looking safe, where he kept the secret files from top cases and his own police file containing information on the murders he committed after the war.

A surviving yearly plan for 1978 has Stiller responsible for working on an important "object" called "Weapon" and for running the agents to meet information needs. "Weapon" was in fact the Society for Nuclear Research in Karlsruhe, an institution in which the MfS was interested. He was also assigned to analyze the developments in "Lighting" – laser developments. Stiller was assigned to use his agent "Klaus" (Reiner Fülle), an employee at the nuclear research center whom he had inherited from a colleague in 1976, to gather information.[11]

The goal for analyzing Weapon was to establish a personnel base at the institution. The department already had a few leads on employees susceptible to recruitment based on monetary motivation. Stiller could use his domestic unofficial staff member (IM), an instructor code-named "Rosemarie," a retiree permitted to travel to the West, to recruit someone with a cover story. In addition to these covert methods for acquiring information, Stiller was instructed to look into a "legal possibility" for information gathering and to "establish focused accidental contacts," by using IM "Secretary," who was in reality Robert Rompe's personal secretary, Peter Nötzold.[12]

Stiller was also instructed to use his base of agents to meet existing information needs. By the time he defected, Stiller ran six Western agents and a staggering thirty domestic East German IMs. His Western agents, the sources that stole the secrets and really counted in operations, included three West Germans and three East German migration agents. By contrast, the East German domestic IMs were the instructors, recruiters, and couriers used for communication; they either lived in, or traveled to, West Germany and met with agents to pass on instructions or collect information. Another group within the GDR served as rank-and-file informants. Stiller assembled an impressive network of East Germans who worked at various physics institutions. Some of them were also potential candidates for migration to the West.

Stiller had inherited most of his Western agents, including his first, "Sperber" or Rolf Dobbertin. "Sperber" was one of those refugee agents sent to the West in the late 1950s. Robert Rompe's connection helped Dobbertin secure a position in France.

But Stiller's greatest achievement, according to his memoirs, his personnel file, and the file of the agent, was his recruitment of a professor from Göttingen, Karl Hauffe, code-named "Fellow," who was a physical chemist. Hauffe, a West German, was originally from the East and had apparently already worked for the Soviet Union's Committee for State Security (KGB) under the code name "Wagner." His motive was monetary, and his file notes that he owned a house and drove a BMW, which he later traded in for a Mercedes. Stiller recruited him using a cover as a Ministry for Science and Technology staff member and slowly revealed his real identity.[13]

Stiller's most important agents, because of their placement in key institutions (or objects) and due to their collection of valuable scientific-technical information, were Gerhard Arnold ("Sturm") and Rainer Fülle. Stiller has called Arnold, who worked at IBM, Stuttgart, the "father of data processing" in the GDR. According to the yearly plan from 1978, the documents obtained by IM "Sturm" relating to software and database systems had "much economic and also military importance." Indeed, he collected important internal IBM information that was successfully integrated into the GDR military computers. Fülle, also called the "slippery ice spy" because of his escapades fleeing his captors, worked at an important MfS object – the Nuclear Research Center in Karlsruhe. The department head also underlined the importance of his material: "He delivers important documents . . . on atomic technology . . . and statements on the FRG's [Federal Republic of Germany] ability to produce its own atomic weapons."[14]

An agent from the Siemens Company, "Hauser," G. Sänger is portrayed as the least productive of all the agents, in part, because of personal problems, including a divorce.

Completely absent in Stiller's memoirs – because he wanted to protect her against prosecution – is a West German agent code-named "Gabi," Annemarie Gutschmidt, the only woman in the group. Streubel suspected that she was working for the other side: "The enemy could be involved."

Stiller and his co-worker on the case may also have been encouraged to start an affair with her in the style of Markus Wolf's Romeo spies, but she had a boyfriend and "showed no interest in them." Initially recruited by Stiller in March 1976 as a "contact" under the cover of a staff member at the Ministry for Science and Technology, she worked at the Ebert Foundation as a secretary and seemed to supply political, not scientific, information, though she had been a secretary at an atomic institution previously. The case officers knew that "Gabi," whom they described as "pleasant," "good-looking," and "attractive," enjoyed flying glider planes, and they recruited her based on money, which she received in exchange for information several times. Case officers were attempting to "stabilize" her and procure information in Bonn from a wide variety of people.[15]

Being a case officer was not simply a desk job. When in Berlin, Stiller met with his agents at restaurants and cafés or in his safe house, called "Fortress," where they were sometimes met with MfS hospitality. Stiller also enjoyed the job travel. Meetings with agents often took him to the major East Bloc capitols, such as Budapest, Prague, and Moscow, and even several trips West to the soccer game in West Germany and to Finland. On one of these trips, Stiller uncovered information about a very secret spy ring in Vienna, which he called the Vienna Residency. The spies there procured computer information, smuggled embargoed goods into East Germany, and had shady connections that reached as far as Silicon Valley, California.

A GIRLFRIEND

While on a business trip to southeastern Germany in January 1978 to meet with his Siemens agent, Stiller stopped in at a hotel's bar restaurant in Oberhof, a small town near the border of West Germany, for a nightcap. He struck up a conversation with the attractive waitress. She had just been declined a visa to travel to her brother's wedding in the West and was very angry and annoyed at the state. Stiller speculated that she was either a "real enemy of the state or some kind of decoy." The woman interested him. He concealed his real identity and introduced himself as a scientist working at a ministry for technology in Berlin and invited her out for a drink after work.

To determine whether or not she was an MfS employee under cover, he looked up her name – Helga Mischnowski – in the district office the next day. She was clean. He called her again in mid-February and said: "I have to see you." He waited for a few weeks to tell her his real identity.

During one visit to Oberhof he pulled out his Stasi ID as a test. He had expected her to shake from fear, as most citizens would have. Instead, she said, "get out of here." Fifteen years after his defection, Peter Fischer described the incident: "Then I told her the truth. I said, "I'm looking for someone who can create a contact to the West for me. Can you help me?" Helga thought about it for a week, called him and said, "I'll help you."[16] She had started to fall for him.

Fischer related that he had been systematically looking for a Helga for many years: "it could have been someone else . . . but the constellation [of events] were favorable." Making contact with the other side is always tricky; it is hard to know if a potential contact is in fact one of your own people. In divided Germany it was even more difficult because East Germany had so thoroughly penetrated the West with informants and agents. Stiller had determined that Helga was a "genuine enemy of the state" with a "desire for revenge": "And these days Helga has an ambivalent relationship with me. On the one hand, it was an important period in her life. On the other hand, she feels used by me. Her point of view now is that 'he only used me.' And she's partly right. She's not totally right, though, because I had been looking for a Helga. When I found her, she also became important to me as a human being."[17]

The two quickly became romantically involved. Helga recalls wonderful times together, walking through the snow in Oberhof. He had convinced her that there was no chance for them in East Germany with her political leanings and that their future together lay in the West. "This will go down in history," he told her.[18] Things began to get messy for Stiller on the home front. He told his wife about the affair, although he had not told Helga about his wife, and began to spend a lot of time in Oberhof. On 13 February 1978 his wife gave birth to their second child, a boy. In the car on the way home from the hospital Stiller told her he could no longer live with her and was going to leave her. Later his wife threatened to tell his boss at work about the affair, and Stiller partly moved back home and told his wife he needed time.[19]

To add to a tense and complicated situation, Horst Vogel, his boss, had seen Stiller and his new girlfriend together in Oberhof in February. At the office, Vogel asked Stiller: "Who was the woman?" At a meeting at work a month later he warned Stiller: "to behave correctly and to think of his family."[20] Although the MfS in general is not known for performing moral acts, paradoxically, staff members were required to lead a moral life, refraining from extramarital affairs. Not only this, but it was possible that Vogel's intelligence intuitions made him suspect that the woman was more than a girlfriend – Stiller was never sure.

SPY VERSUS SPY

Meanwhile, Helga's brother, Herbert Kroß, from Coburg, West Germany, visited Helga in Oberhof with his new wife on 29 April 1978. Helga arranged to have Stiller meet him. Stiller asked Kroß to deliver a letter to the BND, and he agreed. Memories conflict at this stage: Fischer recalls that he asked Kroß to deliver the letter directly to the BND, but instead Kroß gave it to a federal border control officer. Kroß recalls a brown wallet with a secret compartment, which he was asked to give to the border control officer. In the letter Stiller offered to work for the BND.[21]

"Walk-ins," or intelligence officers who offer their services to the other side are always suspect. It is hard to know if they are genuine or sent by the enemy as part of an operation. During the Cold War, hundreds of intelligence officers defected to the West from the Soviet Union and other East Bloc countries. How they did it varied.

However an intelligence officer makes contact to the other side, he or she always has to establish his or her bona fides. According to Kroß, a BND case officer named "Ritter" visited him twice in May 1978 to find out more about Stiller and if he was genuine.[22]

By July 1978, the BND established direct communication with Stiller. On July 5th "Ritter" arrived at Kroß's door in Coburg with a text for Stiller that described a park in Berlin with a dead letter drop containing a stash of material. Kroß learned the text by heart and recited it to Helga on his last visit east. Stiller called Helga from Hungary, where he was vacationing with his wife and family, and after hearing the news quickly left early with an excuse and met Helga at the park. They searched the park for the hidden stash on 25 July 1978 and found the described plank of wood, a clever concealment, under a pile of leaves.[23] It contained all the spy paraphernalia that could be used in court as evidence to convict a spy.

They returned to Stiller's safe house, the "Fortress," and cracked open the piece of wood. Inside they found a very nice letter from the BND greeting them, a code table, jars of invisible ink, ten prewritten letters with envelopes addressed to cover addresses in West Germany, and information on radio frequencies but no radio. That evening Helga went out to an intershop and bought a West German shortwave radio, a "Telefunken International 101."[24] The same day, the BND sent them their first message through its Agent Broadcasting Service. Like the MfS, the BND conducted one-sided communication (from headquarters to the agent) with its agents using a specific frequency and time. Once the agent named their personal frequency number (in this case Nr. 688), the BND sent an encrypted radio message using the five-number-group method, which encrypted letters with scrambled groups of numbers.

In July 1978 an intensive communication and cooperation began between Stiller and the BND, with Helga responsible for deciphering the encrypted messages. Helga's role in communicating with the BND was pivotal but ignored in Stiller's 1986 memoirs.

The BND still needed hard evidence that Stiller was for real and not some sort of MfS operation. They demanded that he "deliver all of [his] people [agents], in order to have [him] totally hooked.... [He] was then totally committed to them and dependent on them." Helga recalls that they "demanded material" and then it began to get exciting. In his memoirs, Stiller describes some qualms about naming his agents. He was worried that the West German police might arrest them right away and place him in danger. During the Cold War, this was the name of the game: in order to earn their bona fides, defectors named names. At the time, Stiller did not think too deeply about the consequences for the agents.[25]

Meanwhile, about a month after the BND gave the couple the communication materials, on 28 August 1978, the Stasi's spy catcher department received a suspicious letter from the mail intercept department that they thought had earmarks of spy activity. In the course of a routine search of mail called "Net," the mail interceptors came across the couple's letter with a fictitious return address. The spy catchers sent the letter to the specialists in the technical operations sector. They found invisible ink and the telltale five-number-code group of columns and speculated that the letter was prewritten. These communication methods were all hallmarks of BND activity for the seasoned spy catchers. On that day counterintelligence opened a new file called "Bristle" and launched an intense spy hunt.[26]

Ever since February Stiller had been slowly stashing away microfilms and microfiches stolen from the department in a hole in the ceiling of his safe house, "Fortress." By the end of November, the BND demanded to see them. They told the couple to deposit a package containing the microfilms in the toilet of a transit train. Helga tried to board the train, which was headed for Denmark, but police surrounded it because it was a transit train and did not stop in the communist East; she aborted the mission, returned to Berlin, and wrote a telegram to the BND. The telegram could not be delivered to a forwarding address, and therefore the West German post office sent it back to the GDR as undeliverable. The spy catchers intercepted this telegram as well. Now they had another sample of Helga's handwriting and could compare it to the other letter.[27]

Most spy agencies suggest an alternate meet or appointment time for safety reasons. Helga's second attempt a week later was more successful. She boarded an interzonal train traveling from Leipzig to the West and deposited the material in the bathroom, then exited the train in Erfurt, East Germany. She wrote another telegram to the BND with the good news and sent it from the post office near the safe house: "Helga sent the travel papers on 7 December at 10:30 in Leipzig. Greetings, Gisi." But because that telegram was returned to sender and did not reach the BND, the MfS immediately began to look for the "rolling" (i.e., on a train) dead letter drop, which had not been serviced. They spent two nights looking for the stash and took apart eleven train wagons and twenty-two bathrooms but found nothing.[28]

As a result of the intercepted telegram, the Stasi also increased its postal investigations by using the technique "Eagle Flight." Initially developed in 1968, it entailed a series of operational and technical steps in order to identify who deposited a letter in a mailbox. They observed and then took secret films of each person who deposited a letter, a precursor to modern video surveillance systems.[29] From then on, all mail in downtown East Berlin was monitored. Because this took place several weeks before Christmas, this kept the Stasi very busy. They investigated 462,500 letters.[30]

On 20 December, the spy catchers received another piece of information from the radio intercept department, which they began to link with the operation "Bristle" and their pursuit of Helga. The information report stated that there was increased radio activity on the BND Agent Broadcasting Service, specifically with number 688, which the spy catchers and the radio interceptors had been following since August 1978. They found out that radio number 688 had received 15 radio messages with 1,841 five-number groups since 25 July.[31]

AN ESCAPE PLAN

The package with microfilms was the proof the BND needed to establish that Stiller was for real. Soon after, they hatched an escape plan. Stiller's personal life had become a continual balancing act, and plans were made to exfiltrate the spy couple in mid-December. The first escape date was delayed because the false passports created by the BND indicated that Stiller had blue eyes instead of brown. Meanwhile, the Stasi was getting warm as it pursued Helga's trail. About a week before Christmas she prepared a package containing her crystal to send to her brother in Coburg. She used her real name and return address in Oberhof. The Stasi found this package too, compared the handwriting to the two telegrams, and started to search for Helga more intensively.[32]

Finally, on 11 January, the spy catchers sent a staff member, Nowack, to Oberhof to investigate and find Helga. When he arrived at the Hotel Panorama it was closed until 21 January because the heating system had broken on New Year's Eve. Nowack heard that the boyfriend lived in Berlin and, not being a particularly persistent worker, did not attempt to visit Helga in her apartment, although the Stasi had her address. With the weekend coming up, he instead drove back to Berlin and missed Helga, who was still in Oberhof. The Stasi's initial seemingly good investigative work faltered with this careless step.

Even with luck on their side, time was running out for the mysterious spy couple, and a new escape plan was hatched. A new passport was issued to Stiller so that he could board an interzonal train destined for Hanover, West Germany, while Helga would travel to Warsaw, Poland, where she and her son would stay at a hotel and wait for the arrival of false passports by a BND courier.

On 18 January 1979, Stiller prepared to leave his homeland. He sent his wife a farewell letter with ten thousand marks slipped in the envelope. Stiller began, "By the time you get this letter, everything will have happened ... the worst is behind me. ... I was already working for the other side when we met ... at the beginning of 1978 I made a mistake and told you about Helga. ... Then Vogel saw us in Oberhof. It makes no sense to bring you along. You have developed too much along the lines of this state. The children will be safer here. ... I don't understand a lot of this myself."[33]

After the Stasi offices closed for the day, Stiller made his way to headquarters to find more loot for the BND. At the time security was fairly lax. He simply grabbed the keys from the hook hanging in the office and entered his boss's office with a chisel to crack the cabinet. After considerable effort the department head's cabinet proved impossible to open in a short period of time, so he moved on to the secretary's safe. There he found the pass officers used to cross the *Friedrichstrasse* border in order to deposit material in the train station lockers for their agents. Stiller had already done it several times. Uneasy about putting his life in the hands of others, especially with the mistakes the BND had already made, he spontaneously decided to change plans and simply cross the border with these papers.

The drive from Stasi headquarters to *Friedrichstrasse* took about twenty minutes in the evening. He arrived at the border crossing around 9:30 p.m., entered the secret door disguised with a sign marked "for train employees," and slipped the border guard the papers at the window. The border guard did not look happy and said the paperwork did not have the appropriate stamp on it required since the beginning of the year. The pass had not been updated to include a special notation about crossing borders, but Stiller convinced the border control officer that the dumb secretary at the office was to blame. Because the officer had let many MfS personnel through to deposit material in West Berlin train station lockers, he buzzed the door, and Stiller quickly made his way through the underground maze in the subway station. After passing through what seemed an endlessly long passageway, he was at the platform for the train headed to West Berlin. He tried to avoid sitting in view of the Stasi's observation cameras while he waited for the train – he later described this as the "longest six minutes of my life." Fifteen years after his defection, Fischer described how he felt: "it was as though I was standing next to myself and observing everything."[34]

After boarding the train he watched as it passed through bombed-out subway stops never renovated after Berlin was divided. He exited the train station in West Berlin and flagged down a taxi to the airport. When he arrived there at 10:30 p.m. all air traffic had stopped for the evening. So he made his way to the airport police station, where he encountered several typical German police, who had to confer with the bosses before making any decisions.[35] He was then spirited off to a room in the counterintelligence offices. Slowly, the room filled up. First a French intelligence officer arrived; the district of Tegel was still under French jurisdiction. Eventually, the room was packed with ten officers from various intelligence agencies, including an American (a Mr. Ford). There were also several counterintelligence officers from the regional office of the Federal Office for the Protection of the Constitution. Could one of them be an informer for the Stasi? This did not appear to cross Stiller's mind at the time; instead he appeared relaxed.[36]

While the officers tried to contact the BND in Pullach, Stiller tried to reach Helga's brother in Coburg. The officers in the room looked at some of the material, but Stiller insisted that most of the material was earmarked for the BND. He did give the French intelligence officer some files immediately – presumably those related to "Sperber," who lived and worked in France. All of this was described to the Stasi three years later, in 1982, by a West Berlin counterintelligence officer who defected to the East. The anonymous witness listed all eleven people in the room by name and title. He described a pile of microfiches ten centimeters high, a folder labeled "Gabi," Stiller's handwritten notes, the material-accompanying lists, and 10,000 to 15,000 West German marks in cash. Stiller's comments to the officers: "that's if you don't give me enough – I need capital."[37]

Taking fate into his own hands and getting on a different train to the West proved to be wise last-minute changes. Long after his defection, we can read in the Stasi files that counterintelligence had detected increased radio activity in December and identified a lot of movement in Hanover by the BND the day of Stiller's defection. Stasi agents planted in the West could have nailed Stiller's coffin shut.[38]

Meanwhile, the Stasi did not order telephone taps and wiretaps and an apartment search of Helga's apartment until 19 January 1979, the day of Stiller's defection. Simultaneously, a news story appeared in *Neues Deutschland* warning citizens to be on the lookout for the fugitive Helga Michnowski.[39] It was too late. She was already in Poland, waiting to be exfiltrated to the West.

AFTER THE DEFECTION

The morning after defecting to West Berlin, Stiller flew to Pullach and then Köln for immediate debriefing on the agents to be arrested. His defection made headline news in Germany and even made the *New York Times*. On the West German nightly news, the announcer reported that Stiller defected with a woman and child. In fact, this was disinformation thrown in by the BND to protect Helga and her son, who were still stranded in Poland. Despite Stiller's stressful escape, West German officials were impressed with his ability to wade through the material with them to quickly make arrests and prepare material for court.

In East Berlin, the morning after the defection, Sector for Science and Technology (SWT) staff discovered the empty, mangled safe-cabinet with a chisel next to it in the boss's secretary's office and began to investigate. Markus Wolf's deputy called him in Karl-Marx-Stadt on the 19th of January, Wolf's birthday, to tell him the news. Like most in his position would, he cursed, but his method of letting off steam did not match Erich Mielke's reaction when he called Wolf to inform him that his speeches were now in enemy hands. He screamed in Wolf's ear on his emergency line: "What a f——g shambles! We might as well just invite the enemy to attend our meetings and have done with it! You all make me sick."[40]

Panic reigned at the ministry. Agents were notified and recalled from the West and domestic IMs interviewed. Lists were made of the material taken from the safe, including code names and border passes. An intense damage assessment began.[41]

Stasi interrogators arrived at Stiller's wife's door. She heard the news from the Stasi: "Your husband has fled the Republic." She promptly fainted, with the newborn in her hands. A grueling interrogation followed. She was pumped for information about the months preceding his defection. She reported in detail, as much as she knew, about Stiller's affair with Helga. Major Schröder's notes detailed Erzsebet's intimate observations about her husband's strong sex drive and the signs her rival left: scratches on Stiller's back.[42]

Erzsebet never received Stiller's farewell letter with the ten thousand marks; the Stasi intercepted it. It turned out that the BND drafted the letter, which was handwritten and signed by Stiller. They had already begun the myth that Stiller had cooperated many years *before* his defection. Erzsebet was forced to move, change her job, and never again utter a word about her ex-husband or recent events.

After they were done with Erzsebet, the Stasi turned to Stiller's domestic IMs for questioning. The MfS seemed interested in Stiller's behavior immediately preceding his defection and even earlier. Many IMs characterized Stiller as "superficial" at meetings, always in a "hurry" and "hectic" in general. These characteristics seemed exacerbated several months before his departure. He even told two IMs that he would not be around any more in about half a year. Even though he had been a model political leader, an IM noted that at their last meeting he commented, "It's not so golden here either." The women found him "open," and "funny" (he "told jokes"), whereas some of the men commented on his weakness for women and primarily described the professional side of the meets.[43]

In the West, Stiller was taken to a BND safe house in the Munich area and debriefed. Helga arrived the day after. The reunion was disappointing for her. She noticed immediately that it was over and that he just wanted to be friends. Many years after the defection, Helga commented that she felt betrayed by Stiller: "He betrayed everyone."[44]

Stiller, Helga, and her son were also housed together at a BND safe house – on the top floor of a high-security high-rise – in Munich surrounded by barbed wire; at the beginning they reportedly had twenty body-guards. Stiller's debriefing lasted a little more than a year, with sessions often running five hours a day. Work was punctuated with weekends in the mountains. Stiller climbed the Bavarian Alps and learned how to windsurf with his new buddies from the BND on the weekend; two BND bodyguards lived with the couple. The BND and BfV not only questioned him on his own department and area, but also asked about more general GDR and HV A issues. Fifteen years after his defection, he admitted that he had not had a comprehensive view of the HV A but his "knowledge expanded through the discussions in Munich and Washington."[45]

As part of the debriefing process, the BND laid some pictures before him, and, for the first time, West German intelligence knew what Markus Wolf looked like. Until 1979 Wolf had been dubbed the "man without a face," because of his success at eluding West German intelligence (reportedly, American intelligence had an older picture taken at the Nuremburg trials when Wolf was a reporter). Now Wolf's image was plastered all over the German news media, including a cover story on Stiller's defection published in *Der Spiegel* in March 1979.

Western intelligence was elated; the Stiller defection was a real coup, and they celebrated it for many years after. Their enthusiasm and triumphalism is reflected in the subtitle to the major *Der Spiegel* article used by the BND for propaganda purposes: "The most important defector from spy central in the GDR lugged suitcases full of secret files and microfilms to the West – a painful defeat for General Markus Wolf's East Berlin foreign espionage unit."[46] In this article too, the BND perpetuated the myth that Stiller had worked for them for many years.

Stiller's defection was the most damaging event in the history of the HV A. The harm done was not limited to the loss of agents or the enemy's acquisition of general information on the HV A and MfS. Any defection ruins morale and agent trust as well. Until the dust settles, it is difficult to recruit agents because of their fear of being unmasked and sent to jail. Agents in place were told to remain inactive until things normalized.

After the fall of the Berlin Wall in 1989, it became easier for Westerners to assess the magnitude of the damage caused to operations as a result of the defection. In addition to the obvious tightening of security and loss of agents who were either arrested or recalled, Stiller's former department became weak. Since many of the agents run by that department were blown, collection in that area diminished, and lost agents were not immediately replaced. Internal security was changed so that no one could flee from *Friedrichstrasse* and so that the identity of agents would be harder to detect.

Stiller's counterintelligence file was code-named "Jackal," and the phrase "Stiller's betrayal" was littered through the files. The BND aggressively recruited East German scientists while they were in the West, and tried to turn agents already in the West or at the embassies.[47]

The defection yielded seventeen convicted agents and one hundred legal investigations. Five of Stiller's own agents were arrested and convicted ("Gabi" was spared, and her name never made the news). At least fifteen agents were pulled back to the East. The other agent arrests came from leads Stiller provided, from the code names in the material-accompanying list and from the SED membership list he possessed as the department's party secretary. In addition to several of Stiller's agents featured in the celebratory *Spiegel* article, two who were not run by Stiller – Johannes Koppe and Karl-Heinz Glocke – figured prominently in the news.

Koppe, who had been a migration agent from the East, worked at the Hamburg Electricity Works as a nuclear physicist; they reportedly had one of the biggest reactors in the world. When the police came to his door to arrest him, Koppe was fast on his feet: "You have the wrong apartment; Koppe lives two floors up." He quickly exited the apartment building with his wife and fled to the East. Ten years later, the MfS honored their star "scout for peace" in a miniature volume on agents printed for the MfS community shortly before the Wall fell in November 1989. The West never knew that Koppe, who had allegedly fled to the West in 1952 at the age of twenty, was in fact sent by the MfS to study physics. On his return to the East in 1979, he used the knowledge gained in Hamburg at his new job in the Bruno Leuschner nuclear power plant.[48]

While agents were being rounded up, tried, and convicted, Stiller, who was not allowed to appear as a witness in court, continued to be debriefed in Munich. Stiller could not provide them with many answers to the military technology issues, which interested them greatly, because he had been in a basic research unit. However, they were surprised that Stiller knew so much about counterintelligence in the Stasi. Unlike the West, the Stasi united intelligence, counterintelligence, and police work under one roof. The BND was also interested in MfS communication methods with agents and other operational technology. Stiller's defection made clear that economic and scientific-technical information was a key East Bloc collection area and that West Germany had been heavily penetrated.[49]

Many years after Stiller's defection, Helga recalled her time in Munich and compared it to being in prison. After being cooped up so long, one day, around the time of Oktoberfest in 1980, Stiller announced to Helga that he was going to Gardasee in Italy to go windsurfing alone (with two male bodyguards). While on the vacation, Stiller met a young nineteen-year-old Italian woman and had a brief romance. When his bodyguards finally found him, they quickly collected him and returned to Munich because Stiller had told the woman everything: "I'm not the harmless West German you think, but in fact that defector you saw on the news." Europe was no longer safe for Stiller, and he was shipped off to America the next day for resettlement. When he arrived, he was debriefed again for about three months and took a semester of English classes. For his services, the CIA paid him $250,000, which he quickly lost in the stock market.

By that time he was thirty-three and did not have a future profession. An MBA was a quick degree and held promise for a secure financial future. The CIA resettlement officers showed him some brochures, and he selected Washington University in St. Louis to study. He liked the idea of being on that side of the Mississippi, and there were not that many agents out there.[50]

ON THE RUN

After Stiller's escape he was reportedly sentenced to death in absentia. Erich Mielke wanted him back, dead or alive, and there were rumors that the Stasi sent killer commandos to find him. As a result, Peter Fischer had continual nightmares that the Stasi was chasing him; he was never caught.

Despite the Stasi's successful penetration of several West German intelligence organizations and capture of other traitors, information on Stiller, especially his whereabouts, was sparse. After the Wall fell, the West discovered that the Stasi had two major and important sources in the BND and counterintelligence: Gabriele Gast in the BND and Klaus Kuron in counterintelligence. But Gast was in the evaluation department of the highly compartmentalized and secure BND, and as a result she could not pinpoint his location, despite frequent, urgent radio messages for information on his whereabouts. Klaus Kuron did not start working for the MfS until 1982. Hans-Joachim Tiedge, a counterintelligence official who defected to the East in 1985, reported on Stiller's interest in "women in Gardasee," but this was not enough to catch him.[51]

Perhaps one of the most incredible post-Wall discoveries about the Stiller case is that his BND courier worked both sides of the fence – he was a double agent working for the Stasi and the BND, yet he did not betray Stiller. He apparently strictly compartmentalized his work for each side and earned a double spy income. The Stasi, however, found out about him through their "Jackal" investigations, and he was given a life sentence, but released after four years.[52]

Unlike many defectors, who lead broken lives filled with alcohol and unemployment after their defection, Stiller did amazingly well while hidden behind the identity of Peter Fischer at Goldman Sachs in London. He was a golden boy there and very successful at managing his German clients' finances. He made millions for himself and the firm. During Germany's year of unification in 1990, Fischer, who was eager to return to his homeland, moved to Frankfurt, Germany, and took a promotion as a bank manager at Lehman Brothers, which had eagerly recruited him. His marriage to the young American New Yorker with Mafia connections began to unravel. She did not follow him to Frankfurt from London, and he began to see other women. Although Stiller had told her about his spy past, he failed to mention that he had been married in East Germany and had two children. On his return to Germany, Stiller sought out his old family. He finally told his American wife about his Hungarian wife in an evening car ride. She was shocked and jumped out of the car and ran. The news was like having "a cold bucket of water thrown in your face." She also described his behavior as selfish: "He knew that she [his Hungarian wife] would be interrogated and tortured. They split up the family, and she ended up scrubbing out toilets ... if I had known, I wouldn't have married him." Despite this, the seven years of marriage were the "greatest part" of her life.[53]

Fischer was a bit disappointed upon his return to Germany. He was still an anonymous bank manager. According to his American wife, he did not receive the hero's welcome he thought his past deserved: "he thought the West Germans would give him a parade in his honor."[54]

In 1992 a major *Spiegel* series appeared in which Stiller told a little about his life after the defection; the story was dressed up with photographs of the dashing Stiller, and, like the earlier BND-influenced *Spiegel* article, he was still portrayed as a hero. Soon after, Stiller began to appear in public. His first public appearance was at a podium discussion on "Death to Traitors." In 1993 he came to my conference on "Science under Socialism" as a surprise guest and met with one of his former agents who took part in the project. The Berlin newspapers eagerly reported on his assessment of the use of espionage in science as well as his seemingly adventurous life.

The post-Wall portrayal of Stiller soon began to look less flattering. Former Stasi officers and leaders saw him as a traitor. When I mentioned his name in an interview with the former head of the sector, Horst Vogel,

4. Peter Fischer (formerly Werner Stiller). Pictured in 1994 in Frankfurt am Main, Germany. (Kristie Macrakis)

he turned red in the face with anger. In a calmer moment he remarked: "One loves treason but not traitors." Markus Wolf was cooler: "He's not my friend," he replied when asked if he would meet with Stiller. An exception to the hostility was spy catcher head Günter Kratsch, who would have taken part in Stiller's execution if the department had caught him. The two former enemies met for an interview in 1994 brokered by *Stern* magazine. Stiller's first words to Kratsch were: "I'm glad to have first met you now."[55]

Whereas in 1979, the West gleefully reported on all the caught West agents, after the Wall, reporters and historians questioned Stiller's character, because he betrayed his own agents. His reply was usually that they took a risk taking on the job, just as he took a risk fleeing. After the fall of the Wall he characterized most of the Stasi people as "criminals." During the Cold War, however, the fate of his agents did not seem to be foremost in his mind, and in the West's eyes it was heroic to capture agents working for the communists. In the 1986 memoirs, Stiller is also portrayed as a hero damaging an evil organization with his pirated information.

The years following Stilller's outing consisted of interviews, public appearances, and even a German movie about him. Employees at Lehman Brothers Bank House were displeased about having a former spy amongst them, and he was slowly pushed out of that job, but was ready for some time off and took advantage of unification opportunities in the East. He started his own real estate business in Leipzig, punctuated by scuba vacations with attractive women in exotic locales, such as the Maldives. His marriage to his American wife ended in an expensive divorce. In 1995, Goldman Sachs hired him again in Frankfurt under the condition that he no longer appear in public discussing his spy past. Simultaneously, he met and married a sexy young blond from Kazakhstan whom he had met through a video introduction service. But things started to go wrong for Fischer. He began to get death threats. Former Stasi colleagues had probably become jealous of his success while they were smeared in public. He disappeared. Goldman Sachs fired him in 1996 for sexual harassment, a charge he disputes. He moved to Hungary, closer to his old roots, and started another new life alone. Soon he met a nice young Hungarian woman and acquired a handsome Rottweiler named Sophie. He was quickly back on his feet and with the little capital he had left started a successful real estate company and then turned to establishing clothing stores with his girlfriend. He started working twelve-hour days capped by drinking a bottle of red wine every night, but he hopes to retire by the time he is sixty years old.

ON MOTIVATION

Motives for defecting vary, but a review of defectors in history shows that their own representations of motivating factors are often contradictory and unconvincing. The enormous number of defectors from the Soviet Union and the East Bloc to the West offers some clues. Surely a common denominator among this group was disillusionment with one's own country and the search for a better life in the West. But often accompanying personal factors played a larger role. By the closing years of the Cold War, the stream of defectors to the CIA was so great and the desire for a new identity and a house in California with a pool so paramount that the CIA started to turn some away.

At the time of the defection, it appeared that Stiller defected partly because he could not tolerate the lifestyle demanded by the MfS and the GDR. It was too moralistic. Hans-Joachim Tiedge, a high-ranking counterintelligence official who defected East in 1985, offers some insight into Stiller's motivations: "According to his own [Stiller's] judgment there was no future for him at the MfS anymore. He was noticed in a negative way by the internal security organs because of his lifestyle, especially his relationships with women."[56]

Stiller's life story and his post-defection lifestyle certainly offer credence to this explanation. After the Wall fell he emerged as a James Bond–like spy: fast sports cars, plenty of money, pretty women (he loves them and leaves them, using them along the way), and a house in an area of southern France popular with jet-setters.

His own explanation for his motivation long after the defection was that after the Prague Spring in 1968 he became disillusioned. This motivation seems unconvincing, because he joined the East German Communist Party in October 1968 and joined the MfS willingly in 1971. Although no single motivation for defecting is outlined in the 1986 memoirs, there too it is implied that he became disillusioned and wanted to cause the hated system much damage by defecting.[57]

WRITING ABOUT SECRETS

The true Stiller story was one of the Cold War's most closely guarded secrets. It would have likely continued to be so if not for a constellation of factors. Stiller resurfaced in Frankfurt in 1990 under his assumed name of Peter Fischer, and the media found out, most likely through his Hungarian wife. Simultaneously some of the participants had developed a desire to come to terms with the past. This coincided with the falling of the Berlin Wall, the opening of the Stasi archives, and the nationwide reckoning with the past. It was not until 1992 when Stiller told a little about his post-defection life in America to the glossy West German magazine *Der Spiegel* that the true history started to be revealed. In that article, however, Stiller still remained mute and loyal to the BND on the issue of how long and in what capacity he had worked for them. Furthermore, until this day, he has never criticized the BND, even though they made so many mistakes, and as Helga pointed out many years after the defection: "We are still alive in spite of the BND, not because of them."[58] Peeling away the layers of truth has taken years.

Fischer reportedly sold the manuscript to the BND for $150,000; in fact, they had encouraged him to write it. After the BND acquired the manuscript, they rewrote and edited parts to incorporate the myth and make it more popular. The "memoirs" relate that contact with the BND occurred for many years and began with the meeting of a businessman at the Leipzig Trade Fair, a plausible story. This alleged mole activity is woven into the book as a theme. In fact, Stiller worked with the BND merely for the six short months described here, in order to change sides. The disinformation was thrown in to confuse the enemy, to throw more salt in the Stasi's wounds, and to make the case even more important than it was. In addition, Helga's pivotal role in communicating with the BND was overlooked. BND's operational mistakes in communicating and organizing the exfiltration were brushed over. Instead the BND is portrayed as superior to the MfS. It placed "his own personal safety at the forefront while intelligence success came second." Stiller continues in the memoirs: In comparison to the MfS's "shameless" use of human weaknesses "my experiences with the BND are a positive contrast."[59]

The myth that Stiller worked for the BND for many years as an agent has persisted until today with several exceptions. It is present in *Der Spiegel*'s three-part series on Stiller published in 1992. In his numerous post-Wall TV interviews and public appearances he never mentioned the revised BND version of the story. The American translation of Stiller's memoirs perpetuates the double-agent myth in the introduction to the 1992 volume. There is even an additional ghostwritten "epilogue" in the book that makes no reference to Stiller's closely guarded life after the defection but reflects on the opening of the Stasi files in 1989 and the democratic fight against totalitarianism.[60]

Each generation rewrites history. Contemporaries experience the events within their own worldviews. Participants find it difficult to change sides of a battle they were on even many years after the war. Post-Wall Germany saw a struggle between the "victims" and the "perpetrators," especially regarding the Stasi files. Many wanted to repress that past or still take sides when they wrote about it. Dissidents used the Stasi files to ferret out the Stasi's wicked deeds while Stasi officers often relativized the past or brushed the abuses under the rug. Few commentators attempted to view this story through the lens of intelligence history. And even fewer commentators have drawn attention to the extent to which such episodes draw attention away from the initial goals of the spy agency. The black-and-white image, or polarization, among Germans of the general Stasi issue is similar to the way in which we see Stiller or Fischer or "the Jackal." Was he the Cold War hero celebrated in the West or a traitor who poisoned his victims with betrayal?

4

The Crown Jewels

The Washington Post has described it as "one of the greatest coups of Cold War espionage" and among the "CIA's greatest triumphs," yet the CIA still remains officially silent on how they managed to acquire the Stasi's foreign department (HV A) agent card files after the fall of the Berlin Wall.[1] Unlike the miles of files from the repressive, internal-security Stasi apparatus that were secured by the opposition movement, the foreign spy files were legally destroyed, with the sanction of the German government, in early 1990. Intelligence officers were especially loyal to their agents and felt morally obligated to protect the identity of their sources.

One of the most loyal patriots, a tall Saxon with a paunch whose appearance was reminiscent of George Smiley, was Major General Horst Vogel, deputy head of the HV A and longtime leader of the Sector for Science and Technology (SWT). After the fall of the Berlin Wall he described how his staff "destroyed everything" by shredding or fire and how he threw many of his files into a bonfire in his backyard and took the charcoaled paper to the dumpster himself. He even refused to endorse the story circulating in the late 1990s that they handed over the filmed agent card file to the Soviet Committee for State Security (KGB): "One doesn't hand over files to strangers." His superior and the successor to Markus Wolf, the always well-dressed, dapper, and white-haired Major General Werner Grossmann, denied that he penned an order to pass the microfilmed agent index files to the KGB, yet the designated Stasi official, Rainer Hemman, admits taking the microfilms to the Soviet compound in Berlin-Karlshorst.[2] The microfilm tin containers were then allegedly spirited off to Moscow in a special transport plane.

Major General Vogel had good reason to wish the files destroyed and buried: the CIA materials reveal that almost half of all agents planted in Western institutions belonged to his Sector for Science and Technology.

This astounding fact demonstrates the significance of science and technology collection for the East Bloc during the Cold War as well as the division's success at placing and recruiting agents.

The large number of science spies is even more surprising because so
few of them were brought to public light and prosecuted. Both the public
and West German counterintelligence were more interested in political
cases. As a counterintelligence official put it: political espionage "hurts
the most." On top of that, Western companies and managers had no interest in unmasking spies; it could damage their image. The industrial sector
wanted to sweep the cases under the rug. As a result, many Stasi science
spies continued as usual after the prosecution phase in the 1990s.[3]

THE CIA'S BIG SECRET

The thousands of dossiers on agents and support staff, the officer's personnel files, and all the operational files and reports were destroyed primarily
to protect the agents' identities (and also presumably to cover up wrong-
doing). All the valuable historical files were destroyed, yet we know who
the secret agents were because the CIA managed to obtain a gritty, barely
readable microfilm copy. The securing of the complete agent card file
allowed the Stasi's adversaries to realize the spy agency's worst fears: the
revelation of the identity of all their agents, including their cover and real
names. This subsequently led to a massive hunt for agents and attempts
to prosecute them.

President George Bush inspired the CIA to go hunting for the Stasi files.
As the revolution had been televised on CNN, the whole world, including
President Bush, had seen the storming and looting on *Normannenstrasse*.
He asked the CIA in January 1990 if it was "getting its hands on the
documents floating out onto the streets of East Berlin." When CIA director
William Webster heard that the answer was no, he asked Milt Bearden,
head of the Soviet/East European Division, if they "needed new people in
Berlin." Inactivity quickly turned into frenzied, aggressive recruitment of
informants and the search for interesting files.[4]

Because phone calls to Stasi officers were not effective, the CIA began to
knock on doors, offering cash for information. They did manage to find
some low-level officers who provided material, but leaders like the head
of the America division and Markus Wolf proved to be recalcitrant and
turned down lucrative offers and the promise of resettlement in California
in exchange for big agents or names of Americans working for the Stasi.
The CIA's pitches had become so aggressive that the head of the American

division invited Werner Grossmann to come to his apartment to threaten CIA officers. David Rolph, the CIA's East Berlin station chief, was "dumbfounded" when Grossman told him that they would go to the police if the harassment continued and then to the press. He was relieved that he was not arrested or ambushed and kidnapped by Stasi "goons."[5]

Whereas CIA officers have described two "dumps" of material they obtained from the Stasi, they have never acknowledged the existence of the most secret and important operation: how they acquired the foreign spy files and who handed it over. The first "dump" of Stasi material into the hands of the CIA came in January 1990 from a counterintelligence officer, Rainer Wiegand, who sold three "red folders" on American agents working in East Germany. Through these files they learned that every agent they had in East Germany had been a double agent working for East Germany. In the spring of 1990 the CIA obtained thousands of wiretap orders recorded on 17,000 index files documenting the telephone intercepts of a large number of prominent West Germans.[6]

But the files the CIA really wanted – sensitive operations involving the HV A and the KGB – were "still out of reach." In his monumental book, which told the "inside story" on the "CIA's final showdown with the KGB," the colorful, cowboy-boot-wearing bear of a man, former Soviet/ East European division chief Milt Bearden, was disappointed about the "banal, neighborly betrayals" that filled the file drawers dissidents had yanked open. It was only later that the CIA realized several trusted Stasi officers had already transported the most sensitive files to the East Berlin airport, where they would be flown to Moscow. But Bearden tells us nothing about the most important Stasi material – the foreign spy files – or how the CIA obtained them. He leaves us hanging at the East Berlin airport as he watches a plane take off to Moscow.[7]

Everyone who has been interested in this mystery of mysteries has either followed the trail of the microfilmed agent card files to Moscow or speculated that they were obtained directly from a Stasi officer, Rainer Hemmann. Once the files were in Moscow, the CIA then allegedly bought them for a sum of 1 million dollars from the Soviet liaison officer Alexander Prinzipalov, by means of an agent posing as a military historian, James Atwood. Yet that story was hard to trace because the protagonists had one thing in common: they were all dead.[8]

Another plausible version of how the CIA acquired the coveted agent card file was set forth by Robert Gerald Livingston and deflates the image of a brilliant operation or the theory that the agency had a mole placed in Moscow. Instead, it reflects the way in which many successes were achieved by the CIA during the Cold War: through a walk-in – a disenchanted KGB officer allegedly walked into the American embassy in an Eastern European capitol in 1992 carrying a briefcase with the microfilms and offered to sell them for a mere $75,000.[9] Yet this story could be disinformation. It is also possible that Prinzipalov simply walked into the embassy in Berlin or that the CIA bought the files directly from him at KGB headquarters in Karlshorst and the files never arrived in Moscow. After all, he died under murky circumstances: supposed "heart problems."

This still-anonymous KGB officer was not alone in seeking money and asylum in the West after the fall of the Berlin Wall. Whereas there had always been a trickle of Soviet walk-ins during the Cold War, the torn-down Wall was like a breached levy: a flood of Soviets flowed into the East Berlin U.S. embassy in the summer of 1990, seeking political asylum. David Rolph was screening four Soviet walk-ins a week – usually tourists who had bought a ticket for a bus vacation in East Germany.[10]

As the Soviet Union began to collapse, the flood of asylum seekers spread themselves out to other East Bloc countries, and some even tried an escape from Moscow through secret services. The most spectacular Soviet defector in 1992 was Vasili Mitrokhin, who was exfiltrated to England by MI-6. He had actually gone to the American embassy in Moscow first but was turned down. Luckily, the CIA did not turn away the KGB officer – if this story is true – who offered the copy of the HV A microfilms – a treasure trove for any spy agency.

ROSENHOLZ

Dirk Dörrenberg, a slender, bureaucratic-looking, blue-eyed, white-haired gentleman with a dry sense of humor, had been fighting the Stasi through counterintelligence for much of the Cold War. Despite his deadpan exterior, Dörrenberg should have been very excited when he and his colleagues from German counterintelligence obtained a few select cases that Milt Bearden had delivered personally to the federal chancellor's office in 1992 on a silver platter. Dörrenberg and his colleagues, however, became very irritated with the state of the material. It had been "laundered" by an outsourcing firm, which retyped it with numerous spelling and typing errors. When the Federal Commissioner for the Records of the State Security Service of the Former German Democratic Republic (BStU) received the material in 2004 it demanded the originals and had to re-do the database mask. German counterintelligence later code-named the operation "*Rosenholz*" (Rosewood), after they were allowed to go to Langley and take notes on the files in pencil. Like the "Venona" decoding operation against Soviet espionage in America, the term was a random, computer-generated word. And, like Venona, the secret files would soon uncover an army of secret agents operating in the West.

Rosenholz demonstrates the primacy of scientific espionage, but the material also reveals some surprising patterns about agents, motivation, and the Stasi's practice of human intelligence gathering. It allows us to reconstruct agent networks and to determine where agents were planted in the West, who they were, why they spied, and how they communicated.

As part of its secret bureaucratic system, the Stasi maintained two sets of index cards on its unofficial staff members: one card, labeled F 16, contains their real name, birth date, address, registration number, and where they worked or studied. The other card, labeled F 22, simply lists their code name, registration number, the name of the case officers who recruited or ran the agent, and the number of files on the agent. It is only when the cards are viewed together that one can attach a code name to a real name. But piecing together identities had one obstacle – a number of unofficial staff members and agent acquaintances were listed under the same registration number; one can only correctly determine the actual agent by comparing the birth date.

Yet another document – the agent data sheet – can help solve the puzzle of which real names matched up with which code names, because it lists the birth date. Domestic unofficial staff members were not included. The data provided a way for the HV A to obtain an overview of all their agents in the West, including information on how they were recruited, their motivation, their profession, the type of agent they were, and the communication methods used and where they worked.

In the early 1970s, the HV A began to annually microfilm its files and cards. With heightened military tensions and the fear of nuclear war in the early 1980s, they began to differentiate Western agents into three categories in case of international crisis or war – the so-called "mobilization" file. Situation I applied to an agent of lesser value who need not be contacted in case of crisis or war. Situation II meant that contact should be maintained in a period of high tensions, and Situation III meant that contact should be maintained with the agent in time of war.[11]

Initially, the CIA used the card index to neutralize former agents by ensuring they did not continue to work for the KGB, since presumably the KGB had seen the file and maybe even had another copy. The CIA also

(a)

(b)

5. CIA-captured *Rosenholz* material. The F 16 card (a) lists the agent's real name, and the F 22 card (b) lists the agent's cover name. The practically illegible state reflects the poor quality of the materials obtained. Oswald Peter Cyron ("Rode") was an East German agent who the Stasi planted in the West in 1956 with the stream of refugees. He worked at Siemens in Erlangen.

may have turned some agents to work for them. But they never imagined their secret espionage coup would become public knowledge.

As arrests of former Stasi agents made headline news, rumors began to spread that the CIA had obtained secret foreign spy files previously thought destroyed. In 1997 the arrest and trial of three Americans – the so-called radical trio – made headlines news in the *New York Times* and *Washington Post*. In Germany, the arrest of Rainer Rupp ("Topas") in 1993 fanned fear among all the former agents who still remained hidden. Whereas early spy catching and prosecutions had occurred because of defections and tips from case officers, a second phase of roundups happened after West Germany obtained the *Rosenholz* material.

As the public became aware of the CIA-acquired card index popularly called *Rosenholz*, pressure began to mount for them to return the microfilms to Germany. Again, the primary pressure came from German dissidents and citizens' groups who thought more domestic informants could be unmasked. After many years of negotiations and strained American-German relations, in 2003 some of the *Rosenholz* material – only the German nationals – was returned to Germany and to the BStU on CDs. Researchers could obtain some information starting in 2004. During a luncheon, Milt Bearden quipped that "we'll return all the material when they return the Egyptian Art at the Berlin Island Museums."[12]

German security officials had already collected a number of leads on former agents from case officers willing to turn them in or testify as witnesses in trials. When the CIA cards surfaced, the German FBI – the Federal Criminal Office (*Bundeskriminalamt* or BKA) – and counterintelligence were still knocking on doors, offering immunity from prosecution in exchange for information. Through this process they had identified three hundred former agents. After obtaining access to the CIA-acquired card file, a second wave of investigations and arrests began. The courts could hardly handle the number of cases: out of thousands of investigations only 257 convictions followed. Interestingly, only about a dozen of those convictions were in science and technology.

Even though a former officer responsible for rocket science, Frank Weigelt, acting subdepartment head of SWT XV, had defected to Western counterintelligence in 1990, Rainer Engberding, chief spy catcher at the BKA, complained that very few science officers were providing leads and testifying compared to their political counterparts.

The value of the agent-identifying information increased significantly with the emergence of yet another foreign spy database in 1998 – this time at the Stasi archives. The *Spiegel* cover story dramatized it as "Markus

Wolf's last secret" and a "sensational discovery."[13] The System for Information, Research and Evaluation (SIRA) contained a database coded on old-fashioned reel-to-reel magnetic tape that listed and rated all the material delivered by agents, including a description of the company the material flowed to in East Germany. Whereas SIRA helped us measure the type and quantity of material, *Rosenholz* fleshed out those bones by providing us information that can answer the questions of who the spies were, where they worked and when, and even why they spied.

WHO WERE THEY?

In 1999 the SIRA database left us with a tantalizing list of cover names attached to thousands of pieces of scientific, technological, or military information. But a cover name does not tell us anything about the person who volunteered or was persuaded to betray his or her country. Such information stimulates curiosity: Who was hidden behind the code name "Dora," "Zelter," or "Test"? Who did they plant at Siemens or IBM or Hewlett Packard? Were professors or leading managers stealing secrets and passing them on to the East? Were they migration agents from the East or a West German recruited as a student who wormed his or her way into a company of the Stasi's choice?

The *Rosenholz* material helped us personify the cryptic code names by revealing the real names, addresses, and workplaces of agents and backup staff. Despite potential tediousness, the recovered foreign department skeletal material lends itself best to statistical analysis.

At first glance, the most striking image that emerges regarding who the sources were is the number of small fish in the large lake run by the sector. There are very few prestigious German sources. Aside from lacking many stellar sources in key institutions, few professors or bank managers or leaders in their fields emerge among the three hundred sources and backup staff in the West. This may be more surprising to the layman than to the intelligence professional.

Among professionals it is common wisdom that the best source is low level – a secretary with good access to secrets, a chauffeur or, as the classic novel *Our Man in Havana* by Graham Greene depicts, a vacuum cleaner salesman who becomes a spy to earn extra money. Similar to Greene's literary spy, who concocts an imaginary world of secret agents, the real-life science spy often exaggerated the importance of the scientific material passed on. Seemingly valuable blueprints could turn out to have belonged to an item as everyday as a vacuum cleaner.

The sector aimed a little higher than vacuum cleaner salesmen. About twenty-five agents were secretaries, students, production workers, and repairmen – not highly qualified scientists or engineers – but some of them had access to secret material. One agent was a German assemblyman at the U.S. Army in Augsburg ("Acker"), one a locksmith at a factory ("Bauer"), another a book binder at the Max Planck Institute in Göttingen ("Protokoll"), while a librarian with a degree in library science ("Irmgard Krüger") at the massive library in West Berlin – known as the Stabi – could win a prize for delivering the most material – some three thousand pieces of information – in nineteen years of spy work. Of course none of it was secret, just unavailable in the East and therefore received average marks from the evaluators (mostly IIIs). Nevertheless, it is amazing what you can find at the library: her collection activities were all over the map, from information on ballistics, aerodynamics, uranium, metals, the space program, military technology, and the environment to a milk economy research report (that received a low grade of V).[14]

The majority of sources were male salaried employees at companies at which electronics played the leading role. Professionally, that group consisted of many engineers or men with college degrees in science. But a number of sources also worked in personnel departments, were businessmen, and a few were officers at the U.S. Army base in Augsburg.

Top sources were not necessarily leaders in their field or heads of departments or even scientists. Several of the most important sources were salaried employees like engineer Dieter Feuerstein ("Petermann") at MBB, who passed on top-secret military plans, Peter Alwardt ("Alfred") at AEG/Telefunken, who worked as an engineer, and Peter Köhler ("Schulze"), who worked for Texas Instruments and earned half a million marks in ten years from his agent salary.[15]

A well-regarded physics professor at the University Bielefeld, Peter Stickel (code-named "Pfeiffer"), was a most curious case. Born in Leipzig in 1932, he was a member of the East German Communist Party (SED) and was recruited in 1955 while he was a physics student at the Humboldt University by one of the sector's founding fathers, Willi Neumann, on the basis of ideology. He was sent to the West in 1956 and studied physics, becoming a professor of high-energy physics at the University of Bielefeld. When Werner Stiller defected in 1979, "Pfeiffer" was detained and questioned but never prosecuted. Although there were seven volumes of material in his file by 1984, he stopped passing on information in 1980, after the Stiller blowup. He may have provided the Ministry for State

Security (MfS) with information on other physicists but he passed on very little material that was of minimal importance.[16]

Although there were few professors in the lot, the Technical University in Aachen seemed to be a special target because of its excellence in the applied sciences and engineering. None of the three professors recruited there in the 1980s was especially productive or important. Two of the sources – "Natur" and "Test" – did not deliver much material and had the same case officer, a development engineer, Thomas Ruß. "Ahrendt" delivered some information for four years then quit. Several West German sources became professors after their spy career was over and were not caught or prosecuted during the capturing wave of the 1990s. Particularly noteworthy is "Friese" (Manfred Bartel), recruited in 1974 on the basis of ideology; he delivered copious and valuable material when he worked for Siemens and the Technical University in Berlin from 1980 to 1988. He later became a professor at a leading trade school for electronics.[17]

There were about as many agents who were "leaders" as there were agents who were lower level or not scientists, but on closer inspection it turns out that many of these sources simply owned their own firm. Two of the division's most productive sources in computing during the 1980s – "Zelter" (Fritz H., a physicist [last name not legible on card file]) and "Dora" (Peter Dölling, an engineer) – owned their own firms and escaped prosecution. "Zelter" was recruited in 1986 based on greed, knew Arabic, and delivered more than a thousand pieces of valuable information in three years on microelectronics as well as an implanter in 1988. "Dora," recruited in 1978 also based on monetary interest, passed on more than seven hundred pieces of information, including timely material about the VAX machine from DEC (Digital Equipment Corporation). In 2000, Peter Dölling founded Defense AG, an IT-security firm, whereas Fritz H. disappeared.[18]

Many of the sources had some sort of connection to East Germany – some left for the West with their family as children, some had relatives there, and some had business to do there. That connection may have made them more sympathetic to a pitch by an East German playing on that sentiment. Like other spy agencies, the HV A preyed on human weaknesses, but simultaneously those with problems often simply volunteered. Several volunteers had drinking or personal problems or were womanizers.

The agent in an interesting place – an enemy spy agency, high-profile companies like IBM or Siemens, a defense contractor, the foreign office, or the chancellor's office – was, of course, at the center of the web of humans.

In addition to these "object sources," who were planted or recruited at institutions, the HV A had "information sources" and contact people. Information sources (or *Abschöpfungsquellen*) could either be pumped for information about a topic like science or technology or they sometimes were similar to object sources. Contact people were simply contacts, not official, and officers approached them either with a cover story or false-flag operation. Sometimes contacts were high-profile figures that refused to sign an agreement indicating that they worked officially for the Stasi. By 1988 the SWT had 68 contact people and 146 object and information sources. A source at an important institution was the most highly prized type of agent.

About as many people served as support and backup staff as those who stole secrets from the institution. Although there were about 146 object and information sources, there were another 120 West German support and backup staff. The backup staff consisted of recruiters, couriers, helpers, "security IMs," and a handful of people who offered cover addresses and safe houses. This does not include the instructors, who were all East German.[19]

Most of the women involved played supporting roles as couriers and assisted their husbands' spy activities. A third of all backup staff were women. Wives were also often brought in to support their husbands as a security measure – to ensure that they would be involved and have a motive to not turn their husbands in to authorities.

Even though the HV A's secretary spies made headline news during the 1970s, and this would lead one to believe that the MfS used many women spies, only about one-fifth of all unofficial staff at the Science Sector (54 out of 260) were women.

There were only ten women object sources. Five of these sources were secretaries and another five white-collar employees, including one Ph.D. biologist, "Ramona," (Dr. Cornelia Nauen) who worked at the European Union in Brussels. Of course, secretaries can be the most valuable agents, since they have the same access to secret files as their bosses. The MfS was notorious for recruiting secretaries at the Bonn governmental offices through male "Romeos," who recruited them using love. Most of those duped secretaries made headline news in the 1970s; one committed suicide. None of the secretaries at the SWT were recruited through Romeos; rather a mix of ideology and materialistic interests were at play. They were important agents, and object sources, like "Ilona" (Katherina Straub), who worked at MBB, the defense contractor, as a secretary and office manager. She was recruited by the rocket science department on the basis of ideology in 1963 and between 1972 and 1982 delivered more than 280 very valuable pieces of information on sensitive weapons systems, secret military satellites, space program polices, secret NATO files, secret military plans, and even sensitive American aerospace secrets and cruise missile information.[20]

WHERE WERE THEY?

During the thirty-five years of its existence, the HV A managed to penetrate West Germany's most sensitive institutions, institutions ranging from the chancellor's office and foreign office to intelligence and security agencies to their most prestigious scientific and technical establishments. In 1989 the SWT had agents planted at internationally competitive companies like IBM, Siemens, AEG/Telefunken, SEL, Texas Instruments, and DEC.

The defense contractor MBB was particularly hard-hit throughout the Cold War, and its secrets were quickly passed on to the Soviet Union. Dieter Feuerstein was not the first agent the MfS and the KGB had placed at the prestigious MBB firm. It was one of the East Bloc's main targets. One of the most important and damaging agents, Manfred Rotsch, was caught in 1986 after he had agreed to work for the KGB and MfS more than thirty years before, in 1954. Rotsch, a mechanical engineer, was sent to the West with the stream of émigré's fleeing the East and worked at various airplane-building firms before taking up a position at MBB in 1969 in space research. At his trial he justified his actions by saying that once he gave the KGB an inch they wanted a mile.[21] Another important post-Wall agent was Frank Musalik, an engineer who worked for the MfS for twenty-four years and delivered information on the *Starfighter* and *Phantom* and an MBB helicopter project.[22] MBB was clearly an important object successfully penetrated by the MfS, ultimately for the KGB. In fact, the SIRA files reveal that the MfS had nineteen sources from different departments who had access to and provided material from MBB in the 1980s.[23]

The SWT ran a sprinkling of agents at Max Planck Institutes, TH-Aachen, and TH-Berlin; a number of agents at smaller, often independently owned businesses; and a large contingent of self-employed businessmen.

Perhaps the most striking find from *Rosenholz* and SIRA materials is the large number of agents planted at Siemens's companies in West Germany. This is surprising because of the East Bloc's previous interest in IBM. In earlier years, particularly in the late 1960s and 1970s, the MfS ran several important agents at IBM, such as Gerhard Praeger and Gerhard Arnold, who were caught, and "Bill," an American, who was not. By 1989, there appeared to be only two main sources at IBM – "Birke" (Wilhelm Paproth) and "Stein" (Lutz Rodig, a volunteer who presented himself at Robtron).[24]

Although Siemens had always been an important target, the West never knew that it had been heavily penetrated, because the chief migration agents sent to the West in the 1950s were never caught. By 1989, the SWT ran ten major object sources at various Siemens companies, and a number of other sources also delivered material from this prestigious institution, which was sprawled throughout Germany and the world. Information stolen from Siemens was not limited to computer technology; other companies, including Siemens communication and medical technologies, were penetrated as well. In addition to recruiting West Germans, the HV A had managed to plant several major East German migration agents at Siemens during the 1950s, including two engineers – "Rode" (Oswald Peter Cyron – emigrated in 1956) and "German" (Günter Gerson – emigrated in 1954). The electrical engineer migration resident "Gustav" (Charlie C.) moved to West Germany in 1958 and worked out of Siemens's largest office in Munich.[25]

"Günter" (Eckhard Schlobohm) was one of the few Siemens agents caught, tried, and convicted of espionage in 1995, after West German officials were allowed to review the *Rosenholz* material. Originally from Thüringen in the East, "Günter" opted to move to West Germany in 1957 after he failed to get into an engineering program. While he was studying electrical engineering in Karlsruhe, he made frequent trips home to visit his mother in the East. Because of these trips he came to the attention of the MfS and was targeted by Dieter Gladitz, an SWT officer posing as an official from the Ministry for Higher Education, who claimed to be interested in material about higher education in West Germany. "Günter" did not complete the engineering degree but obtained a B.A. in economics and soon secured a position at Siemens in Munich in 1969 in the area of data processing. Despite his university spy scholarship; his spy training in radio, codes, and secret writing; and an agent salary of almost 100,000 DM over the thirty years of cooperation, Günter's material was not considered especially valuable by SWT evaluators. During his twenty years at Siemens, he only delivered 212 pieces of information, the majority of which only received the low grade of III in the rating scale (I being the highest grade, V being the lowest). His material was passed on to Robotron in Dresden, but the HV A was more interested in IBM and later DEC. His espionage career did not cause much damage to the West, and he therefore only received a light sentence of one year and three months.[26]

Not surprisingly, given the espionage emphasis on computing, electronic companies had the largest number of agents. During the 1970s and 1980s the HV A shifted its computer espionage focus from IBM to two other American firms with branches in West Germany – Texas Instruments and DEC. One of the most important computer espionage sources was Peter Köhler ("Schulze"), who collected material from Texas Instruments.

The HV A had had a long-standing interest in SEL (Standard Electric Lorenz), one of West Germany's most important firms that worked on communication technology, and had already planted two migration agents there in the 1950s: "Otto" (Gerhard Müller) and "Jürgen" (Andreas Berndt), who were both convicted after the fall of the Berlin Wall.

Like Siemens and SEL, the "Gorbachev" case highlighted the Stasi interest in AEG/Telefunken. When that source started to dry up, two HV A agents were recruited in the 1970s: "Alfred" (Peter Alwardt) and "Filter" (Horst Lang).

WHY DID THEY SPY?

When spies were unmasked both during and after the Cold War, their personal motivations for spying fascinated both the public and espionage professionals alike. Early Cold War spies like the Cambridge Five were often paraded as ideological spies, and, by the 1980s, they were seen as the last of a special breed. Increasingly, spies' motives focused on their need for money. Especially in America it seemed that spying was an easy way to make tax-free income. High-profile cases like the John Walker spy ring, exposed in 1985, drew public attention to the greedy, naval officer who traded secrets for more than a million dollars from the KGB. When Aldrich Ames, the CIA officer, was caught in 1994, his Jaguar, big house, capped teeth, and enormous credit card bills were flashed on TV as his motive for spying. He was likely the highest-paid agent in history, collecting 2.7 million dollars in agent salary in ten years. As a top Russian official commented: "There's no romance here.... Americans do it for money."[27]

In Germany also, it seemed as though there was a shift from ideological to materialistic motivation. After the fall of the Berlin Wall, cynics retorted that the many caught Stasi agents spied for the money. They could point to

Klaus Kuron, head of counterintelligence in the West, who needed money to finance his children's education and to supplement his meager salary. Peter Köhler ("Schulze") is considered one of the HV A's highest-paid agents; he cashed in half a million marks in eleven years (1978–89).[28] Those spies who helped import embargoed technology to the East most likely drew in the biggest profits. Even so, none of the West German Stasi agents made as much as their American counterparts.

On the other end of the spectrum were the voices of the agents and HV A leaders, who claimed most of their spies were motivated by ideology. Their agents were "scouts for freedom," not lowly "spies." Writing in 2003, the group calling itself "Scouts for Freedom" claims ideological reasons for spying. The opening quotation of the book, which was written by Klaus von Raussendorff, an HV A agent who worked at the West German Foreign Office, claims to summarize the thirty-one agents' motive for spying: "All of us had the same motivation – to make a contribution to protecting the first socialist state in Germany and thereby serving peace."[29]

With the return of the *Rosenholz* documentation, the dispute about agent motivation can be settled. The results for the SWT are surprising: a count reveals that the recruitment motive for Germans was split almost evenly between ideology and money, with ideology as a basis for recruitment leading by a handful.[30] In about a dozen cases, both ideology and money played a role as a motive for recruitment. There were also other motives outside these two chief reasons: several agents were recruited using a false-flag operation (the recruiter pretends to work for a friendly spy agency of another country) or personal affection for the recruiter or case officer.

Whereas some, like the HV A, like to use the "bipolar" explanation – either money or ideology – as a motive for recruitment or spying, others refer to the more differentiated MICE model: money, ideology, compromise, and ego.[31] On closer inspection of specific cases, motives for spying often become more complex. Whereas the agent candidate might have appeared to have spied for ideology, he or she may also have had a personal reason attached to the ideology.

As a supplement to the terse one-word summary contained in the *Rosenholz* material, we can use trial testimony and agent memoirs to add some flesh to the bones of the issue of motivation. On numerous occasions, a science spy was recruited with the question, "Would you like to do something to contribute to peace?" Recruiting an agent using ideology was a patient process; it did not happen overnight. Case officers and instructors spent hours discussing politics with their agents, and it was through the gentle art of persuasion that they convinced their targets that the East was a peace-loving nation resisting the aggressive, militaristic imperialists in the West.

The argument for supporting world peace worked surprisingly well with agents who were guided into military installations. Peter Alwardt (code-named "Alfred") had numerous political discussions with his case officer, Günter Blayer, who he met at the Leipzig Trade Fair, before he agreed to spy for ideological reasons. He was also invited to numerous barbecues at an East German safe house and given a tour of the country from head to foot. When he was studying physics in Hamburg during the early 1970s, he became friends with other students who were members of the German Communist Party and considered joining. Meanwhile he had met Blayer and then had another alternative: "Slowly, I came to the conclusion that I could most effectively contribute to world peace through secret service activity in the GDR [German Democratic Republic] in the military area." Although he "loved differential geometry" and theoretical physics, he shifted his emphasis to more applied areas to better serve his new masters. He then landed an engineering job at AEG/Telefunken in 1984 working on developing propulsion methods for torpedoes.[32]

Dieter Feuerstein recalls that his case officer once quipped, "If the enemy is no longer there, they can't disturb the peace."[33]

Whether they were misguided or misled idealists or greedy, crass materialists, after the fall of the Berlin Wall, "Stasi spy" had become a term of opprobrium in Germany, because of the conflation of domestic snitches with foreign agents. However hard they tried, the foreign agent had an image problem. This is far from the case in Russia, where a former KGB man, Vladimir Putin, rules and where Richard Sorge adorns postage stamps and is lionized with large statutes in Moscow.

Among American intelligence professionals, ideological conviction is considered the best way to motivate someone, but it is also considered very rare.[34] Those American handlers would be surprised and envious of the number of spies in Germany who were allegedly motivated by ideological conviction. There is clearly a country-specific cultural and social difference for motivation.

THE HUMAN WEB

When the CIA returned to Germany copies of the *Rosenholz* material relating to German nationals, newspaper headlines blared that the Stasi had planted 280,000 agents in West Germany since the 1950s; that was the number of card files electronically reproduced on the CDs labeled *Rosenholtz* (the *t* was added by the CIA). There is no doubt that the Stasi had an enormous number of agents, but this figure astronomically inflates the reality. Whereas the number of names mentioned in the material may have reached a quarter of a million, very few of the names or code names are actual agents. Many of the names mentioned are people who either knew the agent or were associated with him or her, and the other names belong to the vast web of backup staff developed to support the agents. The support staff was the recruiters, the instructors, the couriers, and the residents. There appear to be 63,000 case files opened in the course of the HV A's history.

The Stasi File Authority reported that there were likely 6,000 West Germans and 20,000 East Germans catalogued in the index cards who had worked for the HV A since the 1950s.[35] The CIA did not return copies of cards on U.S. citizens or citizens of other nationalities. The enormous backup staff quietly helped recruit, run, and handle agents as part of a vast web of people in the East Bloc style of human intelligence gathering and communicating with headquarters. Although the flow of scientific-technical information from the West to the East seemed efficient, *Rosenholz* reveals a surprisingly bloated human intelligence network.

Part of the reason for the emergence of such an intricate web of spy handlers was that East Germany had no Western embassies until 1972. Traditionally, case officers work under official cover at an embassy, where they are protected by diplomatic immunity. Because the MfS did not have a legal base for its case officers, it developed a large support staff to recruit and handle agents. This also reflected the KGB's style of running its illegals.

Before the establishment of embassies, the HV A often set up illegal residencies in the West to run and handle agents. Even after it had embassies to work out of, it relied more heavily on illegal residencies than on the traditional spy residencies at embassies. The Vienna Residency for microelectronics featured in earlier chapters was just one example of a high-profile illegal hub for spying.

The anchors of the residency – the "residents" – were East Germans who were resettled in the West – the so-called migration agents – and ran about three agents each. By 1989, there were only five SWT residents left in West Germany, and most of them had migrated there before 1961. "Gustav," an electrical engineer who had been a migration agent sent to the West on Stasi orders in 1958 and planted at Siemens in Munich, was one of the most important residents still surviving by 1989. "Weißkopf" (Manfred

Wittig), another migration agent sent to West Germany in 1961 after studying at the Technical University in Dresden, was a valuable resident for chemistry and even worked at Leybold in Köln. He directed three other sources in companies such as Hoechst and Bayer. Although "Reise" (August B.) was a less important resident in the service sector, he was tried but not convicted in 1994. All residents were liberally equipped with all the communication technology and methods available, from secret writing to shortwave radios, codes, *mikrats*, and train dead letter drops, in order to be able to communicate with headquarters. In fact, they received the most spy paraphernalia of any part of the network.[36]

Because case officers were not allowed to recruit and handle agents in West Germany themselves, several new and important types of unofficial staff members emerged that recruited and handled agents: the "recruiter" and the "instructor." The instructor took on the handling role of the case officer and the recruiter took the spotting and enlistment role. Whereas an agent met with the case officer only several times a year in either East Germany or abroad in a city like Vienna or Budapest or even Zurich, the instructor met with the same agent on a regular basis, either near the agent's home or in a third country like Yugoslavia, Austria, or Italy. This was done to avoid dangerous trips to East Berlin.

About half of all SWT agents and recruiters had instructors to handle them in addition to a case officer. An instructor functioned like a case officer and was responsible for meeting with an agent abroad and providing political and personal coaching to keep the agent motivated. The instructor trained the agent, gave him or her written instructions from headquarters, passed on agent technology, and handed over the agent salary or travel reimbursement. They also retrieved the material and brought it back to East Germany. All the instructors were East Germans who could travel to the West. Once back in East Germany, the instructor met with the agent's case officer, passed on the material, and wrote a report about the trip and the meeting with the agent. Instructors received extensive training often lasting up to a year.[37]

Many of the instructors were part of the state's "travel cadre" – highly reliable Communist Party members who were allowed to travel to Western countries. In the Sector for Science and Technology, most of the instructors were highly qualified scientists, scholars, and professors, but also technicians. In fact, one is likely to find more Ph.D.'s and professors in the group of instructors than in the sources themselves.

Wolfgang Holle (code name "Hilmar Kohl") was an instructor for several agents, including "Günter" (Eckard Schlobohm), a source at Siemens, and is an example of a prominent East German scientist motivated by ideology and advancing his career. After receiving a B.S. in engineering specializing in CAD/CAM data technology from the Technical College in Ilmenau, Holle rose in the ranks there, becoming a professor in 1985. He had already come into contact with Western visitors in 1970 and 1971 and was therefore recruited to become a courier, later instructor, to agents living in West Germany. After stepping down from his professor chair in Ilmenau in 1993, Holle opened an engineering office, Montage-Design-Studio, in Suhl for assembling products using software.[38]

Used to complement the role of the instructor and to cover the functions of an absent case officer, the recruiter was another type of staff member developed by the HV A. In 1988 the SWT had at least thirty-three recruiters living in West Germany from a wide range of professions, including students, production workers, white-collar employees, and university personnel. The large Working Group 3 for the acquisition of military technology had six recruiters, and the U.S. division of basic research maintained the most recruiters – four – in one subdepartment; several of these recruiters targeted students at the West Berlin universities or anyone who potentially had access to American technology.[39]

Kurt Blaschke was a recruiter for the SWT computer department (Department XIV/2). Like many Western unofficial staff members, he had had a familial relation with the GDR. Although his parents fled the East in 1956, they were socialistically inclined. Blaschke followed them to West Germany in 1957 after he was told, and refused, to distance himself from his disloyal parents. He moved to West Berlin in 1964 to avoid the draft. While living there he traveled to East Berlin frequently for political discussions. An MfS case officer was present at one of these discussions and suggested that Blascke do something "active for securing freedom." His first test run was to photograph U.S. military installations near the U.S.-occupied "Devil's Mountain."[40]

Shortly before Blaschke returned to West Germany, he signed an official agreement in which it was clear he was working for the Ministry for State Security as a spy and was given the code name "Litze." The recruitment was based on ideology. In 1970 Blaschke got a job at AEG/Telefunken (later ANT) as a laboratory technician. Although he did not have access to secret material, he was actively involved in the Work Council at AEG/Telefunken and chair of the IG Metal Labor Union and therefore had many contacts and personal information on potential recruits. As a result, he emerged as a recruiter for the SWT. He was told to provide reports on possible agent candidates for recruitment who had access to secret material.[41]

Blaschke sent the MfS many names, but most of these leads turned out to be fruitless. He did, however, have success in recruiting a friend from the labor union who also worked at AEG/Telefunken, Horst Lang ("Filter"), who had been having marital problems and recently separated from his first wife. He was an electrical engineer and had access to secret material on pulse code modulation, a method for converting analogue signals to digital. Lang was officially recruited as an object source in 1978 on the basis of ideology after Blaschke took him to a meeting with his case officer in Berlin.[42]

With the Blaschke case we come full circle back to a seemingly insignificant figure – clearly an advantage in the area of recruitment. In addition to revealing who the spies were, where they worked, and why they did what they did, the *Rosenholz* material unmasks an incredibly bloated human web of recruiters, instructors, couriers, and residents. The spiderweb was designed to support an agent, but was not cost-effective while it ensnared the secrets of the West. The Stasi simply overestimated the power of stolen technological secrets to solve its economic problems, and the enormous spy infrastructure investment produced a very small return.

Like the KGB, the Stasi had a formidable foreign intelligence arm. Whereas bookshelves have been filled with volumes on the KGB's foreign operations, the Stasi is still predominantly known in the West for its internal repression of enemies of the state. In the secret intelligence world, however, the HV A was widely respected and admired for its achievements. Even so, no one suspected that science and technology played such a large and pivotal role in its operations. Despite the fact that the secret *Rosenholz* material was analyzed by Western officials and used to prosecute agents, no one revealed the extent to which the MfS penetrated Western science. Why not? After all, Russia continues to pursue its old habit of stealing scientific-technical secrets, even in the early twenty-first century. It was the Soviet Union that breathed life into the MfS during its beginnings, it was the Soviet Union that was the sole beneficiary of the stolen military secrets, and it was the Soviet Union that was behind the East Germans' success.

5

"Kid" and "Paul"

The American students are spellbound. The charismatic lecturer has had their rapt attention for half an hour but has not revealed his identity yet. He asks them which intelligence agency they consider the most effective. Their top three choices are the CIA, KGB, and National Security Agency (NSA). The lecturer writes his top three on the blackboard: the Mossad, Stasi, and the NSA. The students assume the lecturer is a recruiter from the CIA. He circles his top choice – the Stasi – and mentions that he worked for them. He has not told them his biography yet. When they hear it, their mouths drop open. He ends his story dramatically: "What I did was wrong. I'm not a hero, I'm a criminal."

Downstairs in the front office as the lecturer is ready to sign the paperwork for his honorarium he notices that the wrong name is typed on the papers. "Jeffrey M. Carney is not my name," he tells the administrative assistant. "I changed it several years ago: it's Jens Karney." He does not ruffle her efficiency but later I hear speculations about how I spend my weekends away from the office. The administrative assistant quipped to me: "The people you know. I had to rip up the paperwork and type it all over again."

Carney seems to be a born teacher. He mentions that he was an instructor in the air force. The older pictures of him on the Internet, in newspapers and magazines and in his file, do not convey a live wire. He looks much more dour and serious – he is not smiling and is wearing intellectual-looking round gold-rim glasses. After his release from prison in 2002, he grew a small goatee that forms wisps on the bottom of his broad, round head, and he projects a more athletic, youthful image.

The case of Jeffrey M. Carney first came to public light in 1997, when the West German magazine *Focus* reported that he had been kidnapped without the knowledge of outraged German officials. There was a rumor circulating that he had been abducted by the CIA in 1991 and brought back to America for a secret trial. Like most rumors, this was not quite true. He had, in fact, been kidnapped by the air forces' Office for Security (AFOSI). The case was intriguing because he was an American and had worked at one of the mysterious U.S. electronic listening stations in Berlin. That station was run by an even more secret agency in Washington, which preferred working in the shadows rather than in the spotlight, like the CIA. The National Security Agency was so secret, its acronym – NSA – reportedly stands for "no such agency." Carney was, in fact, one of a handful of Americans who betrayed the United States' electronic secrets to the Stasi during the 1980s – the other well-known case being James W. Hall. And a third is still hiding behind the code name "Optik."[1] They were likely the most damaging American spies who worked for East German intelligence.

Whereas Jeffrey Carney already served his sentence, by 2006 James Hall was still in prison at Fort Leavenworth in Kansas, carrying out his forty-year sentence. Fort Leavenworth is a huge self-contained city, complete with a movie theater, schools, a historic chapel, a military college, a bank, apartments for army personnel, houses for officers, a shooting range, an airfield, and a shiny, massive, new silver prison, built in 2002. The new prison is hidden at the back of the compound past the airfield and rifle range on a track of land that used to be farmed. But when Hall started his sentence in 1989 he was deposited in the old prison, built in 1877 closer to the military campus, called the "castle" by inmates, but razed to the ground when the new prison was finished. The remaining facade is a combination of a Western cowboy Hollywood set and gulag. It is surprising the extent to which the exterior resembles the Stasi prison in *Hohenschönhausen* – especially the way in which the entrance is framed by the imposing watchtowers.

James Hall does not mince words: during a visit, the first sentence out of his mouth, tinged with a New York accent, was: "I did what I did . . . and thought I wouldn't get caught. . . . It was stupid." His own explanation is that he did it out of "greed, avarice." "I am as guilty as this table is brown." He makes no attempt to portray himself in a positive light: "I am a treasonous bastard, not a Cold War spy."[2] By 2006, Hall had settled into middle age – he is a bit rotund and of medium height and has a broad face, graying short hair and a mustache, a pug nose, and striking blue eyes that are accentuated by his blue prison garb, stenciled with his name and prison number. Because the prison had no special program to reform spies who steal and sell secrets, Hall went through the larceny program.

He also learned two trades – welding and cabinet making – and received a B.A. in European history through a correspondence course. I was his first visitor, with the exception of his parents and government officials, since his imprisonment in Fort Leavenworth in 1989.

Between the two of them, Carney and Hall betrayed secrets from the United States' most important eavesdropping installations in Berlin: Hall worked at the NSA's Field Station Berlin, located at *Teufelsberg* (Devil's Mountain) in the posh Berlin-Grunewald district between 1982 and 1985 (later in Frankfurt), and Carney was stationed at the NSA's unit run by the U.S. Air Force's electronic 6912th division in Berlin-Marienfelde between 1982 and 1984.

Devil's Mountain (*Teufelsberg*) towered over the Berlin city landscape. Although only 115 meters tall, the "hill," as veterans called it, was the highest point in Berlin. Built from the rubble of World War II – truly the Devil's work – and officially known as Field Station Berlin, its existence aroused curiosity, and it was an open secret that Western allies eavesdropped on the East Bloc from there. Located in the popular Grunewald forest, Cold War Sunday strollers gawked at the buildings and radomes and towers dotting the hilltop and speculated about its mysterious activities.

Truly a surveillance architecture landscape, complete with pockmarked golf ball radomes, the hill was outwardly run by the U.S. Army and Air Force, but, in fact, the real string-puller of this spy marionette was the National Security Agency's military branch. The installation of mobile listening posts in 1951 staked postwar territory whereas the 1964 permanent bubble, research and development tower, and three-story brick building showed they planned to stay for a while. By 1979 they had made themselves comfortable with the addition of a mess hall, offices, and a warehouse for its thousand workers (they worked in shifts of 230). The British and French soon joined the surveillance landscape with the installation of a tall eavesdropping mast and a prosaic building on the site, but their modest efforts were overshadowed by the U.S. superpower presence.[3]

In contrast to Devil's Mountain, the U.S. listening post in Marienfelde was one of the Cold War's most closely guarded secrets. Run by the U.S. Air Force's Security Service/Electronic Security Command and built between 1962 and 1965, its geodesic domes on the outskirts of Berlin were less conspicuous than those on this hill. Its cover story was that the station monitored air traffic and "atmospheric phenomenon," when in fact it conducted electronic warfare, like its better-known big brother.[4]

The spy landscape of geodesic domes, antennas, and towers intrigued Ministry for State Security (MfS) spies early on. They started taking pictures in 1962 for their reports and document an apparent building boom between 1968 and 1972. Although *Teufelsberg* looked impressive, the MfS guessed that its reach only extended to East Germany, West Germany, and Poland. Although the MfS knew of the installations general missions, during the 1980s Carney and Hall provided the Soviet Bloc with secrets that could have changed the course of the Cold War if it had turned hot.[5]

Hall and Carney's lives overlapped, converged, and diverged, but they did not meet until they were both prisoners at the Fort Leavenworth Military Prison in Kansas in the 1990s. Both of them joined the military instead of going to college, both were stationed in Berlin in the eighties, and both volunteered to work for the Stasi. Despite the similarities, their cases are markedly different when it comes to motivation, personality, and damage done. Whereas James Hall worked for both the Soviet Committee for State Security (KGB) and the Stasi, Jeff Carney not only provided the MfS with information as an agent, but also defected to East Germany in 1985. Whereas Hall's motive for spying was seemingly the money, Carney's was psychological. Of the two, Hall passed on a vast amount of damaging material; although Carney's material was interesting, he did not have the same access as Hall.

CINCINNATI "KID"

When Jeff Carney enlisted in the U.S. Air Force at the age of seventeen he never imagined that he would become a spy or that he would be kidnapped and thrown into jail. Shortly after his release from prison he recalled having "top security clearance but couldn't even drink beer yet."[6] Born in Cincinnati, Ohio, in 1963, he was sent to West Berlin, the front line of the Cold War, at the age of nineteen. He trained as a linguist and communications specialist and was sent to the air force's language school in Monterey, California, to study German, for which he had a natural aptitude. He would learn very quickly why Berlin was commonly called spy city. Divided after the war, the Western allies had carved up the Western part of Berlin into French, British, and American sectors of occupation. The Soviets ruled in East Berlin and East Germany. It is not surprising that the United States intelligence community developed two prime eavesdropping stations in Berlin, as its strength in spying always lay in technical spying, not in human spying. By intercepting and listening to radio and telephone conversations on land and in the air, Carney was indeed on the front lines of the Cold War espionage. He could see and hear the enemy.

After the first year of getting to know Berlin and the job, he became increasingly disgruntled. He also began to discover his sexuality. He was confused; he had a relationship with a young black male officer. He was worried that the hidebound air force would find out he was homosexual.

On a fall October day in 1983 after too many beers at a West Berlin Irish Pub, Carney made his way to East Berlin through the *Friedrichstrasse* border crossing. When he tried to return to West Berlin, he discovered he had missed the midnight curfew for one-day guests and went straight to the MfS officers at the border. As he related to the students: I just went to the border and "rang the doorbell...let me in!" The on-duty officer at the border quickly called headquarters, and they sent an officer from the HV A's (foreign intelligence arm of the Ministry for State Security) American department (XI/9), which was responsible for U.S. forces. The officer was astonished that the American, unlike most army personnel in Berlin, not only spoke fluent German, but he hardly had an accent. Ralph Dieter Lehman could tell that the young man was in psychological trouble and took advantage of this weakness for his own ends. Carney began to see his handlers as new friends. They immediately recognized his youth and appropriately code-named him "Kid." Lehmann, who had spent time in the United States, later told Carney that he chose that name after his favorite movie, *Cincinnati Kid*.[7]

Carney passed on approximately sixty-five pieces of information to the Stasi between 1983 and 1986. His material received high marks – twenty-four received the highest rating, I. Initially, most of the material was passed on to the Soviet Union. Later copies also went to the HV A Department IX for work against enemy intelligence organizations.

Carney passed on information about his unit's listening activities in the German Democratic Republic (GDR), electronic espionage activities against Soviet and East German targets, and orders from the NSA to its Berlin stations. During Carney's 1983–84 tour of duty, the MfS was glad to have received the Handbook of the 6912th Electronic Security Group, the operational plans of the air force in West Germany, and an overview of the NSA's activities in electronic espionage. The East Bloc was particularly interested in the educational training of the technicians in electronic warfare and the "radio communications analysis technician career development course." From the material the MfS determined that American intelligence was listening to the SED's (East German Communist Party) conversations, monitoring GDR air traffic, and conducting electronic warfare.[8]

Six months after his first meeting with a Stasi officer, Carney was transferred to Goodfellow Air Force Base in Texas, where he became an instructor at a U.S. Air Force service school in April 1984. He continued to pass on material to his case officer during meetings in Mexico until September 1985. During the period 1984–85 he passed on highly rated documents on the NSA's electronic security communications for the 6912th group at Tempelhof Central Airport, a Berlin long-range radar replacement program, activity reports, a cryptological station profile of West Berlin and Augsburg, a DOD capabilities handbook, and U.S. Signals Intelligence directives.[9] Carney claims this was material he found in the library and was not highly classified.

Stasi leaders were amazed by some of the United States' technical capabilities and plans. Carney's documents allegedly showed that the United States had cooked up a plan to intercept Soviet ground-to-air commands at their base in Berlin-Eberswalde while substituting their own orders through taped voices. Marienfelde had apparently collected a taped database of all the Soviet commanders' voices. If this worked, the MiG pilots would have received American orders via the Soviet commanders' voices. To the MfS it seemed like science fiction, but the reality was that this program cost millions of dollars to develop.[10]

According to Markus Wolf, "Kid" began to get paranoid after he found his lover dead in a bathtub and decided to flee America.[11] In fact, with an impending polygraph test, Carney was worried about being exposed as a homosexual and a spy. 1985 was also the year of the spy. Arrests were rampant: Navy warrant officer John Walker, the most celebrated Cold War spy for the Soviets, was arrested in May 1985. Other high-profile cases included the arrests of Robert Pelton, a low-level communication specialist at the NSA who also spied for the Soviets, and Jonathan Jay Pollard, who spied for an ally, the Israelis. Finally, Hans-Joachim Tiedge, a high-ranking West German counterintelligence official, defected to East Germany in August 1985.

According to Carney, he bought a round-trip ticket to Mexico City, went straight to the GDR embassy, and asked them to "tell Berlin I'm here." This was apparently without the authorization of his case officer or Berlin.[12] They were taken by surprise. Officials at the embassy immediately called the central office, which relayed back the reassuring message: "Greetings and welcome from central."[13]

A plan was soon hatched as to how to get Carney back to East Germany. The nearby Cubans had proven to be loyal friends of the East Germans, and they gladly agreed to help. Carney was smuggled out through a laundry shoot and flown to Cuba in a Cubana Airliner, where he stayed for a week at a safe house in Varo Dero. The Cubans rolled out the red carpet and their hospitality. Fidel Castro said hello. Carney felt important.

During the week in Cuba, the East Germans made his situation clear: "You can never go home; you're dead; you died in Mexico." Carney was then flown to Prague, where he was met by a driver in a Mercedes Benz and driven at top speeds back to East Berlin.[14]

After initial debriefings, Carney lived with a couple in the socialist Berlin suburb of Marzahn. Soon he received his own apartment in Berlin-Friedrichshain, near *Alexanderplatz*, the center of town. It was freshly painted and furnished by the HV A and came complete with modern Western electronic entertainment like a stereo and a JVC TV and VCR. A shiny new Soviet Lada automobile followed – a prestige item in socialist Germany. He even received a phone immediately – another luxury in the GDR.[15]

With the new merchandise came a new identity. Jeffrey M. Carney was transformed into Jens Karney. He received a GDR identity card claiming he was an American born in Dessau. The minor changes in name were easy to get used to but adapting to his new life in the GDR was slow. He was totally cut off from old friends and family. The people around him reported that he was "depressive."

The Stasi did not trust him. The phone he received so quickly was tapped, his mail was monitored and controls placed on him at the border. According to Carney, they threatened him: "If you betray us like you betrayed your own country, you're dead." The Stasi disapprovingly observed his homosexual lifestyle. They commented on his large circle of friends. They even sent him on a blind date to check on his "political reliability."[16]

Carney and his case officers thought about what he would do with his life. He considered studying in Leipzig – perhaps religion. But he dropped that idea when he found out that they wanted him to become an informant on the other students. Instead he was given the piquant job monitoring his old unit, the 6912th Electronic Security Group, and the embassy in East Berlin. Markus Wolf reports that this was done to "stabilize him." "It was low-level work."[17] He received 1,500 marks a month as a salary.

Carney lived in the GDR for four years until it collapsed in the fall of 1989 and was absorbed by West Germany in 1990. The Stasi gave him 15,000 East marks and closed the file on him. He was apparently offered the option of resettlement in South Africa but decided to go underground in the Eastern part of Berlin.

He literally went underground by becoming a subway train driver for the Berlin subway service – the U-Bahn. But the changes in Germany were far-reaching. Despite the loyalty of many leaders and officers to their former sources, some were opportunistic. They either defected to the West for money or provided West German officials with information in exchange for immunity from prosecution. Carney was unlucky. His former case officer betrayed him; he took two Samsonite suitcases bulging with files to the West.

Carney's ultimate betrayal came when an unnamed officer sold two German journalists, Paul Limbach and Heiner Emde, thousands of pages of Stasi files from their electronic intelligence and surveillance unit during the chaotic days after the revolution of November 1989 and before unification in March 1990. This included directives, manuals, and documents passed on by Carney and Hall. The officer did not know Carney's real name, just his alias – Jens Karney – and where he lived in Berlin-Friedrichshain. The journalists in turn passed this information on to the West Germany counterintelligence service, the Federal Office for the Protection of the Constitution, which informed the American embassy.[18] The United States was slow to take action.

More than one year later, on April 1991, the game was suddenly over. Six armed air force security officials from the Office of Special Investigations (AFOSI) surrounded, grabbed, and threw Carney into a van in front of his Berlin apartment at 9:00 a.m. as he was on his way to get his breakfast rolls from the corner bakery. He was taken to Tempelhof Airport and flown back in an air force jet to the United States for court-martial. German counterintelligence officials were shocked that democratic America undertook such an operation in post–Cold War Berlin and commented that "the U.S. intelligence services are acting like cowboys again.... They can't simply grab people with a lasso."[19]

Carney was almost relieved to be caught. He knew it would have to happen some day. He confessed and received a thirty-eight year prison sentence, which was commuted to twenty years. He was released from prison after eleven years, four months and three days. Once released from prison, Carney secured a job at a plastics factory, while supplementing his income with part-time jobs like mowing lawns. He related that it was difficult to get a job, even at a fast-food restaurant, with a felony record. He nevertheless managed to secure a better job selling tickets in a theater, where he worked with his new lover.

Homesick for Berlin, Carney went back to retrieve his cat and tried to reactivate his German citizenship. Former leaders and officers like Werner Grossman, last head of the HV A, and Gregor Gysi, the unorthodox lawyer, were supportive of his efforts. Although repentant for what he did, he still felt betrayed by his case officer, with whom he had developed a relationship of trust. His last words to Carney were: "I'm sorry you had to serve such a long sentence."[20]

"PAUL"

If Carney was young, confused, and vulnerable, James W. Hall was ambitious, mature, and greedy. More importantly, he had greater access to super-secret documents, as he was in the Special Access Program (SAP). Even nuclear secrets were not as tightly held as the prized eavesdropping to which he had access. When he arrived in Berlin in 1981, Hall was twenty-four years old and had recently been transferred from his first posting in Schneeberg on the West German border near Czechoslovakia to Field Station Berlin. Hall was born in the Bronx in 1957, grew up in Sharon Springs in upstate New York, and joined the army when he was seventeen years old, where he was trained in signals intelligence. During his stay in Schneeberg he met a young German waitress named Heidi, who became pregnant in 1981. Heidi and their daughter Jessica joined Hall in Berlin in 1982, and the couple got married, despite Hall's ambivalence.

According to spy catcher Colonel Stuart A. Herrington, the military counterintelligence official who conducted a thorough investigation of the Hall case that lead to his arrest: "He had quickly established a reputation as a diligent and talented analyst" in Berlin and had a professional, if not arrogant demeanor. He received excellent yearly evaluations.[21]

Hall would later characterize himself as a patriotic man, but his army pay was hardly enough to keep him comfortable and to cover the expenses of a family and his hobbies. Selling secrets was an easy way to make money. And this is exactly what he told the Turkish auto mechanic–instructor Huseyin Yildirim, "the Meister," at the army's auto craft shop. As Yildirim's nickname suggests, he was a master mechanic. The Meister, as he was known among the troops stationed at *Teufelsberg*, was a colorful, well-liked, outgoing low-life character who came into contact with many servicemen and servicewomen stationed at *Teufelsberg*. Like Hall he was interested in making extra money and had a talent for spotting people with the same weakness.

Yildirim also worked for the Stasi, primarily as a recruiter and courier. He had initially volunteered to work for the MfS in 1978, when he was working at an automotive company near Stuttgart, hardly a prime intelligence target for them. The MfS told him they were not interested unless he could find himself a job with the Americans in Berlin. In 1979 Yildirim took his master mechanic license to the auto shop at the Berlin Andrews

Barracks, the former Hermann Goering barracks, and contacted the MfS again. They were delighted to hear from the Meister again. By 12 May 1980 he was registered as unofficial staff member (IM) "Blitz." In the course of his MfS career, Yildirim managed to recruit about five servicemen or servicewomen.[22]

When Yildirim started buying secrets from Hall, he told him they were for a Turkish relative who worked for Turkish intelligence, a NATO ally. At first the MfS ran this as a false-flag operation, in which the operatives say they are working for another country. While Yildirim was testing Hall out during the initial recruitment phase in 1983, the preliminary file was called "Devil." Once Hall became official in the bureaucracy, his code name was changed to "Ronny." Klaus Eichner, who was the evaluator for Hall's material, relates that he was run under false flags for quite some time before his real handlers were revealed at a Berlin meeting, at which point Hall selected the code name "Paul."[23]

Hall must have realized very quickly that his real partners were not Turkish. Reportedly, Yildirim took Hall to a secret hole in the Berlin Wall at the southeast border in Zehlendorf, where agents were smuggled into East Germany, and he met his future case officers, Wolfgang Koch and someone known as Horst.[24] Hall usually met with his case officers in East German safe houses, one of which was located on a river outside Berlin. An elderly couple took care of the grounds and cooked elaborate meals. Sometimes Hall would stay overnight, and the case officers talked about politics late into the night, emphasizing disarmament. Because the Germans were so pleased with Hall's material, they conferred a medal on him at a secret ceremony in the basement of the safe house in the presence of his case officers. It made Hall uncomfortable because they took his picture – they said – for his file. Long after his espionage career was over and he was doing time in Leavenworth, Hall could imagine American counterintelligence agents throwing darts at the picture.[25]

James Hall did not tell the Stasi that he had already volunteered to work for the KGB at the end of 1982. He had simply gone for a walk in Grunewald and slipped a letter in the consulates' mailbox, offering to spy for them in exchange for money. The encounter with Yildirim two to three weeks later was a coincidence. Hall began to make double copies of the documents for both new masters for double the money.[26]

There is no doubt that Hall thought he needed the money, but motivations for spying are rarely so simple. It usually takes the accumulation of other personal crises to cross the Rubicon. His move to Berlin and his decision to spy coincided with his marriage to his pregnant girlfriend (the choice was "pay child support or get married"), and the child presented huge worries in his mind: she had a rare bone disorder and needed surgery, and the thought of paying for college down the line loomed large. The child's illness soon led to a marital crisis as well. Although every SIGINT (signals intelligence) officer wanted to be stationed in Berlin, it "felt like misery at the time."[27] He could have also been disgruntled about the low army pay, even though he became an overachiever at work while moonlighting for both the KGB and the Stasi. He always had a strong work ethic.

The first document Hall delivered from the Berlin Field Station to the MfS was an eye-opener. It was an "Allied communication publication" depicting all the NSA's installations worldwide and its radio and electronic targets. For the first time the MfS could identify all relevant NSA locations in West Berlin and West Germany. Until 1983, the MfS's main source on the NSA had been James Bamford's 1982 bestseller *The Puzzle Palace*.[28] There was nothing in that book about Berlin or detailed operational knowledge.

Hall was stationed in Berlin until April 1985, when he was transferred back to the United States for a year. During that time, the KGB ran Hall, as the MfS did not have as much experience in America. Hall found servicing the dead drops time-consuming and cumbersome and broke off contact. He preferred the MfS's style and found them more amenable, though the Soviets were more security-minded. By 1986, Hall was transferred back to the Frankfurt 302nd Military Intelligence Battalion of the Fifth U.S. Army Corp, where he was promoted to head of electronic warfare and signals intelligence. Fearing an impending polygraph test, Hall returned to the United States to attend a warrant officer training school. He completed the training in February 1988 and was assigned to G-2 (intelligence) at Fort Stewart, Georgia, near Savannah. By that time Yildirim had moved to Florida with an American woman he had met in Berlin.[29]

During the Berlin and Frankfurt period, Hall passed on hundreds of highly sensitive documents. Surprisingly, the MfS did not know what they wanted, and Hall was not provided with a shopping list; it was not targeted collection. They told him to use his judgment, because he knew what was there and worth passing on.[30] Despite this ignorance on the part of the MfS, Hall did not pass on chicken feed in exchange for cash, but sold the most sensitive secrets in the store. As part of his daily routine, he photocopied the daily brief in duplicate and passed it on to the KGB and MfS.

One of the most notable documents was Project Trojan, a worldwide electronic surveillance program that could determine the locations of military vehicles and missiles through their signal emissions.[31] At first he copied the material at the office's copying machine, but it was so copious that he soon began to use a step van outside of headquarters and then returned the original classified material.

Whereas the Soviets told him to go out and buy whatever cameras he wished, the East Germans gave him the best of their spy cameras: from the rollover camera to the *mikrat* to the Super-8 home video camera to be used on its still, single-shot setting. The Soviets did offer him a camera in a stapler and another in a pen, but he declined because they could only take a few pictures at a time. The Soviets also provided him with a thermos as a container, whereas the Germans modified a blue gym bag container with a false bottom to hide documents. That compartment, however, was rarely big enough to transport the copious material he collected. Hall stole such a large volume of material that he preferred using the photocopier over the cameras. By the time he returned to the United States and his collection activity declined, he used the Super-8 video camera as a still camera. Hall had such a lack of interest in using the cameras that he even forgot the tiny *mikrat* camera in a desk drawer for three months while he was stationed in Frankfurt.[32]

Among the most important super-secret documents Hall obtained for the East Bloc was the National SIGINT Requirements List. This was a voluminous four-thousand-page catalogue filling ten big three-ring binders on how to use SIGINT to optimize intelligence gathering. It was a worldwide intelligence community wish list for electronic intelligence funneled to the NSA. The White House, the Department of Energy, and the State Department were all interested in obtaining specific information from various countries on topics like economic policies, raw materials resources, the position of armies, possession of weapons of mass destruction, atomic policies, and military research. Of course, information about enemy intelligence agencies was included as well. General topics not specific to a country, such as international terrorism and non-proliferation of weapons of mass destruction, were also on the list. Another interesting result was that the MfS discovered the United States did not only spy on enemies but also on friends such as France, England, and Canada. This enabled the MfS to develop some "active measure" activities to tell those allies of the American interest.[33]

In his memoirs, Markus Wolf recalls that he found this document of particular interest because the East Bloc intelligence agencies could infer where the U.S. intelligence community was "lacking knowledge" and where the East Bloc should "increase their activities and then take relevant countermeasures."[34]

Hall obtained this document while he was stationed in Frankfurt. Because Hall's deliveries had become so vast, the MfS instructed Yildirim to rent a small apartment in Frankfurt and buy a small copy machine. Eichner describes the acquisition of the complete NSRL as a "huge achievement of the 'Blitz' and 'Paul' team." "Blitz" stood at the copier for hours with sunglasses on because he had removed the protective cover to copy the documents more quickly. "Paul" came to help in the evening, and "Blitz" drove back to Berlin with the loot.[35]

"Canopy Wing" was another document so important that Erich Mielke personally handed it over to the KGB when he visited the Soviet Union. Although the United States did not wish the details of the super-secrets to be revealed to the public, the New York Times referred to this program in an article, commenting on how it cost hundreds of millions of dollars and was "designed to exploit a Soviet communications vulnerability." The article featured a telling headline about the damage James Hall caused: "U.S. Says Soldier Crippled Spy Post Set Up in Berlin."[36]

Canopy Wing was one of a number of ruthless electronic warfare plans prepared by the NSA targeting the East Bloc. The document listed a number of methods for eliminating the Soviet High Command's use of high-frequency communication when giving orders to its armed forces. Some examples of plans developed to paralyze the Soviet and Warsaw Pact command centers included identifying leadership centers in case of all-out war and acquiring intelligence on locations, structures, personnel, and technical capabilities with exact parameters and coordinates. Specific measures to electronically block work before the first strike so that no counterreaction was possible were in the planning stage. The NSA was also cooking up a scheme to spray microscopic particles or dust on enemy machines to shut them down. Finally, a computer simulation of voices was going to be used to provide false commands to airplanes or atomic submarines.[37]

Klaus Eichner, head analyst in the Stasi's foreign counterintelligence got "goose bumps" when he read the report, which he interpreted in the context of Gorbachev's reforms in 1986, when it was drafted. It was not the first time that such a document had crossed his desk, but he described it as "compact material presenting active preparation of aggression against the Warsaw Pact ... demanding the development of technology and software for a nuclear first-strike." The working group for this project recommended investing $14.5 billion into the project and hiring 1,570 people to work on it.[38]

Compared to the amount of financial and national security damage Hall was causing the United States and his value to the East Bloc, the payments he received from the MfS and KGB were small. He reportedly received a total of $300,000 from both his East German and Soviet spymasters over six years. For an army sergeant and warrant officer, however, the extra spy salary was enormous: it amounted to about twice as much as his $25,894 warrant officer's yearly salary. By MfS standards he was a very well-paid agent; in one productive year alone he received $30,000.[39]

It was not Hall's greed or Yildirim's loose-cannon personality or even good counterintelligence work that lead to the end of Hall's espionage career. In 1986, a low-level East German instructor was sent to West Berlin for an operational support mission. Like many other East Germans who tasted the fruits of capitalism in sparkling West Berlin, the Stasi instructor walked into a department store and longed to have the consumer goods it offered. As the MfS had only given him a modest allowance, he simply helped himself to what he wanted. The fifty-two-year old balding man was not especially furtive about the theft, either. A store detective caught him immediately and detained him. During the meeting the man, who was Professor Manfred Severin and taught English and languages at the Humboldt University, asked to see the *Staatsschutz* – the equivalent of our FBI – and told them who he was and that he had really staged the incident to create an "opportunity to talk." He told the *Staatsschutz* that he supported activities against the United States. Not especially interested in what they perceived to be a tall tale, they passed him on to the CIA, which in turn gave him to army counterintelligence. The professor expressed great bitterness and dissatisfaction with his life in communist Germany and told an army Foreign Counterintelligence Activity (FCA) agent that he was willing to tell them about his life in the MfS in exchange for resettlement in the West. The FCA agent explained to him that to "obtain sponsorship" he would have to contribute "something big" to his new American masters. The officer quickly recruited him under the code name "Canna Clay" and sent him back to the East. The FCA did not hear from him for two years.[40] Meanwhile, Severin had been brought in to act as translator and courier for James Hall, as Yildirim had moved to the United States in 1987 and Hall's German was not proficient enough to communicate effectively.

Out of the blue on 22 August 1988 Severin called the telephone number the officers had given him. This time, he did have "something significant." Two FCA agents picked him up at a West Berlin street corner and debriefed him in the car. Clay excitedly told his new masters that he had been called in by the MfS to act as interpreter at secret meetings in an East Berlin safe house in January and July 1988. Two case officers – Wolfgang and Horst – were debriefing an American soldier who was spying for

East Germany. The unidentified soldier, code-named "Paul," handed over classified documents from the office and described the activities of his intelligence unit and his duties there. Severin knew the soldier was a signals intelligence expert and divulged enough other details to make it possible for the FCA to quickly identify the man: James W. Hall III.[41]

The case interested Colonel Stuart Herrington, and he opened an investigation on 24 August 1988. A team of agents, later cooperating with the CIA and FBI, launched a manhunt and developed a trap that took four months to complete and almost half a million dollars to finance. The team first placed James Hall under surveillance at his current army job in Georgia and tapped his phone. Aside from keeping an eye on Hall in case he planned to flee the country, Herrington was hoping to catch Hall in the act of stealing documents. Herrington was struck by the affluence of the warrant officer, who lived in a nice house most personnel at that level could not afford. He also noticed the new Ford 150 truck and Volvo in the driveway.[42] Sudden affluence is a signal of spy activity but it is often not noticed or acted upon too late, as was the case with Aldrich Ames.

Meanwhile Manfred Severin had to be brought out of the cold, because the moment Hall was arrested the Stasi would seize the U.S.'s prize source. Initially, Severin asked to bring along thirteen family members, including his two sons, wife, and dog. He finally agreed to just bring his wife and dog. Because the CIA was the expert at defector exfiltrations, Herrington turned to Gus Hathaway in Berlin to undertake that operation.[43] It appears as though the family was smuggled to West Berlin in the trunk of a diplomat's car while another diplomat's car was used to create a diversion to distract the border guard's attention.

The next stage of the plan involved setting up an elaborate false-flag "sting" operation to make Hall confess. The FCA enlisted an experienced FBI officer, who would playact a KGB agent named Vladimir. As Severin was now safely in the United States, he was brought into the plan, which had to be executed quickly, because the Stasi would soon notice his absence.

On 22 December, Severin called Hall and set up a covert meeting at a nearby Day's Inn in Savannah. The FBI had installed their surveillance cameras, and Severin and "Vladimir" were waiting for Hall when he arrived. What followed was a two-hour confession of his work for the East Germans and, a surprise for investigators, his work for the KGB! "Vladimir" egged Hall's ego and greed on and handed him bundles of cash adding up to $60,000. Hall described his work with Yildirim, his methods, and the material passed on. For example, he described a plan to release dust over enemy communications to shut them down: "When it goes into electronic equipment, it implodes it. Like if you blow dust into a TV and turn the TV on, it just puff, it shuts it down." "Vladimir" then asked: "So before you turned it on, our side knew already." Hall replied: "I hope so. Don't know personally.... As long as I get my money, you can do what you like with whatever it is I give you." This gave Vladimir an opportunity to elicit insight into Hall's motives: "So you did it just for money?" Hall replied: "Oh yeah. It's not because I'm anti-American. I wave the flag as much as anybody else."[44]

As Hall exited from the motel room and walked to his car, the FBI pushed him against the car, put handcuffs on him, and made the dramatic arrest. Herrington was very pleased with the course of the investigation and the ruse to capture Hall. Yildirim was rounded up in Florida simultaneously. And Manfred Severin was reportedly given a million dollars and a new identity.[45]

At a secret court-martial in February 1989, Hall pleaded guilty to espionage charges and was sentenced to a forty-year prison term, a $50,000 fine, and a dishonorable discharge. Hall's "remarkably candid self-portrait" on video would provide the jury at his trial on 19 July 1989 with a glimpse of a "new breed of American spy" whose motive was money. Yildirim's arrest followed in 1989 and at the trial the FBI rolled in a cart piled high with ten thousand pages of documents found buried in a graveyard in West Berlin. The Stasi reportedly valued their courier so highly that they rewarded him with an interest in a diamond mine in Sierra Leone, Africa, but diamonds did not prove as lucrative as peddling secrets.[46] Yildirim received a life sentence without parole, yet he was freed in 2004 after fourteen years in prison.

After Hall was thrown into jail, he was debriefed for eighteen months by the army and the NSA. The case both fascinated and repelled investigators. At one point, a debriefer asked Hall why he didn't just become a "dope dealer" to earn extra money. Hall's reply was that he had never met a drug dealer and that he was dealing in secrets.[47]

Selling secrets to the enemy can be stressful, though Hall seemed to be nonchalant about it. During the debriefing process, Hall passed the polygraph in every area but one: he was asked if he told anyone about his spy activity. He answered no. After some coaxing and in front of a video camera and with tape recorders whirring, Hall confessed that he told a prostitute in Berlin at a brothel near the popular jazz club in Berlin-Dahlem, the *Eierschale*. She reportedly gave him a blank stare and said "I guess you should stop."[48]

Hall's arrest on 20 December 1988 came about a year before the fall of the Berlin Wall and the collapse of East Germany. The topic of the material he passed on to the Stasi came up again in the media in 1990, when two enterprising journalists, Paul Limbach and Heiner Emde, bought files from an officer in the Stasi's unit for electronic intelligence and counterintelligence (Department III) and published excerpts in the now-defunct West German magazine *Quick*. American officials were not happy to see the fruits of Hall's espionage made public knowledge, even though the Cold War was over. One of the conditions of Hall's sentence was that he would not reveal to the public the material he passed on to the East. The end of the Cold War has allowed us to uncover the extent to which the United States' prized technical intelligence gathering had been compromised. Other Americans, such as John Walker, sold technical secrets or knowledge to the East. FBI special agent Robert Hanssen, who was caught for spying for the Soviet Union, compromised many technical secrets, including a highly secret tunnel project in Washington, DC, designed to spy on the Soviet embassy.

Hall was considered the "perpetrator of one of the most costly and damaging breaches of security of the long Cold War."[49] His case was equally as damaging as that of John Walker, who had volunteered to spy for the KGB in 1968 and did not get caught until 1985, despite the fact that Hall's activity did not last as long.

Together with some other lower-level agents, Carney and Hall allowed the MfS to uncover the secrets that had been hidden behind the fences at the Devil's Mountain and Marienfelde. The new knowledge allowed them to develop strong countermeasures and to gain insight into the United States' powerful and far-reaching electronic espionage program and electronic warfare plans.

During the time Hall, Carney, and Yildirim were handing over secrets to the East, Markus Wolf wrote to deputy chief of the MfS, Lieutenant General Neiber: "By order of Comrade Minister I am sending you 13 original documents of the U.S. Intelligence services. The material deals with vital information concerning the basic organization of signals intelligence collection by the U.S. intelligence services in peace and in war, about specific plans for the European theater of war, and about the special role of West Berlin in the enemy's electronic warfare."[50]

Horst Männchen had always been an enthusiastic admirer of the United States' capabilities in electronic espionage and warfare. When he established the blueprint for the MfS's own Department for Electronic Espionage and Counterespionage in 1973, he emulated the American model, wanting to reverse it to work for the MfS (see Chapter 10). When he was asked to evaluate the material Hall brought, his comments were:

The material consists of some of the most important American signals intelligence directives... [it]... is timely and extremely valuable for the further development of our work and has great operational and political value. It consists of NSA directives and working documents, the leading organization of the USA for signals intelligence. It also includes plans and analysis of the DIA and the Intelligence and Security Command. The contents, part of which are global in nature, some very detailed, expose basic plans of the enemy for signals intelligence collection into the next decade.[51]

There is no doubt that Hall's material was more copious and damaging than that of Sergeant Carney's. On the other hand, with Carney's defection to the East, debriefers there had plenty of time to squeeze out any knowledge Carney had about air force intelligence. In many respects, Carney was more loyal to his communist bosses in the East, whereas Hall, the double-dipper, saw his East German and Soviet paymasters as his partners in a business deal. Carney felt betrayed by, and angry at, the case officer who turned him in, whereas Hall did not care and had no rancor against the East German defector who reported his spy activity.

The 1980s saw a proliferation of enlisted men and women who were ready to sell secrets to the communists. Their Soviet and East German spymasters preyed on the double human weaknesses of greed and ego. With low pay and low self-esteem, they were easy targets. Hall and Carney's harm to Western military intelligence was equal to the damage the infamous John Walker caused to the navy during the seventeen years he spied for the Soviets. Once the American hiding behind the code name "Optik," who also worked in electronic intelligence, is unveiled, the trio should be considered collectively the Cold War's most damaging spies. Unlike their small-fry German counterparts featured in the previous chapter, these were major and damaging sources.

From the air force and army to the marines and navy, the East Bloc had an impressive overview of United States military intelligence, and it provided them with foreknowledge to prepare effective countermeasures. Had the Cold War turned hot, the spy information would have been more damaging and these military men would have become supervillians.

6

The Computer Fiasco

At 5:10 a.m. on 5 December 1989, Artur Wenzel was found dead in his jail cell at the central East Berlin police station. He had hung himself on the cell window with his leather belt. He was a tidy man who attended to appearances, and his shoes were placed neatly in a corner. He usually wore a businessman's suit and tie and had dyed jet-black, slicked-back hair, which did not match his fair complexion and blue eyes. When police detained the well-dressed, corpulent fifty-five-year-old "businessman" outside of his *Alexanderplatz* "House of Electronics" office in the heart of the city the day before, they seized two suitcases containing more than half a million West German marks and 100,000 East German marks – more than a quarter of a million dollars.[1]

Was Wenzel planning to flee the country and go underground with this large amount of money or was he merely carrying out a business transaction as he told investigators the next day? No ordinary citizen, and not even a real businessman, Colonel Wenzel had faithfully served the Ministry for State Security for thirty-five years and had been head of internal security's microelectronics unit, where he had worked on countering economic espionage since 1981.[2] It is not surprising that Wenzel had access to large amounts of money, given his position. The Stasi had established good relations with Alexander Schalck-Golodkowski, Secretary of State for Foreign Trade, who provided East Germany with the hard currency it needed for expensive technology. Computer technology had assumed great significance in the waning days of communism in the East Bloc. Leaders spared no costs to pursue the development of their own computer industry. It became the final battlefield.

Wenzel's suicide would suggest that he had been involved in a high-stakes game consisting of shady business deals and that he committed acts for which he would rather not go to trial. Whatever his individual

6. Artur Wenzel. Wenzel was the director of the Ministry for State Security's counterintelligence microelectronics division. He hanged himself in a Berlin jail cell and was found dead on 5 December 1989. (BStU)

guilt, the state quest for scientific-technical prowess in computers had led to large-scale corruption, money laundering, abuse of power and position, and extensive use of illegal smuggling and espionage. Not only were Easterners involved, but Westerners, especially West Germans, Austrians, and Americans, supplied the embargoed technology or know-how to the East at exorbitant prices. Wenzel was just one cog in a large wheel of corruption bent on acquiring computers, plans, and blueprints through espionage and trade organizations. Schalck and his Commercial Coordination Unit (KoKo) empire bankrolled and imported machinery, while the HV A's (foreign intelligence arm of the Ministry for State Security)

Sector for Science and Technology secretly stole the documentation. The cost of harnessing these enormous human and material resources may have been a factor in the final collapse of East Germany. Ultimately, the Ministry for State Security (MfS) overestimated the power of secret technology transfer to help create an indigenous, competitive computer industry.

Espionage in the area of computers is probably the most well-known aspect of Soviet and East Bloc hi-tech espionage. By the late 1970s and early 1980s, stories about agents caught and machines smuggled littered the pages of the *Wall Street Journal*, the *New York Times*, and other leading newspapers. Several books on the topic of Soviet hi-tech espionage came out in the mid-eighties. From the early sixties until the late eighties, half of the agents caught in scientific-technical espionage were in the area of computers. The number of agents in this area reflects the extent of the effort. As the Soviet electronics industry failed to take off in the sixties, it increasingly turned to smuggling computers, especially IBM models, to copy and manufacture in the Soviet Union. By the late seventies and eighties, breaking the embargo in the area of computers was one of the highest priorities for acquisition agencies.[3]

In his 1986 book, *High-Tech Espionage*, Jay Tuck examined half a dozen cases of massive international rings of professional smugglers who shipped electronics equipment to the Soviet Union. The rings spanned continents, from Silicon Valley and Hong Kong to South Africa and West Germany. Several West Germans, such as "Megabucks Müller" and Werner Bruchhausen, were involved in these rings. Whereas Tuck mostly examined cases of illegal technology transfer to the Soviet Union through seemingly innocuous business deals, the role of other East Bloc countries in this transfer, especially East Germany, was crucial.[4]

Tuck's story stopped in 1986, the year the computer frenzy began to escalate in East Germany. The feverish pace continued until the fall of the Berlin Wall in 1989, one year short of the end of the five-year plan period. When looked at teleologically, the outcome of the quest for an indigenous computer industry seems inevitable. The final years became a battle between the embargo makers and the embargo breakers, with the embargo makers winning the war.

The American intelligence community watched the hi-tech espionage program with alarm, and "Operation Exodus" was launched in 1981 to stem the flow of illegal CoCom (Coordinating Committee for East-West Trade) items to the Soviet Union and the East Bloc. The program was installed soon after the Reagan administration had begun to investigate the extent of Western high-technology transfer to the Soviet Union.

On 10 July 1986 a top secret 1984 CIA study on "West Germany as a Target of the East Bloc for the Acquisition of High Technology" landed on the desk of Major General Dr. Alfred Kleine, the head of economic counterintelligence. It was a harsh critique of West Germany. In essence, the CIA argued that West Germany, with Chancellor Helmut Kohl leading the pack, was turning a blind eye to illegal technology transfer because of trade interests with the Soviet Union.[5]

Despite the Stasi's tardiness in acquiring and passing the secret 1984 report on to the spies in the department for the protection of the economy, it provided them with foreknowledge in the battle over technology. Harry Schütt, head of foreign intelligence's department for counterespionage, sent on the report with the further information that it was likely that there would be stronger export controls as a result of the CIA's criticism. This would include a closer examination of questionable firms that had already been involved with illegal transfer or of unknown companies who applied for export permission. Schütt also forewarned Kleine that there would be "direct physical controls" of the goods. He warned that these measures were going to be accompanied by a public relations campaign in the media about technology acquisition methods.[6]

The U.S. pressure on West Germany did indeed lead to tougher border controls, more arrests, and accompanying publicity. It is no wonder that Horst Vogel recalled after the fall of the Wall that "it became increasingly more difficult to break the embargo."[7]

Western intelligence's increased vigilance coincided with Erich Honecker's illusionary drive to achieve technological world-power status through computers and the production of East Germany's own one-megabit chip. In 1981 Honecker announced a ten-point program at the Xth Party Congress to "draw the bulk of its microelectronic needs from domestic production by 1985."[8] The wish to attain world-power status in computers reached a feverish pitch in 1986 on the occasion of the XIth Party Congress, during which microelectronics figured prominently.

Although Honecker's predecessor, Walter Ulbricht, had already been interested in computers during the sixties, the party leadership's interest increased dramatically in the seventies. The Central Committee of the Communist Party produced a steady flow of resolutions during the late seventies, and, by the eighties, there was a new resolution each year.

In 1964, the Central Committee had already decided to develop a program for electronics during the period 1964–70. By 1968 the data-processing machines named "R 300" (presumably the IBM copies) were being introduced in the most important companies and institutions in East Germany.[9]

During the late seventies, East Germany realized how far behind it remained in computers and developed intensified programs to move forward. The MfS was instrumental in advising government leaders. In April 1977 they prepared information on computers in anticipation of the Sixth Meeting of the Central Committee. They informed leaders like Otfried Steger (Ministry for Electronics), Schalck, and Markus Wolf. The MfS supported the Ministry for Electronics's suggestion of buying complete factory equipment for the production of modern electronic hardware, a plan that was exceedingly important for the eighties, because "every area of life is increasingly influenced by the state and application of microelectronics."[10]

The MfS advised the Central Committee to turn to Japanese corporations (and maybe "non-socialist" countries in Western Europe) for cooperation, because American firms were out of the question due to strict embargo regulations. They recommended simply buying the licenses and complete factory setups. Although East Germany had signed numerous bilateral agreements with the Soviet Union, they did not prove to be cooperative partners. Soviet "development and production potential" was shared in only a limited way with socialist countries, because of "military-strategic considerations." This program was to be carried out in strict secrecy because if the "enemy" was to discover its existence, sabotage was very likely. With the launching of this Microelectronics Program in 1977, the Western computer industry emerged as the MfS's main target. Its goal was nothing less than constructing an indigenous self-sufficient computer industry.[11] Money was not a problem.

Although bilateral treaties to work on a one-megabit chip in 1982 had been signed in the area of computers between East Germany and the Soviet Union, the Soviet Union had again proved uncooperative, forcing East Germany to move ahead on its own. Honecker saw the one-megabit chip as a symbol of technological world-power status for East Germany, a goal that later proved to be illusionary. The MfS was aware that it was an unrealistic goal and considered it to be a power move on the part of the Politburo.

IBM CLONES

One early success story to which the MfS contributed a great deal was the cloning of the IBM 360. A top-secret team in Moscow, with the assistance of East Germany's Robotron Computer Center in Dresden, began working on the project in 1968. By taking apart stolen IBM machines and reverse engineering them, the Russians were able to bring their own version, the "Ryad-1" (Series-1) to market in 1972. The Russian series used the IBM operating system DOS as well as IBM peripherals and software. When these models were delivered to East Bloc countries they came with a Russian translation of the IBM service manual.[12]

From the late 1950s to the late 1970s the Soviet Committee for State Security (KGB) had a star source at IBM's European headquarters in Paris code-named "Alvar." East Germany also had several dozen changing sources over the years, some of whom, like "Ring," "Zentrum," "Rabe," and "Sturm" (Gerhard Arnold), contributed a great deal to the IBM project during the late 1960s and 1970s. Hungary and the East German Army also shared a copious amount of IBM information with the Sector for Science and Technology (SWT). Between 1971 and 1989 MfS sources contributed more than 11,000 pieces of information relating to IBM. They even had several American sources, including "Bill," who was recruited in 1964 by the SWT U.S. unit. In 1971 he provided three major deliveries of material related to the IBM 360, including program logic manuals, the disk operating system, and software.[13]

East Bloc support for the IBM project was pivotal. East Germany also integrated high-tech espionage into its own computer industry. By 1970 they had acquired, taken apart, and reverse engineered at least a dozen computers, and by 1973 Robotron was producing computers at a rate of eighty to one hundred per year.[14]

The IBM project had been part of the "Unified System of Electronic Computing Technology" (ESER) launched by the Soviet Union in 1968. It was a consortium of all the East Bloc countries and the Soviet Union to work on the development of computers, peripherals, and software. In East Germany alone, 20,000 scientists and engineers were hired as a result of the program and another 300,000 employees worked in 70 companies and factories.[15]

As we saw in the case of Agent Gorbachev, it was not just the famous Markus Wolf–led foreign department that contributed to scientific-technical espionage against the West and to acquiring embargoed goods. When the ESER was launched in 1968 to develop electronic data processing, the counterintelligence unit for the "protection of the economy" quickly mobilized it resources. That year marked the twentieth anniversary of East Germany and Walter Ulbricht's 75th birthday. IBM figured prominently in the acquisition program.[16]

Although ostensibly involved with economic counterintelligence and internal security, Department XVIII had foci in electronic data processing and semiconductor or microelectronics collection. In 1968 they had acquired "all necessary material for the electronic industry."[17] They also had several sources in the "area of operations" (West Germany) who had access to either IBM or CDC (Control Data Corporation) documents. According to officers, the CDC system was similar to the IBM system and was therefore useful. Both companies contributed information about the use and application of integrated circuits.[18]

Scientific-technical intelligence gathering for the MfS usually meant recruiting agents who had access to important Western companies like IBM. Occasionally foreigners volunteered to contribute to the MfS's scientific developments. An unusual offer came in the mid-sixties from an American computer specialist, Henry Sherwood, who wanted to help East Germany's data processing industry. Born in Berlin under the name Heinz Weizenbaum, he fled the Nazis in 1936 and arrived in America, where he changed his name while in the U.S. Army. His brother was the famous MIT computer professor Joseph Weizenbaum. Sherwood was invited to direct the Diebold European research program in 1966 and invited the East German Data Processing and Business Machines Company to take part in the program.[19]

Suspicious that Sherwood might be an agent for a capitalist company, the Stasi set four informants on him at the Diebold Conference and between 1966 and 1969 as part of the "computer measure" operation. On top of that they launched "Action World Stature" to try to use the material from the various conferences. Unfortunately, the Stasi staff members did not know English and could not effectively use the material. When Sherwood visited Erfurt, he brought IBM manuals and other material with him, which the Stasi photographed. When there was an opportunity for a German to go to America to acquire more knowledge about data processing, the Stasi vetoed the trip because they were worried that the scientist might be recruited and never come back.[20]

And that was the main contradiction the Stasi presents us with: on the one hand, they vigorously supported state programs by acquiring the needed embargoed or secret technology. On the other hand, security concerns made them work against their own interests by restricting the needed international travel of scientists and by imposing other harmful security measures.

During the 1960s the MfS continued to acquire material ordered by industry and often shared it with the Soviet Union. Although it was difficult to estimate the value of the material, the MfS guessed that they saved East German industry about 75 million marks in research and development expenses and imported embargoed goods worth 6.5 million West German marks. Specifically, internal security provided two magnetic bands and information on the DOS operating system in addition to the conference material for the IBM clone project.[21]

East Germany was not only a conduit for technology transfer from West Germany to the Soviet Union, but it also integrated high-tech espionage into its own computer industry. The most well-known company for computer technology was Robotron in Dresden, although Carl Zeiss Jena and the Dresden Institute for Computers were comparatively more important. Frankfurt an der Oder in the sixties and Erfurt in the eighties were home to semiconductor factories.

During the pre-1989 era, West German intelligence had become increasingly aware that the Soviet Union and East Germany had targeted IBM in Stuttgart as a source of high technology. In 1970 Gerhard Prager, an IBM employee, was caught copying magnetic tapes and passing them on to the MfS. In 1979 Werner Stiller betrayed Gerhard Arnold. Stiller has always maintained that Arnold's material was the most important of any of his agents, even though it was mostly internal IBM company plans, designs, equipment, data sheets, and software. His material apparently helped modernize the East German Army, and Stiller considered him the father of computing in East Germany.[22]

IBM-Stuttgart, however, was not the sole source for the East German computer industry. By the late 1970s, Intel and Texas Instrument microchips had already been integrated into East German computers on a large scale. This is not surprising, for the MfS had had major sources at Texas Instruments since at least 1978, as well as at Siemens and the Digital Equipment Corporation (DEC).

COPYING DEC

The cloning of DEC's VAX 11/780, a thirty-two-bit processor, was a computer story from the 1980s that was an ambiguous success. During the mid-1980s the Ministry for Electronics saw a need for increasing work capacity as a result of worker shortages. There was also a sense that the economy would collapse without the support of computing. One of the ways to replace workers and to prop up the economy was to introduce computer-assisted design or computer-assisted manufacture applications (CAD/CAM) into companies and firms. Although Robotron had already produced a sixteen-bit computer processor, this was not a powerful enough machine for use in CAD/CAM applications, therefore the

Ministry for Electronics asked Robotron to copy the DEC VAX 11/780, a more powerful thirty-two-bit machine. Importing the DEC VAX 11/780 in order to copy it was tricky in itself because it was "strictly embargoed." Along with the order came lavish support from the party; Alexander Schalck, who illegally imported the VAXes; and the MfS. The project was code-named "0023" and was designed to help East Germany become more self-sufficient in this area and decrease dependence on imports from the West.[23]

Despite state initiative and support, Robotron did not think this was the right project to undertake, because by the time the machine was completed it would be ten years behind state-of-the-art computing. Even with the initial hesitations, Robotron engineers moved quickly to clone the embargoed VAX (based on two VAX 11/780's acquired by Schalck and his people for Robotron), and the machine was put into production by 1987. SWT had at least three sources at DEC during the 1980s – "Dora" (Peter Dölling), "Zelter" (Fritz H.), and "Seemann" (Hans Kauther). "Dora," recruited in 1978, delivered material in 1980 and 1981 on the sixteen-bit machine PDP 11/44, and "Zelter," recruited in 1986, delivered material in 1988 relating to the VAX machine 11/780 and delivered more than a thousand other pieces of information during his whole spy career. "Seemann" delivered a staggering amount of material – 4,881 pieces of information between 1976 and 1988; during the later years much of it was related to the VAX 11/780 machine and thirty-two-bit processors, but most of the material only received ratings of III, indicating that it was not of much value for the project.[24]

But the MfS also had important sources for the VAX project run by internal security, including unofficial staff member (IM) "Saale" (Gerhard Ronneberger), IM "Messing" (Dietrich Kupfer), and "Leo" (Siegfried Stöckert).[25] In reality, all these three sources worked for the Foreign Trade Ministry and Schalck, but the MfS controlled them and influenced their activities. The spies watched the spies.

To celebrate the successful completion of Robotron's K 1840 (the DEC copy), an East German TV show (*Aktuelle Kamera*), filmed Günter Mittag's visit to Robotron in 1987. The TV crew shot a secure area but they were not allowed to film DEC computers at the company. Although a great number of DEC machines were used in East Germany, the official story was that they were imported from the Soviet Union, when in fact they were acquired from the West by bypassing the embargo rules. The Communist Party newspaper *Neues Deutschland* paid tribute to the staff at Robotron for their "scientific-technical world class achievement." Scientists, engineers, and foreign trade officials were also honored for their "extraordinary achievements" with prestigious state prizes like the banner of work (*Banner der Arbeit*), awarded personally by Erich Honecker at a special ceremony. Schalck also urged Mielke to award six MfS officers and agents ("fighters on the invisible front") with military prizes. The major role of internal security and counterintelligence as an acquisition organ for the DEC blueprints is reflected in the fact that four members of Department XVIII, along with two from the regular scientific-technical intelligence gathering unit, the SWT – Klaus Rösener and Horst Müller – received one of those secret Stasi awards.[26]

It was no secret in the West that East Bloc countries stole and reverse engineered Western embargoed computers. The East often bragged about it in the press. East German scientists scratched their heads when they came across a DEC chip with a message written in Russian: "CVAX.... When are you going to stop stealing?"[27]

ONE-MEGABIT ILLUSIONS

During the mid-eighties East Germany's efforts to develop an indigenous microelectronics industry reached a climax: the goal was to produce its own chips by 1989. A massive program for microelectronics code-named "Maximum Integration" (*Höchstintegration*) was developed using KoKo and the MfS as part of a system to acquire computer hardware and software. A major part of this program involved illegally importing goods on the embargo list at prices 30 percent to 80 percent higher than normal. Money was not a problem: Western currency was made available by Schalck and by revenue from East German firms. In April 1986 1.3 billion West marks was earmarked for microelectronics over five years, but a lot more was spent.[28] To cover the costs of the rest of the expensive program, East Germany did what capitalist countries and people do: it went into debt.

By the eighties (and earlier) Japan and the United States had emerged as leaders in the world of computers, and even highly industrialized nations like West Germany had trouble keeping up. In the West the computer industry had mushroomed from individual company initiative, which generated its own capital and innovative strategies. In contrast to Western countries, East Germany's computer effort was centrally orchestrated and financed by the state. It is no wonder that the East German economy was so strained: by the time of the collapse of communism in 1989 it had invested 14 billion marks in microelectronics. And by then it had not come close to producing a one-megabit chip, even though this had become a focused national goal. Honecker saw the one-megabit chip as a symbol of technological prowess and an expression of East Germany's abilities. When East Germany collapsed, communist leaders recognized that their efforts had been futile and that they had dug a billion-mark microelectronics grave.[29]

The microelectronics program operated within a state security regime; this power structure involved close cooperation among the Politburo, KoKo, the Ministry for Microelectronics, the Ministry for State Security, and several key scientists. Schalck worked closely with the head of the Ministry for Electronics, Karl Nendel, who provided him and the MfS information and wish lists from scientists and industry. Schalck and his KoKo empire provided the hard currency and illegally imported machinery. The microelectronics program required an especially high number of imports on the embargo list at a time when Western vigilance had increased. For example, in order to produce the 256 K RAM circuits, 60 percent of the equipment needed was embargoed imports.[30] Gerhardt Ronneberger, acting director of the Foreign Trade Electronics Company, was the head of its imports division and directed the import of equipment and know-how for the 256 K RAM circuits from non-socialist countries. In fact, he became a central figure in all import activities for microelectronics during the 1980s.

As Ronneberger admitted in his memoirs, published in 1999, he and the foreign trade unit never acted without the input of the MfS. The MfS had at least seventy-seven agents and informants in the Ministry for Foreign Trade; Ronneberger was one of them. His code name was "Saale," the name of the river and region in southeast Germany from which he came. He had been recruited in 1964 and run personally by Artur Wenzel, whom he called "Arthur the Angel." It is not clear whether Ronneberger's 1965 arrest for hitting and killing a woman in a car accident while he was under the influence of alcohol provided the MfS with leverage and control over him. The charges were mysteriously dropped.[31]

During this period of intense concentration on microelectronics, scientific and political leaders made claims exaggerating East Germany's potential ability to become a competitive nation in computers. Wolfgang Biermann, general director of Carl Zeiss Jena and a member of the Central Committee, wrote to Erich Honecker in the party newspaper, *New Germany* (*Neues Deutschland*), proclaiming that Jena had achieved the preconditions necessary to produce a one-megabit chip. As a result, political leaders and the MfS began to assess East Germany's technological level in computers, and ways to improve it. As part of this assessment the question was asked whether it was in fact possible to develop a one-megabit chip. Although the MfS and the Central Committee had heard from informants that the answer was no, East German leaders persisted in pursuing this national political goal. Informants reported that there were political reasons for proclaiming that the one-megabit chip could be produced.[32]

The logical step was turn to the Soviet Union for help, but despite efforts at deepening cooperation, the MfS reported failure on the one-megabit project due to the Soviet Union's "unwillingness" and East Germany's "insufficient conditions." As usual the Soviet Union had profited (as it had in other areas of science and technology) more from its alliance of expediency and proved a wanting partner. As a matter of fact, Zeiss Jena had built the Soviet Union an electronic ray exposure machine (ZBA 20) in 1985, which was useful for producing chips, yet did not keep one for itself. As it turned out, the ZBA 20 machine was only part of the machinery needed to produce the chip, and East German was missing other necessary elements.[33]

If Warsaw Pact help was not forthcoming, East Germany had to turn its gaze west again, despite their reluctance. In December 1985 Schalck proposed a project that involved importing 256 K RAM circuits and equipment from non-socialist countries into East Germany through the Ronneberger-led Foreign Trade Electronics Company. Rather than conducting its own research and development work, East Germany would import the know-how and production facilities of a complete factory to produce 20 to 30 million 256 K RAM circuits yearly. This was the riskiest computer project East Germany had ever undertaken, and there was no guarantee for success. Strictly enforced embargo laws protected the equipment. The personnel involved would be taking a risk, because Schalck planned to work with a well-known company and not simply a trade or consulting firm. The final goal of the project was for East Germany to produce its own chips, and eventually a semiconductor industry by 1989. In order to realize the ambitious project, the proposal contained suggestions for working with four countries and several major firms: Japan (Toshiba), Korea (Samsung), Taiwan, and China. Because East Germany had successfully worked with Toshiba before in the area of embargoed computers, Schalck favored that company. He found them flexible and cunning about ways to bypass the embargo. Their motive for helping East Germany, according to Schalck, was the hope of receiving more big contracts for business, such as the sale of color TV vacuum tubes.[34]

In March 1986 Toshiba agreed to cooperate with East Germany, as long as no official contract was signed. The plan was to realize the project covertly and in two steps: Toshiba would first deliver a complete original template, including a description of the way in which it worked and parameters for a 64 K circuit, because in this way it could gain experience with the technology for 256 K RAM production. In the second step, Toshiba would complete a special sketch of a 256 K RAM circuit, which would differ from Toshiba's well-known one. This step would occur a year later. Toshiba suggested that East Germany use its own production facilities (whether imported or self-made) for this, but was ready to provide assistance. Toshiba insisted on visiting Jena and Dresden's computer institutes when no East German citizens were present.

"The door was always open at Toshiba," recalled Ronneberger after the fall of the Berlin Wall. He had had close business ties to Japan for many years and traveled there often, especially after 1985.[35] The Japanese seemed to have an affinity for Germans and Ronneberger enjoyed their company style: business was often conducted in Japanese hotel bars at midnight, and deals were celebrated with Ronneberger's favorite cocktail – gin and tonic.[36]

As the project was coming to completion in 1987, Toshiba faced close scrutiny and criticism because of its widely publicized and well-known sale of milling technology to the Soviet Union, which allowed the installation of super-quiet submarine propellers. The U.S. Senate voted to ban Toshiba imports and members of Congress smashed a Toshiba boom box on the Capitol lawn. The Japanese government responded by barring Toshiba's machine-tool company from doing business with the Warsaw Pact for one year.[37]

Though Toshiba's semiconductor project with East Germany was not well-known at the time, Republican congressmen alleged that Toshiba also made illegal sales to East Germany in 1986 by exporting an assembly line to produce semiconductors. By 13 March 1988 this allegation could not be proven.[38]

Meanwhile, representatives from East Germany had several conversations with the general managing director and manager of Toshiba and with the assistant general manager of Mitsui in Japan in November 1987. Toshiba representatives told them of their knowledge about investigations by the U.S. Congress and that the CIA might have sources in East Germany. Toshiba warned the East Germans not to use the Toshiba masks for 64 K chip production in Erfurt.[39]

Because the spotlight was on them, Toshiba and Mitsui requested that all material relating to 64 K and 256 K technology be destroyed immediately. The 64 K templates were also to disappear. In addition, they asked for assurances that institutes in East Germany would not produce 64 and

256 K chips using Toshiba technology. On 9 February 1988 representatives of Toshiba and Mitsui met with Ronneberger and several scientists in Erfurt at the microelectronics combine and destroyed all the material at a nearby garbage dump; the template was mechanically and later chemically destroyed.[40]

Ronneberger, however, did not tell the Toshiba representatives that they had only destroyed copies. Toshiba technology was still in the hands of Dr. Rolf Hillig and for a cheap price, too: the Japanese returned the 7.8 million dollars after the material was allegedly destroyed.[41] East Germany may have ended up with a financial deal on the 256 K project, but it also was given old technology – the original price was highway robbery.

By the mid-eighties East Germany's attempt to build its own chip industry in Dresden had failed miserably. It simply did not have the technical know-how and equipment to do it. By the time East Germany had produced the chips, they were outdated, and capitalistic countries were already using the new generation. By 1989 East Germany was able to produce 90,000 256 K RAM chips, whereas Austria, a small country, had produced 50 million. By contrast, Japan was already mass-producing one million megabit chips per month in April 1986.[42]

Erich Honecker had been especially eager to move East Germany into a position of technological prowess by latching onto computers. He was delighted when Biermann wrote to him in January 1986, announcing that Jena would be able to produce a one-megabit chip by 1989. He called it the "nicest New Year's present" that he had received.[43]

In the fall of 1988 Biermann wrote to Honecker again, announcing that he was presenting him with the first functioning model of the one-megabit chip, one year earlier than he had promised in 1986. Biermann thought East Germany had joined the "international elite" in science and technology with this achievement. Several weeks later Honecker met with Gorbachev in Moscow. Horst Vogel had brought along a prototype of the chip in his briefcase and gave it to Honecker, who then presented Gorbachev with the first "sample" of the one-megabit chip allegedly developed in Jena. Although there was discussion of cooperating on large-scale production of the chip, by the time of the fall of the Wall, East Germany had not produced any one-megabit chips. It turned out the sample was just a dummy acquired from the West.[44]

The Sector for Science and Technology also contributed a great deal to the one-megabit chip project and began to target sources with the right secrets soon after the launch of the microelectronics program. There were several steps to the process. On 27 November 1986, Professor Dr.

Dr. h.c. Wolfgang Biermann applied to the MfS for "documents and samples of the one-megabit chip" as part of the state program "Maximum
Integration." His application was given the number 51.87.00086 (51 was
for Carl Zeiss Jena, 87 the year it was to be realized, and 86 the number of the application). The SWT procured several pieces of information
that helped to "partly realize" this application. On 3 September 1988, a
source code-named "Joker" acquired the technology for the one-megabit
chip. On 27 May 1988, "Zelter" (Fritz H.) delivered logic technology
and information on the manufacture of highly integrated circuits, and on
22 June 1988 he delivered a "wafer" for a one-megabit chip. Robotron
also placed an order for information on the one-megabit chip and received
material.[45]

Peter Köhler, a West German engineer and head of the microchip department for Texas Instruments, was spotted and recruited by the SWT during
a business visit to Erfurt. Lured to Berlin by the promise of profits from
intelligence officers posing as trade representatives, he met with his future
case officer and the subdepartment head at Hotel Stadt Berlin on *Alexanderplatz*. A top source, he continued to sell company secrets related to chip
manufacture for eleven years (1978–89); he must have quickly caught on
that they were MfS officers.[46]

Köhler's primary motivation to spy seems to have been financial; he
could also visit his new girlfriend in Erfurt while on a business trip. In
the course of his spy activity he made about half a million marks of easy
money, which he invested in real estate. He primarily passed on information related to low-power Schottky circuits during the years 1980, 1981,
and 1988. This information was primarily passed on to the company in
Erfurt working on semiconductors and chip manufacture.[47]

THE FINAL BATTLE

Although the East had acquired a sample of the one-megabit chip in 1988,
this did not mean it could mass-produce it. Mass production required
expensive, strictly embargoed machinery from the West. The Toshiba line
had also dried up in 1988 with the incident at the garbage dump and
renewed international attention focused on their illegal activities. As a
result, Schalck and the MfS pursued new acquisition lines.

The United States administration's enforced embargo policy had struck
a deep blow to the East's attempts. Even though acquisition activities were
still occurring in 1988, the MfS reported that deliveries had been reduced
to half that of previous years. The MfS assumed that if a line was being
used, it was under observation, and that most embargo smugglers would

be approached for recruitment by Western intelligence. Using dummy front companies was no longer possible, and everyone knew about the Swiss, Austrian, and Swedish transit routes; as a result new routes in Asia had to be developed. The rule of thumb was that all negotiations had to take place in East Germany and business was to be conducted with little paper, no written contracts, and no telephone calls. Most importantly, all deals were closed with cash.[48]

Mega-money and mega-machinery characterized the activities of the late eighties. Deals were brokered involving millions of West German marks. The machinery needed to mass-produce chips was big, heavy, expensive, and strictly embargoed. Targeted machinery included etchers, testers, wafer steppers, crystal-making machines, and the crucial high-current ion implanter.

KoKo's trade division imported the bulk of the machinery, but SWT's special acquisition organs (SBO) handled the "most explosive" embargoed goods. In 1986, the year the super-program to develop microelectronics was launched, a separate trade division for Western imports was created within Ronneberger's bailiwick and the import division of the Combine for Microelectronics. In 1986 there were approximately sixty embargo smugglers active in acquiring imports in those divisions.[49] There was competition between the various import lines to be considered the best; everyone wanted to be the first to tell the Politburo that they acquired the needed equipment by breaking the embargo.

Western businessmen were attracted to the easy money that could be made selling embargoed goods, but it increasingly became a very risky business. The United State's administration had been successful at galvanizing other countries to enforce the embargo, including West Germany. The late eighties were characterized by arrests and publicity surrounding illegal technology transfer.

Leybold-Heraus, a firm specializing in vacuum technology, was one of East Germany's closest West German partners. During the eighties it boasted annual profits of more than one billion West German marks.[50] During the late eighties, the company made headline news because of sales to Lybia; later, it was implicated in providing equipment to Iraq's weapons program. Clearly trade with the East Bloc and Middle East customers boosted its profits.

During the last six years of East Germany's existence, Leybold delivered more than 96 million DM worth of embargoed equipment, such as crystal-making machinery, cathode equipment, and plasma etchers.[51] The company conducted brisk and successful trade with both East Germany and the Soviet Union. Some of the business was legal, but much of it was connected to embargoed goods. The company simply modified the declaration form if they delivered machinery with slightly different measurement parameters. Custom officials never bothered to check.

By 1988, Leybold was becoming paranoid that their shipments would be checked because of the increased controls. Yet East Germany still sought to become free of Western imports by building their own machinery, which in turn would help to develop their own microelectronic industry. To solve this problem, the MfS sent Siegfried Schürer ("Burmeister") from the trade division to Leybold to scout out possibilities.

Because embargo smuggling had become difficult, Leybold agreed to sell the technical documentation for making a plasma etcher machine, along with some machinery and engineering help. They were even going to transfer the license to East Germany. This operation soon acquired the code name "Pipe" (*Röhre*). Leybold delivered the material to Schürer in Berlin. The first shipment of the documentation arrived in eleven loose-leaf binders in April 1989; six more binders came in September. The material was soon transferred to Horst Vogel at the science sector, and the evaluation department became responsible for "neutralizing" it before it was sent on to Carl Zeiss and the microelectronics firm in Dresden.[52]

Leybold continued to deliver the necessary material for copying and building the etcher. The embargoed etcher machines were shipped through the Taiwan route and from there to the Carl Zeiss Jena Company. Software followed. Unlike some other machinery transfers, this project appeared to have gone well. East Germany did not have to pay the three million DM for the documentation. Ten years after the fall of the Berlin Wall, Ronneberger explained the reason for the free documentation in his memoirs: because Zeiss's research center in Dresden shared the know-how produced there with Leybold, it was considered an even trade. He saw this deal as "one hand washes the other."[53]

Leybold's greed was limitless. In March 1988, they even agreed to obtain a high-current ion implanter prototype from their competition in America and have the West German Fraunhofer Institute work on copying it. They planned to work together with Biermann from Carl Zeiss Jena. After studying the files on implanters from the two leading U.S. firms – Eaton and Varion – they discovered the idea was harder to realize than they thought and abandoned it.[54]

In the last years of East Germany's existence, all acquisition organs were frantically trying to obtain the high-current ion implanter needed to mass-produce one-megabit chips. The MfS and KoKo had already been successful at acquiring medium-voltage implanters since the late seventies, but the high-current implanter remained elusive. It was the most guarded embargoed computer technology, and only two companies in America produced it: Eaton (Beverly, Massachusetts) and Varion Corporation. Difficult to smuggle because of its large size, the implanter weighed two tons and could not be taken apart.

The implanter caused a lot of heartache for KoKo and the SWT. Initial attempts to acquire it through trusted embargo smugglers and dependable lines faltered when the manufacturer found out that the end user was not in fact a Western country but a communist country. Providing a fake end-user certificate had become more difficult because the American companies now wanted proof that these end users were bona fide chip manufacturers not based in embargoed countries. The CIA and other technology-transfer protection centers worked together with American companies to prevent illegal transfer to the East Bloc. They doctored up the machinery or put sand in containers instead of the goods.

On the eve of the collapse of communism, the acquisition organs made final attempts to acquire the implanter. KoKo had a trusted embargo smuggler in Paris, Yvon Pellegrin, who had acquired 20 million DM worth of embargoed goods for East Germany. Initially Pellegrin ordered a stripped-down Eaton implanter from the French plant, which would presumably meet the CoCom specifications. When that request was denied, he developed a route using intermediary countries. This attempt began in April 1988, as controls tightened worldwide. This time the plan was to order two fully functional Eaton implanters from their Boston plant and have them flown to Algeria via Argentina. Pellegrin charged Ronneberger $5 million for each implanter. When the Algeria route failed, Pellegrin bribed a firm in Argentina to give him an end-user certificate; that cost an additional $100,000. Once the U.S. agencies informed Pellegrin that the export license was granted, Schalck provided the necessary funds in October 1988. The idea was that KoKo would be the first to acquire the very sought-after and needed high-current implanter and show what a good job they were doing.[55]

The Argentineans received the implanter on 6 December 1988 and estimated it would arrive in Berlin between 14 and 20 December traveling with a Boeing 747 from Buenos Aires to Morocco, then to Belgrade, and finally to Berlin-Schönefeld. Rumors began to spread in KoKo about the implanter. At the end of January 1989, "Leo" (Siegfried Stöckert) reported to his MfS case officer that the implanter was in Portugal and could not fly out until the crew was bribed to fly the plane further and that a representative from the import trade ministry gave the French partner all the money for that bribe in cash at the Check Point Charlie border crossing. By May the implanter was still held in Portugal in a special transporter.[56]

Ronneberger kept the details of the fiasco close to his chest. Meanwhile he received a strange telegram in broken German from Portugal: they were not going to get the implanters in part because "Pelerin [sic]" was under strong surveillance. After paying more bribe money, the implanter was supposed to fly to Lybia, but, given the political situation, that did not happen either. Instead, Ronneberger heard that Canadian NATO control officers had found the delivery suspicious and it was not delivered.[57] KoKo never got their money back.

While KoKo's attempts at importing the implanter failed, SWT was also trying to acquire high-current implanters in 1988. Because they destroyed most of their files after unification, not as much evidence remains about their attempts. According to bits of archival evidence, the special acquisition organs (SBO) had ordered several high-current implanters with funding from the trade organization and the Ministry for Electronics. They paid 9 million DM for one implanter, which appears to have come from the Eaton Corporation in Beverly, Massachusetts. The asking price was $3.6 million, and the embargo smuggler added 40 percent for his services, making the cost a total of $5.4 million. According to specialists the asking price should have not been more than $1.2 million.[58]

One West German businessman, Werner Scheele (alias IM "Rhein"), was brought to trial in 1997 because he worked for the SWT between 1988 and 1990. He had worked with them through a dummy front company since the mid-1970s and founded a cover firm called OCOM Trade AG in Switzerland to acquire embargoed goods. He allegedly agreed to obtain a high-current implanter in the spring of 1988. By the end of 1988 he succeeded in acquiring the implanter through an Asian branch of an American firm in Hong Kong. Because he did not want to be caught ordering such a hot object, he asked an intermediary to order it and send it to Indonesia so that the SWT could use their Thai line. As was the case with KoKo's implanter story, intelligence agencies and the company quickly became suspicious. This time they doctored up the machine with self-destructive parts. It was actually delivered to East Germany in December 1989 but did not work.[59] It self-destructed around the same time as East Germany itself!

Object Coat of Arms

The HVA spearheaded another expensive computer project during the late 1980s called "Object Coat of Arms." Also run under the code number "Object 0030," it entailed building a factory for the production of hard disks. The factory, modeled after, and using components from, the American Microscience Company in California, would be built in the same town as one of Robotron's installations – in Thüringen, in south-east Germany. Schalck bankrolled the project with 130 million DM worth of hard currency.[60]

Martin Schlaff, a Viennese businessman who was the SWT's main man in Vienna after the residency there was blown by Werner Stiller in 1979, led them to the right partner. Strictly enforced embargo laws made it difficult to acquire individual parts for the factory, because they were dual-use components. Therefore the Stasi planned to smuggle the parts into East Germany through West Germany, Switzerland, and Austria.[61]

In March 1986 Schlaff and a partner from one of his companies – Data Production Modules (DPM) in Vienna – met three businessmen, in Zagreb, Bulgaria. In fact, the "business" partners were three high-ranking HV A and SWT officers: Klaus Butte, Klaus Rösener (SWT V), and Gottfried Gietl (head of the front company Interport). It soon became clear to Schlaff that the project initiators came from East Germany and were officials from the Ministry for State Security. The HV A officers were impressed with Schlaff, his extensive holdings, his various compa-nies, and his access to the needed American technology. After this meeting Schlaff was given the code name "Landgraf" and the registration num-ber 3883/86. Klaus Rösener had recruited Wendelin Simonis, director for research and development at the Robotron branch, in 1985 and in 1986 and worked closely with their agent on a special mission code-named "Hermann."[62]

Because the components needed for the project were so heavily guarded, the conspirators hatched a double-game: DPM would first build a factory in a suburb of Vienna, but the components would be bought in duplicate – one set would stay in Vienna, the other would be smuggled to the East Germany factory. The idea was to slowly take apart the Vienna factory, burn the rest, and cash in the insurance policy to cover expenses. The Vienna hi-tech suburb was touted in the press as the new Silicon Valley in Austria. Because of delays and problems, they decided to stop the project in 1987. Instead, they planned on smuggling the components through one of Schlaff's companies in Singapore. The MfS officers and agents visited the factory there to obtain ideas on how to build their own factory with the second set of components.[63]

The Object Coat of Arms remained a tightly held secret even after the collapse of East Germany. A written contract has not been found, the factory was allegedly only partly built, and the clean room was taken apart.[64]

BLURRED BOUNDARIES

Mirroring the MfS's under-one-roof principle, both the HV A's Sector for Science and Technology and internal security and counterintelligence's Department for the Protection of the Economy (XVIII) were intimately involved with the state computer program. The boundaries dividing their roles blurred, especially in the area of computers. Although Department XVIII was in the MfS's internal security and counterintelligence division, its electronics unit often acted like foreign intelligence – it ran agents in the West and acquired embargoed goods and secret plans from the West like the SWT. Conversely, the SWT passed on information for security needs. Functions were often expansive. As we saw, internal security even recruited, controlled, and spied on leading members of KoKo, including Schalck and Ronneberger, the state's most loyal servants. No one was trusted.

Internal security's official task was to "protect the economy." By the eighties, this charge had become a very broad function, but in the area of microelectronics, "protecting the economy" began to entail securing embargo lines against enemy attack and making sure the personnel involved – from travel cadre, to scientists, to embargo smugglers – were honest. The department's work reveals a dizzying array of security activity involving files and people. The core of their activity was bureaucratic – either opening an OPK (operational person control file) or an OV (operational file). This paperwork was, of course, supported by technical methods and by extensive fieldwork by agents and informants. Agents were one of the MfS's main tools, or weapons, for carrying out its work. Recruitment, testing, and placement of IMs were therefore major activities. They were not immune from the state security system, either. Agents and informants were also vetted and spied on to determine if they were honest and dependable. No one was spared. It came as a great surprise to Gerhardt Ronneberger when he read his file and discovered that he too was tested to determine if he would make a trustworthy agent.[65]

The stated goal of much of this file building was to determine who was who. This was not just a communist version of looking at a reference guide, such as *Who's Who*, to find out more about a person. Once the person became "known" through file work – using informants and technical methods for information and reports – they could determine if he or she was an enemy of the state. Whether they were friend or foe, they could still be recruited.

The MfS did not usually randomly select people to spy on, unless they needed to vet a whole group working on a state secret. Usually there was a trigger – a person was suspected of being a spy, came into contact with a suspected spy, had too many contacts, was involved in subversive activity, had embezzled money, or traveled to the West too often. If evidence was found that someone had broken an East German law, the proof could be used in court.

During the late 1970s and early 1980s there was growing concern in the MfS that Western intelligence agencies were "brutally" working against East German microelectronics. To combat this perceived threat, internal security opened several files focusing on espionage against East German science and technology.[66]

Leonhard F., a British subject and member of the British Ministry of Defense, was a chief suspect, along with several traveling scientists listed in the file "Operation II." Ever since 1978, he was suspected of spy activity in electronics.[67] The case was part of a larger MfS concern that the British service was working against important East German areas of electronics. The MfS suspected that they were attempting to gather intelligence on defense production in the Warsaw Pact. The West was indeed "spying on science" in the East, but had little reason to acquire civilian science, though they were interested in acquiring military technology plans.[68]

FOLLOWING THE MONEY

Computers, microelectronic components, and machinery are all expensive. Illegally obtaining the same technology and transferring it from the West to the East was even more expensive – involving a 30 percent to 70 percent increase in costs. During the 1960s and 1970s reverse engineering IBM computers and creating the RYADs or Robotron machines was relatively economical, because technicians could use blueprints and a few IBM prototypes to do it. By the 1980s creating a microelectronic industry required illegally importing very costly components and machinery.

During the early years a moderate amount of money was available for operations. By the 1980s, the state quest to create an indigenous computer industry had generated huge financial resources from the trade organizations and intelligence. As we saw, single transactions occurred that involved millions of dollars. Reportedly, the computer program cost the state some 14 billion marks, but the amount could be much higher.

Illegally acquiring Western technology and blueprints must have also cost billions of West German marks during the last four years of East Germany's existence.

The Ministry for State Security's annual budget in 1989 appeared to be about 4.2 billion East German marks.[69] Under communism, it is not always clear where money for such state institutions comes from. Because citizens were not taxed, much revenue for the state came from foreign trade, especially with other East Bloc countries. Schalck was responsible for acquiring a large amount of East Germany's Western hard currency through legitimate and shady deals with the West.

The MfS also generated its own income. In the area of scientific-technical intelligence, revenue for paying agents often came from the East German companies that had received stolen scientific-technical blueprints. During the 1980s Artur Wenzel (who hung himself in 1989), head of the economic counterintelligence department for microelectronics, developed an easy way to make money from the many businessmen he dealt with when illegally importing embargoed machinery. He called it "reparations" (*Wiedergutmachung*).

Wenzel claimed in his reports that the millions of West German marks he generated through "reparations" always went directly to the Ministry's finance department. No proof survives to document whether he skimmed some of the money for himself. Did he embezzle enough to fill the suitcases he was found with after the fall of the Berlin Wall?[70]

According to Wenzel's deputy, Willy Koch, such reparations brought in a yearly income of around 10 million West German marks. Evidence survives showing that in 1987 Wenzel generated more than 3 million West German marks from businessmen based in the West. If he procured more money that year, it is not clear where it went or if it was simply not documented.[71]

If counterintelligence discovered cases of blackmail or cheating or espionage, they demanded that the businessmen pay reparations. If the businessmen intended to continue their lucrative sideline, they paid the money. Even if the sum was large, secret sales involving millions of dollars dampened the blow. In 1987 several interesting cases generated large amounts of money. An Iranian business partner with Ronneberger's Foreign Trade Electronics Company who lived in West Germany and who had already quarreled with his handlers was required to pay 549,720 DM because of "corruption" and "manipulation" to achieve a high price. Together with his last payment for blackmail, in 1983, he had contributed more than a million DM. Alfred Kleine, head of Department XVIII, wrote personally to the Minister of State Security, Erich Mielke, about transferring the funds to the Department for Finance. Mielke approved the request with his signature.[72]

In another case, a Canadian citizen had been delivering embargoed goods for the Technical Operations Sector (OTS). When the machinery arrived, it did not meet the quality and performance standards agreed upon. Because the goods were embargoed, they could not be returned or repaired abroad; instead East German industry tried to make the machines work and acquired parts from other companies. As a result, the MfS decided to break contact with the Canadian. Agent "Messing" (Dieter Kupfer), who had been working with the businessman importing embargoed electronics, blocked the Canadian's access to the bank account in Vienna where the millions had been transferred for him.[73]

There are dozens of other "reparation" cases, mostly involving West Germans. AEG had a very close business relationship with the Foreign Trade Electronics Company from 1971 to 1982. The AEG representative in East Germany also developed a close personal relationship with a woman at the company. The MfS accused him of using that relationship to acquire company secrets such as negotiating strategies and prices. Both employees were jailed. Because the business relationship with AEG was so important, Wenzel developed a reparation deal so that both suspects would avoid a court case and imprisonment. AEG paid 300,000 DM and 100,000 U.S. dollars to get their employee out of the mess.[74]

THE CIA'S PRESSURE

The full story of the CIA's side of the spy-versus-spy technology war in the East Bloc is still shrouded in secrecy, although there are numerous articles and white papers on its technology war against the Soviet Union.[75] Information about the CIA's methods and sources in the Stasi files are not made available to researchers, and their material remains classified. Most of the East German CIA and West German intelligence agency (BND) agents were in fact double agents working for the MfS. The CIA was primarily interested in procuring information about East Germany's relation to the Soviet Union, Carl Zeiss Jena, military technology, laser technology, and microelectronic technology.[76]

The CIA's primary target and enemy was the Soviet Union. It felt that it was West Germany's job to work on its neighbor in the East. During the mid-eighties, however, the CIA thought West Germany was not doing enough against the East Bloc to stem the flow of embargoed Western technology to the East. In fact, they saw West Germany as a hub for the East Bloc's activities. In the 1984 report criticizing West Germany for not enforcing the embargo because of trade interests with the Soviet Union, the CIA catalogues some computer cases in which West Germans were recruited by the KGB or GRU (Russia's Military Intelligence Division) in West Germany. One of the biggest cases involved Lothar Haedicke, who worked for a subsidiary of Honeywell, an American company.[77]

The Americans had a good reason for concern about East German espionage in West Germany. After all, the Stasi's target was really U.S. technology. During the Cold War, American companies had begun to dot the West German landscape; subsidiaries of Honeywell, IBM, DEC, or Texas Instruments were set up there. West Germany provided easy access for the Stasi because of its proximity to East Germany, their common language, and their trade interests with the Soviet Union.

The CIA was primarily critical of Helmut Kohl and his political and economic policies in the East, but their assessment also included a discussion of what they saw as a passive attitude by the BND and other security organizations, such as the Federal Office for the Protection of the Constitution. Given the thousands of MfS agents the Federal Criminal Office (BKA) investigated and helped bring to trial during the Cold War, the CIA's critique is puzzling. It would seem that the Federal Criminal Office and counterintelligence had more experience with pure espionage rather than illegal technology transfer through trade organizations. West German custom officials also worked together with the United States in capturing one of the biggest Cold War embargo smugglers – Richard "Megabucks" Müller – who used a diversionary measure to export a DEC VAX 782 to the Soviet Union. The CIA documented some of its claims with a list of 243 proven illegal technological export diversions between 1966 and 1982.[78]

Whereas individuals were often prosecuted for embargo smuggling, German companies were not. One such case involved Albert and Dietmar Scholz and their Bavarian firm Alltranistor. Although the CIA did not know it at the time, the "businessman" whom they thought was really an "agent of the East German secret service" was in fact Gerhardt Ronneberger, the MfS-controlled trade official from the Foreign Trade Electronics Company, who was imprisoned for several months! They did know, however, that this small firm did brisk business with the Soviet Union on the order of 15 million U.S. dollars between 1980 and 1982. A representative of the subsidiary of an American firm in West Germany turned them in because he was suspicious. All three businessman involved in this case denied any intelligence connection and were therefore not prosecuted. Ronneberger always wondered whether the West really knew that he worked for East German intelligence.[79]

By 1984 the CIA knew how the Soviet system of illegal technology transfer worked: it was a combination of illegal trade and intelligence operations or simply illegal trade. The CIA had charted the export channels – what it called "diversionary measures" – to the Soviet Union through intermediary countries like Switzerland, Austria, Amsterdam, Stockholm, and even West Germany. As a result, U.S. export controllers began to demand end-user certificates.[80]

United States' pressure on West Germany seemed to have been successful. The last years of East Germany's existence are littered with arrests and publicity against the East's illegal technology transfer as a result of enforcing the harsher CoCom export policies. American and West German newspapers were filled with accounts of illegal technology transfer and arrests. During the late eighties a number of conferences and public lectures were held by people such as Jay Tuck, the journalist-author of *High-Tech Espionage*, and Herbert Hellenbroich, the former head of the BND and industrial espionage expert who debriefed Werner Stiller after his defection in 1979.

Stasi informants monitored, attended, and took notes on these events. During the November "Productronica 87" fair in Munich, sources provided information about Tuck's lecture on "The Consequences of Forbidden Technology Transfer." They saw this lecture as part of a tendency toward a "massive coordinated influence of the USA" on enforcing the embargo.

Four days after the Hellenbroich-led conference on "Industrial Espionage – A Nightmare? Minimizing Risk through Know-How Protection" in West Berlin on 21 November 1988, intelligence officers put out a six-page single-spaced information report with a detailed summary of the lectures. They found the lectures "politically very biased and slanderous." One lecture reported that East Germany launched the lion's share (72 percent) of East Bloc espionage operations against West Germany. East Germany also led the East Bloc pack in scientific-economic espionage cases – they were responsible for more than half of all cases. In the years 1985, 1986, and 1987, the lecturer calculated that 33 percent of all espionage tasks were in the area of electronics and data processing.[81] Whether wittingly or unwittingly, these lectures and conferences provided propaganda for the CIA's goals of stemming the flow of illegal technology transfer and thus winning the Cold War.

BENEFITING FROM THE TECHNOLOGY

Breaking an embargo and stealing the West's technological secrets is only part of effective scientific-technical espionage. Integration into the science system is the test of its ultimate success. Several leading scientists profited from, and worked closely with, the various ministries and the central committee. In addition to Wolfgang Biermann, Volker Kempe was another well-known scientific leader who profited from the support of the MfS.

Kempe, code-named "Norbert," was director of the Academy Institute for Cybernetics and Information Processing. Kempe had been a patriotic communist for many years before he was recruited by the MfS. Initially reluctant to become a secret informant, he nevertheless signed a pledge and chose a pseudonym. During the first ten years of his informant activity, Kempe attended numerous space research conferences, informing on the behavior of colleagues and recruitment activities of "enemy" spy agencies. Staying in the good graces of the MfS paid off. By the 1980s the MfS began to support Kempe's work. The MfS acquired journals and equipment for his work through their illegal import pipelines. Kempe also officially worked as an "evaluator" for the SWT, even though he was already an informant for internal security. In exchange for this support, Kempe was to work on solving software problems, including neutralizing a software package called "Medusa," which had been acquired from Vienna, and adapting it to East German conditions. This was just the beginning of the establishment of a central institute for software.[82] After the collapse of communism he turned up in Vienna and was named manager of the year.

A wheeler and dealer, Kempe made contacts with German Democratic Republic (GDR) leaders, such as Erich Honecker and Günter Mittag, who heeded his advice about the microelectronics program for the XIth Party Congress in April, in which microelectronics figured prominently, and around the same time as the Toshiba and Biermann story unfolded.

Kempe's institute was just one of many in East Germany that received the embargoed thirty-two-bit VAX 750 and 780 computers for CAD/CAM (computer-assisted design/computer-assisted manufacture) use. Two hundred and seventy-five sixteen-bit personal computers came from IBM, and a few systems were imported legally from Siemens. Forty-seven of the embargoed computers were acquired from the strictly embargo-protected American firm DEC.[83] Horst Müller, head of the SWT computer department, was awarded the "Banner of Work" for his achievements in acquiring DEC VAX computers.

In addition to the secrecy surrounding methods of illegal acquisition, all personnel who used the computers in any way, especially CAD/CAM computers, were sworn to secrecy. Secrecy began to be slowly lifted in some areas, such as the legally imported Siemens computers. Nevertheless, many scientists who worked outside of secret military projects and who would have been normal civilian scientists in a Western country were called "Bearers of Secrets."[84]

Of course, secrecy created problems. Often machinery did not work when it arrived. Because it was acquired illegally, calling a service repairman was a problem. Sometimes only bits and pieces of information were available, when the whole puzzle was needed intact. But more fundamental problems arose because of secrecy.

The MfS's cult of secrecy clashed with the scientific ethos of openness. Although most scientists were afraid to speak out, at least one science agent wrote a telling but critical report in October 1986, at the height of the computer frenzy. The MfS officer's handwritten conclusion on the top of the page was that the "IM is uninformed." The agent reported that computer specialists with whom he had talked thought the technology was often delivered randomly and not effectively. For example, a VAX 11/750 was delivered to the semiconductor factory in Frankfurt/Oder, when they really needed a VAX 11/780 because of problems with compatibility and service availability. A representative from the Ministry for Electronics responsible for such deliveries reportedly said: "Either you take what we give you or you don't get anything."[85]

The agent reported that hardware and software were delivered secretly in all cases and no one had an overview. As a result it was hard to understand how to use everything, and cooperation in both areas was impossible. The MfS penciled comment was: "Thank God! Specialists are there so they won't have an overview." When the agent reported an opinion that secrecy led to a lack of mastery of CAD technology and only protected the acquisition paths for embargoed technology, this led to the comment: "This man is more than dangerous." The agent correctly concluded that the Western offers of technology were motivated by "maximum profit" and that they sold the East old technology.[86]

Computer technology was alluring, but the state had overestimated the power of secrets to propel its computer industry forward. East Germany's quest to latch onto the computer revolution of the 1980s through espionage and illegal technology transfer failed miserably. The computer had large symbolic value; it had turned into a wonder weapon for the Cold

War. Intelligence officers believed that whoever won the technological battle would win the Cold War. And they were right.

Even with their highly perfected espionage system and seasoned embargo smuggling organizations, East Germany forgot one thing: A scientific establishment based on pirated and cloned technology can never be a leader, especially in such a fast-moving field as computer technology. The sense of trailing behind the West continued to gnaw at the East German leadership, particularly after 1981, when the Reagan administration launched "Operation Exodus" to stem the flow of embargoed computer technology to the Eastern Bloc. The unrealistic goal of catching up by stealing secrets, together with the embargo, led to one of the greatest fiascos in the history of scientific espionage.[87]

PART TWO

SPY-TECH

7

James Bond, Communist-Style

Taking a Sunday stroll through the streets of the relatively posh northeastern Berlin district of *Hohenschönhausen* (literally "high pretty houses") in the late 1990s, I come across attractive neighborhoods once inhabited by the East German elite: the generals and high-ranking officers of the Ministry for State Security. Bourgeois-looking bungalow-style houses surround an inviting lake called Obersee. South of the Obersee district, modern, bright, steel-and-glass-style apartments have replaced old socialist housing. A particularly attractive apartment complex overlooks a well-kept cemetery, but the grounds have an unusual bulge in the center. Was this where bunkers hid the workshops and offices of the Stasi's technical division? I peer down one of the shafts and still have not found what lies beneath. Circling to the road I see a big gaping hole – the entrance to an underground parking garage.

It is hard to imagine that during the Cold War this area housed an enormous printing press that produced forged documents and that houses across the street from the peaceful cemetery were really workshops for developing Q-like technology for agents sent on secret missions to the West. By the time Western intelligence arrived on the scene, the printing presses had mysteriously disappeared.

About a mile east of the cemetery, after traveling first on cobblestoned streets, then onto the *Freienwalderstrasse*, there is a more ominous-looking set of buildings with courtyards: the feared and hated *Hohenschönhausen* Stasi prison is the most prominent, with its watchtowers, high cement walls, and barbed wire. During the late 1990s tour buses lined *Genslerstrasse*, but most tourists do not realize that, in fact, the whole area surrounding the prison was a Ministry for State Security campus and restricted area. On old Berlin maps dating from the 1980s, the secret area is shaded yellow, and a freight train station is marked at the

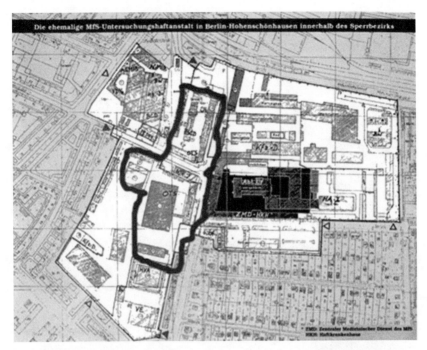

7. Map of the Technical Operations Sector campus. The technical division (circled) was in the Stasi's northern Berlin campus, across the street from the prison (in black), in a restricted area. (Kristie Macrakis)

northern end of the complex. Residents and former prisoners report that the area was surrounded with lift gates, and people could only enter by flashing a valid ID. *Normannenstrasse* in Lichtenberg made headline news as the infamous headquarters of the Stasi, but their northern complex, *Hohenschönhausen*, is usually only associated with the feared and hated prison.

Entering the courtyard of an enormous L-shaped building across the street from the prison, it is hard to fathom what went on here. There are huge warehouses and buildings with electrical voltage warning signs: "High tension equipment – danger." At the back end of the courtyard, a huge, bent, old Zeiss Ikon key tops a small kiosk-like building on the external side. The area is not totally devoid of everyday life: the corner of *Freienwalderstrasse* and Conrad Wolf is adorned with a typical East German restaurant, the *Elfinger*, where hungry staff members could have lunch of *soljanka* and other Eastern European fare, before the technical division opened its own cafeteria.

(a)

(b)

8. The Technical Operations Sector buildings. The OTS's major building (a), which was across the street from the prison, and its interior courtyard (b) are pictured here in 1999. (Kristie Macrakis)

Building plans and descriptions indicate that the L-shaped building belonged to the Technical Operations Sector (OTS) and was built in 1964 with the help of the prisoners living next door. A modern building sporting shielded windows followed in the 1970s, and in 1989 engineers built a sauna in the basement, where staff members could relax in between experiments as a "preventative measure."[1] It was at the technical division that more than one thousand staff members – scientists, technicians, cabinet-makers, leather workers, printers, and handymen – developed the James Bond equipment of the spy trade: some analyzed enemy invisible ink while developing their own; others trained printers to forge passports; technicians invented or modified tiny spy cameras; and criminalists analyzed body fluids of enemies of the state. These are just a few examples of the myriad of research and production projects. Like the fictional Q branch, this was the research and development division of the Ministry for State Security.

Ian Fleming's fiction and the James Bond films were indeed based on fact; most spy agencies have technical units. The CIA's Office of Technical Service (OTS), based within the Directorate for Science and Technology, is one of the world's most technologically sophisticated divisions. Q, James Bond's technical man, is a fictional portrayal of the quartermaster, traditionally a military unit that supplied troops with equipment. Whereas it is well-known that the CIA uses spy gadgets and technology to collect information, the Stasi's and other East Bloc countries' use of technology has been overlooked and underestimated because of their prominence in human intelligence gathering.

The Technical Operations Sector was one of the largest Ministry for State Security (MfS) divisions. In addition to the 1,079 staff members, it maintained many large buildings within the *Hohenschönhausen* campus, in villas in Berlin and other East German cities, and even had its own vacation homes for staff members. The division was also one of the most important, because it serviced the foreign espionage unit with miniature document cameras and containers for hiding equipment. Internal security and counterintelligence were supplied with observation cameras and outfitted minivans, telephone tapping units were given listening devices, and border control received radioactive human sensor devices.

During the 1950s servicing agents and departments with spy gadgets and equipment was slightly less bureaucratic and more casual than it became in the professionalized years of the 1960s and 1970s. Most of the "agents for the future," sent to West Germany during the fifties to start new lives and bury themselves in a company with interesting secrets, received training from the precursor Department S or K in handling spy cameras (*mikrats*), working with codes, and receiving radio messages from headquarters. They simply met with the gadget man, who instructed them on how to use their spy tools.

Harald Gottfried was one of those future agents sent to West Germany in 1956. He received training in how to use invisible ink, a *mikrat*, and code tables and was provided with a flashlight outfitted as a transport container. The container, created to hide material while traveling, was a hollow battery with screw threads inside the flashlight. The distribution of this container in 1959 was documented in "Record Card A for Issued Containers," Nr. 292. Even in the fifties everything had to be documented and accounted for. Later, when Gottfried was caught in 1968, the department could reconstruct what incriminating spy tools he had been issued.[2]

In the fifties intelligence and state security did not have their own pool of technical specialists on whom they could draw to develop, build, and acquire equipment and manage the departments. Therefore the technical department (K) farmed out some equipment-building tasks to scientists, engineers, and technicians in civilian institutions. Although the ministry paid for these services, it was done surreptitiously, and its name did not appear in the dealings.[3]

The Technical Operations Sector was officially founded as a sector in July 1960, when several technical departments operating since the mid-fifties merged together under one roof. The three new departments – 31, 32, and 33 – were responsible for the development and production of chemical and physical technology. Department 32 was also responsible for scientific-technical expertise and was almost identical to the criminal technical institutes in police departments and similar to the FBI's crime lab.[4]

Most leaders at the Ministry for State Security were apparatchiks. The first head of the sector, Colonel Herbert Hentschke (1960–70), was no exception: he had no technical training, but sterling political qualifications. His spy career began when he conducted illegal work for the Communist Party of Germany (KPD) and then emigrated to Czechoslovakia and the Soviet Union with his father in 1934 to flee Hitler's Germany. He was jailed by the Soviet Secret Police in 1937, was released, became a locksmith, and then attended the Soviet Communist International (Comintern) Training School in 1942/43, becoming a spy and partisan in Belorussia in 1944. Upon his return to Germany after the war, he was active in the Communist Party of Germany and was an assistant in the Politburo. After a brief stint working for the police department, he joined the fledgling foreign espionage unit, the Foreign Intelligence Service (*Aussenpolitische Nachrichtendienst* or APN) in 1951, becoming head of political espionage. In 1959 he switched to the counterintelligence and security unit as its deputy head, a position he kept until 1963, while leading the technical division after 1960. After attending the Soviet Communist Party School in 1965/66, he matriculated at the Stasi's Law School as a night student, received a B.A. in law in 1968, and completed his thesis on the best way to plan spy technology. He left the sector in 1970 and was replaced by his deputy, Günter Schmidt, who had a strong technical background as well as sterling political credentials. Hentschke retired in 1981, the year after he became a major general.[5]

Hentschke's political leanings entered into his vision for improving the quality of the technical departments. He called for "stricter planning, coordination and control" and developed a communist-style bureaucracy. Maintaining secrecy and keeping the technology hidden from the population and enemy spy agencies became a major theme throughout the period of the Cold War. Even within the technical departments, cover names were developed for the technology for use in interdepartmental communication. In fact, Hentschke thought the goal of the division should be to "increase secrecy [*Konspiration*]" by providing technology for secret communication or to help internal security.[6]

If OTS was the Q branch, the deployment department (called Department E for *Einsatz*, which means "mission" or "deployment"), was the place to find a number of socialist Q's – the gadget people who trained agents on how to use the equipment. Developed in the 1950s, it acted as an intermediary between agents and the technical division. Most of the agents it serviced and trained initially worked for external counterintelligence against the West, but it also serviced agents run by the foreign department in the provincial offices. By the 1970s, it increasingly served counterintelligence and security within East Germany.

After the building of the "anti-fascist wall of protection" on 13 August 1961, Mielke concluded that the "enemy" would be forced to use more technology to communicate with agents in East Germany, because personal meetings would become more difficult. He sought to expose more agents and spies and beefed up the counterintelligence unit, postal interception, radio surveillance, scientific-technical expertise, and codes. Although the technical division had already been told in 1953 to collect and analyze all enemy communication technology, this activity increased considerably in the early sixties, as Mielke ordered the collection and analysis of all spy technology. In the early months of 1961, the ministry had already recognized that "enemy" spy agencies had increasingly turned to using technological devices for spying, and this inspired the East Germans to emulate them.[7]

In fact, the enthusiasm for science surrounding the "scientific-technical revolution" permeated the whole decade of the sixties internationally. Science historian Derek de Solla Price characterized an "exponential growth" of "big science" in the post–World War II era, especially by the 1960s.[8] This embrace of science and its exponential growth greatly increased the status of the technical division. Whereas in the fifties technology was used occasionally, by the early sixties it had become an active staple of practical spy work, mirroring developments – with some time lag – in America and other Western nations.

At first it was difficult to reconcile the demands of secrecy and socialist planning with the practical need to prepare and make technology available at short notice for use by an agent or in an operation. The short-term needs seemed to clash with socialist long-term planning ideas and the mandate by Walter Ulbricht in the early sixties to prepare "prognoses." Hentschke handled this problem by having some items available immediately as a series. For example, a container to hide tools of the spy trade would be mass-produced and made available from the warehouse. He also started to shift the unit away from its yearly plans to long-term planning (prognosis) in order to achieve the highest level of scientific-technical achievement. This would be done through research and development within workshops and in cooperation with civilian scientific institutions. To further strengthen the quality of the scientific-technical work and to provide consumers with the product they needed, Hentschke started to develop cooperative arrangements with the socialist "brother organs" (other East Bloc countries' security services).[9]

Hentschke was a practical man. He stressed that the gadgets needed to work when needed: "Modern technology as such, even when it embodies the highest level of science and technology, is useless for operational work when it does not contribute to solving the secret task at the moment it is supplied."[10]

He defined "operational technology" in its narrow sense as "special and secretly created technical instruments or devices." But because some of the secretly created spy technology used commercial technology as well, he emphasized its practical application.[11]

Maintaining secrecy while servicing the consumers effectively was a problem. Socialist long-term planning clashed with the need to maintain

9. Günter Schmidt. Schmidt was the director of the Technical Operations Sector from 1970 to 1989. (BStU)

secrecy, because in order to plan, managers needed an overview of the full range of technology. The technical division also needed to farm out some of its technical problems to civilian institutions, and they needed to know enough about the problem to solve it. Similarly, science had become so specialized that the sector needed a number of its own scientists to solve a problem, and this could only be done effectively if the specialists knew enough about the concrete application. This account clashed with the secrecy and compartmentalization principles.[12]

Hentschke tried to limit the number of scientists who knew about the problem by developing a strict need-to-know policy. He never passed on concrete details about operations, like the name and address of a target. A large production series was advantageous for secrecy because technicians could disguise the technology by changing the design of the containers and the camouflage of cameras.[13]

Exponential growth of science and the accompanying specialization meant that the era of the tinker was gone. As Hentschke put it, "universal golden hands" were not enough for solving technical problems. He found that people either underestimated the value of technology because they did not use it in operations and relied on old methods, or overestimated its power by seeing it as "wonder technology" and a "cure-all."[14]

Some of Hentschke's contributions to the OTS that lasted until its demise included developing an internal library for the study of the scientific literature and working groups for cooperating with industry, finance, and their socialist "friends."[15]

Although Hentschke was the first head of the Technical Operations Sector, Günter Schmidt, his deputy and right-hand man, presided over most of its development and led it officially from the time he became chief in 1970 until the fall of the Berlin Wall in 1989. Schmidt was a tall, imposing man with a paunch and a confident manner, nothing like the eccentric white-haired Q, played by Desmond Llewelyn in the James Bond films, who is happiest wandering through his lab and supervising the tinkers. Instead, he had the air of a bureaucrat. His highly successful career paralleled the development of the Stasi, as he joined in 1953.

Born into a worker's family in the region of the Erzgebirge (eastern part of Germany) in 1929, Schmidt was in the Hitler Youth between 1943 and 1945. After the defeat of Hitler's Germany, Schmidt, under the influence of his parents, joined the Communist Party of Germany and the East German Socialist Unity Party in 1946. When he was a teenager he became an apprentice in telecommunications and received training at the Post Office and Telecommunications Ministry school in telegraphy, dialing technology, and repeater technology. He attended the post office's engineering school between 1948 and 1951 and studied electronics engineering. Before joining state security in 1953, he had been a department head at the Ministry for Post and Telecommunications, in the department for "special questions," presumably spying.[16]

Starting in Department S, for technology, he quickly rose in the ranks, and when the department split up into O (for telephone tapping and bugs), F (for radio), and K (for instrument construction) in 1956, he was made acting head of telephone tapping. It helped that he was recognized as "politically the strongest comrade" that year. A vacancy emerged in the telephone tapping and bugs department when the head, Comrade Adolf Viehmann, was dismissed from the MfS for not adhering to the socialist code of ethics and morals and was branded "dishonest and undisciplined." Schmidt replaced him on 1 September 1960. He was thirty-one years old.[17]

During the sixties the organization of scientific-technical areas solidified and merged as they grew in size and importance. Schmidt had the necessary technical training that other politically qualified staff lacked. This had been the main shortcoming with Hentschke. At first Schmidt assisted him as deputy head from 1963 to 1968 and as acting head, 1968–70. In January 1970, Schmidt replaced Hentschke, who took on other duties as a valued political comrade. The personnel department justified the appointment in this way: "Because of new tasks in the technical operations sector of the Ministry for State Security as a result of the galloping scientific-technical revolution, it is necessary for the director to have excellent scientific-technical knowledge.... Comrade Colonel Hentschke does not have these qualifications and is no longer suitable for these tasks."[18]

Along with his loyal party attitude and training, his political dependability, and his strong technical training, Schmidt brought an enthusiastic endorsement from the cadre department. The party organization monitoring the unit – by 1970 they had firmly established themselves within the MfS – endorsed him because he implemented party resolutions and served as first party secretary in the party organization. But Schmidt was not just an apparatchik, he was also completing a bachelor's degree in criminalistics at the Humboldt University's night school to supplement his technical background.[19]

During his career Schmidt collected a staggering amount of medals and honors for his work: seventy-three commendations. Other countries also honored his work as part of the division's international cooperation with the brother organs – East Bloc communist security services. He received three medals from Cuba, including one for twenty years of service in the Cuban Ministry of Interior, and a friendship order from North Vietnam. When the head of the Department for Cadre and Education nominated him for his second medal in gold "for service to Folk and Fatherland" on the occasion of his fiftieth birthday in 1978, Mielke himself crossed out that order and named him major general instead.[20]

Schmidt was well-versed in Marxist theory and the communist ideals of the Socialist Party. His fluent knowledge of Marxist organizational theory, popular in the 1960s, is reflected in the 1970 bachelor's thesis he completed, together with Claus Hillenmaier, an OTS departmental head, entitled "The Formation of Analytic Prognosis Work as Part of the Leadership and Directorship Activity in OTS." They completed it for the MfS university in Potsdam in 1970, the year Schmidt officially took over as head. This thesis became a blueprint for the way Schmidt ran the division until the end of the German Democratic Republic (GDR), and it demonstrated that he had thought long and hard about how to run a unit along socialist lines.[21]

On first glance, the thesis seems to be a bewildering socialist tract, setting the stage for the emergence of a rigid and highly bureaucratic structure with directors, deputy directors, departments, subdepartments, groups, and so on. But in this respect the bureaucracy probably does not differ from structures in Western Cold War spy agencies.

Unlike Hentschke, Schmidt had no qualms about embracing long-term planning, rather than relying on the previous short-term monthly, quarterly, and yearly plans. Whereas short-term planning meant that the technology was in use within a year, long-term planning required a development time of two to four years.

Both Hentschke and Schmidt saw the need to establish close ties with industry in order to cover technical needs. Hentschke proposed infiltrating socialist companies with "officers on a special mission," ("*Offiziere im besonderem Einsatz*" or OibE's, as they were known). These officers worked at a company, but were actually employed and paid by the MfS. Schmidt used the new and necessary partnership with industry as a way to justify and integrate long-term planning and prognosis into OTS. By their very nature, companies and scientific institutions needed to keep abreast of, and even anticipate, trends in scientific-technical developments.

THE OTS: A SPY-TECH UNIVERSITY?

By the time Schmidt had assumed leadership duties, the main scientific areas embodied in the departments resembled a science college at a university or scientific research institution. There were fields for fine mechanics or optics, for electronics, for secret writing and marking material, for "document preparation" (aka forged documents), for scientific-technical expertise, and for material-technical equipment procurement. All these fields became departments.[22]

By 1989 the division was one of the largest units at the MfS, with a dozen departments: 31, 32, 33, 34, 35, 36, E, SF (containers), RZ (computer center), AB (machine building), ZB (central photo lab), and the Institute for Technical Analysis, officially a civilian scientific institute. But as the following chart indicates, the department numbers had been rearranged into lettered groups. The first group was subordinate to Günter Schmidt and included planning, the computer center, and Department 36 for securing materials and buildings. The second group, C, encompassed Department 32 for scientific-technical expertise (including the vast fingerprint collection); Department 34 for chemical and physical methods, primarily secret writing and chemical marking material; and Department 35 for analysis and reproduction of documents. The Institute for Technical Analysis followed and focused on electronics and spy radios for communicating and for countermeasures. This unit primarily worked for

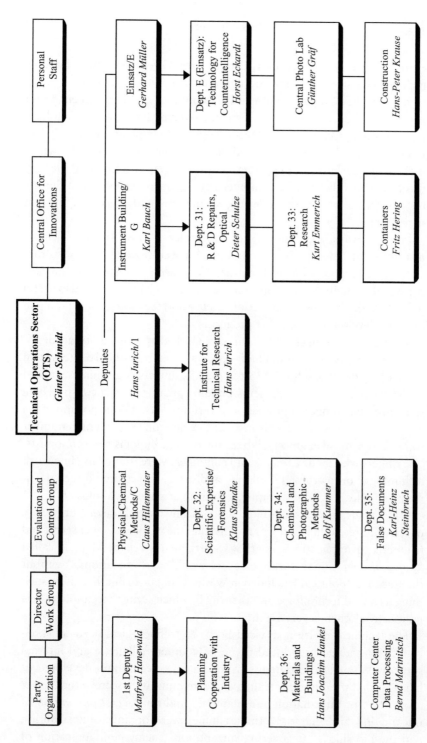

CHART 3. The structure of the Technical Operations Sector in 1989.

Horst Männchen's electronics empire. Area G for instrument building included Department 31 for photographic technology, visual observation technology, key copying, and security technology and Department 33 for research and development on electronic circuits, hard drive technology, tape recording technology, TV technology, and cooperation with civilian industry. Area G also encompassed the container department (SF), which made concealments. Finally, Area E (for *Einsatz*) encompassed Department E, which distributed equipment and trained agents to use the spy technology; the photo lab for developing pictures; and a special equipment department.[23]

In other ways, too, the division resembled a university or scientific institution. It developed and maintained a well-stocked library so that staff could keep up with the literature. Qualified scientists or technicians consulted the literature like ordinary scientists. The library was also useful to leaders for charting the direction science and technology was taking in order to develop their socialist prognosis.

Most of the technical staff could have worked at a university, academy, or in industry. By 1986, about half – 495 staff members – held degrees from a university or trade school. Most of the 284 university graduates worked in the electronics and instruments-building area or were chemists. There were an equal number of physicists and criminalists. A large portion of the 211 trade school graduates also worked in electronics, but a high number were also chemical engineers, lab technicians, or biologists or economists. The tinkers who made cameras and containers were trained in "fine work technology" or instrument building, and those who created forged documents had degrees in polygraphy, graphics, or paper technology.[24]

OTS's goals, of course, differed dramatically from those of a university or scientific research lab. It was not just that the work was super secret and had practical applications, but they were there to serve the MfS's so-called "*political*-operational work," or, as we would say, "operations," without the adjective "political" included in Western language. But there is no such thing as naked technology, and the way in which security technology was politically clothed is very clear.

The technical division serviced both the technological needs of intelligence gathering abroad and domestic counterintelligence and internal security. What differentiated it from civilian research and development labs was that it supported stealing and communicating secrets: the "*secret acquisition* of information and material" and the "*secret passing on* of information and material" (italics mine) were organizational rubrics, and the flip side – "uncovering surreptitious enemy communication of information and material" and "security for protecting secrets" – was also part of the plan.[25]

Predictably, foreign intelligence and the deployment department (Department E, the Q people) had the most voracious appetite for spy gadgets, because of their communication needs. This does not mean that the telephone eavesdroppers, surveillance, mail snoopers, border control, and the host of other departments did not need technology. They were also consumers and kept the division busy with requests for devices to spy on people and to gather information and material. While creating inventive communication technology, technicians also contributed to intercepting enemy communication channels. And, of course, they had their bread-and-butter job – providing security technology, such as surveillance cameras to secure governmental buildings, including the Ministry for State Security.

By the mid-seventies, cameras and containers topped the list of gadgets developed for foreign intelligence and the deployment department. Since it was a research and development lab, division leaders filed these requests under the category of fine mechanics and optics. In one year alone, more than a hundred *mikrat* cameras – real technological wonders – were made for their agents, as well as some mobile infrared cameras for taking pictures in the dark. In that same year the division delivered 1,216 containers, mostly made out of leather, though some were mechanical containers.[26] Most of this equipment was used to gather intelligence, by taking pictures of documents (document photography) or by transporting and hiding the communications material. While the foreign intelligence arm of the Ministry for State Security (HV A) mostly worked abroad in intelligence, E worked in external counterintelligence and intelligence, which meant the devices they used also entailed surveillance activities. Although HV A staff, such as Markus Wolf, claim that this unit only undertook intelligence gathering abroad, some of the technology, like the infrared cameras, indicate that they were not immune from informant-like activity.

In order to communicate, foreign intelligence and external counterintelligence also received a number of items in the area of electronics, which mostly translates into radios, transmitters, receivers, and burst transmitters. More than a hundred shortwave agent receivers were given to foreign intelligence, whereas the deployment department's top item was a burst transmitter for shortwave agent transmitters.[27]

The enormous number of forged documents developed reflects the extent of foreign intelligence activities abroad and number of agents they must have had. Three thousand and seven hundred passports and identity cards were developed in one year alone. The agents also needed a number of other documents, letterhead, stamps, and other printed matter, such as index cards.

Secret writing is a staple in a spy's toolbox. In 1973 alone, agents working abroad received enough secret writing copy paper to write several books (1,080 impregnated sheets) and 870 portions of developer for making invisible ink visible, as well as more than a hundred prepared textiles (such as scarves) and invisible ink cartridges for pens.[28]

If foreign intelligence and counterintelligence primarily received technology for collecting, passing on, and communicating secrets, other units needed technology to gather information surreptitiously to be used in operations involving a suspected spy, dissident, or other form of "criminal" activity. Internal security's telephone tap and observation department took the lead in these areas. Most of the items for the telephone taps, bugs, and video department involved electronics, such as a long-playing tape recorder for remote control telephone listening and amplifiers for listening devices (1,425 amplifiers were delivered in 1973). The eavesdroppers received 1,976 carrier frequency transmitters for busy and open telephone lines and special lines for bugging. One of the most inventive listening devices came installed in an ashtray. The caption to a picture in the file reads: "More sensitive than an ear."[29]

Of course, the radio counterintelligence also needed electronics, specifically, shortwave surveillance receivers for surveillance of radios and for finding the direction from which the radio was transmitting, antennas, radios, and receivers. The communications department (N) received thousands of antenna units.[30]

Observation, surveillance, and investigation require a fair amount of technology. As a result, the observers were voracious technical consumers. If agents needed small spy cameras to take pictures of documents and household containers in which to store them, observers needed observation cameras and more mobile containers in which to hide them. In 1972 alone they received hundreds of camera concealments in various bags, cars, and even umbrellas. Electronic items include transmitters and receivers for wireless alarm systems.

The sheer number of technical devices prepared for the consumer departments demonstrates that technology was an essential part of spy work for the MfS. It also provides clues to the type of work departments did, when other evidence no longer survives. Later chapters will survey the technology in greater detail and assess the extent to which the high quality technology made a positive contribution to operations.

SOCIALIST Q'S

Gerhard Müller was an unlikely Q, but he became a quintessential communist leader of a stable of Q's, the gadget people who supplied and trained agents with spy paraphernalia. Born into a worker's family in Dresden in 1930, he joined the Ministry for State Security in 1955 at the age of twenty-five, after learning the trade of typesetting and earning a degree in engineering graphics at the Trade School for Graphics in Leipzig. With his printing background, he was a shoe-in for working on forged documents and joined the technical department's document section when he was hired.[31]

Once at the MfS, Müller became a political activist. He was not just a requisite member of the communist party, the SED: he went to the Ministry of the Interior's evening school and studied Marxist psychology and pedagogy, he became part of the leadership of the basic party organization at work, and he belonged to all of the relevant political organizations, including the Free Youth Movement. His activism did not stop at the office: at his apartment complex he was a party agitator, and during his free time he read books on the workers' movement. He even lived according to the rules of "socialist ethics and morals" with his wife and two children. Although he had above-average knowledge in his field, it was his "developed class consciousness" and his model socialist life that helped his rise in the ranks. By 1959 he headed up the documents department at the newly created deployment department (E), became acting director in 1960, and became leader of the whole department in 1961. Under his leadership his staff became "socialist patriots and chekists."[32]

By 1959 the staff's main mission involved preparing everything related to the use of spy gadgets in counterintelligence and security for "work towards the West." This was a period of institutional flux when Mielke's security division covered similar territory as foreign intelligence, which had recently been placed under the same roof. Whereas foreign intelligence had its own units (HV A VIII and VI) for technology and documents, E also serviced the district office's foreign intelligence department. It advised all consumer departments on how to use the gadgets; it supplied them with the techniques or instruments. It led and outfitted groups of agents who were trained to undertake technical operations in West Berlin and West Germany, and it disguised certain technical devices for concrete use.[33]

Utmost secrecy guided this unit as well, and Mielke declared that the "chief principle in solving operational technical tasks is the strictest maintenance of secrecy." Planning played a major role early on. A distinction was made between long-term orders, which were part of the plan, and short-notice orders, which were acted upon immediately. Founded with three sections, by 1968 Department E had expanded to four sections: Section I for radios and electronics, Section II for containers and lock technology, Section IV for documents, and Section IV for cameras, secret writing, and marking material. Specialists for technology were placed in all counterintelligence and internal security units. The number of orders processed per year varied, but in the seventies between seven thousand and eight thousand technical devices or combinations were delivered per year. By the time of the collapse of East Germany in 1989, the department employed about 170 staff members.[34]

The year of the Prague Spring, 1968, was a turning point for the deployment department. Until 1968 citizens could cross the border with their identity cards. This changed in 1968, when the two Germanys instituted mandatory passport and visa regulations. As a result they had to develop 440 new West German passports; a large portion of these passports went to East German agents. In order to forge the passports, they had to acquire two new crucible printing presses to print numbers on the passports and a passport typewriter with the necessary type. They were able to produce passports from twenty-eight different West German cities as a result of obtaining copies of West German passports used as models. That year alone, staff members distributed 3,411 East and West documents, including Federal Republic of Germany (FRG) passports, GDR passports for retirees and business travelers, and West German and West Berlin identity cards.[35]

Because agents had to hide the passports, they also needed containers. As a result there was an increased demand for containers. That same year E handed out a total of 1,161 containers, including some they made themselves to meet the unexpected demand.[36]

Even with these new demands, the department continued its routine work in the late sixties. Radios, cameras, containers, and secret writing were developed together with OTS, and agents were trained how to use them. Department E used both infrared and decimeter radio channels and two-sided radio contacts (from headquarters to the field and from the field to headquarters). They worked on a technique so that tape recordings could be played on the radio.[37]

In the area of photography, there was a demand to develop concealments for observation reasons (more than a hundred were distributed in 1968–69). Another focus was document photography; in 1968 agents received thirty-four Minox cameras. Infrared photography was also a hot new area, but they were not able to acquire the cameras from Japan at that point because of the embargo. The plan was to start using infrared photography – it was very useful for work in the dark – in 1970.[38]

The seventies can best be characterized as the decade of the "authority of the plan" and a decade in which the tasks of the department shifted from an external focus on the West to an internal focus on the GDR. Even with the broad shift to internal use of technology, E continued to provide innovative and adaptive communication technology to agents stationed in the West or on a mission there.

The "authority of the plan" coincided with an increasingly bureaucratic structure. Whereas the director had been writing yearly reports on the accomplishments of the department for many years, in 1970 he wrote his first prognostic plan for the coming year. In a department characterized by short-term deployment, long-term planning is almost an oxymoron. Problems arose when the department developed certain technologies because of projected needs. Instead of that technology, however, the consumer departments demanded short-term technology needed for an operation they could not predict far in advance. Staff often recognized that the planning had been unrealistic in relation to actual need.

In 1974 Department E complained that the planning by the district offices was very unrealistic in relation to needs. That year they were over-prepared, although in the case of containers, they did not develop enough in relation to the demand (26 planned, 83 ordered). Tinkers developed too many West documents, like FRG passports, in relation to demand (637 false passports created, 112 ordered), too many shortwave receivers (106 planned, 14 ordered), and too many camera concealments (186 planned, 58 ordered). The reverse problem occurred the next year – the technology had not been developed and had to be prepared at very short notice and required a lot of extra work by staff members.[39]

To make matters worse, increased cooperation with industry during the early seventies meant more long-term planning, because the communist economy had a plan for industry. If industry planned on contributing to intelligence and security technological needs, then OTS would have to adapt and plan four years in advance instead of just one.

The diplomatic recognition of the GDR as a separate German state in 1972 created a new political landscape and new demands for technology. Embassies could now operate abroad, and they needed technology. But this also created a new political situation at home. Counterintelligence increased its surveillance of Western diplomats stationed in East Berlin as well.

The gradual shift to internal surveillance began in 1972, when there was a 291 percent increase in requests for observer technology such as radios, cameras, and tape recorders. For the next five years this pattern continued in requests from the counterespionage department and from the observation department. They claimed they needed more observation technology to guard military objects and to keep track of diplomats in the GDR. But this was also a period when East Germany cracked down on people attempting to flee East Germany either through smuggling groups or through the border.

In 1974 requests for eavesdropping devices increased sixfold. In this case orders were made for tape recorders and radios, as another department handled bugs and telephone taps. Müller's department responded to this demand by developing women's handbag concealments for small tape recorders. In 1977, Department E delivered 56 small tape recorders with 30 concealments, and by 1980 a total of 643 different types of tape recorders were in "operational use," including 467 small cassette recorders.[40] The increased demand for some kinds of technology mirrored social and political developments in the GDR and the emergence of a security state.

By 1973 entire observation teams were outfitted with needed technology, primarily radios to communicate amongst one another and tape recorders to tape conversations. These teams were used for big operations like "Action Banner," which involved security in case of attack for the 1973 World Games in East Berlin. This entailed using long lists of technology. Department E bragged that it could meet all the operational departments' needs on short notice. They tried out fourteen new technical "combinations" using radios and eavesdropping technology; they developed thirteen new types of locks (secret mechanisms to open a container) for containers, produced ninety-four containers and concealments, and developed five secret writing methods on their own for observers and couriers.[41] The operation was so successful that Günter Schmidt received yet another award for OTS's good work.

Even with this startling new development in the seventies, E's traditional role of developing communication technology for agents in the West continued. The seventies saw an increased sophistication and adaptation in communications technology.

X-ray-safe containers were an adaptive innovation. As border security began to use X-ray technology in response to terrorism in the early seventies, containers containing metal parts set off alarms. As a result, tinkers began to develop X-ray-safe containers in 1972. To avoid detection, mechanics either developed containers with no metal parts or matched them with a legitimate item. For example, a leather container outfitted for a passport would be set up so that the metal ring on the West German passport aligned with the buckle on the handbag. Or there would be no metal parts whatsoever. Leaders soon discovered that there was no such thing as a completely X-ray-safe container.

Department E kept abreast of technological developments and tried to incorporate innovations into its tools. During the early seventies, most radio communication with the West was done through "decimeter" radio. They set up stations along the Western side of the border (in *Heiligenstadt*, for example) so that agents could receive messages. The early seventies saw increased use of infrared and ultra shortwave radio technology; by 1979, decimeter radio communications had been phased out. Infrared and light radio technology could be implemented at short ranges – up to three kilometers – and worked best over the border.

DEPARTMENT 32: LIKE THE FBI CRIME LAB

Unlike the American system, in which foreign intelligence (CIA, DIA, etc.) is separated institutionally from crime fighting and internal policing (e.g., the FBI), the MfS combined these areas under one roof. The under-one-roof principle was embodied at the technical division. Preparing technology that allowed agents to communicate was one side of the coin. The flip side of the coin was providing technology for security and crime scene investigations and analysis of evidence for operational departments.

Although the East German police maintained the Criminal Technical Institute (*Kriminaltechnisches Institut* or KTI) located in the heart of Berlin near *Alexanderplatz*, it was not appropriate for them to handle all the secret forensic science needs of the MfS, therefore a separate forensic science unit was set up in the mid-fifties; this unit became Department 32 for scientific-technical expertise in 1960. Like the FBI crime lab, Department 32 provided forensic and technical services, but unlike the FBI, which services federal, state, and local law enforcement agencies, the OTS's unit worked for the MfS's operational units, for its investigative Department IX, and for customs.[42]

Like the FBI crime lab and other German criminal technical institutes, the MfS's unit provided expert analysis in chemistry, biology, fingerprinting, ballistics, questioned documents, voice analysis, criminal photography, and explosives. By the early 1980s the unit provided on average 2,300 examinations and evaluations yearly for other MfS units and for customs.

On occasion it also supported the police's KTI efforts, for example, in a murder investigation.

Items to be evaluated by the experts ranged from documents with secret writing on them to saliva of dissidents. In 1983 their work focused on five broad areas: general criminal investigations relating to handwriting, blood groups, voice identification, fighting enemies of the state (spies and dissidents), and terrorism. The latter focused on fighting terrorism through ballistics and the examination of suspicious objects that could be explosives. Spectacular border escapes also occupied their attention that year, as well as the examination of "enemy communication" through chemical analysis.[43]

One of the scientific expertise department's most innovative contributions was an automated fingerprint system undertaken together with the police department's Criminal Technical Institute and the Academy of Sciences launched in 1979 and completed in the early 1980s called the Automatic Interpretation of Dactylographic Prints (AIDA in German). The project used electronic data processing to compare fingerprints from the MfS's collection.[44] After the fall of the Berlin Wall many Western criminal technical institutes were interested in learning more about this project. In fact, the United States Secret Service obtained a copy, and the FBI developed a similar automated fingerprint system in 1999 called the Integrated Automated Fingerprint Identification System (IAFIS).[45]

UNDERCOVER CONTRACTS

The late 1960s and early 1970s saw the development of a number of crucial cooperative arrangements with prestigious East German socialist firms (called *Volkseigenebetrieb* or VEB). Since OTS did not have the necessary labs, equipment, and other material needed to support all of its work, it sought out institutes that could provide both material and personnel support. The pattern of establishing contact and covertly working with industry was similar to the pattern used when working with the academy. First it was necessary to find institutes working on areas useful to the OTS, such as electronics, photography, or isotope production. When investigating a potential partner, staff looked for politically active and reliable directors who would be open to an approach.[46]

One of the first companies successfully co-opted was the VEB for Radio and Television in Dresden. The company's director was very cooperative when Schmidt approached him and was ready to establish a special development and production center in their scientific-technical research center

in May 1969; he promised fifty staff members and twenty engineers by
1975. This inspired Schmidt to create a base for OTS within the Dresden
district office for companies, which agreed to cooperate with the MfS,
using a method similar to that of the Pentacon relationship – the leading
GDR camera and film company – an old partner.[47]

The VEB for Radio and Television, known as RFT, was one of the best-
known electronic equipment companies in the GDR and produced much
more than TV sets, radios, and tape recorders for East Bloc consumers.
Surveillance technology and measuring equipment were also RFT products. The equipment was used by the MfS in a large-scale surveillance
network spread over crucial areas in East Berlin: international hotels,
cafés, restaurants, airports, and other places such as *Alexanderplatz*, a
crossroad for East-West contact and an East Berlin landmark. RFT even
had an advertisement on one of the towers on Karl-Marx Alley in East
Berlin: "Measure – Surveillance."

In 1971, the MfS established a very secret cooperative agreement
with the department for radioactive preparations at the Central Institute for Nuclear Research of the Academy of Sciences of the GDR in
Rossendorf, home of East Germany's major nuclear reactor. And, in 1972,
Schmidt completed an official agreement with the two most prized socialist companies: VEB Combine Pentacon in Dresden and VEB Carl-Zeiss in
Jena. By the end of the GDR, OTS had established cooperative agreements
with at least nineteen socialist companies or scientific institutions.[48]

By the mid-seventies, the OTS had also courted and penetrated as silent
partners many institutes at the prestigious Academy of Sciences. Even
the academy president was a willing partner and offered services to the
Ministry for State Security, seeing it as another state ministry to serve.
Although an official contract with the general academy was not signed
until 1989, OTS had already created working groups in individual institutes such as cybernetics, space research, computer technology, and electron physics.

Although official contracts existed with most of OTS's partners, only
the institute director knew of the arrangement, and the cooperation was
kept very secret and undercover. No one else was privy to the fact that
the MfS was a contractor and user of the scientific research undertaken
at a civilian institute. Because official contracts existed, the content of the
research done under the aegis of the contract could become a state secret.

The organization of the undercover work followed the MfS's basic principles for "conspirational work": OTS planted OibE's and unofficial staff
members with "key positions" at the target institutes and used them as

liaisons, as informants, and as agents of influence. Internal security in the economy (Department XVIII) was then responsible for spying on personnel in the OTS's scientific group and asking the "who's who" question.[49]

Officers on Special Missions were MfS employees who worked at institutes as though they were regular employees of that workplace. There were reportedly 3,030 OibE's who worked at jobs in the GDR.[50] They received their salary from the institute and MfS and long, convoluted orders regulated the work relationship in order that the OibE would also receive a pension upon retirement. Officers received a whole new identity and cover story to disguise their previous work for the MfS. Only "scientifically highly qualified" and "experienced technical operations specialists" were selected to work at the nineteen institutes with which the OTS maintained cooperative agreements.[51] They coordinated communication between the institute and OTS, made sure strict secrecy was maintained, and above all, worked undercover for the MfS.

The coordinator for cooperation with industry, Wolfgang Reimann, saw this "conspirational method of cooperation" as a "higher form of secrecy for the realization of technical operations tasks." He acknowledged, however, that it would be difficult to keep the contract work secret because the group that knew about the project was fairly large.[52]

The OTS used the partner institutes' equipment and research and development results. More sinister was the way it tried to "influence civilian developments" in order to use the results later. This part of the relationship did not require extra money, but some research and development, commercial deliveries of special instruments, and construction of prototypes did require money. To keep that work secret, MfS had to create "front companies" and use their unofficial staff to pay for material. The MfS also had its own cover institute, the Institute for Technical Research, which was primarily made up of OibE's but was run like a civilian institute.

THE BROTHER ORGANS

Even with the help of industry, OTS could not cover all the needs of the consumer departments. Another source of support was, in theory, the other East Bloc spy technical divisions. OTS had the oldest relationship with the Soviet "technical operations administration" in their Committee for State Security (known in the West as KGB, in the East as KfS). During the early years, the KfS sent advisors to East Germany to shape and influence the creation of a ministry for state security in their image, and in the course of the fifties the two technical divisions worked closely together. By the 1970s OTS had established cooperative relationships with the technical divisions of almost all the East Bloc security services, also known as the brother organs (Czechoslovakia, Poland, Hungary, and Bulgaria), and had had long-standing relations with Vietnam and Cuba. By the early eighties it was in the position to offer generous "solidarity gifts" to Nicaragua.

All of the East Bloc countries' technical divisions were similar in size and structure to the OTS. Unlike OTS, however, they were part of their respective ministries for the interior. OTS shared, sold, and traded technology with the other East Bloc brother organs. It was constantly making deliveries and payments for technology. One of the most ingenious and interesting spy gadgets it received from the Czechs was the David, a pen camera. Other more common, mundane exchanges included security technology, radios, antennas, and the like.

TECHNOLOGY IN THE TROPICS

Like the Soviet Union, East Germany and the MfS supported communist regimes in the Third World. They helped train security personnel and provided other communist countries with advisors and material. Unlike their relationships with the other East Bloc brother organs, these relationships were often characterized as "solidarity contributions" and involved one-sided support instead of mutual exchange. Three communist countries are notable for the amount and quality of technical assistance they received: North Vietnam, Cuba, and Nicaragua.

North Vietnam

North Vietnam appears to be one of the first communist countries to have received extensive technical material, training, and support from the OTS. Already in the late 1950s a large shipment of listening devices for telephone and room surveillance arrived in Vietnam. By the mid sixties, OTS and Department 26 were advising Vietnam on how to develop a modern technical department to help them combat "USA-Imperialism" and its state-of-the-art technology. The new Department for Surveillance Technology was to employ 150 staff members. By the 1970s and 1980s, the Vietnamese technical services department (H 18) was a mirror image of OTS, though it was anchored in the Department of the Interior: it had subdepartments for fine mechanics and optics, chemistry (secret writing), biology (including saliva, blood, and hair analysis, as well as smell differentiation), toxicology (including the synthesis of toxins), bomb detecting, and forged documents. The Vietnamese seemed especially interested in drug analysis, although secret writing was also an active topic. OTS supported secret writing by providing material and instruments as well as training in gas chromatography. The Vietnamese were also eager to learn more about radioactive marking substances and the use of dogs in smell differentiation. East Germany was generous with their Vietnamese comrades: their Ministry of the Interior had built up Vietnam's entire service dog unit, and the MfS provided supplementary information on performing smell differentiation.[53]

In 1984 OTS provided the material for, and helped build, a state-of-the-art container and disguise workshop for the Vietnamese security services, all within two weeks. The MfS completed the electrical work; put in a water source; installed all the machinery for metal, leather, and wood; and decorated the workshop with benches, desks, stools, tables, and storage cabinets. They did not cut corners and provided the Vietnamese with the best technical equipment, including Western Ricoh and Robot cameras and an Aciera milling machine with a price tag of 191,389 West German marks. The Western Swiss-made Aciera was one of the most desirable and best small milling machines for micromechanics used by watchmakers.[54]

Cuba

Although not much is known about KGB operations in Vietnam, historian Christopher Andrew describes the KGB's great success in creating a "foothold in Latin America" and found that the KGB's code word for Cuba was "bridgehead."[55] Soon after the Caribbean island of Cuba became communist in 1961, it began to receive extensive technical support from Soviet and East German intelligence and state security. Whereas it is well known that the Soviet Union maintained one of the world's largest signals intelligence facilities in Lourdes, near Havana, since 1962, it is less known that from the early sixties until 1989 the MfS also provided much technical equipment and support in the areas supported by OTS, for telephone taps and bugs and communications.

In his memoirs, spy chief Markus Wolf describes his 1965 trip to Cuba via an unintended stop over at JFK Airport with two other senior intelligence officers. Although he does not identify these officers by name, one of them was a technical officer, and without a doubt, it was Günter Schmidt. Reportedly, the group came "armed with information and technical help."[56]

The Cubans were interested in acquiring German spy technology early on. Initially, they were fascinated by James Bond–style bugging devices and spy cameras and "poison-spitting pens and knives hidden in the heels of shoes." They showed Wolf Western catalogues but were disappointed in him as a "traveling salesman of espionage equipment." Although Wolf mentions this technical interest in his memoirs, he does not offer a full-scale discussion of the extent and kind of East German technical support.[57]

The Cubans ended up receiving large-scale technical support from both the Soviet Union and East Germany, and later, more modest help from some of the other East Bloc countries, such as Bulgaria and Czechoslovakia. At first, each side was in the dark about what kind of technical help the other supplied, but later East Germany and the Soviet Union consulted with each other and divided the labor in order not to duplicate efforts. For example, the Soviets supplied the Cubans with agent technology, an area OTS did not cover for them.

It was not until 1979 that the Soviets and East Germans exchanged topics and lists of equipment delivered to the Cubans. Like the Germans, the Soviets sent specialists to Havana to train the Cubans. Some of the other areas they worked on were: development and production of radio electronic devices, repair and servicing of tape recorders, cameras, questions related to "people control," and some areas of document technology, though this was not as extensive as the German's support. The Soviets advised supporting the Cubans enough to achieve an "acceptable high technical level" like that received by the security services in other countries, but being careful not to "harm" the "technical operations interests" of the GDR's and Soviet's state security.[58]

Between 1965 and 1972 Cuban colleagues traveled to Berlin for numerous meetings and study trips, and the Cuban specialists were trained so that they could become independent. From the early seventies through the end of the eighties, delegations consisting of OTS leaders and their counterparts in Cuba – the General Directorate for Technology (GDT) – shuttled between Havana and Berlin for annual meetings, viewing of labs and facilities, training sessions, and tourism. In addition, there were annual technical specialist meetings in Havana and Berlin.[59]

The Cubans were warm and welcoming hosts when the German delegation came to Havana for meetings. During a 1980 trip, the Cuban hosts hung banners in the entrance of the building with slogans like "Warm welcome, worthy OTS comrades" and "Friendship between the GDR and Cuba lives!" The Germans found their Cuban colleagues well prepared for the working sessions, and they were also impressed with extensive social events for the evenings and weekends – two weekend excursions, nine evening programs, rich and plentiful food, and a constant supply of rum and drinks in the hotel rooms. By 1989, the Germans had been to all the best restaurants and nightclubs in Havana and Cuban resort towns and had seen all the major tourist sites. The Berliners were also good hosts, but their so-called "social measures" reflected a less fun-loving, tropical nature. The Prussians took the Cubans to a show at the *Friedrichstadt-palast*, a stroll to the Brandenburg Gate, and bowling in the Palace of the Republic.[60]

The German delegation – always headed by Günter Schmidt – usually stayed in suites at the Hotel Riviera, located on the famous Havana Sea Wall, with a view of the glistening blue-green Caribbean water at the bay in the Vedado district. Built in the 1950s with Mafia money, the Riviera resembled a socialist high-rise with 1950s décor, but was considered a four-star hotel. During the day, the colleagues met at a Cuban intelligence safe house called "Trigal" (wheat field); nighttime entertainment included visits to Cuba's best restaurants, such as 1830 and the famous nightclub The Tropicana, also known as "paradise under the stars."[61]

Lively discussions at the safe house lead to a signed contract with Schmidt about the terms of the cooperation. Meetings with dignitaries such as the representatives of the KfS in the Soviet embassy were punctuated by visits to GDT technical operations installations at "Trigal."[62]

OTS taught the Cubans how to forge documents and develop secret writing. In essence they sired these units in Cuba's General Directorate for Technology (GDT) in the Ministry of the Interior (MININT) in the early 1960s. From the end of the sixties until the mid-seventies, they helped build up the hardware necessary for producing fake documents – technical equipment for paper production and processing, reproduction photography, and polygraphy. The heavy-duty equipment – items such as a Hollander, a two-zone reproduction camera, a vulcanizing press, an engraving mill machine, and galvanic equipment – was installed by OTS specialists; OTS staff also trained Cuban staff on how to use the equipment.[63]

OTS's false document section (Department 35) spent 15 to 20 percent of their time working on technology or developing false papers for the Cubans. By 1983 they were no longer willing to prepare complete fake passport for the Cubans; they made it an exception rather than the rule. OTS was only willing to have their people work on individual components of the passport "reproduction" process. The Cuban little "brothers" could no longer order complete passports.[64]

Unlike the work they did together on secret writing, forging documents largely remained a one-way street. In 1985, OTS thought they were beginning to profit from the "cooperation" when the Cubans provided them with reviews of the literature and material related to problems of retro-reflection foils. The Cubans hoped to be able to reproduce passports from ten different countries, as 1 million Cubans lived abroad. In 1989, the Cubans reported that they were considering buying an offset printing machine called PLANA from West Germany; instead they may have taken OTS's offer of two Mailänder offset printers they had in the warehouse.[65]

OTS rarely asked questions about how the technology was going to be used, unless this knowledge was needed to produce the technology. That was not their job. Because most of the technology was also used in East Germany, they could easily guess the Cuban applications. The main difference between using the technology in Germany and in the tropics was the effect the tropical weather had on the machinery. This was particularly true with the cameras and photography material. The specialists at Carl Zeiss Jena worked on making the cameras "tropically safe."[66]

OTS, together with the Soviet's technology unit, became the Cuban's technological lifeline and life support. Though disappointed that no poison darts or James Bond gadgets were in the huge containers that were shipped from the OTS warehouses to the *Hohenschönhausen* freight station and overseas via a freighter ship, the Cubans could not help but be grateful for the free equipment. After 1976 the Cubans were sent a bill, which was not always paid; during the eighties it was cash-on-delivery. Shipments ranged in value from 300,000 marks to more than a million total marks yearly. When work began, Cuba had no working industry to speak of, but the Soviet Union propped it up in the course of the Cold War.[67]

At the beginning the Cuban Ministry of the Interior received large amounts of commercial instruments and material from the East Germans, including document and papermaking technology, photography lab material, cameras, electronics, semiconductor technology, cables, and instruments. It was not until the beginning of the 1970s that OTS also began to deliver large amounts of secret spy technology, including instruments and methods relating to reproducing documents, uncovering secret writing, and studying enemy secret writing. By the late eighties the shipments included both commercial and secret spy technology, and the list of goods expanded to include items such as Morse code machines, telescopes, periscopes, and infrared communication devices.[68]

Although OTS seemed pleased with the Cubans' preparation for meetings and their increasing mastery of technological espionage, they often characterized the "cooperation" as "one-sided." OTS primarily delivered technology and information to the Cubans, while the Cubans offered their hospitality, but no technological knowledge. The relationship did not remain a one-way street, however. By the 1980s OTS saw a glimmer of hope and began to characterize the Cubans as "real partners." This new partnership developed as the Cubans became more sophisticated in the two key areas of OTS support: document technology and secret writing. OTS was especially interested in the information Cuba could supply about enemy secret writing methods.

As early as June 1975, the Cubans passed on an original American multi-color ribbon for a U.S. visa stamp. OTS was delighted because they had just completed some development work on a method for copying a three-color visa stamp half a year earlier. That same year the Cubans shared two samples of secret writing from a CIA operation; this aided OTS in decoding all the formulas needed to uncover secret writing. Secret writing soon became a chief focus for real cooperation between OTS and the GDT. The OTS used the Cuban connection to learn more about the "techniques and tactics" of U.S. intelligence secret communication methods using the post office. By the late 1980s, OTS had a "complete overview of enemy" secret writing, because the Cubans shared what they found.[69]

Because Cuba has been considered technologically backward and is known for its fun-loving salsa-infused "be happy, don't worry" attitude, Western intelligence has largely underestimated Cuban intelligence's technical capabilities. With the help of their communist friends, Cuban intelligence managed to turn a largely backward technological standard into a first-rate technical services division.

The Cuban relationship with the OTS offers a window into Cuban intelligence and reveals a surprisingly large and effective technical unit. By 1985 it had at least eight hundred staff members and a large departmental structure with administrative, personnel, equipment, and subject areas. It was not a carbon copy of the Soviet or East German technical operations units but blended Cuban needs with Latin organization. Electronics was the largest department, with 220 staff members, and the Cubans were in the process of building an electronics factory together with Bulgaria in 1985.

Very little is known, or has been written, about Cuban intelligence, counterintelligence, and security except for the basic structures and material gleaned from defectors and the agents caught in America. The size and capabilities of its technical unit would suggest that Cuban intelligence is a much greater threat to Western interests than previously thought. Like East Germany, its intelligence services were very large in proportion to the population (9 to 10 million in the seventies and eighties) and size of the country.

Interestingly, public information available on Cuban intelligence in the early 2000s describes a technical support unit "responsible for the production of false documents, communications systems supporting clandestine operations, and development of clandestine message capabilities."[70] There is no doubt that East Germany's OTS played the pivotal role in building the Cuban's forged documents section into a first-rate outfit. Not only was false document technology one of the chief areas of support in terms of machines and equipment delivered, but OTS also offered a lot of manpower and often spent ten thousand hours of work time yearly working on fake passports for the Cubans.[71]

General Cuban intelligence and state security was not just a carbon copy of a repressive system of informants, as East Germany was often portrayed after the Wall fell. The two areas – document technology and secret writing – in which the services worked together most suggest a strong force in foreign intelligence and foreign counterintelligence. The Cubans most likely outfitted the many Cuban refugees who were, in fact, spies for Fidel Castro with false passports in the U.S. and other countries in which Cuba was active. As has become clear, the secret writing material the Cubans uncovered for the Germans was usually related to an operation directed against America or a caught American spy in Cuba. Much of the electronics was also used for agent communication.

Of course, a lot of the technology was used for surveillance and security purposes. The Cubans were very interested in the Stasi's informant system and transferred the technique to Cuba. Like East Germany, the Cubans had their share of dissidents and critics. In fact, there were reportedly seventy dissidents on trial in the year 2000.[72] They also had their share of traitors and spies. The surveillance equipment, such as telephone taps, bugs, marking material, periscopes, TV monitors, video technology, and so on, could be used against those internal enemies.

Nicaragua

Exporting spy technology and sharing knowledge did not stop with Cuba. Both the Soviet Union and its closest East Bloc ally, East Germany, enthusiastically supported communist "liberation movements" in Third World countries. Immediately after the Sandinistas seized power in Managua, Nicaragua, in 1979, Erich Honecker, the Politburo, and Erich

Mielke pledged generous support for the Nicaraguan Revolution. Colonel Siegfried Fiedler, head of the MfS's department for border control, was charged with organizing the project, and he sent a contingent of about seventy officers to the Managua outpost in July 1979. Fiedler was familiar with security at the border and was chosen because the Nicaraguans wanted to tighten security at the airport. Over the years, support ranged from huge shipments of food, motorcycles, manpower, training of security personnel, and spy technology. Within ten years of supporting Nicaragua, Mielke had delivered spy technology worth millions of marks.[73]

While the Soviets concentrated on military, financial, and ideological support, the MfS organized and trained security personnel and intelligence officers. In March and April 1980 Tomas Borge visited both the KGB and the MfS, requesting help. After that he merely had to make a request and both services responded immediately.

Unlike the other East Bloc countries, the Soviets saw Nicaragua as a useful espionage base to target all of Central America. Therefore they thought its intelligence agency should be supplied with agent communication technology like invisible ink, containers, one-way radio transmitters, and cipher training. The Soviets also suggested the creation of facilities to develop forged documents and electronic surveillance equipment.[74]

As a complement to the KGB, between 1982 and 1989 the MfS provided a generous supply of surveillance and security technology at the Managua airport, Minister Borge's home and office, and the prison.

The Nicaraguan security service requested technical equipment to "control border traffic," specifically the delivery of technical equipment for a TV surveillance system at the Sandino International Airport, the installation of the system by MfS specialists, and the training of Nicaraguan personnel on how to maintain and use the technology. The project was run under the code name "Object M."[75]

In 1981 two OTS specialists from the department for equipment building were sent to the Managua airport to survey the scene. By 1982, OTS had delivered and installed "remote observation equipment" worth 500,000 marks plus 128,000 DM as a "solidarity gift." The equipment consisted of a total of fourteen cameras outfitted for panning, swivel, and tilt for inside and outside observation and with all-weather cases. It also provided the central command desk with eleven monitors.[76]

The tropical weather conditions caused a great deal of premature aging to the equipment, even though specialists had considered the weather when developing the all-weather covers and applying extra lubrication to the gears. This required frequent visits for repairs, and on those trips specialists were warned to behave "morally" and not to drink too much.[77]

Soon after the "M" project, Minister Borge asked the MfS to provide him with a new security system for his new home and office. In 1983, a full-scale internal and external security system was delivered as a solidarity present – the Nicaraguans did not have to pay the 95,000-mark price tag. This project, code-named "Object R," developed in a peculiar way. There were apparently constant building projects at the minister's home and office, which disturbed or damaged equipment such as the underground cables and emergency calling system. The German donors were very patient with the Nicaraguans.[78]

In 1987 OTS staff involved with the project doubted that the security system was ever switched on. According to the specialists there was "only partial evidence for operational use" by 1989. The minister's security detail denied this and assured the Germans that it was being used.

By contrast, the Nicaraguans used their requested prison security and TV surveillance system effectively. In 1984 security officials wanted to increase "security and order" at the general directorate for state security's remand prison in Managua. State security detained "leading counter-revolutionaries, state criminals and dangerous criminals" at this prison.[79]

OTS delivered both a TV surveillance system and security system valued at more than 500,000 marks to the head of state security and other security officials in 1986 as a solidarity gift (Object H). This system contained nine cameras, two monitors, fifty security lines, and a conference line telephone connection. Some of the equipment, like the TV system, had never been used under the highly stressful tropical conditions, and some minor adjustments had to be made, but this project had fewer problems than the other ones.

In addition to the three security system projects, OTS provided Nicaraguan state security with chemicals and equipment for a photography lab. They also provided them many different OTS observation cameras, like the half-format and quiet 35 mm, as well as more than eighty GDR commercial Praktika cameras.[80]

SUPER-SECRET SPY COMMANDOS

In October 1969, the twentieth anniversary of the German Democratic Republic, Minister Erich Mielke himself had a special request for the technicians in his ultra-secret "Minister's Working Group/S" for special missions: start a car with a remote control, accelerate it to twenty kilometers an hour, and explode it. Did Mielke have a specific car in mind from the MfS's garage? Was it a Bentley, an Aston Martin, a BMW? Were these technicians so advanced that they could operate a car remotely as featured in the 1997 James Bond film *Tomorrow Never Dies?* Hardly! Product placement, of course, played no role in the GDR, even though the technicians were given a Wartburg to work with – a step above the mass-produced Trabant (or Trabi), the single-track car with the power of a lawnmower.

After spending months on testing and experimenting, the group used a then-novel method of initiating the explosion – electrical contacts. Then a more traditional napalm explosive charge imitated the electrically caused blast. The technicians had a reason to be nervous: it seemed like East German technology only worked half the time, and they had to develop a demonstration for none other than Erich Mielke. As the day of the demonstration approached, they set up an arena with box seats for the minister. A technician described the scene in 1982: "All the comrades asked the question: 'will it work?' When comrade Minister pressed the start button [on the remote] and the Wartburg was set into motion, it went up in flames in a few minutes. We all had tears of joy in our eyes because the effort had been worth it."[81]

The success of the demonstration provided inspiration and led to even more imaginative and sophisticated modes of destruction, the most unusual being explosive towels and socks. The explosive material was actually impregnated into the textiles and could either be stored as disguised explosives or activated when touched. The special technicians also worked on more common weaponry like silencers for submachine guns and other small weapons.[82]

These were not OTS scientists and technicians. Instead they worked for the aforementioned ministerial working group for special missions in a technical "service area 2" (DB2). The projects they worked on were so secret that they were forbidden to cooperate with the technical division or industry. By 1970 an elite group of eleven technicians developed military-style technology for *Einsatz* groups to use on missions planned for the West German area of operations. Their goal was to develop, test, and produce small weapons for offensive use, including "explosive technology, fire and special weapons technology." Slowly departments emerged covering mechanics, electronics, and chemistry. They developed remote control detonators and sensors, containers for weapons and vehicles, electronics, remotely controlled radios, and irritants like mace. Gradually, they even acquired several Western vehicles, such as a VW bus and car and an Opel, presumably to use for missions in the West. By the 1980s they had 14 large trucks.[83]

The name of this group is, of course, reminiscent of the Nazi's mobile killing unit, whose victims were mostly Jews. But their mission was slightly different: "active measures against the enemy" and "diversion, kidnappings, liquidations, acquisition of technical materials," and so on. It is not clear if this group ever conducted any missions in the West. The surviving evidence documents the training of the fighters but no substantial examples have been found of their actions.[84] It appears that they were trained during peacetime to be used in time of war.

Typically, such military-style actions did not belong to the Ministry for State Security, but, in 1962, along with expanding power came the army's military intelligence unit for diversionary measures against the West. In many ways the group resembled the real and imaginary "death to spies" group SMERSH, immortalized by Ian Fleming. In fact, the inspiration for the MfS version of the *Einsatz* commandos came from the Soviet Union, with whom they worked closely on the conception and training of the group. Between 1963 and 1964 they conducted a joint mission with the Soviets against Soviet émigrés in Frankfurt at the NTS (National Alliance of Russian Solidarity) radio station and printing office. In 1969 Scholz visited both the special KGB school in Moscow and the Soviet Army's airborne troops school in Rjasan for advice.[85]

The minister's group did not limit itself to hunting enemy spies and soon planned "active measures against the enemy" with actions targeted against "political centers, military institutions, the armaments industry, communication, electro-energy, the transportation system and gas and water installations."[86] They developed a rigorous program of training for select officers and agents at secret installations like the one in Wartin, a town north of Berlin in Brandenburg, known for its castle. By the year 2000 only vestiges of a training camp remained: areas were set off for target practice, mounds of sand were set up to absorb gun shots from practice dummies, and mysterious wires and destroyed technical devices made the area look like an archeological site.[87] The elite group learned how to parachute, scuba dive, and ignite explosives. Everyone had to learn how to detect bombs in suspicious packages using a variety of techniques, such as the use of metal detectors. They also learned the rudiments of common agent communication methods such as employing invisible ink, camera techniques, and loading and unloading a dead drop. Emphasis was placed on radio communication, especially one-way radio communication.[88] In some ways, this group resembled the CIA's special forces, with the explicit mission of learning how to kill if necessary.

By 1986 the group had been absorbed into the MfS's counter-terrorism department (XXII), and activities like detecting bombs in suspicious packages and providing security services on the occasion of events such as the 25th celebration of the "anti-fascist wall of protection" in 1986 increased. That same year, the department leaders lamented the fact that they had no sharpshooters and developed a position to train one.[89]

In addition to the Wartin training camp, the Stasi trained and harbored left-wing terrorists like the notorious Red Army Faction (RAF) in another training camp in Franfurt/Oder called object 74. At the height of Ronald Reagan's "Star Wars" program, the Strategic Defense Initiative (SDI), in the year July 1986 to 1987, there were seven terrorist bombings, three assassinations, and five suspicious suicides. The RAF took the blame for murdering the CEOs from firms, such as Siemens, working on SDI. It cannot be a coincidence that the foreign department kept information on West German firms working on SDI. The Stasi or the KGB may really have been behind these murders, as the East Bloc found the program repugnant, and the RAF may have taken the blame to cover the actual assassins. After all, one of the Cold War's most spectacular espionage killings was the famous joint Bulgarian Secret Service/KGB Markov umbrella murder. A Bulgarian dissident, Georgi Markov, was poked with an umbrella outfitted with a release mechanism that shot a ricin pellet into a thigh on the Waterloo Bridge in London in 1978.[90]

This leads to another mystery of who attempted to assassinate the GDR critic and border smuggler, Wolfgang Welsch, not only once, not twice, but three times. While riding in a minivan in England with his friend Peter Haack, an unidentified sharpshooter attempted to shoot Welsch but failed when he suddenly jerked away to find his missing pipe. Was the sharpshooter a hired gun or part of the *Einsatz* group? This mystery was never solved. The second time around, Welsch was in a car accident as a result of a plastic explosive going off in his car, but remained unhurt. The third attempt was perhaps the most chilling.

In 1981, Peter Haack, the friend from the previous vacation, invited Welsch and his family to Israel for a communal vacation. While lounging at a seaside resort, Haack made hamburgers for the family, laced with thallium, a highly toxic heavy metal often found in rat poison and insecticides. Haack was in fact an informant for the Stasi code-named "Alfons" and involved in "Operation Scorpion," headed by Major General Fiedler from the border department. Whereas the thallium sickened Welsch, it did not kill him, but it took weeks before doctors determined what had caused his illness and hair loss.[91]

Tasteless and colorless thallium has often been the poison of choice for spy agencies. One of the first cases involved using radioactive thallium on Nicholai Khokhlov, the KGB spy who refused to carry out a contract murder of a dissident in Frankfurt, Germany, in 1954. Because thallium at that point was not widely known, Khokhlov's life hung in the balance for many weeks before they found an antidote. The CIA thought about dusting Fidel Castro's shoes with thallium salt as they were being polished before a planned trip, thus causing his hair and beard to fall out, but the scheme was abandoned when Castro cancelled his trip.[92]

Peter Haack, who had befriended Welsch in Greece on the order of the Stasi, was convicted of attempted murder in 1994 and received a six-year sentence, the only known case of an MfS poisoning. Although OTS had a department in which poison chemicals were kept, they were mostly dual-use chemicals for other work, like marking and secret writing. And poisons were never part of the planning documents. Because it went beyond their own area of expertise, the minister's group had a list of poisons it acquired from the criminalists at the Humboldt University. Dr. W. Katzung prepared a database entitled TOXDAT in 1987 containing a listing of poisons and their effects, as well as cases in the GDR. Under thallium is written: "especially hard to detect . . . long incubation period."[93]

Sharpshooters, explosive experts, poisons, and liquidations were not the everyday bread-and-butter functions of the technical services division. Such extraordinary activities were left to a top-secret unit under the arm of a high-ranking minister. This survey of the OTS, the Stasi's James Bond–like department, reveals a highly organized outfit developing tools and techniques for traditional espionage needs as well as for the requirements of a paranoid state security surveillance system.

This chapter also demonstrates that the gadgets and technology were not developed in a vacuum. The context of communist East Germany determined who the leaders were and often frustrated their efforts to develop and distribute state-of-the-art technology. As we saw, leaders always had sterling political qualifications and were invariably loyal servants of the state. But contrary to popular belief, this did not mean that party hacks without any scientific knowledge were at the helm. On the contrary, OTS leader Günter Schmidt was brought in precisely because the previous leaders lacked the technical background he possessed.

The notion of planning clearly frustrated tinkers' attempts at distributing the needed spy tools in a timely fashion or in the right amounts. Despite these obstacles, it appears as though consumers of the product received items when needed. Later chapters describe whether political concerns were in some way built into these technical artifacts.[94]

8

Communicating Secrets

During the Cold War, East German intelligence kept West German counterintelligence busy in the spy game of hide and seek. Despite the East's massive and successful penetration of West German politics, industry, and intelligence services, Western counterintelligence caught and convicted thousands of East German spies before 1990.

The technological artifacts from these arrests can be found at the evidence collection of the German Federal Criminal Office (the *Bundeskriminalamt* or BKA), which is similar to our FBI. A back room there is stuffed with shelves upon shelves of old radios, briefcases, cameras, and other household items. A few dozen more tools of the spy trade, such as Minox cameras on stands, super-miniature cameras, false passports, and an impressive statuette, are displayed in three glass showcases.[1]

Helmut Regenhardt, a friendly Rhinelander and director of the office, shows visitors the collection at the heavily guarded, gated federal building. He is like a magician as he pulls out the bag of tricks he uses to educate future investigators. At the beginning of our session he opens a seemingly airtight candleholder. He hands it to me and asks if I can open it. Feeling foolish, I twist and turn, yet nothing happens. He takes a simple sewing needle and pushes it into a microscopic hole, releasing a mechanism, which pops the candleholder open.

The same pin principle worked with the well-worn blue-gold chrome-surrounded 1970s ashtray. When this one popped open, it revealed a Minox camera embedded in the cavity. In Germany, spies called these intriguing household hiding places "containers," whereas in the United States they are typically called "concealments."

Regenhardt goes through a boxful of containers, opening them and finding the surprise inside. When a smaller candleholder popped open and

10. A storage room at the Federal Criminal Police's office filled with shelves of containers for hiding secret material. (Kristie Macrakis)

revealed nothing inside, he picked up a subminiature camera and placed it there. It was the right match.

Regenhardt indicates that some of the collections' nicest items are on loan at various exhibits or other offices. For example, the collection is missing the famous subminiature matchbox camera that belonged to "Sonja Lüneburg," which was hidden behind a handkerchief that had a small opening for the camera lens. If someone walked in the room while Lüneburg, a secretary, was taking a picture, she simply put the handker-chief camera near her nose or stuffed it in her purse or pocket.

One of the most beautiful containers, which was on exhibit at a travel-ing Hamburg museum show, was a hand-carved wood deer statute with a hiding place for a Minox camera. Such a container would be ideal for a hunter or a spy with a country cottage.

The Schultheiss beer can container at the evidence collection looks very old, perhaps dating to the late 1950s. Heavy enough to actually contain

(a)

(b)

11. A deer statue container. This hand-carved deer may look like a normal statue (a), but it has a secret compartment for a Minox camera (b). The release mechanism to open the container is activated by inserting a pin in a minuscule hole on the bottom of the base. (Rana Brentjes)

beer, the bottom has liquid in it to make it seem more realistic. Inside the beer can is another Minox camera. Most of the containers up to that point have had cameras or film inside them.

For something different, Regenhardt hands me a manicure kit to inspect. With the pin ready in hand, I search the woman's kit. The holes are so small and hidden that I return the set to Regenhardt. He presses the pin in just the right place and pulls out a false passport. This one belonged to a spy couple arrested during the mass arrests after the fall of the Berlin Wall in 1989. Joachim Preuß worked for the East German military intelligence services, the *Verwaltung Aufklärung*, for twenty-three years while he was deputy director at the printing office of the air force. Gisela, his wife, was a secretary and acted as a courier. Preuß passed on everything that came through his hands about the West German Army's conferences, plans, and exercises, as well as some NATO material hot off the press.

The Preuß case is interesting because he had so many containers – about ten of them – at his apartment when he was arrested. He clearly needed a lot of storage for his stolen material on film. Even though this is incriminating evidence for a caught spy, the crucial materials in this case were the myriad of documents he hoarded in his apartment; he never used the money his case officer gave him for a paper shredder.

Technicians made Preuß an elaborate and stylish black-and-white striped breakfast tray with a hidden compartment underneath with cavities for a Minox camera, a stand, and twelve Minox film cartridges. The release mechanisms are carefully designed and executed. Preuß was a productive agent, delivering some five hundred photographs per meeting. In addition to the tray, which is a household container, his wife used a cream container outfitted with a false bottom to hold developed Minox film (8×10 mm) when she traveled to Berlin to deliver material. If someone at the border opened the cream container, their hands would get messy with hand cream, and it would be unlikely that they would find the false bottom with the film strip.

In addition to his Minox, Preuß obtained a standard 35 mm camera in 1967 (an Edixa), was given a spy-agency-made *mikrat* camera in the mid-1970s, had a Braun Nizo Super-8 movie camera, and bought a Minolta in 1984. In court testimony, he stated that the *mikrat* broke a lot and never worked properly and that he simply used the Minolta and developed the film himself.[2]

Less visually intriguing and imaginative, but equally important for communication, were radios. Not only shortwave radios, but radios for sending and receiving coded messages. The classic five-number code was

(a)

(b)

12. Gerhard Preuß's spy technology and secret container. Preuß's material was so copious he needed this breakfast tray (a) with a hidden compartment (b) to hide his film cartridges (left and right), camera stand (lower left), and Minox (lower right). (Kristie Macrakis)

usually typed on tiny sheets of paper. These secret pads were also hidden in containers as big as a walnut or small as a coin.

A case dating from 1976 showcases quite well how some fourteen pieces of paraphernalia, including a Minox spy camera, container, and radio, helped Western investigators find damning material and convict the agent couple for high treason.

Lothar Lutze, whose family had fled to the West in the early fifties, was recruited by the foreign intelligence arm of the Ministry for State Security (HV A) while he was in the air force in 1959. By 1966 Lothar had recruited his friend Jürgen Wiegel, and in 1972 he recruited his wife, Renate, a Ministry for Defense employee, to also spy for the Stasi. In 1973, Lothar also joined the Ministry for Defense and began to pass on very secret material to the Stasi.[3]

West German counterintelligence had observed the couple, code-named "Charly" and "Nana," meeting with their resident, Frank Gersten, many times in 1976. Counterintelligence had come across Gersten through an operation called "Registration," which used computer technology to examine all German registration records for false identities.

On the morning of 2 June 1976, BKA officials rang the Lutze's doorbell and entered a house filled with spy gear. It did not take long to find a Minox camera with sixteen exposed pictures of secret documents from the Ministry of Defense, a movie camera (a Bauer C1 M Super) with four films of confidential NATO material, several storage containers, code sheets, Nivea crème containers, thirty undeveloped Minox films, a green tea set with paper codes inside, photo accessories, false passports, and a key impression kit.[4]

The agent technology itself is evidence, but, in this case, the exposed and unexposed films contained in the cameras and containers provided more precise evaluation of the damage done to national security because of the secret documents stolen. Lawyers could display facsimiles of documents relating to the West German Army, its structure, its military strategy, its weapons, and its weaknesses.[5]

Raiding an apartment and uncovering agent technology as evidence is one way to convict an agent, but the agent's technology plays a role in actually finding the agent as well. Perhaps the most famous case in this regard is Günter Guillaume. Since 1956 West German counterintelligence had been monitoring East German radio messages. In the late 1950s, they had already intercepted a message and cracked a coded message intended for an agent code-named "Georg." The Ministry for State Security (MfS) had sent "Georg" their traditional birthday greetings on 1 February (Guillaume's birthday) and on October 6th (his wife's birthday); another congratulatory message was sent when their son was born on 8 April 1957. For many years these messages were forgotten because counterintelligence had not figured out who agent "Georg" was. While investigating another case in 1973, Western spy catchers focused on Guillaume, because his birthday matched the greeting date.[6]

Luckier agents destroy all materials if they become paranoid that they are under observation or if they have been instructed to do so by headquarters. After the fall of the Berlin Wall, most agents were told to destroy any incriminating evidence. For example, top agent Gabriele Gast, who was placed at the West German intelligence agency, the BND (*Bundesnachrichtendienst*), describes how she destroyed her material, including a microdot camera hidden in a pen.[7]

Unlike James Bond, agents did not present themselves at the Q lab to obtain gadgets and receive training on how to use them to get out of a bind. Instead, once spies were given their license to steal, they met with a technician, who trained them how to use the tools of the trade in order to communicate. The East Germans sent to the West as "illegals" or migration agents received the most extensive training on how to use all spy gear, especially how to encipher and decipher messages and how to use a camera. Not only were they instructed on how to use miniature cameras or the microdot system, but sometimes they would receive extensive training on document photography in general. Instead of returning spy gear in "pristine order," agents were encouraged to destroy it if they were in danger of being caught.

COMMUNICATING AND STEALING SECRETS

Given that agent technology was risky and used as prime evidence to convict an agent, why was it employed so often? Stasi chief Erich Mielke recognized that communication between an agent and headquarters was the most vulnerable aspect of tradecraft, but also at the heart of operations: "The constant secret contact between the Ministry for State Security and the IM [unofficial staff member] . . . in the operational area, is the nerve center and simultaneously the most sensitive area of attack of operational work."[8]

Despite the dangers, then, communication between the agent and headquarters is essential for spy work. Spies need to collect information, copy it, hide it, and pass it on secretly. They also need to communicate with their handlers for future meetings, danger signals, and instructions. Like all spy agencies, the HV A used both personal and impersonal communication, or a combination of the two. The personal kind involved meetings in the West between the agent and a courier or resident, usually an East German illegally emigrated to the West under a false name or an East German traveling to another country for a meeting.

Impersonal communication involved spy technology and meant that the agent and case officer did not actually meet personally – often a courier serviced and maintained the connection that served to pass on "operational material like information, instructions, money and operational-technical methods without the parties involved getting to know each other personally."[9] It could also involve using technical methods for communicating and passing on secrets. In some ways, impersonal communication could be safer than the personal kind, because the agent and his or her contact could not be observed meeting and sometimes did not know each other. Of course, both types of communication were used together in operational plans: one needed impersonal communication to arrange a personal meeting!

Secrecy was the watchword and principle behind communicating throughout the four decades of spying. It was the backbone of all espionage communications, and finding ways to hide and disguise secrets was its lifeblood. Communication methods evolved from the 1950s to the 1980s and increasingly involved refined technical methods and a breakaway from the Soviet methods. By the 1980s, the HV A developed separate and more detailed instructions on spy technology that were not imbedded in agent instructions on communication. To maintain secrecy, staff used creative code names for spy technology. All these developments reflected a more seasoned, creative, and mature HV A in matters of agent technology, an HV A increasingly caught up in the trappings of the spy world.

The five main components of agent technology – containers, cameras, secret writing, codes, and radios – were not only developed to aid communication, but they were also designed to obtain the needed information and to provide camouflage for the agents and the technology itself. In addition to the five areas mentioned above, creating false documents also belonged to the rubric of spy technology. This was the ultimate disguise for agents, and the MfS's technical unit produced thousands of false documents a year using secret printing presses.

During the 1950s communication methods between headquarters and the agent were still influenced by the Soviet style. Communists who had come back from "illegal work" against the Nazis were recruited to train new students, and, in general, the Soviet Union had "advisors" on hand to help the East Germans.

During the 1950s two "hiding places" were essential to impersonal communication: Foremost in importance were dead letter boxes or dead drops (*tote Briefkasten* or TBKs), but containers were also important. Soviet intelligence favored the use of dead letter boxes. In 1959 the MfS considered them to be the most important element of agent communication. The classic dead letter drop during the early Cold War was a cemetery. An agent could either store materials like a camera or film in a container by burying them in the cemetery or hide a message his or her courier or resident would pick up. The courier could also leave money there. There were "storage" and "moving" TBKs. The agent and courier decided whether they wished to use the TBK as a place to continually pass on information or as a longer-term hiding place for technical devices, money, and documents. Hollowed-out stakes driven into the ground were fairly common for smaller items, but bigger hiding places, like a hollowed-out brick in a wall or tree stump, were needed for larger objects. These are all common everyday things that most people would not find suspicious.

Cemeteries were just one popular place for a dead letter drop. The MfS also found parks, walls, trees, and other outdoor objects good hiding places. Indoor objects, or what they called "closed spaces," such as restaurants, museums, or vehicles like trains, ships, and trucks, were also good concealments.

Agents were asked to prepare a sketch of where the dead letter drop was located and, if possible, a photograph. These were often placed in the agent's file. Security signals were agreed upon and placed near the site to determine if the TBK should be approached. The Soviets became known for using chalk as a signal, especially post office mail boxes in the Washington, DC, area, as was the case with Aldrich Ames. The Germans did not use chalk as often because it washed off easily. Other security measures included ways to determine if strangers had examined the TBK or container during the time between its servicing and emptying.[10]

Moving-train dead drops became so popular it is a wonder that spies did not bump into each other in the lavatory, a favorite hiding place. In the West, trains were called moving dead drops, in the East they were designated as Z-TBK (Z for the German word for train, "*Zug*"). Trains typically crossed the German border. Each side could inconspicuously drop off or pick up an item hidden in a hollowed-out toilet paper holder or doorstop, for example.

Because the MfS understood that the communication system was the most "vulnerable" part of spy activity for all intelligence agencies, it tried to "penetrate" the "enemy's" system. It was particularly interested in the BND's use of dead letter boxes, especially after the building of the Wall, when all Western spy agencies became more dependent on these boxes for impersonal communication. The MfS observed the hiding places, took photographs of them, and questioned caught spies about them. They learned details about the courier's system for servicing dead letter boxes and that they were mostly in East Berlin. They used criminalistic methods such as observation, fingerprint analysis, and chemical marking material to try to catch the couriers.[11]

Containers

Officially and initially containers were described as "specially prepared objects for the secret storing and for secret transporting of intelligence material" such as documents, money, and instruments. The tinkers themselves defined containers as "objects with a secret compartment to store, transport or destroy information." It was considered a spy agency's "safe" and was similar to hiding money under a mattress. The most important features of a container were that it resemble an everyday or household item without being recognized as a container, that it fit its purpose, and that it fit the person to whom it belonged. In 1970, Major Gerhard Müller, the deployment department's gadget man and head, cautioned his technicians that a non-smoker should not be given a cigarette pack holder as a transportation container or a bald man an outfitted hair spray can to transport film.[12]

Lack of imagination is the only limit when thinking of container possibilities. Transportation containers could be anything from false teeth, toothpaste, or a cigarette package to a piece of clothing or a shoe. At home, containers needed to be made for things like cameras and radios and were often made of household items.[13]

By the late 1970s four different types of containers had been developed and used to either store or transport materials:

- Containers for continual use with different locks and security systems; these were typically made out of leather, metal, and wood
- Disposable containers for one-time use
- Destructive containers
- Test containers to determine if someone has tampered with it

By 1970, the MfS began to develop so-called X-ray-safe containers because of problems at the border when metal detecting X-ray technology would find the metal locks in briefcases or other containers. Nevertheless, in 1979 staff members were advised not to use containers when traveling by plane.[14]

The leather briefcases, leather handbags, and other types of carrying cases were so common and ubiquitous in the MfS's container shop that they line shelves upon shelves of the enemy's evidence collection room. It is not surprising that leather handbags were the most common type of container; they were easy to outfit with a hidden compartment for stolen papers or false passports, and they are a common fashion accessory. The technical services division (OTS) often developed and produced a thousand of them yearly. OTS's forty-staff-member container department, headed by the imaginative and well-liked Fritz Hering, had an eleven-member *referat* devoted solely to developing and producing leather containers; it employed purse makers, leather workers, and leather engineers.[15]

During the mid-seventies the HV A discouraged agents from using leather briefcases as transport containers because several agents had been caught with them. This did not deter all agents, however. In his 1979 memoirs, Werner Stiller describes his astonishment that agent "Hauser" was using a leather briefcase transport container in 1975, when he had recently received instructions to discontinue use.[16]

Style, of course, played a role, and East Berlin tried to keep up with fashions in the West. To a modern Western viewer many of the items seem like they are out of a tasteless historical fashion show. This may be explained by the fact that the OTS sent undercover staff members to "consumer goods fairs" in the East (Budapest and Lodz) that featured exhibits from "non-socialist countries," instead of directly to the West, where more up-to-date fashions may have been displayed.[17]

Unlike the West at the time, the leather industry in East Germany had increasingly turned to artificial materials instead of real animal hide. Gerhard Müller noted that the "scientific-technical revolution" produced changes in industry, such as increased "chemicalization," that had an affect on operational technology: "If, for example, the leather industry uses foam material instead of animal hide, then we must act accordingly in container making and adapt."[18]

Many of the Bonn secretary spies were given leather handbags. Gerda O., convicted in 1977, did not find her old-fashioned big handbag stylish enough and threw it away after a colleague teasingly told her "that looks like a Sütterlin handbag" (a Bonn secretary convicted in 1968).[19] It may well have been stamped "Made in the GDR [German Democratic Republic]."

Destructive containers were developed to be secure against enemy attack during personal or impersonal transportation. The information was either stored on film or a magnet, which would be destroyed if an unauthorized person opened it. Examples of destructive containers include a can of Vasenol baby powder, a statute, or a hair spray canister outfitted with a battery and flash bulb. If someone opened these containers without knowing how to deactivate them, the flash would go off and destroy the film. A West German member of Parliament, Alfred Frenzel, who worked for the Czech services, used both the booby-trapped statute and baby powder container for film; he was caught in 1960.

If some leather handbags seemed out of style in the West, one courier complained that the containers he was instructed to pass on to his agents were relics of the "Ming dynasty." One of these Ming dynasty artifacts was a deodorant spray can. Despite the fact that West German counterintelligence had confiscated many of these, they continued to be used throughout the Cold War. As a result of the courier's concerns, his source, none other than star spy Gabriele Gast, received a new container – a compressor for pumping car tires – to hide her film.[20]

Photography

Spy cameras are almost synonymous with spying and spies. Photography, of course, was the central way to obtain, reduce the size of, and pass on information. Even James Bond, who rarely used authentic agent technology, was given a Minox camera to photograph secret documents in the movie *On Her Majesty's Secret Service.*

In the 1950s, East Bloc agents used miniature cameras and the microdot system to reduce photographs and pass on documents and other secret information. With the microdot process, agents could reduce a negative to the size of a period in a book and pass it on through the post office (under a stamp, for example) or a courier.

By 1958, *mikrat* cameras also came into use in East Germany. A *mikrat* camera should not be confused with the microdot process. A *mikrat* camera was as small as a quarter and usually used round negatives with about fifteen shots on each film; the *mikrats* were 1.4 mm by 2 mm in size and could photograph paper up to A4 size. Some *mikrats* had a modified

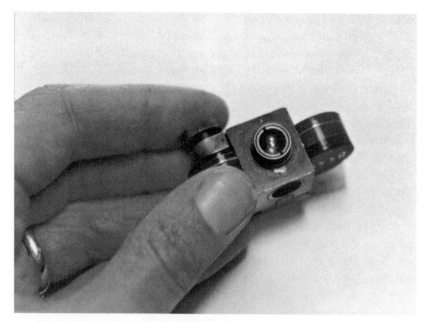

13. A *mikrat* camera with a modified Minox cassette. (Kristie Macrakis)

Minox film cassette attached to or inside of them, which could take up to 240 shots (called the Rigel). The spy took a picture and sent the negative to headquarters.

In 1972, specialists at the OTS developed 125 *mikrat* cameras for HV A agents. They code-named it "*Meise*" (titmouse) in external correspondence. By 1984 the *Meise* M, which had fifteen microdot pictures on each round negative and also came with a viewer, had become so well known among the Stasi's "brother organs" that the Cuban security services requested twenty *Meise* M cameras, an enlarger, and a film cutter; OTS sent them five.[21]

Perhaps because the spy cameras were the OTS's most sparkling achievements in the spy technology firmament, they all received planet or star code names when referred to by internal staff members. In 1986 miniature cameras were called "Venus" (B or Z), *mikrat* cameras were named "Uranus" and "Rigel," and commercial cameras, including pocket cameras, received names like "Mars." The Minox was code-named "Jupiter."[22]

Like the *mikrat* cameras, the Venus Z and Venus M were developed by the OTS in cooperation with Carl Zeiss Jena, the renowned optical firm, which developed and provided the 3.5/8 mm lens. The Venus resembled an elongated matchbox or fat lipstick container and measured 58 by 20 by 15 mm and could take about sixty pictures on a modified Minox film cassette. Although the Soviet Committee for State Security (KGB) developed a camera inside a lipstick container and gave it to a West German secretary (Margeret H.) convicted in 1987, the MfS did not use lipstick containers. They did, however, use a lighter.

Both the *mikrats* ("Uranus" and "Rigel") and the Venus cameras did not have viewfinders; therefore, the Venus needed to be about 250 to 300 mm away from the object, and the *mikrats* needed to be 75 cm away. Manfred Roski, who hid his camera in a razor kit, had a Venus outfitted with "light wells" so that he could better determine the distance to the object.

On the eve of the fall of the Berlin Wall, OTS asked Zeiss Jena to develop a lens small enough (3.5/5 mm) to hide in a felt-tip pen. It took optical engineers from 1983 to 1988 to do it, at a cost of 1.5 million marks, but they developed ten prototypes (code-named "13104") as communist East Germany began to collapse in October 1989. The Carl Zeiss optical specialists submitted a secret patent to the patent office. The scientific-technical "peak performance" item was presented to the head of the Ministry for State Security.[23]

Although the *mikrats*, the Venus cameras, and the felt-tip pen camera are fascinating as technological artifacts and embody high technical ability in optics, agents tended to use the standard 35 mm cameras, the Minox, or the Super-8 movie camera on its single-picture setting. This was in part because it was difficult to take quality pictures with the super-mini cameras, and they sometimes broke or did not work. The commercially available cameras were also less conspicuous as spy paraphernalia; the BKA's shelves are filled with these, although they may have been confiscated from agents' apartments as possible evidence only.

The Cold War workhorse was still the classic spy camera, the Minox, which the MfS often modified. It is not widely known that in the 1970s Super-8 movie cameras became popular for East German spies because they could take a lot of single pictures on one roll of film. Agents who had a voluminous amount of material to photograph were encouraged to use the film camera on its single-picture setting.

The inventive technicians in the Q-like labs on the outskirts of Berlin developed a highly sensitive document film that was placed in a normal cassette. To disguise the spy film as the store-bought kind, three meters of conventional film were spliced onto the beginning of the film. One caught agent described in court that his film camera had ordinary film footage at

(a)

(b)

14. The Venus miniature camera, closed (a) and opened (b), with a BKA ruler. (Kristie Macrakis)

the beginning of the film in case someone looked at it.[24] A single cassette
of film contained up to 2,200 single pictures. The system was covered by
the code name "Wega" (or Vega, the bright star).[25]

Secret Writing and Codes

Whereas cameras had planet or star-like cover names, different types of
secret writing used birds as code names. For example, secret writing used
between the area of operations and headquarters was called "falcon,"
"pelican," "vulture," and "pigeon."

Secret writing was essential for making secrets invisible so that they
could be passed on. The post office was used most frequently during the
early years because the invisible message was sent to a cover address.
The secret message was usually written between the lines of an official
visible text, and agents were instructed to make the letter look natural.
Sometimes these messages were coded as well.

The MfS developed a number of different secret writing methods and
used a variety of chemicals for ink and in the reagent or developer, which
made the chemical visible again. Sometimes an agent simply used a chemically impregnated felt-tip to write on a postcard, so that no imprint would
be made. The felt-tip pen contained a fluorescing chemical, which became
visible under ultraviolet light.

Many agents were given chemically impregnated blotting paper, which
they placed between two sheets of paper. They wrote the coded message
on the top sheet of paper, and then the text would be transferred invisibly
to the bottom sheet. Then the agent wrote a harmless visible message on
the bottom sheet in between the lines of the invisible text.[26]

Codes and ciphers served to make operational messages unrecogniz-
able. This was especially important for names, addresses, dates, concepts
in operational work, and information leading to the origins of the material. Radio messages were always sent in cipher because the enemy monitored the traffic. After Guillaume was caught in 1974 because the spy
catchers had cracked the Soviet codes, the MfS began to use a modifi-
cation of the one-time pad method, which uses five-number columns to
encipher messages. This method was virtually unbreakable because only
headquarters and the agent had the individually made-up key, and they
theoretically changed it often.

Although it sounds complicated in the abstract, when used by the agent
it is fairly simple: Each letter of the alphabet had a number attached

to it. To encipher a message, the agent first translated the letters into five-number groups. Then the agent placed the five-number groups from his or her individually made-up key under the numbers that contained the message and added them up. The final numbers were then transmitted to headquarters or visa-versa. For investigators, cipher pads with numbers in groups of five linked a suspect to spy activity.

Radios

Radio communications consisted of one-way or two-way radio transmissions. One-way radio contact meant that headquarters sent the agent an encrypted radio message. An agent merely needed a shortwave radio to receive these messages, usually at a predetermined day and time. A-2 meant that headquarters sent a Morse code message to the spy, and A-3 was two-sided Morse code between the central office and spy. In this case, the agent not only had a radio to receive the message but also a transmitter on which to send it. This method was only to be used in emergencies. (West German counterintelligence erroneously believed it was only used with important spies.)

With the one-way radio system, the agent communicated back to headquarters via dead letter drops, cover telephone numbers, or through the post office using a letter addressed to a cover address.

During the fifties two-way radio transmission was reserved for an emergency situation. Even then, it was usually a radioman, not an agent (unless trained as a ham), who made the contact. Two-way radio transmissions were discouraged because the location of the agent could be found through directional antennas. Nevertheless, as two-way radios became more sophisticated it became more common for agents to have them. Radios with transmitters, receivers, and antennas have been found by the BKA, and there are cases of agents who buried them somewhere outside, usually a forest or cemetery.

By the 1980s the HV A had developed a number of high-tech ways to communicate, including an infrared communication system for distances up to 3 km, which was often used at the border; this system was very difficult to intercept or detect. A number of agents were also given a "talking calculator." This innovative device combined a pocket calculator with a universal rapid transmitter (a *schnellgeber*) to speed up the transmission. The spy typed the five-number code into the calculator, found a phone booth, and called the cover telephone number in East Berlin; the message was transmitted in a matter of seconds. At least three important agents used this method: Klaus Kuron, who was head of counterintelligence in Köln; Dieter Feuerstein, an important source at MBB; and Gerhard Müller, a migration agent who worked at SEL.

The West also used sophisticated technology like rapid transmitters. In fact, the MfS may have been inspired to develop it from its own evidence collection of spy paraphernalia. Both sides studied and copied each other's agent technology and used it as evidence in court.

COLD WAR ARTIFACTS

Regenhardt's back room was a fascinating and intriguing, if a bit disorganized, living Cold War history museum. Show-and-tell was punctuated with stories about caught spies through the enemy's eyes and a visit to the cafeteria where blue-jean-clad investigators were investigating post–Cold War terrorism cases.

The principles behind finding and opening hidden spy gadgets were pretty easy to grasp after a day's briefing by Regenhardt. By investigating the story from the Stasi's perspective, outsiders can better appreciate the need for communicating and hiding secrets, but still might wonder why they did not change and adapt the methods more often once agents were caught and the technology found. Sometimes they did. For example, the pin principle, once understood, could uncover many new secrets, and as a result they began to use other methods, like the nail file, to lift a hiding place in a container. But many methods stayed constant throughout the Cold War.

Most of the East German–made cameras, containers, radios, and other spy paraphernalia developed in the super-secret labs on the outskirts of Berlin were destroyed and transported by the truckload to incinerators in the wake of unification. Some items remain at exhibits, were appropriated by various police offices, or were purloined by dissidents or collectors in the confusion following the fall of the Berlin Wall. Therefore the items at the evidence collection and exhibits offer us artifacts from a bygone era.

Artifacts often reflect the ideas, beliefs, achievements, and attitudes of long-lost civilizations; they also mirror their culture. Technology talks; it speaks the language of culture. Even though some documentary evidence about the HV A survives at the Stasi archives, the technological artifacts offer us rare and valuable insight into a very secret culture and community within which, like in a secret cult, every member was trained to keep the methods and sources of their work hidden from the enemy and outsiders.

One of the most closely guarded secrets of that community was its communication method. While some of the communication technology was essential, much of it is evidence of an organization that had succumbed to that insular spy-culture.

The artifacts left at the BKA's evidence collection reveal much about the nature and goals of the spy community, its culture, and its achievements. It is not surprising that hiding things and making things very small is a key feature of these technologies. What other way is there to maintain secrecy and to accomplish the goal of delivering secrets to the other side?

The artifacts also reflect fine craftsmanship and technical skill on the part of the tinkers. In particular, the MfS's cooperation with Carl Zeiss Jena, one of their silent partners, allowed them to produce superior technical optics.

Aside from being entertaining and providing visually interesting artifacts, the containers used to store or transport spy material outwardly reflected the bourgeois culture in which they were embedded. Tasteful or tasteless, they were designed to fit unnoticed in the spy's residence and match his or her lifestyle. Outwardly they were ordinary items; that was their cover story. As hiding places, they stored either enemy secrets transposed onto film or the secret methods used to communicate the secrets themselves.

All modes of impersonal communication were designed to protect the agent from being seen and discovered by the enemy. But the spy gear was a double-edged tool: although it was designed to protect, it could also convict. Unlike American spies, who are often imprisoned for decades or for life, those convicted in West Germany, that land of spies, were usually only sentenced to two to four years or could be traded. The MfS called those agents "scouts for peace" who worked on the "invisible front." Like other common foot soldiers who worked for a higher cause, they too could be imprisoned by the enemy and lose their freedom.

9

Secret Writing Revealed

No one suspected that Dr. Gabriele Leinfelder was a spy for the other side. Her colleagues thought she was too prim and proper for that. They admired her intellect and thought she projected the image and purity of a nun. She rarely wore make-up, had simple, short hair, and wore unfashionable glasses. She was very bright and had landed a coveted position at the West German intelligence service's (BND) Soviet division in 1973 after completing a dissertation on "The Role of Women in the GDR [German Democratic Republic]" with Professor Dr. Klaus Mehnert, the leading GDR studies scholar in West Germany. When her colleagues at the BND heard that she was Markus Wolf's "best spy," they were shaken and felt betrayed. That sense of betrayal was likely similar to that felt by Aldrich Ames's CIA colleagues when they learned he worked for the Soviet Committee for State Security (KGB). The super-spy imagined the scene at work the day after her arrest in 1990: "Have you heard? Mrs. Dr. Leinfelder! No way. We would have never imagined. I am shocked."[1]

The unglamorous, inconspicuous person who blends in with the rest of the crowd has always been the perfect spy and cover. Leinfelder, whose real name was Gabriele Gast, was far from an ordinary spy. It was unusual for a woman to work at the BND; by the time she was betrayed by a defector and caught in 1990, she had advanced to director of the evaluation department.

During a dissertation research trip to Karl Marx City in East Germany in May 1968, Gabriele Gast met a charming Ministry for State Security (MfS) major, Karl Heinz Schneider, who offered to help with her research. He recruited her three months later and ran her under the code name "Gisela." Gast denies that this was a Stasi Romeo story and that Schneider made Gast fall in love with him as a motive for recruitment. In her autobiography, *Scout for Freedom*, published in 1999, she writes that she had political motives for spying. The MfS arranged an "engagement party" in 1970 to further cement the spy relationship.[2]

From containers to a pen camera to a silk scarf impregnated with invisible ink, Gast was provided with some of the MfS's most interesting spy technology. There is not always a correlation between the value of the agent and the communication technology provided, but in this instance, her case officer outfitted her with the very best.

In 1972 Gast received a colorful, thin silk scarf impregnated with invisible ink, which was to be used like carbon paper in between a top sheet used for writing and a bottom sheet with invisible writing, to pass on secret messages, undetectable by the post office, to a cover address in Karl Marx City.[3] Although a handkerchief is an old spy artifact for hiding messages, by the 1970s the MfS had moved beyond the original method – simply writing with invisible ink on the handkerchief itself, which was then made visible with a developer. When Gast passed on messages, she coded them first and then used the secret writing "transfer" method. This meant she used the chemically treated scarf sandwiched in between two sheets of paper instead of the usual impregnated copy paper.

Unlike the traditional "wet" direct invisible ink method, the transfer method usually used a piece of chemically impregnated paper placed in between a top sheet, where the initial message is written, and the bottom sheet, where the writing is transferred invisibly. Gast substituted the scarf for paper. The recipient then used a reagent, a chemical used to develop the message like a photographer developing a picture in a darkroom.

After writing the message, Gast held the piece of paper over steam so that the physical writing of the message did not leave any telltale impressions. Once the paper dried, Gast was ready to write the rest of her cover letter in normal ink: she then wrote the typical German spy letter: "Dear Aunt Erma [or Uncle Max] how is the weather?" When she was done, she sent it to the cover address; an East German agent then passed the letter to the foreign intelligence arm of the Ministry for State Security (HV A). As a return address, she made up a name and address in her city.[4]

Spy agencies are always working on new secret writing methods because they know the other side is continually trying to detect and expose them. As a result, agents are theoretically given new secret writing methods from time to time. In 1979 Gast traded in her beautiful silk scarf for a magic pen. This time she used the "contact principle" using a fountain pen filled with invisible ink. First, she wrote directly on a piece of paper with her fountain pen. She then laid a piece of paper on the written sheet and stacked a pile of books on it. The pressure transferred the ink from the original sheet to the other one. Then she wrote her visible message on the new sheet of paper. Gast was always careful not to leave traces of her secret activity. She never wrote on top of her pad of paper, for example. As a result, when the German FBI searched her apartment in 1990, they found nothing to incriminate her.[5] In this case, though, they had ample evidence to convict her of espionage and sentenced her to six years and nine months in jail.

Millions of agents throughout history have used secret writing methods to pass on secrets, but only a few cases in which unusual methods were used have become public. No spy agency has ever revealed their invisible ink recipes or allowed them to be published. In 1998 Washington, DC, lawyer Mark S. Zaid filed a lawsuit in order to view documents containing German World War I recipes for creating and detecting invisible ink. The six oldest classified documents in the United States are deposited at the National Archives and Records Administration (NARA) and date back to anywhere from 1917 to 1930. Predictably, it was the CIA that objected to, and blocked the release of, these documents on national security grounds. They claimed that the old papers could provide "building blocks" for the CIA's modernized methods of producing or detecting secret writing, that they could aid in identifying current "vulnerabilities," and that CIA agents could still use the invisible ink.[6]

Many of these claims are plausible, even though most secret writing was already conduced electronically and cryptologically or through the World Wide Web when the claims were made in 1999. In our own age of information explosion, some recipes and further knowledge can be gleaned by surfing the World Wide Web, and the CIA's fears can already be realized without access to the World War I formulas. Every schoolchild knows the basic principles behind invisible ink – an invisible chemical substance can be made visible by applying heat or another developing chemical known as the reagent. Countless children have written secret messages with lemon juice then developed them with heat or played with secret decoder pens filled with invisible ink on one end and an ultraviolet light on the other. If it were only so simple!

Secrets from the Stasi files reveal that secret writing methods are more complex. The wet direct invisible writing method is only one method available. More common during the Cold War was the "dry" transfer method, similar to that used by Gabriele Gast, which involved impregnating paper with chemicals and using a reagent to develop the paper. For the first time in the history of espionage, we can now reveal those secrets and some of the chemical recipes and steps the Stasi used to create and uncover secret writing.

The Stasi was not alone in its use of the dry transfer method, but it may have been the first to develop it, along with the KGB. The CIA followed suit and also used the dry method. This reflected a general shift in methodology during the Cold War.[7] Both sides spent a considerable amount of time trying to break enemy secret writing systems.

Like codes and ciphers, invisible ink is one of the oldest methods for concealing and passing on secret messages and dates back to antiquity. In antiquity and the renaissance, shaved heads and eggs were popular places to write secret messages. During World War I French peasants smuggled valuable secret messages about troop movements to the allies. The old women brought their produce and eggs to the market to sell. They would only sell the special eggs to certain buyers. Spies would write messages on the shell with a type of invisible ink developed by heat. The ink passed onto the membrane of the egg and left no sign on the shell. When it was boiled the message was developed.[8]

Common invisible ink substances such as lemon juice, milk, fruit juices, urine, or saliva are known as organic fluids, whereas the more sophisticated reagent-specific chemical solutions are commonly referred to as sympathetic inks. Another method uses colorless fluorescing chemicals that light up under a black light or ultraviolet light. Because of their simplicity, the most primitive forms of secret writing can still be used in a pinch.

Spy agencies can use all forms of secret writing from primitive to high-tech, but since World War II they began to employ a large contingent of chemists to develop new and more sophisticated chemical substances and secret writing techniques. The chemists also developed elaborate chemical analysis for detecting enemy's secret writing. The secret writing production and detection war was similar to the code-making and code-breaking challenge-and-response dialectic that has occurred throughout history. As one side uncovered a secret writing method, the other responded by developing yet more ingenious methods. The chemical makeup of invisible ink is just one element in a system of secret writing that spy agencies use to protect their agents and to detect the enemy's invisible ink.

SECRECY WITHIN SECRECY

Surrounded by steam machines, test tubes, analytic chemistry instruments, and brown flasks filled with secret solutions labeled with code numbers, chemists in white lab coats puzzled over enemy secret writing as they created their own. The Technical Operations Sector (OTS) in the Stasi's North Berlin campus provided the institutional setting for these scientists. Most of the chemists worked in Department 34 for chemical and photographic communication methods, which contained four subdepartments (*referat*) devoted to secret writing. Interestingly, the same chemists worked on chemical marking material. This is not surprising, because the two methods use similar techniques and chemicals and share their basic principle – making an invisible mark visible.

There were about fifty staff members who took on the painstaking task of analyzing chemicals, searching the literature, writing reports, and developing and detecting new secret writing substances and reagents. This included about twenty-four chemists with bachelor's degrees, a number of physicists, several chemical engineers, twelve chemistry lab assistants, and a couple of secretaries. The head of the department, Rolf Kummer, had a bachelor's degree in chemistry and physics and also received an administrative degree from the MfS Law School. The unit for chemical expertise also had a subdepartment with twenty-five staff members who worked on uncovering enemy secret writing and worked closely with MfS counterintelligence.[9]

Scientists who worked on developing new secret writing methods for impersonal communication worked in two units, while even more staff spent their time attempting to detect enemy use of secret writing and its chemical components. The detectors developed new physical, chemical, and photochemical investigative methods for examining secret writing.[10] Counterintelligence and the Department of Investigations asked OTS to conduct analyses of papers, envelopes, and other suspected carriers of invisible ink either intercepted by the post office or confiscated from a suspected spy.[11]

The MfS's secret writing creation and detection effort was very large in proportion to the size of the country. In addition to the technical staff, the mail intercept staff contributed a great deal to pre-screening mail for signs of secret writing. During the 1960s, the CIA had about two dozen technical officers who worked at headquarters and abroad on secret writing and about another dozen who worked on research at home. Unlike the MfS, the CIA also contracted out work for help in developing new systems. Like the MfS, they also spent quite a bit of time on "counter-censorship" operations in an effort to learn more about enemy secret writing and mail intercept methods.[12]

Once OTS developed new methods, new inks, or new secret writing paper, it passed these materials on to either the foreign department, HV

A (*Hauptverwaltung Aufklärung*), or Department E, (for "*Einsatz*" or "deployment"), which in turn gave them to their agents. The deployment department received the lion's share of secret writing material. In 1972 alone, they received 796 sheets of secret writing copy paper, 127 pieces of prepared textiles (like scarves), 760 bags of powder developer, and 55 liters of developer solution for making secret writing visible. They serviced both domestic informants and agents abroad. Their agents did not simply use secret writing to pass on secrets, but they also used it to take invisible notes or to write down assignments. By contrast, in the same year, the foreign department (HV A) received 284 sheets of copy paper, 110 bags of powder developer, and 2 liters of developer solution.[13]

Almost every MfS agent outfitted with communication methods, like cameras and containers, was also trained in secret writing and given invisible ink or a secret writing method. Secret writing was used to communicate through letters and the post office, a courier across the borders, or through a dead letter drop. Most agents used the post office to send secret letters. Whereas OTS was chiefly responsible for the scientific development and detection of secret writing, counterintelligence and the mail opening department routed suspicious letters to them through a huge fishnet operation that searched for mail with earmarks of intelligence activity.

CREATING NEW SECRET WRITING

I have obtained a number of secret Stasi invisible ink recipes and am working together with a chemist and students at my university to reproduce them. We were very excited when the secret writing methods actually worked and we saw the secret writing substance develop like a photograph and take on color. My chemistry colleague, Dr. Ryan Sweeder, and I have developed a secret writing lab using the Stasi formulas. This lab goes beyond the simple invisible inks used by children, like lemon juice, or even recipes on the Internet, such as applying a reagent to the common laxative phenolphthalein. Instead, students will learn that most Cold War secret writing methods involved using the secret writing paper transfer method, not the direct invisible ink method. They will also learn about how and why chemists choose certain chemicals to work with and the role of catalysis and the nature of acid-base reactions.[14]

Layers of secrecy surrounded creating and detecting secret writing. OTS chemists were at the forefront of developing new secret writing substances and methods and experimented with several hundred different kinds of secret writing production and detection procedures. Their efforts were so extensive that they developed a secret writing electronic database in 1987. Only three staff members from the secret writing unit had access to the database, and very strict need-to-know and secrecy rules applied. Other staff members had to fill out a form stating the reason for using the restricted database, which was kept in room 304 B, and were accompanied by the select triumvirate when they used the computer. Even the database itself was constructed in code so that no one could recognize the research and development work. Only the number of the OTS method and the sorting number of confiscated and developed enemy secret writing were listed. In cases in which general research exposing a lot of secrets was needed, a special shielded room in the computing center had to be used.[15]

The obsessive secrecy was even worse at the level of actually working with the chemicals. The bottles of powder substances or solutions were labeled with a letter and a number; for example, L 044 for a solution and F 044 for a powder substance, where "L" means solution and "F" powder. The instructions and steps for producing, developing, and detecting secret writing always used the code numbers. No key has turned up in the archives yet. Occasionally, the chemical name will be in the procedure or penciled in next to the code. From these leads one can match the code to the chemical. I have found several recipes not in code. Creating a protocol for secret writing is not simply a matter of writing up a chemical formula for the substance and the reagent. The way in which the substance was applied to the paper and the type of paper used are both central components to developing a secret writing procedure.

There are hundreds of different chemical combinations that can be used in developing secret writing. The trick is to develop a combination that is not obvious to the other side or easily detectable with an ultraviolet light, silver nitrate, iodine, or heat. In 1977 OTS chemists developed an interesting secret writing method using one of the most common rare earth metals – cerium – as the secret writing substance. They used as a developer a combination of manganese, hydrogen peroxide, ammonia carbonate, and chelaplex, a chelating agent used to create a chemical compound in which metallic and nonmetallic atoms are combined. The cerium in powder form was rolled onto suitable paper to use as the copy paper. Scientists obtained the cerium from a GDR chemical lab company in Apolda, the concentrated solution of hydrogen peroxide (30 percent) at Chemapol, and the chelaplex from a chemical company in Adlershof, the site of the GDR Academy of Sciences.[16]

My colleagues and I started experimenting by mixing all the chemicals together to see how the cerium would act as a catalyst in the developer

342006

Operativ-Technischer Sektor
Abteilung 34

Geheime Verschlußsache
MfS 218 Nr.: _B 38177_
_1.Ausf.___ _2_Blatt

BStU
000003

Archiv-Exemplar
E 23187

Verfahren 41601 - 002

Chemische Grundlagen

1. Reaktionssystem

Mn^{2+} + Chelaplex   [Mn(Chel)]$^{2+}$
Mn^{2+} + yH_2O_2 Kat. pH 6.5   z Mn O(OH)$_2$ + MnO_2 ↓
                         pH

Katalysator = Ce^{3+}

2. GS-Substanz

Cer(III)-oxalat, 9-Hydrat, reinst
$Ce_2(C_2O_4)_3 \cdot 9\ H_2O$
VEB Laborchemie Apolda

3. Entwicklersubstanzen

L 038: Wasserstoffperoxid, 30 %, reinst zur Analyse
        (pro analysimum); H_2O_2
        VEB Eilenburger Chemiewerk bzw. Chemapol

F 006: Chelaplex III z. A.
        (Dinatriumdihydrogenäthylendiamintetraacetat-2-hydrat)
        $C_{10}H_{14}O_8N_2Na_2 \cdot 2\ H_2O$
        VEB Berlin-Chemie Adlershof

(a)

15. A "top secret" Stasi secret writing recipe. This recipe (see "top secret" or "*Geheime Verschlußsache*" stamped on the upper right corner of the first page [a]) comes from the Stasi files and describes a secret writing system using cerium, a rare earth metal, as the secret writing substance. Although the document

342000

MfS GVS 218/B 38/77

- 2 -

Archiv-exemplar

F 108: Mangan(II)-sulfat, 4-Haydrat reinst
$MnSO_4 \cdot 4 H_2O$
Chemapol

F 105: Ammoniumcarbonat, Hydrat, reinst
$(NH_4)_2CO_3 \cdot H_2O$

VEB Laborchemie Apolda

45001-1
~~45121~~1 Ammoniumcarbaminat, z. A.
$NH_4CO_2NH_2$

Merck

4. Das Verfahren entwickelt folgende GS-Substanzen

GS-Substanz Name, Formel	Konz. mg/W/A4	Stärke der Entwicklung auf OF 80A	
		Original	Abdruck
Cer(III)-oxalat, 9 Hydrat	25	+++	+++
	10	+++	+++
	5	+++	++
Cer(III)-carbonat	25	+++	++
	10	++	+
	5	+	∅
Cer(IV)-Nitrat	10mg/100ml	+++	++
Lanthan(III)-carbonat	25	+++	++
	10	+	−
Lanthan(III)-citrat	25	+++	++
Lanthan(III)-tartrat	25	+++	++
Lanthan(III)-oxalat	25	++	−

Die noch überprüften Carbonate und Oxide (Konz. 25 mg W/A4)
sowie die Chloride (Konz. 10 mg/100 ml) der Seltenen Erden
brachten keine Entwicklung.

Eine Reihe anderer Metalle, Metalloxide, Metallsulfide und
Carbonate (Konz. jeweils 25 mg W/A4) gab ebenfalls keine
Entwicklung.

(b)

15 (continued) outlines the chemical reaction system in which cerium is used
as a catalyst and manganese as one of the developers, the concentrations are
not indicated. We had to experiment to reproduce the formula. This recipe was
archived in 1977 and the original instructions destroyed. (BStU, OTS, 2428)

solution. During our first session we used a solution with a high pH because the exact pH level was covered by a secrecy stripe. We found that the solution turned yellow fairly slowly. When we poured in a higher amount of sodium hydroxide, the more basic solution bubbled and boiled and turned black. Dr. Ryan Sweeder, our chemist, thought it was creative that OTS chemists used the cerium as a catalyst in the reaction. In many secret writing formulas, the secret writing substance reacts when a reagent is applied.

It turns out the pH level – a measure of the acidity or alkalinity of the solution – played an important role in the chemical reaction. In fact, most invisible ink formulas developed in the lab involve a complex balancing act between acids and bases. Once we deciphered the exact pH amount – 6.5 (a mildly acidic mixture) – the solution turned yellow at a slow to moderate rate, which told us cerium was slightly reactive. Our next step was to apply the cerium in powder form onto paper. The OTS procedure recommended two German papers (*alte Mühle* or *Europa*). Instead we experimented with filter paper, which absorbs substances well, and fine, one hundred percent cotton paper. The filter paper worked best. We used the low-tech method for applying the powder to the paper because our lab did not have a wringer. Just as a 1965 OTS procedure recommended, we used a spatula and spread 1 mg of cerium onto a small piece of filter paper. We then rubbed it in with our index fingers (while wearing latex gloves), spreading it out in a circular motion. Another feature of cerium was that only a small amount, 5 mg, was needed for one A4 sheet of paper. This was part of OTS chemists' effort to find ways to use a very small, almost undetectable amount of the chemical substance to ensure that the enemy could not find it when they analyzed the paper.

All four of us experimented with different ways of writing on the impregnated filter paper. We each wrote our secret messages. I encouraged the students to use capital, block letters like real spies do, in order to make sure the messages was easily readable when it was developed. We got the best results when we used a dropper to apply the developer solution on the paper so it would not soak in too much. At first we thought nothing was going to happen, because my first messages did not develop instantly or quickly. The sage wisdom of the chemist in our group paid off; he encouraged us to wait a little more patiently. After about ten minutes Kevin's message – DAIRY QUEEN (he was hungry) – turned a nice deep yellow, and we all had smiles of satisfaction on our faces because it worked. Dr. Sweeder's message echoed our sentiments: "This rocks."

We concluded that cerium was a good secret writing substance because it was not easily or quickly detectable using an ultraviolet light or heat. Although the metal manganese is sometimes used in photography development, it is also not an obvious ingredient for the three-part developer solution. If a letter using the cerium secret writing were to be intercepted, enemy secret writing detectors would have to experiment with a number of reagent combinations before finding the right one. In the process, they would probably destroy the secret writing. The slow development time and the initial light yellow color that develops may also throw off an impatient examiner.

Procedures from the mid-sixties for preparing secret writing substances described how to pulverize and prepare the secret writing substance using an agate mill or mortar. Further instructions described how to prepare the secret writing paper. Once the secret writing substance was refined, it was then suspended in an ultrasonic pot (also known as fine suspension). Between 5 to 15 ml of the slurry was then sprayed on an A4-size paper. The amount of the substance had to be measured exactly for the paper size. If it was too little, it was hard to spread evenly; if it was too much, the paper would become too moist. The sheets of paper were sprayed in a cross motif, and the spray pistol had to be straight.[17] A number of other methods were developed for making copy paper. A chemical substance in powder form could be placed on the paper with a spatula, and then rubbed onto it with the middle or index finger, as we did when we used the cerium protocol.

A more sophisticated method was developed in the 1970s using a wringer to impregnate the paper. The "roll method" was fairly popular. For this method one needed two primary pieces of wood pulp paper, on which the substance was spread with a spatula. The prepared sides of the two sheets of primary paper were then placed on either side of the secondary copy paper, and all three pieces were placed between two thin plastic sheets, making a sandwich, and rolled over fifteen times back and forth through a wringer with a lot of pressure. The copy paper could be used thirty times to write a secret message.[18]

By the 1980s, OTS had also developed a more sophisticated spray machine. This machine was used to spray not only paper, but also packaging paper and textiles like scarves.

During the 1970s chemists started using a small gauze fishnet, like those used in personal aquariums, as a sieve for preparing the secret writing substance. Once the substance had passed through the fishnet sieve, it was ready to use in a pen, to create a suspension, or to be rolled onto paper. Other processes were more complicated.[19]

Wet secret writing – the use of an invisible chemical substance in a pen – was the lowest-security method and was usually a category 3 or 4 method, with 1 and 2 being the highest-security methods – that is, hardest to crack. The wet method could be used to pass on information in a residency or to write personal notes.

One such wet method drew on unique resources in the GDR to develop an invisible ink from shellac. Chemists obtained "laccain C," a shellac, from a paint factory in Zwickau and used it to develop an unusual ink. Laccain C could only be obtained from this paint factory. Scientists pulverized five grams of laccain C and mixed it with one milliliter of benzyl alcohol. The resin-alcohol mixture was heated on a hot plate or infrared machine until the mixture became a clear solution. Four hundred milligrams of pyrocatechol was mixed in the clear paste until it turned brownish. The hot paste was then put in a pen cartridge. A syringe and its drain tube were heated with benzyl alcohol. The alcohol was put in the syringe and squirted out several times. About 1 ml of the hot paste was taken out of the pen cartridge, and the syringe was placed in the pen cartridge until it stopped, then it was removed. This procedure ensured that no air pockets occurred in the cartridge filling. The secret writing was developed using the developer substance F 046, was dissolved in 100 ml of distilled water at 20 degrees Celsius, and then was poured into a beaker. A damp but not wet cotton tampon was used to paint over the secret writing, which turned black while the paper turned yellow.[20]

Once the secret message was written, it was important to make sure there were no signs of the indentations made from writing on the paper, just as Gabriele Gast did. Agents were instructed to use steam for follow-up treatment of the secret letter. The agent simply boiled some water in an ordinary pot. The paper was placed over the steam and turned around so it steamed evenly for about four minutes for a standard A4 sheet. The agent had to be careful not to get water on the paper. The process was complete when there were no more writing traces on the paper. To make sure the writing traces were gone, the agent could look at the paper obliquely in light. Once the steam process was over, the agent placed the secret writing paper between two clean sheets of paper and pressed a heavy book on it for up to one hour.[21]

MfS agents used all the secret writing methods available, from the home-grown organic methods, such as lemon juice, milk, or urine, that were developed by heat, to the most sophisticated secret writing paper or new hard-to-crack chemical formula for invisible ink, such as cerium or dyes. The wet method usually was the most simple, whereas the copy method required the most steps – what H. O. Nolan calls in his manual a "compound" method. One of the most innovative methods commonly used by the MfS was a felt-tip pen, because it did not leave indentations on the paper.

Regional Variations

The MfS's technical department had developed basic guidelines for distributing secret writing in 1958, but all units did not adhere to them. The Magdeburg regional office thought the older guidelines were no longer applicable to operational conditions in the late sixties and early seventies. As a result, technical officers updated and developed their own methods of practice based on the regional office's experiences. The outcome was a systematic routine that started before dispensing the secret writing and progressed to the training of the agent or courier, to the actual dispensing, and to the post-deployment control of the secret writing paper and envelopes against enemy detection. The routine combined operational common sense and a heavy load of German bureaucratic paperwork.[22]

Evaluating and rating the agent according to levels of dependability and honesty was considered one of the most important determinations before the secret writing was provided. The most dependable and honest agents received the most technically advanced secret writing system, whereas those with low ratings – often suspected of being double agents – received the most simple and well-known secret writing. Presumably, the enemy would therefore learn less about the MfS's novel secret writing methods. There were four secret writing categories, I to IV. The Magdeburg regional office received twenty-three different types of wet, dry, and micro-secret writing from categories II to IV from the OTS. The dry, transfer copying method was the most popular. No more than twenty agents were assigned to each different secret writing method.[23]

Unlike other MfS offices, Magdeburg had a dedicated secret writing specialist instead of one general technical officer who handled all of the different technical communication methods. Before distributing and allowing an agent to use the secret writing, the officer was supposed to have complete technical mastery of the secret writing method and be convinced that the particular secret writing would be "successful" and "secure." Magdeburg technical officers tried to match the needs of the agent and the operational conditions with the right secret writing method. They considered the way in which it was going to be used, the communication path (from agent to central or central to agent), frequency of use, where it was going to be used, and other conditions. They always considered the "activities of the enemy organs" and possible controls conducted to uncover MfS secret writing.[24]

A full array of bureaucratic steps accompanied the technical: secret writing methods were registered in a list with the secret writing number, category, and distribution date. Department E already had its signature order forms to keep track of distributed secret writing – the so-called D-method – including the agent's file registration number and information indicating that the agent was trained in secret writing; Magdeburg added another more detailed form that listed all the considerations about training, dependability, and use of the secret writing. There was even a form for the type of secret writing paper distributed.[25]

The Magdeburg office tested out the secret writing methods to make sure they worked properly before distributing them to the agents and wrote up the results in a report. The tests included intensive work with the paper. One sheet of A4 paper was divided into two A5 pieces – one for secret writing, the other for comparison. A list of instructions with thirteen steps was made up for a sample test for secret writing Nr. 071. The steps included application of the secret writing solution, holding the paper over steam, and application of the developer. They tested all the chemicals in the same way.[26]

The Magdeburg office was then ready to distribute the material in its own secret writing dispensers. Before doing this it had to match the right type of secret writing method with the agent or informant.

HV A and the Observers

Elaborate code names accompanied the HV A's different types of secret writing. They preferred bird names reminiscent of the apocryphal pigeons that transported secret messages in World War II. Secret writing used between the "operational area" and headquarters was called "falcon," "pelican," "vulture," and "pigeon."

Countless HV A spies were caught during the Cold War, and, like the other communication material, secret writing was used as evidence of spy activity. The German Federal Criminal Police has a baggie full of different kinds of invisible ink pens, including felt-tip pens, and a box full of different kinds of papers used, bottles of invisible ink, and ordinary household items, like cologne, that stored invisible ink.

Since the HV A destroyed most of its files after the fall of the Wall, few concrete examples remain of the specific type of secret writing methods individual agents received, but they were similar to what the deployment department used for agents working in the operation area. The case of Gabriele Gast is typical; other HV A agents also received training but did not necessarily use secret writing very often.

The HV A and the deployment department received the lion's share of secret writing methods, but this did not mean that other internal security or counterintelligence departments did not use secret writing. The observers (Department VIII) received the most secret writing processes, other than the deployment department. The most common method was using a felt-tip pen to write secret messages, notes, and letters. The invisible writing was often developed using a specific reagent, pelican ink, or an ultraviolet light. This meant that the agents often used the simple organic methods. Saliva, for instance, can be developed using pelican ink.

DETECTION

Detection and production of secret writing are inseparable activities. From the intelligence standpoint, detecting secret writing is vastly more important than producing it. Detecting secret writing is a more general process and requires less knowledge than the detailed steps involved in producing it.[27] But more importantly, the process of detecting enemy secret writing often leads to ideas for developing new methods. The MfS tested its secret writing methods with the steps it used to detect in order to determine how secure the agent was.[28]

Most spy agencies use the same principles for detecting invisible ink. During World War I, before the U.S. Army created a department for ciphers and codes, it used the Department of Ciphers at the Riverbank Laboratories in Geneva, Illinois, to examine suspicious letters. One of America's greatest cryptologists, William Frederick Friedman, worked at Riverbank and developed a series of technical monographs on cryptology, which he used to teach classes to army officers.[29]

H. O. Nolan, a technician at the lab, wrote a manual on *The Production and Detection of Messages in Concealed Writing and Images*, published by Riverbank in 1918. Only two hundred copies of this rare manuscript were published. It offers detailed instructions on examining documents that may have concealed writing or images as well as methods for preparing messages. Thorough examination of the paper and its characteristics was central to the process.[30]

Heat, iodine, and exposure to light are the biggest enemies for spies using invisible ink. The well-known household substances like lemon juice, milk, urine, and other organic chemicals can be developed by heating the secret writing paper with a candle, lamp, hotplate, or iron, in order to turn the ink brown. Examiners do not just use ordinary light to examine paper for secret writing. They use either infrared or ultraviolet light. Ultraviolet light will not only allow fluorescing chemicals to illuminate, but it will also capture fingerprints and other marks. During World War I, treatment of the paper with silver nitrate was also very common as a developer or reagent, as was the iodine vapor test.

After investigators examine the paper and apply quick detection methods like heat and light, they undertake more complicated chemical examinations using a variety of chemicals, or reagents. If the spy agency is lucky and already familiar with an enemy secret writing method, they can apply a specific reagent to develop the secret writing. The trick is to develop new inks and to continually change the secret writing substance and reagent needed or to use one that is not of a general nature or very common.

The OTS had a special department for examining suspicious letters, cards, and envelopes for secret writing at the request of consumer departments. The mail opening department usually had already done a preliminary examination of material from West Germany. When the material landed on the desk of the chemists, there was a routine for examining the material and writing up a formal report for the consumer department. Chemists analyzed several hundred pieces of paper a year.

Captain Renate Murk, a chemist and one of the few women scientists in OTS, examined hundreds of envelopes and sheets of paper in 1987. She went through a number of steps when examining a document. Usually the consumer departments wished to know if the paper had characteristics of enemy secret writing. The exam started with a visual examination of the paper using the naked eye, then a slanted light machine and Nyom machine to detect indentations, and ultraviolet light at different nanometers to detect luminescence. Then it was examined with various spectroscopes and finally with a number of chemical developers. The secret writing detectors had a hundred different kinds of chemicals they applied to the paper.[31] Once the examination was completed, the chemist wrote a report to the department that made the request.

In 1972 alone, the mail opening department examined 89,993 envelopes, letters, or packages for the purpose of finding secret writing. Once they identified a suspicious letter, they sent it to the detectors for a closer expert analysis. That same year, chemists found secret writing on 34 pieces of paper. They examined another 171 pieces of paper to

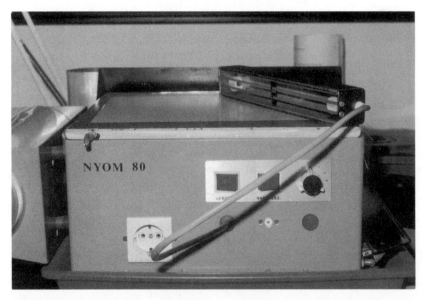

16. A Nyom invisible impressions detector. During the 1980s the secret writing department used this machine to detect invisible impressions on a sheet of paper. Operators spread a graphite-like material on the suspicious sheet, and the device on the top of the machine was scanned over it. The West German Federal Criminal Police obtained this Nyom 80 after the fall of the Berlin Wall. This method is similar to the Western Electrostatic Detection Apparatus (ESDA). (Kristie Macrakis)

determine if they had "imperialist secret services" secret writing on them and identified 15 items that did.[32] The BND and CIA were the most common "imperialist" agencies that used secret writing.

Ultraviolet light (UV or black light) almost became a universal screening method for the mail opening department. Because ultraviolet light emits electromagnetic radiation with wavelengths shorter than visible light, it stimulates luminescence. Black light is shorter than visible light and is between 380 and 315 nanometers. The importance of UV light is underlined by facts and figures: in 1980 OTS developed 480 UV lights and the next year distributed 608 UV lights to their brother organs in Vietnam and Czechoslovakia as well as to other MfS departments like the Postal Search Office. The new UV lights not only made invisible ink visible, but also supported the search for "operational important mail" and for solving criminalistic problems.[33]

The Hungarian-made Nyom machine was an innovative method used by OTS in the 1980s to check suspicious materials for telltale indentations. "Nyom" is the Hungarian word for clue, an appropriate name for

17. A sample from the Nyom machine. (Kristie Macrakis)

a machine that helps provide evidence to solve a problem. It uses similar material as is found inside the American Etch A Sketch toy – an aluminum powder formed into beads that stick to the toy's screen. When the Nyom machine is turned on, the powdered, bead-like substance vibrates down the piece of paper and reveals indentations on it.[34]

During the early 1980s, the detectors became enthralled with the Nyom and its capabilities for screening suspicious mail. They followed a lead to the machine after they learned of a similar machine used by Western intelligence that they dubbed "Crystal" (Kristall), most likely the Electrostatic Detection Apparatus (ESDA). Once they obtained the Hungarian Nyom, they began to study it intensely and modify it to improve the quality. They expanded the known capabilities of the machine to detect indentations in paper to include identifying fingerprints, marking of letters, treatment of envelopes, and micro-secret writing. They could even tell if the letter had been opened with steam. Most importantly, they could tell the difference in writing pressure between the date of the letter and the letter content or address.[35]

Using photographic developers was another common chemical investigative method. This is not surprising, as secret writing and photography share a number of principles and techniques. The most obvious, of course, is that a developer is used to make the invisible visible. OTS produced countless variations on the photography theme. They sometimes simply used GDR developer from the ORWO photographic company; other times they used Western developers like pyrogallol.[36] New secret writing methods were also developed using photographic techniques. Photographic secret writing has been used since at least World War I; this was not unique to the MfS.

The OTS spent much of their time isolating secret writing substances from the coated papers, experimenting with a variety of spectroscopic and chromatography techniques, which produced mixed results. They developed a process in which the first step was to press a piece of black polyethylene plastic on the paper to remove the substance. In 1976 researchers completed an extensive literature review and a 177-page report on this topic in order to find ways to isolate the increasingly smaller amounts of organic substance their adversaries used.[37]

The possibility of using the fruits of radioactivity for investigative purposes had begun to fascinate OTS in the 1970s. From technology at the border to tracking methods, they enthusiastically applied nuclides to criminalistic or spy investigative tasks like secret writing. In 1980 they experimented extensively with neutron activation analysis of enemy secret writing and reported one success in determining the substance on a piece of enemy secret writing paper.[38]

Since the 1970s at least, the MfS had identified the BND's signature secret writing method – it always used prewritten letters sent from cover addresses. Almost all of the secret writing evidence the MfS collected on the BND came from these prewritten letters. The case of Werner Stiller in 1979 is the most well known.

The BND tried to collect the grayish-yellow socialist East German paper through contacts who traveled there, but when that method did not rake in enough paper, they opened their own paper factory at a cost of 4 million marks in 1979.[39] Depending on where the letters came from, or were sent to, the BND, like the MfS, used both East and West paper.

In 1989 OTS succeeded in chemically analyzing and identifying five different types of the CIA's secret writing copying paper. OTS used their branch office at the Humboldt University section for criminalistics to carry out the chemical analysis using old analytic technology. They based their analysis on fourteen different samples from examinations done between 1978 and 1988 from counterintelligence, foreign intelligence, and the Cubans. This left only two more CIA formulas to identify from secret writing samples. With this knowledge, OTS could create a reagent to develop the invisible writing on the paper. It had been using a variant of

this reagent since 1978 and passed it on to the mail opening department
in 1986 to use on suspicious mail.[40]

Steam Street

Finding secret writing in letters sent through the post office is one of those
proverbial needle-in-a-haystack jobs. Even so, post offices and censors
have checked letters using chemical developers and infrared and ultraviolet light since at least World War I. During World War II, 14,462 United
States censors opened a million pieces of mail per day from abroad. Of
those, about 4,600 were passed on to the FBI because they looked suspicious, and 400 contained important messages or used invisible ink.[41]

If democracies resorted to using censorship offices during wartime, the
Soviet Union and East Bloc totalitarian societies were notorious for opening and examining mail throughout the Cold War. This was no secret.
Everyone assumed all letters were read. The East German Post Office
worked closely with the Stasi's mail snooping department. The central
office in Berlin had a surprisingly small staff – 500 employees – compared
to other departments, given the amount of mail they processed a day.
However, the fifteen regional offices throughout East Germany brought
the total number of staff members to 2,177. Reportedly each regional
office examined 6,000 letters and cards a day for a total of 90,000 pieces
of mail a day during the 1980s.[42]

In the early years, mail opening and closing was fairly primitive and was
done manually with very little use of technology. During the 1970s this
changed dramatically as new technology was introduced to improve the
quantitative and qualitative processing of mail. The mail openers established a subdepartment for technology, hired technically trained staff,
and organized innovator's groups to work on new technologies. The mail
openers worked closely with the technical operations division and had
them develop the Automatic Opener 10/10 in 1972, which came into use
by 1975.

The fully automated 10/10 machine could open six hundred letters
an hour as they rolled down a "steam street." In addition to opening
letters with hot steam, an innovative method was later developed using
cold steam, in order to reduce the structural changes in the paper that
occurred through heating. Working conditions for staff improved when a
dehumidifier was attached to the machine.[43]

The beginning of "steam street" began with workers placing between
three hundred to five hundred letters in a loading tray. From there, each

(a)

(b)

18. The 10/10 automatic letter opener. This automatic letter opening machine was developed by the Technical Operations Division. The tray holder could be filled with three hundred to five hundred letters (a). From there the letters went down the conveyor belt "steam street" (b). (BStU)

19. The 3/81 automatic letter closer. This machine was developed by OTS. Once the tray holder was filled, a conveyor belt pushed the letter to the glue station, where the flap was automatically closed. The table press on the right flattened the letters. (BStU)

letter was individually transported down "steam street" by a conveyor belt. A steamer inside the machine reached temperatures of about 100 degrees Celsius, which softened the glue on the envelope. Then an air stream loosened the flap, and warm air dried the letter.[44]

Not only did OTS develop technology to open letters, but, in 1972, it completed the development and production of a fully automated letter closing machine for the mail department. OTS boasted that this "new development" could automatically close 1,200 letters an hour, in contrast to the rate of 600 an hour manually. Workers loaded the tray on this machine with similarly formatted letters. A conveyor belt brought the letters to the glue station, after which the letters were automatically closed. Then the workers flattened the letter with a table press.[45]

In the seventies a special sorting and X-ray machine was developed to uncover cases of so-called political-ideological diversion (PID), while techniques continued to be developed to catch spies. The mail department had always kept an eagle eye on mailboxes when they suspected that a spy was depositing letters with hidden messages in them. In the seventies the department developed a technique to photograph the suspect with remote-controlled radios.[46]

One of the official tasks of the mail openers was to detect secret writing. By 1989 two out of ten departments were devoted to working on "suspicious secret service" mail. After the building of the Wall, personal contact between agents and their case officers became more difficult, and spies had to rely more heavily on impersonal communication methods like secret writing. Most agents used the post office for passing on messages with secret writing; others used a courier.

Until the mid-eighties, the mail openers conducted preliminary tests to determine if a letter had secret writing characteristics. Some of this mail had been detained because a suspect was under surveillance and had a file; other mail was stopped because it looked suspicious. Investigators examined the characteristics of the paper. In the early seventies they started using physical-technical methods to do this. The primary preliminary investigations used a "slanting light machine" (to examine if there were indentations on the paper from pen pressure), ultraviolet light, a stereomicroscope, the wet pressure method, and a method for searching and examining microdots using ultraviolet technology from the Soviet Union. In 1981 the Berlin mail opening department received a Nyom as well.[47]

Whereas the mail openers conducted preliminary tests to determine if letters contained secret writing, OTS was ultimately responsible for technically detecting secret writing. The spy catchers sent the most letters to OTS. They in turn had the mail openers keep under investigation certain letters addressed to specific people or cover addresses.[48]

"Buzzard"

During the 1960s the mail openers worked closely with the spy catchers and uncovered seven spies who used the post office to communicate. With the increased use of technology in the 1970s, investigations led to the unmasking of thirteen CIA and BND spies between 1971 and 1982.[49]

Wolfgang Reif was an East German diplomat who worked at the GDR embassy in Indonesia in the early 1970s. During that time he earned some extra income illegally importing automobiles with and for Indonesians. After a break, he returned to Indonesia in 1977 and contacted the CIA resident at the U.S. embassy because he thought the CIA, which knew of his illegal side business, would blackmail him. The CIA recruited him in January 1978, and he began to pass on information about the GDR embassy and foreign policy.[50]

Reif's problems soon snowballed. His marriage was on the rocks, he drank, and his professional life suffered. He thought about defecting to

West Germany, and therefore let his problems be known to West German colleagues, who informed the BND, as he hoped. The BND took the bait and recruited him in Jakarta in April 1980. Meanwhile, Reif's marriage stabilized, and he decided to return to the GDR. He dropped the CIA, but began to work for the BND, passing on information in exchange for money. He returned to East Germany in the spring of 1981.[51]

On 25 May 1981 the mail searchers intercepted a letter in which the handwriting of the sender did not match that of the letter writer. They found a number of other suspicious characteristics, such as inconsistent writing pressures, that lead them to believe that the letter was related to intelligence activity. Four months later they found another letter in which the handwriting did not match. The mail openers passed the letter on to the OTS secret writing detection department. OTS chemists had recently developed a new technique for uncovering secret writing using specially prepared paper that developed the secret writing when the paper came into contact with spy's secret writing letter. They found the spy through further handwriting analysis and by comparing everyone's handwriting in the same building to that on the letter. They placed the suspect under surveillance and observed him deposit a letter into the mailbox on 15 December 1981 addressed to a well-known BND cover address. The letter was a prewritten letter that the MfS had come to recognize as a hallmark of the BND.[52]

Reif had been trained by the CIA on how to write letters with invisible ink and to read microdots. The MfS found a microdot reader, a writing pad with five pieces of carbon paper, and a cover address. The BND had given him money for a radio, three pads of paper with 195 carbon sheets, ten prewritten letters (five male, five female), a telephone number, code tables, and instructions on how to write secret writing letters. The MfS found many letters written in invisible ink. By 1983 OTS succeeded in determining the type of secret writing substance used on Reif's secret writing copy paper.[53]

Reif was one of several dozen spies who were caught because of the MfS's tightly woven net for catching spies. The newly installed Nyom at the post office also played a role in determining that the letter was not written on the same day as the date, because of variable pressure on the paper. The spy catchers were not always successful, however. As we saw in Chapter 3 the mail department had intercepted Werner Stiller's prewritten BND secret writing letters, but could not decipher the code to read them.[54]

The mail department took a leading role in catching Reif and worked closely with the spy catcher department; OTS offered technical assistance. Detection of secret writing was a painstaking process. It was in part due to the successes in intercepting mail and blanket surveillance of the mail opening department that the MfS had any success in finding spies communicating with invisible ink. But intercepting these letters was only the first step. If a message could not be made visible, or decoded, the investigator only had a suspect, not a criminal. The seventies saw a great period of success in making invisible messages visible. By the end of the eighties there was a precipitous drop in the use of secret writing, as agents started using programmable calculators, like the Casio, or computers to communicate.

West German counterintelligence did not catch Gabriele Gast because she used secret writing, whereas East German counterintelligence did catch Wolfgang Reif because he used secret writing. These were not isolated cases, but are representative of the playing field in the spy game. Although the West caught hundreds of MfS spies during the Cold War, they did not catch them because they used secret writing. However, objects like pens, papers, and vessels used to hide invisible ink were later used in court as evidence of spy activity. By contrast, the MfS seemed to have been fairly successful in catching spies because the spies used secret writing. The censorship efforts of the mail opening department, which had co-opted the post office, certainly played a large role in pre-screening and pre-catching. The number of pieces of mail and suspected material examined belies an operation of enormous intensity and effort. The OTS also used a lot of manpower and poured a large amount of money and resources into creating and detecting secret writing.

It is not clear how great the West's effort was because of secrecy restrictions, but in a celebratory brochure developed on the fiftieth anniversary of the CIA's Office of Technical Services (OTS), CIA historian Benjamin B. Fischer refers to "technological breakthroughs" in secret writing.[55]

Like the code-making and code-breaking war, secret writing methods developed in response to the enemy's challenge. During the Cold War both sides spent a considerable amount of time studying enemy secret writing systems, and both sides reported success in uncovering enemy secret writing methods. OTS chemists on both sides analyzed the paper to determine if there were signs of secret writing. In response, Stasi chemists developed new secret writing methods, like the cerium chemical reaction, which used only a very small amount of secret writing substance on the paper. The

CIA also developed new techniques that employed "almost undetectable quantities of chemical" in the message. A CIA chemist likened this method to "uniformly spreading a spoonful of sugar over an acre of land."[56]

Secret writing chemists are like photographers in a darkroom. They work on developing latent images from blank paper and on applying different developers on enemy secret writing to make it visible. Much like an image in a photographer's darkroom, the real secret writing story has slowly developed and taken on shape and form as we learned about the interconnections between creation and detection, the threat of enemy interception, and the variations secret writing methods take. Most laypeople associate invisible ink with magic pens filled with colorless fluid that develops color when it is heated or when a reagent or light is applied. Secret writing is much more interesting and complicated than the common conception.

The Stasi secret writing experience reveals a great deal about the way in which spy agencies actually developed and used invisible ink during the Cold War. This is material spy agencies like the CIA would rather not reveal, judging from the 1999 lawsuit, their refusal to declassify agency methods and sources, and the lack of published books or articles on the subject. It is only because the Stasi no longer exists that it has been possible to piece together a true story about secret writing, a story told for the first time.

10

Eye Spy

A plastic flowerpot, a hand-carved wooden birdhouse, a man's jacket with a buttonhole opening, a shoebox, and an ordinary looking handbag – what do these various artifacts have in common? They are objects scattered throughout exhibit cases located at the former Stasi headquarters, now a museum. They seem to randomly decorate the real message of the exhibit as bizarre objects. The real message lies in the plaques on the walls – the story of the storming of the Stasi fortress, the suppression of dissidents, the persecution of the Jehovah's Witnesses, violations of civil rights, and so on.

The artifacts are not integrated into the story line as tools used to spy on these victims. Rather than being examples of the Stasi's inventiveness or use of technology, these objects, and other similar ones, such as bugging devices, are all curiosities meant to reflect Stasi perversity. Upon closer inspection, all the ordinary objects on exhibit share something in common: they all have cameras hidden inside and are in reality a disguise for secret photography.

Like the agent spy cameras, most of the observation cameras were destroyed shortly after the fall of the Wall. Stasi staff members drove trucks to Berlin-Hohenschönhausen and loaded them with valuable West German Robot cameras, Swiss Tessinas, Soviet F 21's, and Stasi-designed silent 35 mm cameras, as well as the document cameras like the Minoxes, *mikrats*, and the technological wonders made at Carl Zeiss Jena. The truck drivers then drove off and presumably destroyed the artifacts in dumpsters. Some items were spared and bought by savvy intelligence agencies and collectors. Remaining items not rounded up ended up scattered throughout exhibits on the Stasi as handmaiden of the SED dictatorship. Despite the destruction of much of these valuable and intriguing artifacts, it is still possible to piece together the story of their origins and evolution, including the development of the camera technology, methods for disguising the technology, and techniques for using it in spy work.

The story of observation cameras and the Stasi could easily be shoved into the conceptual box of a German Orwellian surveillance state, characterized by permanent eyes watching its citizens' every move. After the fall of the Berlin Wall, the phrase "all-encompassing surveillance" was the popular term for describing the Stasi's presence. This notion was similar to Michel Foucault's term "panopticism," coined to characterize a development in twentieth-century modern Europe: the "faceless gaze" – "a permanent, exhaustive, omnipresent surveillance" that "transformed the whole social body into a field of perception: thousands of eyes posted everywhere."[1]

Were these cameras – hidden in bags, clothing, and stationary objects – like those "thousands of eyes posted everywhere," watching every move people made in the former East Germany? Walk into a shoe store – the all-seeing eye is gazing at you from a shoebox. Take a stroll down Karl Marx Boulevard – a man with a big coat snaps away. Visit a friend in the countryside – your snapshot is taken from a birdhouse. However, the Stasi did not use observation cameras as permanent surveillance, like the video cameras placed in gas stations or banks in Western society today. It might seem this way, but, in fact, observation photography was usually taken with a specific purpose in mind. The actual uses of covert photography changed and evolved during the forty-year existence of the German Democratic Republic (GDR), as it grew out of its criminalistic roots and became one tool in an effort to watch a broader spectrum of the population.

Even if the Stasi was not watching people all the time, most people who lived or visited drab East Germany thought they were being watched. This was perhaps a more effective tool than actually creating permanent eyes.

IN THE SERVICE OF THE MINISTRY FOR STATE SECURITY

Photography in the Ministry for State Security (MfS) had its roots in criminalistics and the work of the Soviet Committee for State Security (KGB). With the emergence of the field of criminalistics in the 1950s came the recognition that science played a central role in fighting crime. Police investigators saw the Criminal Technical Institute (*Kriminaltechnisches Institut* or KTI) of the German People's Police as a "sharp weapon against crime" whose staff possessed the most "modern instruments" and "latest scientific knowledge" to support the work of criminalists.[2] Photography was also placed in the service of criminalists and used by the East German police force in the same way as in the West – to take pictures of the scene of the crime and especially to secure trace elements. Photography was also used for reproducing documents and for taking mug shots of the criminals.[3]

The MfS quickly adopted criminalistic photography and used it in its own work. This is not surprising, as part of the East German Police Department had been absorbed into the MfS during the early 1950s. The Technical Operations Sector (OTS) developed its own criminal technical institute in the late 1950s – the Technical Research Unit – which was very similar to the KTI. As a result, they also used microphotography, infrared, and ultraviolet light photography. The MfS's work was sometimes similar to that of the police, but they also adapted methods for other work in counterintelligence.

The MfS started using photography in support of its work as early as 1952, when state security was founded. In the early 1950s, photography, including infrared and ultraviolet photography, was primarily used to take pictures of prisoners and to make reproductions, securing traces, object pictures, and scene-of-the-crime pictures.[4]

The MfS did not only adopt technical methods from the police; it also incorporated investigative and observation techniques developed by law enforcement agencies. Observation and photography intersected when observations needed to be documented through pictures.

SECRET POLICE VOYEURS

Most people do not think there is a fundamental difference between observation and surveillance. In fact, the former is a targeted, focused, limited-time effort, whereas the latter is a constant activity. Because East Germany has gained the distinction of being a surveillance state, the general public has made the false assumption that citizens were under some constant form of surveillance by means of technical equipment or agents and informants. This misconception has continued to exist until the preparation of this book. When the observation department was given the task of observing a person, this was always a limited-term effort involving a case file. This is why observer reports exist that reconstruct in painstaking detail the activities of a suspect between specific times. For example, one observation occurred between the hours of 11 a.m. and 2 p.m., when the observation ended.

So many enemies of the state had emerged by 1989 that even targeted observation may have inadvertently created a sense of constantly being watched. There is no doubt that the MfS's observation department (VIII) was one of its largest; in 1989 the central office in Berlin had about 1,618 staff members, not including IMs and regional offices.[5]

Major General Karli Coburger, the last leader of the observation department, had an illustrious MfS career. He spent most of it (1953–84) in the notorious criminal investigations department (IX). While there, he studied criminalistics at the highly regarded police school in Ascherleben (1957–60), took his state exams in criminalistics at the Humboldt University in Berlin in 1966, and finally wrote a dissertation at the MfS's Law School in Potsdam on a sinister-sounding topic with a five-sentence, nineteenth-century title: "Legal and Political-Operational Preconditions and Measures to Realize Penal Responsibilities of Non-Socialist and West Berlin Citizens for Their State Crimes and Other Political-Operational Important Criminal Offenses and Their Strict Observance and Offensive Enforcement by the MfS." In 1984, the same year that he became major general, a rank only a select cadre of seasoned highly patriotic men attained, he became head of the observation department, an appointment he held until the dissolution of the MfS in 1990.[6]

Leaders before and after the fall of the Berlin Wall, such as Karli Coburger, characterized observation and investigations as the MfS's "indispensable classic working methods." Pre-1989 Stasi university dissertations and studies also underline the importance of observation as a "chekist" instrument, thus pointing to Soviet influence.[7] According to the 1985 Stasi university dictionary, an observation is "an operational process for acquiring operationally important information through focused perception of the external behavior and movement of operationally interesting people."[8] Of course, in plain language, this means tailing people to find out if they are committing a crime, political or civil.

The Stasi's bureaucratic machinery would be incomplete without the requisite observation report. But an observation is nothing without pictures to accompany the brief written descriptions of shadowing people. High-ranking observation department officers wrote learned dissertations on the topic and emphasized that the photographic documentation of the report was the most "important activity" for the observers. The report and photo documentation were inseparable. They were ultimately used as proof in file cases and were seen as being one hundred percent reliable in interrogations at prison detention centers, because they were considered to be "irrefutable...and a clear confirmation of what was seen."[9]

Budding secret police voyeurs did not just learn how to take secret snap-shots as amateurs; they first had to go to the observation department's special observation and photography school, where they were expected to master both the theoretical principles behind photography and the practice of taking good secret photographs. Because the photos were sur-reptitious, they also spent a considerable amount of time on how to use the disguises for cameras effectively.[10]

Observers received thorough training on how to use various photo mod-els and masks. There were a variety of ways to disguise and hide a camera in items ranging from a flowerpot to clothing. The Stasi developed many different camera disguises and variants, sometimes using people to display the hidden camera in clothing. The observer was instructed to pick the right photo mask, film material, aperture, and film speed based on where and when the observer was going to photograph. Instructors warned students to make sure the camera worked before hiding it in a mask.[11]

Training would be incomplete without hammering in the utmost impor-tance of secrecy. Everything had to be done to maintain secrecy. Even if the Stasi's techniques resembled those of the regular police, they always added that extra layer of obsessive secrecy. It is therefore not surpris-ing that the spies learned secret, not open, photography. They were also outfitted with all the latest gadgetry to help with secret communication, from radios for communication to state-of-the-art technology vans for stationary observations.[12]

Once the budding spy learned how to use secret photography, he or she was ready to find a base from which to observe. Observer bases were an essential part of an observation. They were hidden or disguised observa-tion posts and helped to maintain the secrecy principle. These bases could be stationary, such as apartments or offices, or mobile, such as vans or trucks.[13]

One of the most fascinating mobile observation vehicles developed by the OTS was a refrigerated truck outfitted with all the Stasi's technolog-ical bells and whistles, code-named "Swallow." The outside of the East German Barkas 1000 looked like an ordinary refrigerated truck, but on the inside it was jam-packed with cameras, video equipment, and video monitors and even had a roomy workplace.

One video camera was hidden behind the ordinary-looking external cooling unit on the front trailer section of the truck behind the cab; another camera was hidden behind the air vents on the side of the truck. Two video monitors were mounted on the desks inside to view the images caught on

Variabler Stützpunkt B 1000 „Schwalbe"

1- Kameratarnung. Kühlaggregat'
2 - Kameratarnung . Luftschlitz' (rechts und links vorhanden)
3 - Einseitige Lichtschranke „ Türhalter'
4 - Außenmikrofone (rechts und links je 2 mal)

20. Disguised mobile surveillance unit B 1000 "Swallow." The numbers on the pictures point out where surveillance equipment was hidden: 1. Camera disguise in cooling grate. 2. Camera disguise in air vents. 3. One-sided light hole in door handle. 4. Exterior microphones. (Detlev Vreisleben)

Arbeitsplatz der „Schwalbe" mit Technik

21. The interior workplace in "Swallow." (Detlev Vreisleben)

tape. Because the "Swallow" was a complete technology unit, it had an external microphone and heat sensor mounted on the side in addition to standard observation technology.[14]

The vans and trucks could either be used as stationary places from which to view a target while the target was stationary or as mobile places to follow a target or support other observation personnel who were on foot.

THE CAMERAS

The Stasi did not invent observation cameras. In fact, their camera of choice was the West German Robot camera. Heinz Kilfit, a watch-repairmen-turned-optical-specialist, completed his prototype of this camera in 1931. He then found a benefactor, Hans-Heinrich Berning, who had the idea of installing a spring-driven motor that advanced the film and activated the counter without the photographer having to re-wind the film. The spring-driven motor was the chief characteristic of the camera, and it quickly became famous as a rush job camera. During World War II it was used by the air force to take aerial surveillance photographs.[15] In the postwar period, the Robot firm was reestablished in Düsseldorf and presumably provided the West German police and intelligence agencies with dependable, motor-driven, relatively quiet surveillance cameras.

The Robot factory made available kits for hiding the camera and there-fore was aware of, and supported, the security and spy uses of the camera. A common factory-ready concealment was a handbag kit, which could be placed in a variety of bags. The kit had an internal frame, battery, remote shutter release, solenoid switch for the remote operation of the shutter, and decorative metal ornament for hiding the camera lens opening.[16]

It is not clear when the Stasi began using the Robot camera, but they adopted it from the police and the Criminal Technical Institute, where it was used for criminalistic purposes. By the 1960s it had become the workhorse for observations. Despite the greater availability of other cameras, the Robot was considered to be the most reliable, and it was the observation personnel's favorite camera. Most operatives would echo Captain Holger Natho's view that it was "very robust and dependable."[17]

In addition to the Robot, observers used several other commercially available Western observation cameras; the Soviet secret observation workhorse, the F 21; and several in-house cameras developed in the 1970s and 1980s as an alternative to the expensive Western cameras.

Another popular commercially available Western import was the Swiss Tessina. Reportedly one of the smallest 35 mm cameras in the world, it easily fit into its classic cigarette package disguise. Like the Robot, it had a spring-driven motor and could take ten pictures without rewinding.[18] Although it could take fewer pictures than the Robot before rewinding, Stasi users liked the Tessina because of its size – it was easy to build into a disguise. It was louder than the Robot but Stasi spies during the late sixties solved this problem by stuffing the disguise with foam rubber.[19] Another way to make the Tessina quieter was by modifying it and installing nylon gears to reduce the noise of the whirring film advance mechanism. Tessina also made a "noise-free version" without the spring-driven motor for those who wished "complete silence."[20] The Tessina was an obvious spy camera and also came in a wristwatch version from the Swiss Concava factory. The Stasi was not the only spy agency to use the camera. In fact, investigators found a black Tessina camera on the "plumbers" from the famous Watergate episode, which was kept as evidence.[21]

During the fifties and early sixties, the Stasi also experimented with the Minox as an observation camera. Although the Minox was considered a first-rate document camera, it was only partially useful as an observation camera, because the picture format was too small. When the film was developed, the pictures were too grainy and not sharp enough to be useful in recognizing people. As a result, the Stasi later adopted the Czech "Milox," a modified Minox with a bigger picture format (10.5 mm by 14.5 mm), which produced better-quality pictures for observation purposes. It also had a spring-driven motor and could take eight pictures without rewinding.[22]

Another important spy agency–made camera developed by the KGB in 1948 and based on the German Robot was the Soviet F 21.[23] The Stasi called this camera "Ammer" (Bunting), and thought its longevity proved its usefulness. It was easy to use, small, and fit easily into a disguise. Its spring-driven motor provided about twenty pictures. It was very quiet.[24]

During the early 1970s, OTS began to develop its own observation cameras to substitute the expensive Western models with indigenous Eastern ones; they either developed cameras in-house or contracted East German companies to develop them. There was a growing need to reduce the amount of hard currency spent and decrease dependency on Western models. The Robot was seen as a product of the "enemy" and was very expensive – 5,000 West German marks per camera.[25]

OTS asked the East German company Pentacon, Dresden, to develop a quiet camera with automatic lighting for secret photography. Work started in the early 1970s, and the "quiet 35 mm camera" (*Geräuscharm Spiegelreflex Kamera* or GSK) began to be produced in 1976. It was similar to Pentacon's Praktica cameras, but adapted for spy needs. Some of the camera's many features included automatic lighting, remote control, date stamp, and a quiet spring-driven motor. Accessories were developed that included a seventeen-meter cassette for 450 exposures and a grey light indicator that released the shutter when a moving object passed. It cost 16,000 marks to develop.[26] Camera collector Detlev Vreisleben estimates that some six thousand cameras were produced.[27]

By the 1980s the GSK became part of the list of standard cameras used with a disguise, along with the Robot, Tessina, and F 21 (Ammer). Not all departmental consumers were happy with the GSK, however. It did not prove as robust as the Robot workhorse. It did not always work in bad weather and broke down frequently. Some consumers, however, used it almost as often as the Robot: in 1987, a district office used the Robot fifteen times in one month and the GSK fourteen times.[28]

During the mid-1970s, together with Pentacon, OTS developed a quiet, small camera to replace the Robot – the Half Format Camera (*Halbformat Kamera* or HFK). Like the GSK, it was a no-frills, functional-looking, rectangular, flat camera. It was 18 (or 24) by 24 mm, electrical, and was designed to use regular or infrared film. Like the GSK it was designed for disguises. OTS leaders bragged that its optical system was world class and that it was unique in socialist countries in part because of the internal lighting control.[29]

The observation cameras were used either in stationary or moving observation posts or in disguises. By the 1980s the GSK, Robot, Ammer, and Tessina were the most popular and common cameras used in concealments. Other commercially available cameras, like Canon and Pentacom and the HFK, were used at observation posts.

In addition to the observation cameras, OTS developed or modified a number of document cameras developed for searches, infrared cameras, and TV cameras. Some of the document cameras were adopted from the Soviet Union or were an amalgamation of GDR-made cameras. Most of the document cameras folded into an attaché case.

The most striking and visually intriguing camera was the OTS periscope, developed for secret hotel observation. With its long, half-meter, tube-like lens, it resembles a sniper's rifle. Made for what was called the "observation complex" (*Beobachtungskomplex or* BEKO), it had unique room surveillance capabilities, especially the second generation model, produced in 1982. The BEKO could shoot photographs quietly through a 1-mm hole and produce quality photographs of people in the room next door; the pictures were round. Binoculars were attached to the camera so it was less tiring to operate. Although it functioned like a periscope, the tube had a downward slope. Despite its capabilities, it did not seem to be used as often as other periscope cameras, and only about a hundred were made.[30]

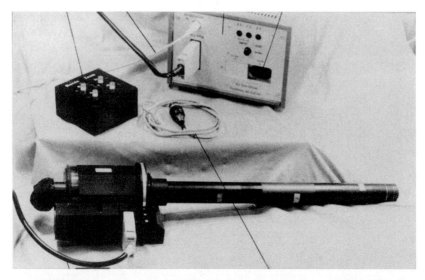

22. The BEKO periscope camera. This observation camera was developed by the technical division in the 1970s and named after the "observation complex," or system. It was primarily used in hotels and could shoot through a 1-mm hole and produce quality photographs. (BStU)

DISGUISING CAMERAS

Craftsmen spent quite a bit of creative energy developing concealments for the spy cameras – the shoebox with minuscule holes punctured in the side, clothes, overcoats, flowerpots, shopping bags, and handbags – to name the objects on display at the Stasi museum. Special "innovator" groups were encouraged to develop ingenious concealments and received bonuses if they were especially creative. In 1987 the MfS lamented that they only had forty-two disguise makers and nineteen in training.[31] The most common cameras used for concealments were the Tessina, the Robot, and the Soviet F 21 (Ammer). There were some standard disguises for each of these cameras, like the classic cigarette pack concealment for the Tessina, but it was better for maintaining security to change the disguises. Coats, handbags, and briefcases were the bread-and-butter concealments, but a wide variety of more unexpected places to hide cameras were developed, such as using a glove, motorcycle helmet, or bra.

Everyday objects with enough space to hold a camera were all candidates for camera disguises. The goal was to find an unobtrusive object that could effectively hide the camera without impairing its ability to take good photographs. Ease of use was another criterion for camera disguises.

Once the disguise was made, staff tested it extensively as they wandered about the streets of Berlin, taking pictures of street scenes to test if the pictures would be useable. They experimented with different film speeds, aperture openings, shutter speeds, and lightings. They were very thorough with the testing and wrote up a brief report on the advantages and disadvantages of each model and how it operated under various conditions. If the lighting was not right the first time, they experimented with the camera's aperture opening to achieve optimal conditions.

Coat concealments and handbags were considered best suited for taking secret pictures of people. One of the most common coat concealments used a waist-belt to hold a Robot camera underneath the coat. A false button was mounted in front of the camera lens to take the picture, with a remote release threaded into the coat pocket. The only problem with the waistband camera was that it produced a worm's eye view of the world. To correct this problem, the innovators worked on developing a coat concealment with the camera hidden in a neck stash travelers often use to store passports or money. This elevated the camera view to breast level. Developed in 1978 and code-named "Purse," this disguise used an Ammer (F 21) camera and a men's jacket. The money holder was attached to the inside of the jacket with two buttons, one of which had a hole in it for the camera lens, which was held in place with a plastic holder. The remote shutter release was threaded from the money holder to the jacket pocket. It was considered easy to use. A similar disguise used a waistband-type holder at breast level.[32]

In addition to women's handbags, a common concealment, one that could be used by men, was the wrist bag – a male handbag with a wrist strap. In Eastern Europe this concealment was almost as common as the cigarette pack Tessina but instead contained an Ammer. Both disguises were used at the photography school to teach spies how to use them.[33]

Whereas the Minox fell out of favor as an appropriate camera for concealments in later years, its shape made for some clever concealments during the 1950s. A leather glove was used as a concealment, with a Minox modified for one-hand use. The Minox hidden in the glove had a spring rod attached to the camera to release the shutter and advance the film. There was a small hole in the glove for the lens.[34]

New disguises were often developed out of necessity. And this old mother of invention produced a number of creative disguises. Women did not have any appropriate camera disguise models to choose from when operating in warm weather, during the summer. As a result, a group of four women in an observation collective in the province of Suhl were asked to develop an appropriate camera disguise in honor of the upcoming XIth Party Congress in 1986.

Under the code name "Wiese" (Meadow), the group began work on the project. Not surprisingly, the women focused on finding a way to hide a camera in a bra while wearing a stylish summer dress. They used the small Ammer and placed it between the two breasts with the lens protruding through a hole in the bra. It was naturally held in place. The remote shutter release extended from the bra to a pocket in the dress.

The women's supervisors were delighted with the new camera disguise model. It allowed women to walk around taking pictures by simply pressing the shutter release in their dress pocket; otherwise, their hands were free.

The four women initially did a test run at a summer market, and the results looked quite good. The bra disguise camera was so successful other MfS offices quickly appropriated it. The first test in a supermarket produced very good quality photographs in which the people and objects were easy to recognize. Because the lens protruded from the bra and was placed flush up to a hole in the lace front of the summer dress, pictures did not contain the fish-eye effect of some other secret photography.[35]

CHANGING TARGETS

Different targets emerged in the course of the development of the GDR corresponding to who was perceived as a major threat or enemy of the state. During the early years, suspected spies and their communication methods were the major foci. This included military and civilian spies. After the building of the Wall on 13 August 1961, West German spies were forced to use a greater amount of agent communication methods. The MfS was determined to penetrate communication channels in order to catch spies. They found that Western spy agencies made enormous use of dead letter boxes. As a result, they targeted dead letter boxes with cameras, because they were often in isolated locations where it would be difficult to plant a human observer.

Other spy targets included military spies who crossed the border; the Western Military Liaison Missions, which traveled east though stationed in the West; the transit highway connecting West Germany to West Berlin; and the spy residencies at embassies or representatives in the East. During the seventies and eighties, major observation targets requiring

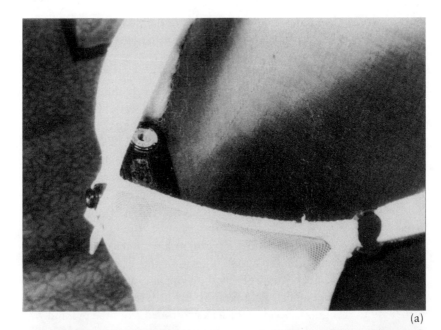

(a)

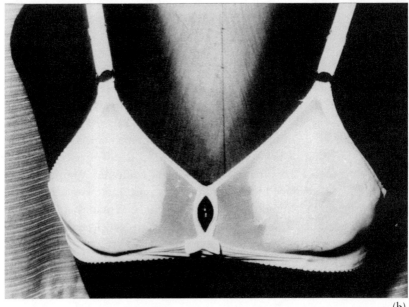

(b)

23. A Soviet F 21 camera disguised in a bra. Innovator groups developed a number of creative disguises for observation cameras, including this bra disguise for use with a summer dress. A Soviet F 21 camera, the Ammer, is cradled in the bottom of a bra (a), and the lens protrudes through a hole cut between the cups (b). (BStU)

photographic documentation included people-smuggling groups, considered the biggest enemy, and so-called political underground activity or political-ideological diversion. Between 1972 and 1974 the observation department claimed to have stopped 44 percent of all people-smuggling attempts made in vehicles traveling through the transit highway, their bailiwick.[36] Dissidents started to become major targets in the 1970s, and as their numbers swelled during the 1980s, the Stasi spent a large amount of their time collecting information and shooting photographs of them as well.

With increased demands for observation, as both internal and external enemies seemed to proliferate, the MfS developed "observer groups." Initially formed to watch suspicious people who might be planning to flee to the West, observation groups were also trained and sent to work in the West. Their tasks ranged from undertaking general observation and photography to specific missions, including penetrating people-smuggling groups.

The observer groups underwent extensive training using all types of gadgetry to communicate and hide secrets, but their special focus was training in photography. One of the star instructors for such a group was code-named "Reiner Bergmann," in reality Bernd Rier, an East German tool maker who became an instructor in 1974. While still living in the East, he made numerous trips to the West to run his group, including agents "Jonny" and "Cornelia," who observed the Jehovah's Witnesses. His case officers applauded his "excellent achievements" with photography during sixteen such operations. He received extensive training in photography and took good, useable pictures with his disguised Tessina, code-named "Trixi."[37]

CATCHING SPIES

Catching spies on camera while they were meeting with their handlers was one way to prove their guilt. Dead letter boxes had become popular because they were impersonal and seen as more secure, but the problem with them was that the spy could be caught in the act of servicing, placing, or emptying a dead letter drop, even if another human being was not there. Locating and putting a dead drop (TBK) out of service disrupted foreign intelligence communication channels, and visual documentation of an agent at a dead letter drop was decisive in court. According to a specialist at the MfS university in Potsdam, "documentation through photography increases the quality of proof." Photographic documentation was not only limited to people. Fingerprints and shoe and car traces could also be photographed and used as proof.[38]

After the building of the Berlin Wall on 13 August 1961, the MfS determined that foreign intelligence agencies increasingly relied on technical methods to communicate with their agents. Dead letter drops were a central part of communicating and passing on secret messages or secret material like radios, code blocks, and invisible ink.

Between 1961 and 1967, the MfS analyzed fifty-six operational files involving spies delivered to the legal and investigatory department, which brought suspects to trial and, like the police, enjoyed executive authority of criminal prosecution by the Code of Criminal Procedure of the GDR. In all cases the spies used dead letter drops. Thirty-three dead letter drops belonged to American spy agencies, twenty-one to the West German intelligence agency (BND), one for French intelligence, and one for the West German counterintelligence office in Köln.[39] The BND, in particular, placed a heavy emphasis on dead letter drops. In addition to routine spy work, the MfS assumed they were preparing for "Day X."[40]

Favorite places for dead letter drops were cemeteries, forests, and highways. It was difficult to keep people under surveillance without arousing suspicion in these remote places. The seemingly peculiar artifacts for hiding observation cameras displayed at the Stasi museum in Berlin, such as the flowerpot, tree stump, and gas can, all fit perfectly at cemeteries, forests, and gas station rest stops on highways. Soon, the favorite sites became known, and the MfS could keep them under observation.

Spies did not just visit remote places like cemeteries to pass on or collect information; they also worked under legal cover at the various embassies, consulates, and permanent missions in East Berlin. There were observation bases littered throughout East Berlin, targeting the U.S., the FRG, and other Western countries. They boasted that, with these observation bases, twenty embassies and three missions could be "kept under control." The observers had eight bases, including the hospital across the street and some nearby apartments, from which they observed the permanent mission of the Federal Republic of Germany on Hanover Street.[41]

DUELING CAMERAS

The Western powers' Military Liaison Missions (MLM) became the largest group of legal spies in East Germany. Established through a little-known 1947 agreement between the Soviet Union and the Western powers of France, the United States, and Britain, the Westerners all had rights to travel to the East to inspect Soviet and East German military installations. All three allied Military Liaison Missions to the commander-in-chief of the Group of Soviet Forces in Germany were based in Potsdam. Conversely, the Soviet Union also had the right to travel freely through West Germany and established their liaison headquarters in Frankfurt, West Germany. Each side was allowed to station sixty-three officers at a time in enemy territory.[42]

It quickly became clear that the liaison function of these military officers was minimal in comparison to their reconnaissance missions. John A. Fahey, a retired naval officer who characterized his activities as a "license to spy," admits that his liaison work took up only 10 percent of his time, whereas "90 percent was spent on reconnaissance and spying."[43] Military liaison officers were armed with maps, binoculars, and cameras, but carried no weapons. In 1978 alone the United States Military Liaison Mission (USMLM) shot 195,000 photographs and 500,000 infrared photographs at dimly lit military installations.[44]

During the height of the Cold War, the Stasi had many successes in seizing liaison officers' cameras and developing the film. In 1960, Walter Ulbricht, then head of state in East Germany, claimed that state security could document nineteen espionage cases between March and July 1960 because of confiscated cameras.[45] The MLM soon developed techniques for destroying the contents of the film as the camera was opened.

There was often a fine line between what was legally possible and what constituted espionage. In cases of doubt, the Soviet military, which was ultimately responsible, was brought in to mediate. Collectively, the three Western missions had photographs of 95 percent of all Soviet and East German military installations. They took pictures of Soviet military installations and vessels, East German shipyards, new antennas, tanks, radar, and communication sites. They crawled around in the woods and hid in forests when they thought they could find military installations. They were involved in a number of high-speed car chases with the "Stasi hoods," as they called them.[46]

Conversely, the Stasi took pictures or film footage of military liaison officers on the streets of East Berlin or other cities and towns, while trailing them and especially while catching them in the act of espionage. If the Stasi could capture espionage on film, they could arrest the perpetrators. By the 1970s they only found about a 1 percent rate of espionage from the four to five thousand yearly missions, a considerable decline from earlier years.[47] With the decline of spying in the East came an increase in internal discontent and dissent.

Some discontented East German citizens tried to leave the country illegally using the underground people-smuggling groups. The Stasi suspected
that the military missions smuggled people in their vehicles, because they
did not have to be inspected. But more often, they found people hidden in
trunks or sometimes even tucked under the backseat bench while crossing
the border or on the transit highway. The observers made detailed photo-
documentations of people caught in the act of popping out of trunks like
crackerjack dolls.

The Stasi particularly abhorred the people-smugglers Wolfgang Welsch
and Kai Mierendorf. They tried to kill the former three times and sent
a letter bomb to Mierendorf in 1982. After they caught the Mierendorf
group red-handed in a smuggling attempt at the border in 1975, they
developed a detailed picture report to illustrate the new methods "the
people-trading organization" – an "enemy of the state" – used for smuggling people through the border. Of interest to them was luggage found
on the backseat of the car, including a sailing bag used as a concealment
for money and a piece of paper with notes. In one picture they displayed
more than 12,000 marks in cash fanlike.[48]

SPYING ON DISSIDENTS

When the Stasi's dirty deeds were exposed after the collapse in 1989, it
appeared as though the Stasi's main function was to silence critics and enemies of the state. Dissidents had been abused, and dissent was squelched.
Revenge and the rule of law took over. But the focus on dissidents blurs
away the other targets. Critics of the regime were only one of various targets. The department responsible for political-ideological diversions and
political underground activity, the universities, and the churches was one
of the MfS's smallest departments, with 460 staff members at headquarters and about 700 IMs.[49]

Many dissidents in East Germany had, in fact, started out as idealis-
tic communists or state heroes and then grew disillusioned with "real-
existing" socialism. Robert Havemann (1910–82), a chemist, communist,
and prominent dissident, was one such hero before he became one of the
state's most embarrassing critics. Resistance was not foreign to him. During the Nazi period, he had become a communist, worked for Comintern
in Germany, and helped found the resistance group European Union. After
the war Havemann became the director of the physical-chemistry institute at the Humboldt University, joined a variety of political groups, and

was awarded the state's most prestigious prizes. He even became a "secret informant" for the Stasi in 1956, reporting on his contacts with Western scientists. But Havemann soon became critical of the Stalinist dogma he saw in the East German brand of communism and began to lecture at the Humboldt University in 1963 on the "dialectics without dogma." By then he had been expelled from the party and prohibited from teaching and doing research at the university.[50] This is when the Stasi surveillance began.

There are hundreds of photographs of Havemann in his one-hundred-volume file. The Stasi even put a secret photo studio in the garage next to his house to support the extensive surveillance activities, which included listening devices and observation units. They used both hidden and open photography, and his file contains numerous photo documentations and reports from his currency trial in 1979 to his funeral in 1982.[51]

Young people confused about the contradictions between the ideals of communism and reality of an oppressive state flocked to the iconic dissident Havemann. During the 1970s other well-known critics of the regime emerged, for example, the singer Wolf Biermann, who had been such a convinced communist that he had emigrated to the East from the West when he was a teenager. By 1976 he was stripped of his citizenship and forced to live in the West after a provocative concert there in 1976. When Jürgen Fuchs, a prominent dissident and writer, protested this action, he was arrested and jailed in 1976, and once released, subjected to psychological intimidation and character assassination tactics by the Stasi. The surveillance of both of these dissidents was so heavy that one of Biermann's most well-known songs describes the Stasi as his personal secretary (his "Eckerman," referring to Goethe's secretary), keeping track of his life.

By the late seventies and early eighties, individual critics like Havemann, Fuchs, and Biermann had been replaced by a second generation of critics who mobilized themselves into peace, environmental, or citizens' movements, often under the roof of the church. The Stasi's work against them became more intense; they expanded their observers into "observer groups," and operatives received extensive training in covert photography. They were often sent out to take pictures of dissidents' apartment houses and their meetings with people in public places and trained to trail them as they left for work or returned home. These observers rarely broke into their apartments unless there was a reason to conduct a search. The informants surrounding some of the dissidents posing as friends took more personal and intimate portraits at home, parties, and even at the nude beach.

Youth and counterculture were Stasi observation targets, but the intensity of the effort did not take off until the 1980s, with the emergence of the skinhead and punk movement. In 1987 the Berlin regional office counted 350 skinheads in Berlin alone. They saw them as threats because of their antiauthority attitude and their antisocial behavior; the Stasi saw them as a symptom of the decline of capitalistic society. Visually, their pointed, exotic hairstyles and hair color; chains; ripped clothes; leather jackets; and punk accessories contrasts starkly with the militaristic, polyester suit–wearing, and straitlaced world of the Stasi. They photographed them at concerts and clubs, on the street, and anywhere else they could easily see them.[52]

HOTELS AND SEXPIONAGE

One of the most iconic images of Stasi spying is that of a naked Western businessman cavorting with a Stasi prostitute while a voyeur views the scene on a TV monitor.[53] Rumors spread that every such hotel room had hidden video cameras, bugging devices, and tapped phones. This was hardly the case! One hotel in Dresden – the Bellevue – had all telephones tapped and rooms bugged, but video and camera observation was limited to special suites or installed on demand. The Stasi used prostitutes to ensnare and blackmail unsuspecting businessmen or enemies of the state in these special suites, but most of the cameras were pointed at the bar area or other public places.

Despite the state's efforts to develop a progressive, socialist society, the Stasi was surprisingly old-fashioned and chauvinistic when it came to women. Only about 15 percent of all staff members were women, and most of them worked as secretaries. Women were seen as too "talkative" to make good agents, but if they were recruited they had to be "intelligent, creative and attractive."[54] They belonged in the bedroom, not the boardroom.

Whereas the KGB became notorious for its sex schools and use of women as "honey traps" to seduce men, the Stasi seems much more prudish but did develop the reverse gender strategy of targeting Western secretaries using male Romeos. Even if there were few Tatiana Romanova's with bodies that belonged to the state and who were "instructed in all the arts of allurement" by a Rosa Klebb character, as immortalized in Ian Fleming's *From Russia with Love*, some women offered their services to the Stasi as prostitutes.[55] One such prostitute, Monika Lustig, has told her story: "I had a great figure and charisma. That attracted the men. I wanted to show it to them all the time." Armed with this motivation, she slept with businessmen at the Leipzig Fair, Arabs in Berlin hotel suites, and Western engineers and servicemen who came to the East.[56]

Voyeurs usually used camera periscopes to peer into hotel guests' rooms through a small hole in the wall from the adjacent room. This was often, but not exclusively, done to obtain compromising material for blackmail: a male guest or businessman is caught on film with a woman, often a Stasi prostitute, and is presented with the compromising material, which will be given to his wife or superior if he does not cooperate. The Soviet "Kedr" camera was used three times between 1970 and 1972 to obtain "compromising material" from rooms at the inter-hotel Newa.

In each case technical officers installed equipment in different hotel rooms for several days and then took it apart when they were done with the job; the rooms were not permanently outfitted with hidden cameras. In all cases a Kedr periscope was used, several times with a Soviet Nyrok camera attached. One case involved a Western visitor, one an economic spy, and another a representative of the evangelical church. Often the pictures were not usable because of bad lighting, but they were more successful with video cases using Kodak recording film.[57]

A prominent male victim of a sexy Stasi swallow was Heinrich Lummer, a popular Christian Democratic politician based in West Berlin. While on a pub tour of East Berlin in 1973, he met a twenty-five-year-old woman who said her name was Susanne Rau and that she was an art dealer. The Stasi took pictures of him lying naked on top of her and eight years later tried blackmailing him when he became senator for interior affairs. He told them to "get lost" and reported the incident to counterintelligence.[58]

Visual surveillance took place in the foyers, hallways, bars, fitness centers, and areas external to the hotel. The observation department covered the hotel television, video, and camera surveillance with which Western Society is familiar – cameras pointed at hotel entrances, foyers, corridors, and so on. They also installed cameras in walls and pointed them at the bar area. The Leipzig Fall Trade Fair drew thousands of Western visitors and hundreds of Stasi observers to follow them. The 1961 Berlin Wall had stemmed the flow of Western traffic to the East; during the 1960s Westerners were not especially welcome, except in Leipzig. As it became easier to travel to the East during the 1980s, Westerners became curious about life behind the Iron Curtain. With this demand and the GDR's increased confidence as a "stable socialist society," the GDR began to build more inter-hotels to house Westerners and bring in Western currency. The Stasi was suspicious of "political tourism" and wanted to keep it under control.

The technical and observation departments installed extensive television surveillance systems in many of the major inter-hotels in East Germany, but targeted the ones being built in order to gain their cooperation early on. Dresden inter-hotels were the most high-tech, whereas Erfurt hotels had no technology.[59]

By the early 1980s, the Stasi already had bases in hotel rooms with monitor walls – usually about fifty television screens – where they viewed the results from the television and video cameras installed in the hotels. The observers also needed a cover story so that they could become invisible in the hotels. Their solution was to look like hotel personnel by acquiring hotel clothing and identification. The way to do this was by co-opting the hotel managers. The MfS convinced the hotel managers that national security was at stake and persuaded them to sign secrecy forms ensuring their cooperation in the ruse. Another element of secrecy was the use of a password phrase to signal to the managers that they were speaking with a security official.[60]

The Stasi tested this system at the Palast Hotel and Grand Hotel in Berlin. They seemed to think it worked well, although there were some awkward situations. A Stasi man disguised as a hotel guest spoke to the manager using a password phrase and received odd looks from hotel guests. Another time, the undercover officers were given a table at a restaurant because they used the password, but the manager asked them not to stay too long because it was already reserved. On one occasion, the doorman asked why they were hanging out in the lobby until 2 a.m. Clearly the undercover security officials were an unwelcome but tolerated nuisance. The Stasi did not see it this way. They thought conversations were "calm and open" and took place in a constructive atmosphere.[61]

The Grand Hotel, now called the Westin Grand Hotel, was an elegant luxury hotel that opened in 1987 in the heart of East Berlin on *Friedrichstrasse*, next to the stately boulevard *Unter den Linden*. It was designed as a showcase, even though its glittering opulence contradicted socialist ideals, but brought in needed Western currency. It featured 358 rooms and many different restaurants. Some, like the *Sichouet*, were hard-currency-only restaurants accessible through the hotel, others could be entered from *Friedrichstrasse* and guests could pay in East German currency.[62]

The Stasi had already started to work with the hotel in 1985 before it was ready to open. They thought it was a "forced necessity" to use TV cameras, because they had to "control" the mass of people coming in as part of political tourism delegations. With the floor plans in hand, they quickly targeted points like hallways, restaurants, elevator entrances, and the lobby to install some fifty, mostly hidden, TV cameras. They received a technology room on the third floor, where they installed sixty monitors to view images from the TV cameras. They also established a base across the street in a building they called the "Stopgap Building" because of its incompleteness.[63]

DOCUMENTING SEARCHES

Different types of cameras were used and developed to undertake secret searches, to document the search process, and to take pictures of incriminating material. The observation department was responsible for conducting searches, primarily to provide proof for the notorious investigative arm of the Ministry for State Security. In addition to providing the investigators with photographic proof, they were supposed to be thorough enough to contribute a "you-are-there" type of photo journal to document what a written report could not.[64] Photography played a central role in the search process, because it was seen as an effective way to collect, store, and present information. In theory, the MfS followed criminalistic photographic methods fairly closely. Investigators were supposed to go through the four steps of taking an orientation photograph, followed by the overview, focused, and detail photos.[65]

An orientation picture could be taken of the exterior of the building using a wide-angle lens. But the real first step started when investigators photographed the whole apartment interior to provide an overview, while keeping every object where it belonged. Then the search could begin. If evidence was found during the search, it was marked with a reminder that it should be photographed later. Because someone committing a criminal act hides incriminating objects or material, investigators were instructed to examine every conceivable hiding place – usually seemingly innocuous household objects ranging from furniture to a vacuum cleaner, musical instruments, or a door frame and occasionally more unusual hiding places, such as bee houses, stalls, and dung heaps.[66]

Once general pictures were made of possible proof, detailed and bigformat photos were made of highly incriminating objects like radios, codes, secret writing material, false documents, or printing material for defamatory material.[67]

Like the procedure in other observations, staff members created a photographic documentation of the process and the objects found. During the seventies, officers still preferred to use black and white film because it offered more clarity and contrast. The type of camera used depended on the crime. Investigators brought suitcases they outfitted themselves with cameras like the East German Praktica or the Pentacon, film, tripods, and a host of other material.[68] During the eighties, it became common to use a Polaroid camera for the overview step. Another common camera used exclusively in searches was a suitcase camera – either the JEL or the Yeschvka. This camera was actually built into the suitcase and folded out for photographing evidence in detail.

"Revisor"

To illustrate the proper way to conduct a search, the MfS produced an educational film about the case of "Revisor" (Auditor). "Revisor" was the code name for an East German citizen who had started to write critical material about East Germany and planned to pass it on to a West German journalist.

On 7 January 1984 several Stasi officers seized and detained "Revisor" when he attempted to meet with a *Stern* journalist at the glossy West German magazine's East Berlin office. The charge was "illegal attempt at contact," a crime in East Germany.[69]

The man first came to the Stasi's attention in December 1982 through routine observation of the West German mission in Berlin. They also learned of his interest in contacting a Western journalist through an informant with enemy contact, "Roland," who had visited a journalist at ARD in March 1983 to procure information for the Stasi. During that visit, the phone rang, and the informant surmised that it was a GDR citizen who was attempting to contact the ARD journalist.

Investigators began to look for the caller. They searched all their files, cards, and computers to find bureaucratic traces of his existence. They gave him the code name "Revisor" and opened a file on him.

In December 1983, the Stasi received another tip about "Revisor" from an informant with enemy contact, "Klaus." "Klaus" was visiting a *Stern* journalist at his office, who left him alone in the office to read Western newspapers. While the correspondent was out, the informant rifled his papers and found a handwritten note about a GDR citizen who reported about unemployment in the GDR and his own situation. "Revisor" had written textbooks earlier, but was now writing poems and stories, which he could not publish for political reasons. He contacted *Stern* because he hoped they could help him publish his material with their publishing house. "Revisor" planned on visiting in January 1984.

The Stasi was worried that *Stern* would write about this case and quickly blocked the contact and transmission of material critical of the GDR. In order to find proof of the man's guilt, the spy catcher department decided to search his apartment. First they kept him under surveillance for several days in order to observe his movements. Then three officers, two disguised as firefighters, entered the apartment to ensure that no one interfered with the team's search. They radioed an okay, and the officers trained in searches and photography surreptitiously entered the apartment with a lock-picking device. The upper lock was not bolted so it was easy to enter the apartment.

A year after "Revisor" was detained, the ministry made the educational film, which provides visual documentation of the search process and the role of photography in it. The technical officers who handled the photography wore white gloves and first made a photographic overview of the whole apartment using a Polaroid camera. In the educational film, the officer prominently displayed the Polaroid camera. Then the officers looked through all the cabinets and drawers of the one-bedroom apartment. They found a note on a table with a reference to an appointment with a *Stern* journalist. They also found a series of manuscripts, which they photographed in the kitchen with a suitcase camera. They used the Yelka suitcase copy camera with a bulk film holder and accessories to photograph these documents. The search lasted four hours.

The movie closes with a scene about the final capture of "Revisor." They film him emerging from the central Berlin subway station on his way to the magazine office. As he approaches the building, at 9:08, he encounters construction at the front door. Two Stasi men disguised as construction workers escort him to the back door, and he is detained.

TECHNOLOGICAL SAFE HOUSES

The Ministry for State Security developed and maintained a number of safe houses equipped with surveillance technology. They ranged from small apartments outfitted with basic listening devices and cameras to elaborate houses fully equipped for total surveillance. They were used to either debrief defectors or to monitor agent groups surreptitiously.

Several houses are noteworthy because of the extent of their elaborate technology. One was in southeast Germany in Jena and the other thirty miles northwest of Berlin in Prenden. The ministry bought the house in Jena in 1972 for 25,000 marks. It was a single-family house with seven rooms and a big garden. Between 1972 and 1981 they invested about another 82,000 marks for renovations, furniture, technology, and repair of the technology. The "object" was run by the subdistrict office of the Jena district office and was code-named "Berg" (mountain).[70]

"Berg" was developed as a secret base for the spy catcher department secret agents, who were not allowed to visit headquarters because of secrecy regulations. Officers anticipated that important "political-operational" discussions would occur in the safe house, and they sought to monitor them without the knowledge of agents. To do this, microphones were built in the wall before it was wallpapered, telephones tapped, tape recorders installed, and cameras hidden behind cabinet doors. The lens of a camera was hidden behind the lock of the entertainment center door.[71]

A more technologically sophisticated and luxurious safe house was developed for the HV A's (foreign intelligence arm of the Ministry for State Security) Department IX for counterintelligence against the Western secret services, thirty miles northwest of Berlin, in an isolated country house in Prenden. It featured total surveillance. In addition to a birdhouse camera disguise outside, the interior was dotted with cameras strategically placed in all parts of the house. Everything was not what it seemed to be. The harmless-looking clock at the head of a hallway facing the living room was in fact an infrared glass-plated disguise for two cameras hidden behind it. One hidden camera was an infrared video for movement surveillance, and the other one was a 35 mm Praktika, which used infrared film and was remotely triggered.[72]

No room was spared – the more private the room, the more surveillance was required. The bathroom had a pinhole camera with a wide-angle lens installed behind the toilet and the ceiling, a pinhole microphone. If a defector or other inhabitant was tempted to flush incriminating evidence down the toilet, officers could shut off the sewer system and retrieve the paper or object outside.[73]

The most famous defector to the East who was debriefed and lived there for two and a half years was Hansjoachim Tiedge. He was head of West German counterintelligence's East German division in Köln, had access to all of West Germany's counterintelligence operations against the East, and specialized in double agents; he defected in August 1985. Tiedge never claimed any high ideological reasons for his defection and admitted he was a traitor, but his personal life was a wreck. He was obese and an alcoholic. His wife had died under mysterious circumstances after a drunken quarrel, and Tiedge was under investigation for murder.

Tiedge simply took the train to Magdeburg and asked to speak to officers from the HV A's counterespionage department; he already knew their first names. He was picked up in a BMW, and the chauffeur drove north, past Berlin, and started to drive past Wandlitz, the famous exclusive forest subdivision for Politburo members. Tiedge began to get excited, because one of his double agents had spoken glowingly of a wonderful safe house there. The driver continued, however, to an even more exclusive area in Prenden, where Markus Wolf also had a country house near a lake. The safe house was code-named "Waldhaus" (forest house) and was used exclusively by the HV A.[74]

Tiedge was awestruck by the house. In his 1998 memoirs he spends pages describing this enchanting place: its location in the middle of a pine forest, the large living room with its comfortable furniture, the study, the bathrooms, and the bedroom upstairs. He describes all the Western entertainment, from a stereo to a VCR, and comments on the wood paneling.[75] Even by 1998, however, he knew nothing of the spy technology hidden behind that splendor.

Tiedge apparently had a mind like a computer. He told the HV A officers about all the double agent operations, including one agent who lived in the East and later died in prison. At the time, he did not know that the HV A already had another mole, Klaus Kuron, from Tiedge's department, who volunteered in 1982 and had already created huge holes in West Germany's operations against the East.[76] Much of Tiedge's information was not new for them, but the fact that the East had a Western defector was a major coup in the Cold War intelligence war.

Tiedge also describes the other nicely furnished and beautifully located safe houses in East Germany from the north to the south. As a Western intelligence officer, he was impressed because West German intelligence and counterintelligence lacked such safe houses. Instead they had to rent hotel rooms in the outskirts of Köln and Munich for debriefing and meetings. The West Germans simply did not have the same access to real estate as the Ministry for State Security. Of course, it was not easy for ordinary East German citizens to live in, maintain, and furnish such beautiful houses. In fact, shortly after the fall of the Wall, word got around that any nice country house must have belonged to the Stasi or Schalck.

There is no doubt that the Stasi's power had increased over the years and with it financial support. In the eyes of state security, the numbers of enemies of the state had mushroomed, and therefore surveillance also appeared to be blanket. But the fact remains that "Big Brother" usually only watched you if they suspected a violation of their restrictive laws. By 1989 the Orwellian "thought police" function of the Stasi had expanded, but so had the power of the people to overthrow it.

II

Big Ears

Major General Horst Männchen's name has become synonymous with the Ministry for State Security's "big ear" – its electronic eavesdropping department. In contrast to his stature within that organization, by the time of his retirement years, the general has become a slight, energetic man with one arm (as a result of an accident). Dark and intense, he is a chain smoker, with a charming, yet down-to-earth manner. During a visit at his posh Berlin-Wilhelmshagen apartment on Lake Dämeritz, typical for Ministry for State Security (MfS) generals, he hacks throughout animated discussions of electronic eavesdropping. He is proud of the successes of his unit during the Cold War, but is equally admiring of the American achievements in technical and electronic intelligence gathering. In fact, it was the Western developments in electronic espionage and electronic warfare that inspired Männchen to develop a new department. He thought everything the West was doing could be reversed and used against them. He had recognized the importance of eavesdropping when he was a young radio operator. The main weakness he noticed was that one could "listen in on everything."[1]

It was only after the fall of the Berlin Wall that Männchen and his empire received any attention as major players in the world of global eavesdropping. Even then, it was the sensation that East Germany had listened in on and recorded embarrassing conversations of Western politicians that came under the glare of public scrutiny, more than the technical accomplishments. Former Western enemies had been as clueless as the public during the Cold War. Even before the veil of secrecy had been stripped from the covert operations of a defunct spy agency, Western espionage agencies had underestimated East Germany's technical capabilities. As a result, electronic technical intelligence gathering became a secret weapon.

Intercepting, listening to, and locating radio communications belongs to radio-electronic *counterintelligence*, and this is where it began, during the 1950s. By contrast, electronic *intelligence gathering* was a "bureaucratic late-bloomer," as CIA historian Benjamin Fischer has noted,[2] and was not institutionalized at the MfS until 1967. Since 1989, attention has been focused only on the intelligence gathering activities of Männchen's empire, while the counterintelligence activities have been ignored.

The radio counterintelligence unit and the intelligence gathering unit merged in 1982, and this also marked a unification of counterintelligence and intelligence under one roof – domains usually kept separate in Western spy agencies. It is not surprising that the MfS was late in establishing a radio-electronic intelligence gathering unit. The East Bloc intelligence style emphasized human intelligence gathering over technical intelligence gathering. It was a style adopted from the Soviet Union. As we saw in earlier chapters, using human sources had high risks: agents get captured and jailed; officers defect and spill the beans. By contrast, technical intelligence has fewer dangers. But it was less the risks of human intelligence than the power of technical intelligence that captured Mänchen's imagination. When the sprawling unit with its nationwide listening posts, mobile units, college, administrative offices, cafeteria, and enormous personnel – more than three thousand staff members – disbanded in 1989, it had kept its secret technical weapon hidden behind the misperceptions of the West during most of the Cold War.

CATCHING RADIO SPIES

Electronic espionage had its origins in World War I and was sparked by scientific and technical developments at the turn of the century. Whereas a number of inventors and scientists contributed to the invention of radio, it was Guglielmo Marconi's work developing wireless telegraphy, tuners and receivers, detectors, and the Marconi stations that launched the wireless age at the turn of the twentieth century.

Very soon after wireless radios were invented, operators discovered that they were not only useful for communicating, but that the signals emitted could be intercepted and located. Operating from a radio intercept truck on 19 August 1914, radio operators in the British Intelligence Service successfully intercepted messages sent by the German Army radio units. Flush with success, the British began to construct and deploy more intercept trucks in the field. This development marked the birth of electronic espionage.[3]

Operators already knew that it was possible to intercept and listen in on a radio communication by tapping into the same frequency, but they also learned how to use radio signals to determine the location of armies, ships, and airplanes in World War I, World War II, and the Cold War. Engineers developed radio direction finders consisting of a radio receiver, loop antenna, and a compass.[4] This simple machinery was at the core of electronic counterintelligence through the end of the Cold War. During the first two world wars, radio direction finders primarily had military applications, although they were occasionally used to unmask spy rings, like the famous Nazi espionage system uncovered by the FBI on the eve of World War II.

During the Cold War, the battle to uncover enemy communications continued, but the arena shifted from military agencies to spy agencies, as the war was not fought on the battlefield but silently through espionage and technology. For the superpowers, targets remained similar – the discovery of the location of armies, ships, missiles, and so on – but on another level a major target became spies communicating through radio, or radio spies.

As we saw in the stories about agents, moles, and defectors, they all needed to communicate with their handlers. Communication, of course, entails much risk. Equipment can be found or messages intercepted and read or the spy located. In fact, spy agencies spend much of their time playing the spy-versus-spy cat-and-mouse game; radio communication is often the weak link used to catch and convict spies. All intelligence agencies have spy catchers and counterintelligence departments devoted to ferreting out spies. During the Cold War, radio was one of the most important communication methods for spies. This was no secret to the Soviets or East Germans or Americans.

Once the Soviets began to allow the East Germans more autonomy in running their own security affairs during the early 1950s, the MfS took over the functions of radio counterintelligence. The MfS's radio department had its beginnings in 1953 as part of a technical unit called S/3, which later developed into the full-fledged Department F (for "*Funk*" or "radio") in 1956. Its primary task was to find and determine the location of spy radio transmissions within the German Democratic Republic (GDR).[5]

Shortly after the 17 June 1953 people's revolt in the GDR, the Ministry for State Security began to hunt actively for those whom they thought were the real men behind the "putsch": "enemy organizations of American and West German secret services." The Ministry of Interior made the GDR's capture of an enormous spy ring in October 1953 public: "Secret radios made in America, weapons, spy material and secret instructions and plans to implement attacks against the GDR population were seized through the arrests in Berlin, Halle, Cottbus, Potsdam and some other places."[6]

They prominently displayed a picture of the small secret spy radio in the propaganda brochure. Each capture of enemy technology increased their knowledge about the level of enemy technology; they often imitated spy devices and displayed them in public. The spy catcher department also collected and catalogued seized enemy technology for evidence and education.

The MfS soon joined the other European socialist countries – the Soviet Union, Czechoslovakia, Hungary, Romania, Bulgaria, and Albania – in an East Bloc alliance for radio counterintelligence, bureaucratically called Coordinating Apparatus. It was officially founded in Prague in 1956 and was located in Warsaw until 1972, when its central location returned to Prague. Romania and Albania soon dropped out, while Yugoslavia aspired to join, and China occasionally took part. Männchen liked to call this organization a "mini-NATO."[7]

The Coordinating Apparatus shared technical knowledge, equipment, and operational knowledge such as the location of directional antennas, as well as cohabitating listening stations, especially on the GDR-Czech border. There was also much cooperation in the education and training of personnel.

1956 was a banner year for the sciences at the MfS, and it also established a civilian institute called the Institute for Technical Developments that made transmitters and receivers for internal use and for the other East Bloc spy agencies. Unlike most of the MfS's installations, this was not a secret place and was even in the phone book. Personnel were mostly officers on a special mission. This meant that they officially worked at a civilian institute but were in fact spies, because the ministry paid part of their salary and pension.[8]

From 1953 until the building of the Wall in 1961, the MfS found two hundred spies on East German territory who transmitted secrets via radio to their handlers in the West. In addition, they determined that another four hundred spies in the GDR and other socialist countries were communicating with central offices in the West with either one- or two-way radios. By 1975 four hundred spies in socialist countries were still communicating with handlers in the West.[9]

Collectively, Männchen's "mini-NATO" learned much about Western agent communication methods and the "imperialist enemy." The East Bloc countries determined that enemy operators almost exclusively used shortwave radio and that transmission was limited to several one-way radio transmissions a year. One-way transmission always occurred from

the central station in the West to the agent in the East in order to communicate instructions. The agent returned the communication through the
mail, a telephone call, or a dead letter box. During the sixties, Western
agencies used burst transmissions to decrease the length of transmitting
time so that it became more difficult for the enemy to intercept the message and locate the spy. During the period of the Cold War, the apparatus
witnessed dramatic improvements in technology as transmission times
decreased to less than one second.[10]

The radio unit operated stationary and mobile vans to observe the
enemies' actions and to catch radio waves in the ether. There were also a
number of radio surveillance stations and radio direction finding stations.
The most important surveillance stations were in Gosen, on the outskirts
of Berlin, and Hohen-Luckow. By 1971 the department had about 705
staff members, and it grew to 1,095 the year before they merged with
radio intelligence gathering.[11]

Radio counterintelligence operators searched the ether for transmissions by manually finding a favorite frequency of the enemy or by using
more scientific methods to tune into the right station. This was part of
radio surveillance. Once a transmission was observed, the next step was
to find its location through direction finding equipment.

Once radio counterintelligence found the radio spies' location, it turned
to its close partner, the spy catchers, to track the spy down. While the
technicians located where the transmissions came from, it was the human
spy catchers' job to "personify" the transmissions by seizing the agent
and finding the evidence to put the spy in jail.[12]

Watching the technical achievements of the enemy spurred the East
Bloc to increase their radio technical capabilities. In 1967 "mini-NATO"
launched a program for "technical reconstruction," code-named "Mineral," that called for developing basic technology to equip all radio counterintelligence services. Over the years several Mineral programs (Mineral
1 to 3) were developed, further improving the technology. The program
was the formal creation of a unified technical system for the East's radio
counterintelligence services. All the members of the alliance were supposed to use the same technology to counteract the unified forces of the
"imperialist secret services." Stationary systems dotted socialist countries,
and mobile stations moved along the borders in specially outfitted vans.[13]

The system of *stationary* technology was designed to determine the
direction of shortwave agent radios on socialist territory and to find
the transmissions of "capitalist secret services." Technically they were
equipped with automated systems for radio surveillance, which could find
and record the radio waves of radio stations in frequencies between 2 and

32 MHz and in AM, FM, and PhM. Their receiver antennas also worked
in the area of 2 to 32 MHz. They planned to develop a stationary system
called "granit," which would automatically fixate, register, and find the
direction of shortwave radio stations with transmissions that lasted two
to three seconds or longer.[14]

The system of *mobile* technology had similar goals, but the mobile
vans searched specific areas to find the location of spy radio stations. The
technology also could search in 2- to 32-MHz frequencies and in AM,
FM, and PhM. They planned to develop a vehicle-automated system for
radio surveillance, reception, and direction finding of short transmissions
in the shortwave area.[15]

In addition to developing technology to find enemy transmissions, the
Coordinating Apparatus spent a considerable amount of time determining what kind of technology the enemy used. The West's technological
achievements in shortening transmission times challenged the East. They
seemed particularly interested in the U.S. – their real technological neme-
sis – use of burst transmission. During the sixties transmission time was
well under a minute and by 1989 the fast, automatic message transmission took less than a millisecond. During the 1950s the West German
intelligence agency (BND) had also already reduced transmission time
to forty-five seconds, using quartz and a cranking device attached to a
mini-transmitter small enough to fit in a cigarette package.[16]

The East Bloc observed that the West always used the most modern
technology, which was small, always ready for deployment, dependable,
and conveyed a lot of information in a short period of time. In fact, 95 percent of all radio traffic from agent to handler used fast, automatic coded
transmissions (burst transmissions).[17]

In 1975 the Soviet Union, with the support of the other East Bloc countries, launched a new research project, code-named "Swesda," to increase
automation for radio surveillance and direction finding. Whereas the system still operated in the 2- to 32-MHz frequency, the idea was to be able to
catch transmissions lasting six to ten seconds. The instruments would have
automatic search and reception of radio transmissions capabilities (code-
named "Pamjat"), two channels for search and direction receiving, and a
magnetic recorder called "Tisa." In many ways, this new automatic system
was a response to analyzing the state of the technology of the enemy.[18]

By the late 1980s, the MfS had trouble keeping up with rapid advances
in Western technology. They only had the ability to observe "antiquated
standard radio transmission methods" and found it difficult to work on
band spreading, frequency jumps, short transmissions, or small band and
extremely weak transmissions. Further, they only worked in frequency

channels and did not observe broadband radio. Automatic signal analysis was limited, and therefore they still needed a large stable of radio
operators.[19]

They did have technical capabilities to work on high-frequency areas
less than 30 MHz and a little in VHF or UHF areas up to 1 GHz; they
had no receivers or direction finders for frequencies above 1 GHz. They
knew that "the enemy" used automatic direction finders and sometimes
commercial technology like that available at the highly regarded West
German electronics firm Rohde & Schwarz; they were particularly interested in the machine PA 2000, which could work on channel times of one
millisecond.[20]

Although MfS radio counterintelligence bragged that they had caught
two hundred spies during the 1950s, it is not clear how many agents they
caught after the building of the Wall. They were successful at finding spy
radio transmissions and had tapped into the BND's Agent Broadcasting
Service. The BND conducted one-way communication – from headquarters to the agent – using a specific frequency and time. Each agent had
a personal frequency number, and the BND would send encrypted radio
messages using the five-number-group method.

The MfS had been hot on Werner Stiller's trail (see Chapter 3) through
its mail intercept and technical departments. Although counterintelligence
had correctly identified the radio number 688, as of August 1978, and
then determined that that number had received fifteen radio messages with
1,841 five-number groups since July 25th, they could not decrypt the messages to find out what they said. This obviously took more skill and time.

The radio spy game soon became a battle between the spies and the
spy catchers. While the West used the most recent scientific and technical
developments to outwit the enemy, the East had to anticipate changes
and act accordingly. It was not just the technical developments that kept
the East on its toes; the other side constantly changed its transmission
frequency and its location and developed shorter transmission times. Over
the years this battle accelerated technological developments for both sides.
The West began to shift from traditional shortwave frequencies to higher
frequencies in the frequency stratosphere of gigacycles, decimeters, and
infrared; the East responded.

WESTERN EAVESDROPPERS

The counterintelligence battles continued steadily throughout the Cold
War. But the flip side of the coin – intelligence gathering – took on a different trajectory. Electronic and radio foreign intelligence gathering started

off slowly but quickly took off. Technologically advanced countries like West Germany and the United States established local and global listening stations and began to rely heavily on technological means for gathering information.

West Germany developed a fledgling electronic-radio intelligence unit in the late 1940s and 1950s. It grew out of American listening stations and influence before the BND was created in 1956 and before West Germany was freed from the yoke of the American-financed Gehlen Organization. Like the East, Western interests began with radio counterintelligence: intercepts, cipher experts, and direction finding. When West German counterintelligence was founded in 1950 in the form of the Federal Office for the Protection of the Constitution (*Bundesamt für Verfassungsschutz* or BfV), the Gehlen Organization relinquished most of its radio counterintelligence efforts to them. Later, other organizations, like the Radio Surveillance Service, took over this function.[21]

The U.S. Army helped the West Germans create their earliest radio-electronic operations in 1945, when the Germans used American equipment for a signals intelligence (SIGINT) operation against Soviet troops in Germany. In 1946 the American Army Counterintelligence Corps (CIC) recruited former German intelligence officers who had worked for Hitler's security organizations and SIGINT specialists from the *Wehrmacht* to develop SIGINT intercept stations for the United States. As early as 1948 the Gehlen Organization's staff moved into Kransberg Castle in Hessen. They quickly constructed a high-frequency direction finding (HFDF) network that zigzagged from the most northern tip of West Germany in Bremen, to Butzbach in the Hessian west, down south to Chiemsee in Bavaria.[22]

Listening posts and intercept stations followed in 1952. One of the first listening posts was established in Tutzing, near Munich, to monitor radio traffic from East Germany. The building was disguised as a commercial company named *Südlabor GmbH*. The U.S. Army opened an intercept station in Lauf an der Pegnitz, on the most eastern part of West Germany, to monitor Czechoslovakian border control traffic and the Czech state security radio networks. Although the Gehlen Organization quickly took control of the station, the United States financed it until 1956.[23]

Even though radio-electronic structures had been developed earlier in the West than in the East, SIGINT still played a backseat role to human intelligence gathering. In 1957, the BND had only two small units – the technology and research department and the telecommunications and radio surveillance unit, Department III. In 1976 SIGINT numbers recorded a small group of 475 staff members. By 1987 SIGINT had assumed greater importance, and Department 2 (technological surveillance) for SIGINT collection and analysis had a staff of about 2,200, which was a large proportion of the total BND staff – 7,500.[24]

The West German Army (*Bundeswehr*) also played a significant role in radio-electronic intelligence and counterintelligence. In the course of the Cold War, there were turf battles between the BND and the *Bundeswehr* for control, but also cooperation. For example, the BND asked the West German Army to develop mobile SIGINT collection units along the East German and Czech borders for monitoring military radio traffic coming from East Germany. Military SIGINT intercept stations did not really blossom until after the Cuban Missile Crisis in 1962. Twenty high-frequency direction finding sites and four new SIGINT battalions were opened. Like the BND stations, these stretched from northern to southern Germany. In the end, the BND gained control over SIGINT operations and even shared them with friendly Western intelligence agencies, although the German Army was responsible for SIGINT against the Soviet and East German armies.[25]

The United States was the undisputed leader in electronic intelligence gathering with the establishment of the National Security Agency (NSA) in 1952. Officially, the NSA is subordinate to the Department of Defense, but it wriggled out of this subjugation early on by emphasizing the word "separately" in its charter: "*separately* organized agency within the Department of Defense." This shift in emphasis from military strategic SIGINT to more civilian tactical SIGINT was symbolized in the modified insignia developed in 1965. Previously the eagle clutching a key (to secrets, presumably) was surrounded by the words "National Security Agency" on the top and "Department of Defense" on the bottom. This bothered NSA director Marshall Carter, and he had a new seal designed with "United States of America" written on the bottom.[26]

West Germany, the United States, and other NATO countries established a chain of radio-electronic intelligence listening posts along the border dividing East and West Germany, between West Germany and Czechoslovakia, and on Austria's borders with Hungary and Czechoslovakia before the MfS.[27] And they had already engaged in electronic warfare against the East Bloc. The development of "physical-technical means" to combat the West was the East's response. More polemically, they viewed the "new and greater tasks" to be taken on by the radio department (F) as the result of the "increased enemy efforts to force electronic warfare and based on the increasingly broad use of radio technology in all areas."

And ideologically they justified their new mission as part of a weapon in the "conflict between imperialism and socialism."[28]

STASI EAVESDROPPERS

When Major Wolfgang Berg joined the Ministry for State Security, he thought his spy activities would involve agents, adventure, and travel. Instead he was assigned to the eavesdropping unit and sent to the Bruno Beater School to learn the skills necessary to listen in on radio transmissions and turn the mass of information into readable dossiers. He learned the "five Golden Ws": Who, What, When, Where, and Why, and he learned patience. The obligatory political education was fostered through a newly created "Tradition Cabinet," an exhibit that paraded the achievements of the great spies in chekist history, such as the postage stamp hero Richard Sorge, who warned Joseph Stalin of Germany's invasion.[29]

Major Berg spent his days with earphones glued to his head, listening to a variety of conversations. He sometimes felt like a Peeping Tom when he heard about private matters such as politicians' extramarital affairs. At least the gossip prevented boredom. Like Markus Wolf's human intelligence collecting department, the eavesdroppers in the ether looked for human weaknesses to exploit. The most promising places to look for weaknesses were in the most intimate areas of life, like sex or money problems and debts or alcohol and drug dependencies or abuses.[30] Whereas sexual deviations could be used for blackmail, money problems provided an opening for recruitment.

Once Major Berg came across an interesting conversation, he notified a transcribing secretary, usually a woman, who was told to type the taped conversation and have it ready in a certain amount of time. The information could be passed on instantly or within twenty-four hours if it was classified as important. As a result, the eavesdroppers thought they could collect a larger quantity of information on people faster than other departments. A flood of information was transcribed and transformed into dossiers. The final reports often obscured the origins of the material and might open with the claim that an agent gathered the information or vaguely state that the information was "operationally collected." Helmut Kohl's file alone contained twenty-five to thirty pages per week, for a total of nine thousand pages between 1982 and 1989.[31]

In 1999 headlines in German newspapers blared the shocking news that Helmut Kohl had engaged in illegal campaign financing. The information had come from intercepts of phone conversations. Although East Germany had this information during the Cold War, they apparently

24. A typical eavesdropper with reel-to-reel tape recorders. (BStU)

did not use it to blackmail officials or to weaken the Kohl government. According to Werner Grossman, the HV A's (foreign intelligence arm of the Ministry for State Security) last head, they "collected the material on finance practices but did not use it for anything.... we kept the small secrets of the CDU to ourselves and never made it known in the West.... we would never have presented it to someone like Erich Honecker." Was this the case or did they overlook this information within the mountain of material the eavesdroppers had collected during the 1970s and 1980s? Reportedly, more than 40,000 Western telephone lines were tapped and 150,000 pages of transcripts produced a year.[32]

Eavesdropping on politicians could provide foreknowledge for future negotiations. The MfS often knew political gossip when it was still limited to two or three people in the chancellor's office. For example, while Manfred Wörner was still head of the Ministry of Defense, Kohl decided that he would offer him the position of secretary general at NATO headquarters in Brussels. The MfS heard this by eavesdropping on a conversation Wörner's wife was having with a close friend. They could not resist noting that the wife was "blond, attractive and natural." The Stasi collected volumes on Wörner's political work and family life.[33]

The eavesdroppers' favorite political target was the federal election candidates. They collected millions of pages of information on them. The facts and data would have been valuable to the rival candidates. They could easily uncover an affair, make it public, and ruin the opponent's chances. In 1990 *Quick* magazine thought the Eastern PDS Party (Democratic Socialist Party) would have an advantage in the 1990 elections because they could have access to the Stasi's information on the Western party candidates. If they did, it did not help the fledgling party.[34]

Tapping Bonn politicians' telephones was just one piece of the information gathering pie, but it looms large in the public imagination. Monitoring and breaking into the West German security and intelligence services communication channels and securing agent networks in the West German area of operations were of equal importance. So-called enemies of the state were monitored, but a larger target was the so-called people-smuggling groups, rather than dissidents who had emigrated or those still in the country.

The politicians were easy prey. The suffered from "telephonitis" and used mobile telephones that were easy to eavesdrop on. Their spy adversaries were more reticent on the phone, but the eavesdroppers still succeeded in listening to many high-ranking intelligence officials, including two presidents of the BND, Klaus Kinkel and Hans-Georg Wieck. Their conversations were secured by the Elecrovox security system, but the MfS could read the theoretically secure Elecrotel telegram system.[35]

The Stasi knew that Kinkel was a candidate for the intelligence czar position in the chancellor's office. When Kinkel visited a BND regional office in Düsseldorf in July 1981, they read his positive report. Not only did they have telephone numbers, they had safe combinations. They found the report in the regional office head's safe; it is not clear how they acquired the safe number. Perhaps there was a mole in that same office. They knew the names, telephone numbers, home addresses, and auto license plates of all the BND staff members.[36]

The Stasi found that the Düsseldorf office head had notable weaknesses, for example, he had an affair with his close co-worker, even though he was married; he also lived beyond his means. They had a difficult time pinpointing possible shortcomings in Klaus Kinkel, who they had under blanket surveillance. They could not find any "special interests, passions or hobbies" but noted that he "loved working" and doted on his dog.[37]

Aside from trying to ferret out compromising material on leading intelligence officials, the Stasi collected reams of seemingly random details. They knew the time and place of a resident meeting in Munich and of a meeting with a liaison spy agency and details of the BND's mobile observation groups' activities.[38]

The armaments industry was another favorite target. The SWT already had many well-placed agents at the Munich armaments firm MBB (*Messerschmidt-Bölkow-Blohm*), while the electronic eavesdroppers spied on the company bosses. They collected details on their private lives and business intrigues and developed detailed profiles of them by listening in on their telephone conversations or intercepting faxes and doing the same with the communication channels of everyone in their circle of colleagues and friends. They knew about the MBB's reorganization in 1987 and the interpersonal intrigues accompanying the discussions on a new helicopter and the MBB production site for the airbus. No details were spared. By reading the reports, one can find out that the MBB company vice president thought he was "overweight for his age."[39] The profiles alone provide useful reference materials on each person's personal and professional contacts and stature within the community. They were a kind of Who's Who in industry for secret purposes.

The Stasi eavesdroppers often come across as the Oprahs of the spy world when they describe the conflicts among the managers, sex lives, money problems, and other juicy gossip. Imagine spending the day eavesdropping on a manager's telephone conversations. For example, the head of the Munich Mercedes Auto Company talked to an official in the Bavarian government about an FDP politician who "needs a well-paid position so he will not become a criminal" and noted that "he told me that he is over his ears in debt... he said, Karl, I can't stand it anymore.... His wife is cleaning him out." The politician received a well-paying job.[40]

Even juicier were intimate details of a Siemen's manager's extramarital affair with a married woman: "He and his intimate partner are keeping their intimate relationship secret. He picks up his mail at the post office. They are both very jealous of each other. He suggested opening a joint bank account so they could finance business deals together."[41]

Männchen's empire did not limit itself to conquering West Germany. The Soviet Union thought so highly of East Germany's capabilities that they considered the MfS's "special radio services" to be the only other worthy SIGINT effort in the East Bloc and asked them to cover Western Europe as well; the Soviet Union blanketed the rest of the globe. The Soviets had also encouraged Männchen to launch his eavesdropping effort in Cuba, which ultimately benefited both Cuba and the East with knowledge procured from the United States.

Whereas the ministry had a vigorous and well-stocked radio counterintelligence operation by the 1960s, it lacked an electronic-radio intelligence gathering and electronic warfare unit. It was not until the late

1960s that Mielke's first deputy, Bruno Beater, enthusiastically promoted and supported the development of electronic intelligence. In 1966 Horst Männchen was asked to organize a group to develop intercept and listening stations along the inner German border aimed at monitoring and collecting information from West Germany.

According to Horst Männchen, Mielke was not particularly interested in technical intelligence; he demanded a lot of information, and he did not care how it was acquired: "whether it was with a fishnet" or more professionally did not matter. Markus Wolf was slow to accept technical intelligence gathering: he initially preferred "spending the money on recruiting more spies," but this attitude changed later.[42]

Surprisingly, Männchen's career does not fit a typical Stasi trajectory. He joined the ministry in 1953 at the unusually young age of eighteen as a radio operator in Department S, but only joined the party in 1957 and failed to conform to the Stasi's conservative moral vision.[43]

His abilities were recognized but he allegedly suffered from "moral weaknesses" and "arrogance." When he was young he had extramarital relationships and drank. He was dismissed from the MfS in 1961 for violating "socialist ethics and morality." He was then demoted to the status of an informal staff member between 1961 and 1963. It is not clear where he worked, but he apparently fulfilled his assignments with great élan and contributed to developing "operational radio services." The ministry made sure that his "moral weaknesses" did not reappear and thought that he had learned from his mistake when he was reinstated in 1963. They felt he was still a bit arrogant and therefore judged things prematurely, but they thought through education these faults could be quickly overcome. In spite of the existing weaknesses, they justified the reinstatement as long as he was under "strict control." In 1963 Männchen began a degree for radio building; in 1965 he completed the degree in high-frequency radio technology. This time the HV A rehabilitated him by letting him join its technical department (VIII), where he tested "special apparatus for the operational radio services" and controlled the efficiency of radio communications. Markus Wolf – someone who also had a weakness for women – approved the reinstatement.[44]

Männchen's career quickly took off after joining the HV A. His evaluations were glowing, he was given the new task of building up radio intelligence, and he collected a long list of honors and awards. The youthful problems never resurfaced.

With his new mission Männchen quickly began searching for qualified personnel to man an electronic-radio intelligence outfit. One rich recruitment pool was the department that worked with and worked on the army. The army needed noncommissioned officers and sergeants with Morse code and shortwave radio training and officers with training as radio operators, in directional radio, as radio measuring specialists, and so on. Once officers with this training left the army, the MfS directed them into their new outfit. In short, his new department needed technically qualified personnel. Department III was officially founded on 26 June 1971 with 187 staff members.[45]

It quickly grew into one of the ministry's largest departments. Within ten years personnel had mushroomed to 1,808 and by the time it merged with radio counterintelligence (Department F) in 1983, the figure was 1,909 without the regional offices. Not only was there an increase in personnel, but the merger also reportedly brought in a 183 percent increase in information.[46] By 1989 it was the biggest MfS unit, with twenty-five departments divided into the five areas of intelligence gathering, evaluation, counterintelligence, technology, and the service department and 2,979 staff members (some estimates are as high as 4,000).[47]

But all these people were not just eavesdropping. The unit had become such an important, independent, and wealthy entity in the bureaucracy that it even had its own large service department and cafeteria, which other departments also used. Bloating the personnel numbers were an inordinate number of soldiers – eight hundred to a thousand – serving as guards and security personnel for the numerous buildings and intercept stations along the border. The central building in Berlin-Wühlheide housed about five hundred to seven hundred workers, and radio counterintelligence's installation in Gosen housed about seven hundred. After the fall of the Berlin Wall, the Gosen installation turned into a shopping center with no signs of its earlier activities.

The MfS leadership looked favorably upon Männchen's projects and richly supported them financially and with the necessary buildings. Männchen quickly occupied the Ministry for Science and Technology building complex in Wühlheide, which consisted of four main buildings and a multipurpose structure. This offered a good cover story, and the building project was presented as the Ministry for Science and Technology's Institute for Technical Developments, even though it no longer owned the complex. By January 1972, the MfS had built an addition and integrated it with the old ministry buildings. They mounted a tower on the multipurpose building and added energy and heating equipment. Telephone lines and data processing capabilities already existed, as the MfS data processing group worked there. Männchen estimated that completion of the project, including furniture, would run about 2.5 million marks.[48]

The cover designation for the building project within the MfS was "W 72," and everyone was urged to maintain strict secrecy and the cover story. The "unplanned sum" beyond the ordinary budget had already been recommended by Männchen's patron, Bruno Beater, and was kept in a special account.[49]

Männchen's unit was not the first to sprout electronic ears along the East German border. Like other countries, military reconnaissance units had largely conducted this activity. The National People's Army (NVA) and its one thousand–man-strong military intelligence arm, the Administration for Reconnaissance (*Verwaltung Aufklärung*), reportedly controlled four hundred NATO institutions' radio signals around the clock during the 1980s. Both Germanies shared their tradition of using the post office for electronic intelligence.[50]

Officially the radio-electronic intelligence unit had the goal of conducting electronic warfare; in fact, it concentrated on information gathering. By contrast, military intelligence did conduct electronic warfare and cooperated to a certain extent with the MfS. There were no turf battles here, and military intelligence ceded to its alter ego: the "special radio services of the MfS plays a leading role in information gathering in the present state of peacetime" though it was not clear what role they would play in case of war. Because the MfS had few electronic warfare capabilities, it used the "power of the National People's Army radio counter-measures," such as jamming, paralyzing, and suppressing, when they were available.[51]

One of the justifications for adding another electronic intelligence gathering arsenal to the existing one was that the "imperialist enemy" had such capabilities and used the results of modern science and technology to enhance its electronic warfare against the communist countries.[52]

The MfS often used the army as a cover story for their installations or missions, as was the case with the intercept stations that sprung up along the inner German border. One of Männchen's first operations in Czechoslovakia in 1972 was to establish listening capabilities along the Czech and West German border, and this involved obtaining army uniforms, cots, and other set-up equipment. The Czech listening post was just one of seventy-three listening posts that dotted the Eastern side of the East-West divide. By the time Männchen had set up his side in the late sixties, the border was lined with complementary base pairs, as the West had had theirs in place since the 1940s.

Superimposing the East and West listening posts on a German map creates an image of dueling listening stations. Opposing eavesdroppers

25. The "Stasi Mosque" on Brocken Mountain. Brocken Mountain was on the border between East and West Germany. The square structure on the right was dubbed the "Stasi Mosque." (Cornelia Kreis)

sometimes even occupied the same mountain regions. All of the major Cold War eavesdroppers had installations in the Harz mountain region, because part of the mountains was in the East and part in the West. The legendary Brocken Mountain was the highest mountain in central Germany, rising to 1,142 meters. By the year 2000, few Stasi archeological remnants existed on the mountain range. A mini-railway station that was used first by the Soviets and then the East German military was still in use, and at the plateau on the top of the mountain a TV antenna mast and a square building with a golf-ball white radome are still visible. This building had belonged to the Stasi between 1986 and 1989 and was dubbed the "Stasi Mosque" by demonstrators who stormed the previously walled-off military zone in December 1989. Its radome was one of seven that occupied the mountain-top plateau during the late 1980s.[53]

The Stasi Mosque listening post – so called because of the white cupola on top of the three-story-high square building – was reportedly built with the help of the film studio in Babelsberg. The dome was built out of fiber-optic fortified polyester resin.[54] Like all radar domes, it was transparent to radio waves. Very little remains of the Stasi's technological machinery, most of it, the best communication equipment, was bought or stolen by the West. Instead the museum that is currently housed there concentrates

on the legends surrounding the mountain, around the witch and devil lore
from the Middle Ages. Remnants of the wall that surrounded the region
and barbed wire dominate the exhibit. The most interesting items left
behind are in the dome itself – a very large cavernous area. Umbrella-like
radars, antennas, and other equipment were still left lying there in the year
2000, like at a garbage dump. The technology used at the Brocken encompassed antennas, parabolic mirrors, amplifiers, tape recorders, computer
technology, and information transfer technology.

The U.S. army occupied the mountain in 1945 but soon relinquished it
to the Red Army when border demarcations were reevaluated. When the
Berlin Wall was built in August 1961, the border area was closed to outsiders and became a military security zone. The Soviets continued to use
mobile units and maintained one building with a radome during the Cold
War, whereas the Stasi had a number of installations, including a directional radio antenna and the mosque. They code-named the site "Urian"
after the devil that reportedly occupied the mountain and stationed
between twenty-one to twenty-six eavesdroppers there, who worked in
three around-the-clock shifts. They spied on the West German military,
spy agencies, and the military-industrial complex. One of the most important Stasi stations, it used directional radio to target the radio lines to
Berlin as well as the north-south axis between Hamburg and Munich
or Berlin.

THE TECHNOLOGICAL SYSTEM

Once personnel were recruited and facilities built, Männchen's goals could
be refined and the technology to achieve them developed. The stated purpose of electronic intelligence gathering was to recognize a "military surprise" attack or plan. The main consumers of the SIGINT product were
the party and state leadership and foreign intelligence (the HV A). Counterintelligence and the MfS army unit followed. The eavesdroppers provided them with material in three main areas: collection of political, economic, and military information from the powerful and influential in the
West; protection of agent networks in the West by keeping enemy activity
under surveillance; and, finally, monitoring of political dissidents.[55]

The MfS's own Institute for Technical Developments and the Technical Operations Sector (OTS), sometimes working together with industry, produced most of the technology needed for electronic intelligence
gathering. OTS worked closely with the eavesdroppers on developing a
voice recognition system. What they did not make themselves they bought

commercially, and what they could not buy legally they stole from the West. Männchen's own assessment of their technology was that it "wouldn't win a designer prize," but it did the job.[56]

Technology was developed to penetrate the public and secure communication channels, networks, and systems of "the enemy." This involved capturing signals and selectively surveilling operational targets. At the heart of the system lay technology to select telephone numbers – the "call selection equipment." Computers were used to process signals for selection and for automation. Large reel-to-reel tape recorders and storage technology captured voice and digital signals, and decoder technology read the coded information.[57]

By the early 1980s the MfS could identify phone numbers from electrical impulses generated as the number was dialed, using special antennas and receivers. The numbers were kept in a database; 30,000 to 40,000 phones were targeted on a continuous basis. Real-time analysis allowed conversations to be monitored and recorded immediately. The 73 intercept stations at the border could monitor 63,000 channels.[58] Each intercept station had the TA-500 machine system developed by the Institute for Technical Developments, which consisted of antennas, an amplifier, a receiver, selectors, and tape recorders to catch the signals passing through East Germany.

Technicians worked on intercepting landline communications as well as wireless mobile phones, directional radio transmissions, and satellite. Most transmissions in West Germany were conducted through cable, directional radio, or satellite. Their easiest targets were parasitic signals that reached home territory. It was more difficult for them to capture signals in the Federal Republic of Germany (FRG), unless they used the stations at the East German embassies. The technology to intercept mobile phone calls was satisfactory, according to a 1988 assessment of current and future technological needs. In general, the MfS estimated that the socialist technological communications industry was fifteen years behind general technological trends in the leading industrialized nations and that the MfS could not rely on industry to meet their needs. They saw an increasing trend toward digitalization and could not keep up. Whereas their technology could select for specific phone numbers, it could not search for concepts or words, as could leading Western technology at the NSA.[59]

Almost half of all intercepted signals came from the West German Post Office's directional radio transmissions. With this system, a connection is made between a transmission antenna and a receiver antenna, often within sight. The signal can be digital or analogue and is transferred through a carrier frequency. Most of these signals passed through the territory of East Germany between West Germany and West Berlin. The MfS had monitored this traffic at its border intercept stations since the mid-sixties.

The MfS had thorough command of connecting to and processing signals and of selecting with analogue landline communication channels and with mobile telephones. In 1988 they still had not achieved command of connecting to and processing signals and of selecting with digital schemes like PCM (pulse code modulation) and light conducting transmissions with very fast transmission times.[60]

Digitalization brought faster transmission times (up to 2.24 Gbits per second) and higher frequencies (up to 300 GHz) in directional radio transmissions. The MfS's key directional radio transmissions could only work in frequencies up to 5 GHz.[61]

Surprisingly, the control card system for processing target requests was not computerized but was a manual, decentralized card file system. If a consumer had a request, they filled out a target control card. Once the request was processed, the information was entered on the card. For example, it was recorded on the card that a certain mobile phone number for an operation had been tapped and monitored for a period of time and transcripts made of the conversations.[62]

As the MfS increasingly fell behind the West in its radio technology, it turned to the HV A's SWT department to steal the technology from the West. Its efforts are very similar to the case of the computer industry as it became increasingly dependent on the West for leading technology. For example, in 1987 the SWT offered Männchen a light wave transmission system produced by Siemens, which was strictly embargoed. With this machine it would be possible to monitor three traffic directions instead of the one that would have been possible if the Institute for Radio Technology developed the technology. The machine cost more than half a million West German marks, and Männchen thought the technology was so important that he convinced one of Mielke's deputies to provide special funds for it. Finance chief Henning was informed.[63]

The most spectacular project, launched on the eve of the fall of the Berlin Wall, was code-named "Saphir A/2" and was designed to use the new fiber-optic cable the West German Post Office and Communications Ministry built between West Germany and West Berlin with the permission of the GDR in 1986. The treaty between the East and the West German Post Office and Communications Ministries made a provision that repairs would only be conducted by the West to prevent planting listening devices.[64]

The MfS saw this cable as a great opportunity to create a new information source. Instead of tapping the line, they attached their own cable, located near one of their intercept stations in Potsdam named "Source I" (*Quelle I*). The project cost 8.3 million East German marks and 3 million West German marks. A million marks were needed to buy thirty kilometers of fiber-optic cable, which was strictly embargoed. They also needed to acquire several digital PCM machines. Technicians then attached this cable to the main cable at a signal-regeneration site. The cable went into commission in June 1987; by October 1989, the MfS could intercept about 6,000 of the 76,800 channels and monitor phone calls, faxes, and data transmissions.[65]

SPIES IN THE WEST

Whereas radio counterintelligence focused on capturing enemy agents, radio foreign intelligence gathering concentrated on penetrating the whole communication system of enemy spy agencies and breaking into their "secure" systems. They also spent quite a bit of energy on securing their own agent networks in the West and launched a number of successful operations against West Germany during the 1980s.

"Rubin," the code name of the listening post built in Czechoslovakia in 1972, provided blanket coverage of observation and radio activity of all the intelligence and security agencies in Bavaria. The knowledge provided the East with a deeper understanding of Western police agencies and the BND. They could protect their agents and find references for attempted recruitments. They even had information on leading personnel at the BND, like presidents Hans-Georg Wieck and Klaus Kinkel, Vice President Norbert Klusac, and others. In 1985 they succeeded in penetrating a BND object code-named "Torfmoos" and found leads on other objects and people at the BND.[66]

The eavesdroppers had already begun to collect data on West German intelligence agencies and internal security organizations in the 1970s. They had accumulated so much information on people and topics that they began a data processing project called "West Investigations" in 1980 that stored information on 200,000 people, 30,000 vehicles, and 1,000 objects of interest. The information was primarily passed on to the HV A and used to protect and support agents in the West. In fact, the lion's share of information was about spy agencies, followed by information on the military, politics, diplomacy, journalism, and economy.[67]

By the 1980s radio intelligence supported the HV A's agents in the West by securing their meetings with couriers and instructors or monitoring the West's observation team radio communications. This operation was run under the code name "Protection" and served to provide a kind of invisible electronic umbrella when agents were servicing a dead drop or around the meet area. They were able to follow the West German counterintelligence agency's radio message traffic and to spot observation vehicles. In 1987 alone there were 263 requests to provide this invisible protection.[68]

The eavesdroppers also gained access to West German security databases. The project code-named "Access" began in 1982. By 1984 there had been 1,255 connections made into West Germany and 52 missions. They were able to identify twelve agents and sixty target and contact people. The operation also helped to improve information collection, dossiers, reports, and analysis by providing more material.[69]

Perhaps one of the eavesdroppers' greatest coups was breaking into the highly secure Western voice scrambling machine Vericrypt. When West German counterintelligence started to use Vericrypt in the late seventies, Männchen thought they might lose the ability to hear Western radio messages. The HV A provided their eavesdropper colleagues with some information about Western intelligence's use of the machines and message traffic so they could be prepared. By June 1982, they had acquired the embargoed Western Vericrypt 1100 security machine at a cost of 60,000 Swiss Franks (29,500 USD) through an agent. The West did everything possible to maintain secrecy and never found out that their adversaries had acquired the machine. It automatically coded mobile radio conversations in vehicles and was used by all West German intelligence and security agencies. Both the eavesdroppers and the codes and ciphers department had tried to break into it, without success, for three years. But once the machine was acquired, their luck began to change.[70]

Working together with the codes and ciphers department, the eavesdroppers planned to reverse engineer the machine. They examined it carefully, and the codes and ciphers department reconstructed the key. The group working on this project got even luckier when they were able to intercept two enemy radio messages in which the daily key had not been changed. Once they knew the key setting, it was easy for the codes and ciphers department to begin to reconstruct it. They began to work closely with the Soviet codes and ciphers group, which speeded up the process, and broke into the highly secure Vericrypt machine by November 1982. They quickly copied the machine and began to use it at the border listening posts.[71]

The eavesdroppers were also successful at deciphering some of the BND's radio messages. In 1984 they listened in on a secret plan, code-named "Stay-Behind," to develop so-called overrun agents in case there was a military conflict between NATO and the Warsaw Pact countries. If the Warsaw Pact invaded, the plan was to let them in – "run over" the territory – and fight them in a subversive way using intelligence. There were approximately eighty overrun agents, who were FRG citizens living along the border. The agents used both one-way and two-way radio communication, and counterintelligence planned to keep them "under control" by deciphering the radio messages.[72]

When Hans-Joachim Tiedge, director of the GDR counterintelligence department at the BfV, defected to the East in 1985, this created another windfall. Not only was Tiedge a major intelligence coup for counterintelligence, but the eavesdroppers rubbed their hands with glee as they took advantage of the "insecure and hectic situation." Männchen predicted it would lead to "increased communication" that in turn would produce more information for them during this period of "damage control" and "massive activities." He was interested in finding out what kinds of measures were introduced, who was involved, and where they were planned. He instructed his staff to "carefully determine every change" in the FRG's security system and to analyze them.[73]

The MfS's reach extended to other spy agencies as well. They worked on the British Observation Services in West Berlin in a project code-named "Charly," which had been in place since 1979, and successfully cracked the British West Berlin cipher. Because the British targeted Soviet people and institutions, their East German counterparts often passed on information to their "friends."[74] Männchen also shared with the Soviet Union copious information on U.S. citizens in Germany and West Germans at embassies abroad in the form of dossiers. He was even considering extending his reach to Washington, DC, in 1985 by conducting an "exploratory radio mission" to investigate the "ether situation" there.[75]

It is not clear if a SIGINT station was set up in Washington, but the eavesdroppers did work together with the HV A abroad, especially at the GDR missions in West Germany. An important base was Steering 1 at the GDR mission in Bonn. It was about thirty square meters and had thirty-five tape recorders and thirty-two receivers, which were always on.

The HV A also had four square meters worth of similar technology. From this Bonn base, East German spies could monitor West German counterintelligence in Cologne, the BND, and West German military intelligence.[76]

DEMYSTIFYING DEVIL'S MOUNTAIN

Some of the most important American SIGINT installations were located in the Ministry for State Security's backyard – West Berlin. It was difficult to hide their existence. Antennas, radomes, and big buildings gave the secret away. The eavesdroppers had known about all three of the U.S. outposts – *Teufelsberg* (Devil's Mountain), Marienfelde, and Tempelhof – since the early sixties, and they had developed photographic documentation of their exterior existence since 1962. They also knew about the British in Gatow and the French at Tegel Airport, but they concentrated on the U.S. presence. It was not until the 1980s that they gained more knowledge about their tasks and capabilities.[77]

The eavesdropper group charted external physical changes and additions when they photographically monitored the development of all three installations in the course of the Cold War. When they first observed Devil's Mountain in 1962, they saw barracks, a metal lattice mast with antennas, and three dish antennas. Between 1968 and 1974 there were extensive renovations and expansions. By 1979 they had pictures of a main building with three radomes, a new antenna mast, and an arctic tower with a radome. They learned a lot about their technical capabilities through visual analysis of the antennas. They knew the size and capabilities of the dish antennas, which ranged from ten to twelve meters and had remote-controlled 360 degree turning capabilities for frequencies in the GHz range and were hidden under radomes.[78]

By 1984 the eavesdropping group seemed to have quite detailed knowledge of the goals and tasks of Devil's Mountain. They knew that the facility was run by the NSA and monitored the communication networks of the East German and Soviet armed forces in East Germany and that they passed on warnings about activities in the Warsaw Pact territories to U.S. political and military leaders. They also knew the limits of how far into the East Bloc this ear could hear – its listening capacity only reached as far as Poland.

The Marienfelde Air Force installation housed the 6912th Electronic Security Group. Visually the buildings and eavesdropping equipment looked more extensive than Devil's Mountain's. Judging from the observed antennas and equipment, the group assumed that the facility had total surveillance coverage of all signal emanations for most of East Germany, Poland, and Czechoslovakia. They had detailed knowledge of what the technology could monitor, knew that the U.S. covered the Warsaw pact air force, and found that the Marienfelde installation could monitor the radio and data transfer systems of the Soviet tropospheric connection.[79]

The eavesdroppers' knowledge of U.S. SIGINT operations in Germany expanded considerably with the recruitment of James Hall in 1983 by the HV A and with Jeffrey Carney's defection in 1985. But it was not until 1985 that the HV A shared some of the information passed on by Hall with Männchen. Markus Wolf sent him thirteen top-secret documents, including six general directives on SIGINT, five documents about U.S. results of reconnaissance on the Soviet Armed Forces, and two documents on the U.S. bases in West Berlin.[80]

The most explosive document was about the Canopy Wing project, the INSCOM analysis of attack possibilities against Soviet strategic high-frequency communications. The idea was to cut off these strategic communications, which were very important for the Soviet Union in securing its troops. The conclusion was that by using weapons, agents of electronic means, they could cut off three-quarters of high-frequency communications and immobilize the Soviet system.[81]

Männchen was in awe of American technical capabilities. His judgment was that Americans were "in love with technology."[82] In 1985 Männchen and his staff discovered another American project – this time on East German soil. They found a sensor as big as a shoebox near a military installation, which they code-named system "Bowling Pin." This was the first time that a sensor system was discovered in the GDR. It consisted of two seismic sensors, a round metal compact body, a long-lasting battery, and a small antenna system. It was buried 30 cm into the earth and only the antenna appeared above ground. It registered every truck that passed and could distinguish between military and non-military vehicles. It would have been impossible to detect it using normal radio counterintelligence search methods. Männchen found the U.S.'s and NATO's increased use of such military-use sensors disturbing, because they were developed in a time of peace. His evaluation was that the sensors "reflected very sophisticated science and technology."[83]

Scientists determined that all of the sensors had been assigned the same frequency, and by disabling that frequency they could intercept the transmissions being sent to the spy satellites. Former CIA officers claim that a German double agent betrayed the sensor, but Männchen insisted that they found it through a tip the Cubans gave them about irregularities in satellite communications.[84]

OPERATION "ROYAL PALM"

The Ministry for State Security–Cuba relationship in electronic intelligence seemed mutually beneficial from its inception in 1982. Mielke had called Cuba "a light house in America with socialist light."[85] With SIG-INT it was possible for the Soviet Union and the East Bloc to easily peer into U.S. operations in Cuba and acquire information about America from Cuba.

Surprisingly, it was the Cubans who provided the East Germans with the first operationally interesting material. Before any official agreements had been developed, Cuban officials visited Erich Mielke at the end of 1982 and passed on information about the CIA's satellite agent-to-headquarters radio communication method. Both countries had little knowledge of, and experience using, satellite technology. In particular, this was totally new knowledge in the area of agent communication used by the "imperialist secret services." The CIA's new agent communication method was technically very sophisticated and advanced, using the military MARISAT satellite. It could pass coded spy messages with "great security and speed (1024 bits/sec)." The eavesdroppers quickly dubbed this CIA system "Pyramid."[86]

In exchange for the information, the Cubans asked Mielke to send GDR specialists to Cuba to explain the agent communication system in more detail. The Soviets encouraged Männchen to take the Cuban's invitation for mutual exchange in the area of radio-electronic espionage. This would be an opportunity for the East Germans to study the CIA's communication system. However, the Soviets warned Männchen that the U.S. code system was "so secure" that it would be impossible to "break it," and they should not bother trying.[87]

The Cubans had shared the satellite information with the Soviet Union as well, and it inspired both East Germany and the Soviet Union to develop their own satellite systems. The East German satellite installation was in Biesenthal, and they quickly set up a working group called "Pyramid" to receive satellite signals. The Soviets' technology to control satellite channels was almost identical.[88]

It was the explosive CIA agent communication information that led to an official bilateral exchange between the Cuban Ministry of Interior and the East German Ministry for State Security on "specific questions of electronic warfare" in 1983. Other areas were also covered, such as radio counterintelligence, decoding, and electronic intelligence. The two agencies agreed upon mutual exchange of technology such as receivers, transmitters, and direction finding technology. The official exchange led to working visits in Berlin and Havana and swapping of materials and personnel.[89]

The eavesdropping specialists who had visited Cuba quickly hatched a bilateral operation, code-named "Royal Palm," in November 1984 to spy on the United States naval base in Guantánamo. The Cubans appeared to have no knowledge about SIGINT at the naval base and thought if they pooled their resources, they could learn more. The eavesdroppers expected to find a radio-electronic setup similar to that in West Berlin.[90]

The goal of the operation was to obtain "complete reconnaissance of the ether situation at the U.S. naval base" and to determine "possibilities for information gathering from radio-electronic sources." They hoped this would contribute to their system of "instant information gathering." They also wanted to find out if they could listen in on other radio communications in the Caribbean. This was a bilateral operation because the idea was to provide the Cubans with preconditions for a "permanent information" flow, while fulfilling Soviet and German information needs.[91]

Staff and financial resources were quickly mobilized. Männchen planned on sending seven to eight eavesdroppers to Cuba, and the Cubans were to provide fifteen to twenty specialists. Major Fritz Gregor, an analyst and English and Russian translator, headed up the East German team. They gathered SIGINT equipment valued at 8 million marks and prepared it to be shipped to Cuba on a freighter loaded with a Russian military truck and two five-ton trailers and a container. Not only was the nature of the material to be kept secret from the Cubans, but it was to be returned to East Germany after the two-month operation. They planned on sending the loaded ship at the end of January or the beginning of February 1984.[92]

A container ship ended up leaving the port of Rostock in March 1985, accompanied by two staff members. The cover story was that it was transporting "geological materials." The rest of the group flew to Havana on 16 March 1985 to receive the ship and set up. Operation "Royal Palm" was initially planned as a two-month operation but was extended to August 1985.[93]

"Royal Palm" seemed to be a great success, and the results had "extraordinary operational value: indispensable strategic and operational-tactical information from the U.S. base became known." It was then possible for the Cubans to keep the whole "targeted object" under "radio control."

They focused their information gathering on all military movements in Guantánamo, including air and sea transport as well as unusual movements in the whole Caribbean, so that deviations from normal activity could be monitored. They gained information on anti-Cuban groups (exiles) and U.S. personnel leaders in civilian, military, and intelligence. As was the case for the target West Germany, the eavesdroppers found communication at Guantánamo to be an open book, for they did not seem to know that they were being spied on through radio-electronic means.[94]

In gratitude for operation "Royal Palm," the Cubans gave East Germany the blueprints to build a ten-meter parabolic satellite dish in 1985. The actual building of this parabolic mirror was a great technological coup for the GDR.

It was impressive that the Ministry for State Security's reach extended as far as Cuba, given the size of East Germany. Whereas East Germany's chief target was West Germany, it was capable of helping its East Bloc allies as they fought the "imperialists" abroad and extended communist influence. Clearly, the eavesdroppers' main focus was not dissidents; instead they took part in the worldwide espionage game of spy-versus-spy and targeted their counterparts in the West. It was a real surprise to unsuspecting politicians when they found out so many of their conversations had been recorded.

Männchen was in awe of the U.S. technological capabilities and thought that the power of technology could be used against the enemy as well. Technical collection may have fewer human risks, but it could also vacuum in a lot more information. During the early years, middle-range technology could effectively cover the needs of their operations. By the late eighties, with the dawning of the digital age, East Germany became increasingly dependent on Western technology and had to import it illegally. Even so, its successes during the eighties are in part due to the West's underestimation of its technical capacity. Regardless of the information gathering successes, the amount of information collected was staggering and too much for analysts to evaluate and certainly more than policy makers could digest.

12

Smell Science

After the fall of the Berlin Wall it became one of the most iconic images of
Stasi perversity: rows of shelves stacked with jam jars stuffed with yellow
dust cloths. The media frequently scanned their cameras past these stuffed
jam jars when they aired shows on the Stasi to display the seemingly
bizarre method used by the secret police to keep track of dissidents –
by vacuum packing their smell in an airtight container. Like other Stasi
techniques, smell science has a history rooted in criminalistics and the
police, and, like the other methods, secrecy was paramount.

During the chaotic days of rage after the fall of the Berlin Wall, a myth,
not grounded in the facts, developed on the topic of the jam jars. That
myth began when Leipzig dissidents opened the door of a storage room
at a local Stasi district office. Their eyes widened when they saw rows and
rows of glass jars with yellow dust cloths in them. These dusters were used
to wipe a surface or person to capture their smell. This was in December
1989. By June 1990 they found the same jars, empty, at the smell storage
facility of the local police's service dog station. The explanation was that
the police wanted to use the jars for other purposes. Despite the removal
of the yellow smell-impregnated dust cloths, dissidents could determine
that the Stasi had a "complete smell collection of the Leipzig opposition,"
because the labels with names still remained.[1] So began the origin of the
myth and image of the dust-cloth-stuffed jam jars.

POLICE DOGS

Reportedly, dogs have been used for tracking ever since the days of the
ancient Greeks. Police dogs also go way back in history, starting as com-
panions to the night watchman and evolving into the working police dogs
used today in law enforcement. Thousands of dogs are on duty every day.

26. The Stasi's smell collection: smell-impregnated dust clothes stored in glass jars. The yellow dust cloths stuffed in jam jars became synonymous with Stasi perversity. However, the police had been using the science of smell to track criminals for many years before. (Kristie Macrakis)

Police dogs began to be part of institutionalized European police departments in the late nineteenth century to aid them in their work. Belgium and Germany took the lead at the turn of the twentieth century in training and using dogs as detectives to investigate criminal cases. The Belgian shepherd, especially the malinois, and the German shepherd were trained for protection and nose work.[2] The United States police forces were slower to use and train service dogs and still import trained police dogs from Germany and other European countries for their K-9 units.

It is less the intimidating bark and more the dog's extremely sensitive nose that police are interested in. A dog's sense of smell is reportedly fifty to one thousand times more sensitive than a human's; some put this figure as high as a million.[3] As a result they are used for search and rescue and tracking. Trained dogs track criminals or missing persons, search buildings, and sniff out drugs, bombs, and suspects.

East Germany's Ministry for the Interior ran a large service dog training school in Pretzsch, a small town northeast of Leipzig, and all police dog training was centralized there. It gained quite a good reputation for dog training, and, after the collapse of communism, police from countries abroad, such as Norway, sent handlers and dogs there for training.

The special school in Pretzsch for police dogs was no secret. In 1983 the *Berliner Zeitung* ran an article about the school and the "dependable helpers" in the policeman's daily work. The article described guard dog training and mentioned that dogs with an "especially developed sense of smell" could receive special training as scent dogs for the criminal police.[4] Although the public knew about the school and some of its activities, one type of scent training remained secret: the science of smell differentiation.

DOGS AT THE MINISTRY FOR STATE SECURITY

Like the Gestapo, the Stasi had a large stable of guard and border dogs. For the general public it is hard not to visualize German shepherds paired with jackbooted soldiers at border crossings when thinking of Nazi Germany or divided Germany. The East German police, army, and the Stasi had their share of border and guard dogs, but they also had a number of service dogs trained for espionage and security purposes, in which the dog's nose, not its bark, played a central role.

By 1988, the Ministry for State Security (MfS) maintained 534 guard and watchdogs and about 55 service dogs. The service dogs included 26 scent and tracking dogs, 15 smell differentiation dogs, and 10 bomb sniffer dogs.[5] There was a distinction made between the more common scent and tracking dog and scent differentiation dogs. Scent dogs were common in police work worldwide, whereas a scent differentiation dog was a unique type based on an innovative method developed at the Central Dog School in Pretzsch. Like the police, the Stasi also sent staff there to be trained as dog handlers; they often bought dogs trained there or had their handlers train a dog at the school.

Dogs had become a fixture at the ministry by 1989, and plans were made to centralize efforts in Berlin. Surprisingly, it was only at this late date that Stasi leaders acknowledged the "operational necessity" of using dogs to solve spy and security problems. A new kennel was built in Berlin, and leaders centralized other departments, such as the observers, counter-intelligence, mail, and even the university and churches, under the internal police department umbrella. There was some resistance against centralization, because some departments thought it unclear whether a dog trainer using a differentiation dog for written agitation could work as effectively in crime scene investigations.[6]

During the first half of 1989 a number of other departments used the service dogs. Eleven cases involved scent dogs with tasks ranging from searches, observations, an escape attempt, and a breaking-and-entry case. Differentiation dogs helped in eight cases involving agitation, robbery, and breaking and entry. The police department even let their service dogs be used for research on narcotics and on how to secure traces with a vacuum pump.[7]

TRACKING DOGS

Tracking dogs used in regular police work led the pack of service dogs. Police around the world, and even leading counterintelligence services like the Royal Canadian Mounted Police, use tracking dogs in their work. They can be trained for tasks as diverse as search and rescue and tracking people.

Initially, tracking dogs at the MfS were used for investigating crimes we normally consider to be under the bailiwick of Western police force activities, such as robberies or finding criminals. In the 1970s the observation department became interested in using tracking dogs for tracking and finding spies and other "enemies of the state."[8]

Like chemical or radioactive marking ("spy dust" featured in the next chapter), tracking dogs were a surreptitious way to track people. Whereas observers following a suspect or outfitted with cameras could possibly be seen, marking materials or tracking dogs involved marking the people in order to follow them or tracking their scent in order to find them. The observation department thought tracking dogs held great promise for following the tracks or scent a person left behind without actually having to follow the person and risk detection. Detection was a problem in open areas with no place to hide, such as open fields, cemeteries, forests, parks, and so on. Because spies, for example, often used remote places like cemeteries to service a dead letter box, tracking dogs provided a surreptitious way to follow their movements but not them.[9]

Surprisingly, tracking dogs were not introduced into the observation department until 1975. Like other observation techniques, the science of criminalistics offered inspiration. Tracking dogs were a regular part of a criminialist's technique and workday. Major Werner Wollarz noted in 1975 that the tracking dog was rarely used in operational work because the dog's abilities had hardly been researched, even though the dog was able to single-mindedly follow a scent with its "highly developed smell organ."[10]

Using tracking dogs to follow the scent of a person after they left the area was a kind of invisible shadowing. Wollarz thought dogs would be useful in tracking the movements of spies such as personnel from the Western Military Liaison Missions who were allowed to visit legally certain areas in East Berlin and Germany. If a spy threw away an item like a cigarette pack or matches, the dog could follow the scent of the object touched or the person who touched it.[11]

The dog could further determine if objects like weapons, explosives, poisons, chemicals, and radios were used for "enemy activity." The observation department was especially interested in securing dead letter boxes using dogs. A dog could also determine if a person had been at an apartment or house.[12]

The observers were interested in using chemical perfumes to intensify the smells. Perfumed scents lasted longer than what a human left behind. This made it easier to track people in places with a lot of people or traffic or where the ground did not have the right constellation of easy-to-detect smells. Car scents worked at a distance of four to five kilometers, and tires were a favored part to mark. The only problem with chemical perfume smell intensifiers was that it was hard to neutralize the smell later.[13]

The Technical Operations Sector (OTS) supported this work by developing scents and doing research in this area. Scientists used items ranging from plant hormones like Oxin to musk and conducted experiments with possible scents that elicited a positive reaction from the dog. Reportedly, they even used female sex hormones – a scent few healthy male dogs would ignore. During the experimental phase researchers sprayed areas in forests or cars to see how easily the scent could be followed; but in actual practice the artificial scent was sprayed in places the suspect was expected to walk on or drive through.[14]

LIVING SMELL ANALYZERS

Whereas scent dogs had been used for decades in Germany to track people, they were not used to identify people by preserving their scent until the Cold War. During the Cold War strides were made in the science of smell – or odorology – in the Soviet Union. In 1965, a Soviet scientist, A. I. Winberg, proposed the notion that everyone has an individual smell that is unconsciously left behind when the smell makes contact with the surrounding environment.[15]

Capturing someone's smell, preserving it, and storing it were the next challenges. The first puzzle to solve was what material to use to capture the smell and how to preserve smells for a long period of time. It was precisely these problems that a team of policemen at the Pretzsch Dog Training School solved while developing an innovative technique called smell differentiation. Not only were smells preserved long-term through this method, but dogs were also trained to differentiate among different human smells. Although the policemen who developed smell differentiation did not make the analogy themselves, the method was similar to fingerprinting, in that criminals could be identified through their unique smell.

For East German criminalists, smell differentiation fell under the topic of traces. Much of crime scene investigation is based on the notion that nothing vanishes without a trace. Traces include bodily fluids like semen, saliva, and blood, or fingerprints, explosives, hairs, and shoe prints. By the 1980s biologists learned how to use DNA as a molecular fingerprint. Because all human cells, including those in bodily fluids, contain the molecule, DNA fingerprinting became an all-encompassing test to find the criminal, but it did not enter the work-a-day world of the criminalist until the 1990s. East German investigators thought micro-traces had information that could lead to the criminal directly or indirectly.[16]

The key to preserving smells in order to create the equivalent of a fingerprint collection lay in finding the right sort of absorptive material and long-term storage. W. Derda, the head of the dog school in Pretzsch, influenced by the teaching of the Soviet scientist A. I. Winberg, hit upon the idea of using sterile dust cloths as the absorbing material. In 1965, together with his police colleagues Krüger and Löbl, Derda developed a method consisting of collecting smell traces (called *Geruchspuren*, GS) and preserving them in airtight glass jars – smell conserves (*Geruchskonserven*, GK). By the early 1970s the technique began to be used by police departments across East Germany, and the Ministry of the Interior issued an internal pamphlet in 1973 with "methodical guidelines" for "using smell differentiation to fight crime."[17]

Humans usually cannot sniff out crimes themselves, because their sense of smell is more limited than a dog's. Therefore the Pretzsch Dog Training School trained special dogs called "differentiation dogs" for the job. Once trained, the dog trainer could compare the smell conserve of a specific person with the smell trace of people and objects by setting the dog loose in a room with the various smells. Dogs also have the ability to find a specific smell out of many different colliding smells. For example, if one places the criminal's sneaker in a pile of one hundred other sneakers, the dogs can find the correct sneaker.

The smell conserves were placed in a collection stored at police headquarters, and well-known criminals were registered.[18] The police gathered
scents for their smell collection from suspected criminals and stored them
in the jam jars in a room lined with shelves. The Ministry of Interior's
Department for Innovations developed a special chair to collect smells at
police stations. A sterile dust cloth was placed on a chair, and a specially
prepared frame was placed on top of the chair seat. The suspect had to
sit on the chair for at least ten minutes for the method to work. The chair
was usually used during interrogations, but it is not clear if every victim
knew that this was a special dust cloth or if they assumed it was fabric
on a chair. In any case, officers were warned to clean the chair afterwards
with fifty-degree centigrade hot water.[19] Another way to capture smells
from a suspect was to wipe the dust cloth on the waistband of their pants.
In this case, the suspect clearly knew that something was being done to
him or her.

When smells were to be collected from the crime scene, the area was
cordoned off, and no other smells were allowed to enter the area. Smells
were secured with the yellow dust cloth – officers were instructed to use
only those issued by the Ministry of the Interior – handled with a set of
long tweezers. The cloth had to stay on the smell for a minimum of thirty
minutes to work properly. To increase the smell, a piece of aluminum foil
could be placed on the cloth. The police then took a picture of the whole
scene.[20]

Back at headquarters, the dog trainer placed six to eight opened mason
jars with suspect's smells on the floor with about 80 cm between each jar.
The glass top and plastic ring was placed on a table. Then the dog was
brought in the room on a short leash. Before making the rounds along the
glass jars, the dog was presented with the smell-impregnated cloth – the
smell trace – and allowed to smell it. Then the dog was taken from jar to
jar; once the matching smell was found, the dog sat in front of it.[21]

In typical German bureaucratic fashion, a special two-page report form
was developed to collect the information gained from the smell comparison. It included information such as the scene of the crime, time secured,
smell traces, weather, and so on. A copy was sent to the German People's
Police Criminal Institute. The registration number, the police station, the
crime, and the dates were noted on a sticker, which was placed on the jar.
The smell traces were destroyed once the crime was solved or the crime
reached its statute of limitations. Smell conserves of registered criminals
were kept until five years after the prisoner was released from prison.[22]

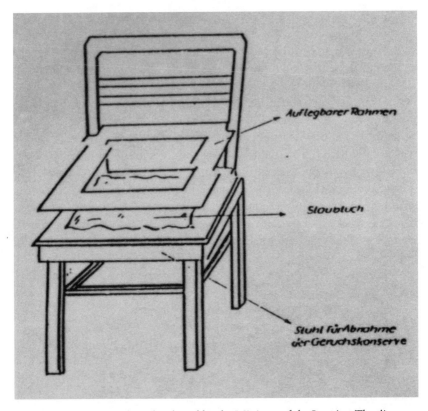

Auflegbarer Rahmen

Staubtuch

Stuhl für Abnahme
der Geruchskonserve

27. The special scent chair developed by the Ministry of the Interior. The diagram points to the frame on the top, the dust cloth in the middle, and the special chair for "smell preserves." (BStU)

The Stasi adopted a number of criminalistic techniques from the police, including spy dust. Like the criminal police, they sought to apply the latest scientific-technical techniques to fighting crime. And the political police division of the Stasi saw much of what they did as catching "criminals." Sometimes regular crimes like robberies, fires, or murders fell under the bailiwick of the Stasi. But more often they investigated "enemies of the state" who distributed what they saw as "inflammatory" leaflets against the state as part of a smear campaign.

Smell differentiation began to be used by various sections of the Stasi at different times. The interrogation department seems to be one of the first to adopt the method, and they used the smell chair developed by the police for interrogations. In addition to using tracking dogs, the observers also began to use smell differentiation. Even the post office surveillance

division employed smell differentiation to catch people sending inflammatory letters against the state.

In 1979 Manfred Brauner was chosen by the Stasi to build up a new
area for training dogs in smell differentiation at the Leipzig district office.
That same year he was transferred to the subject area of "manhunt" or
searches in Department XX, the unit known for hunting down dissidents
and keeping churches and universities under the watchful eye of the Stasi.
From the point of view of the Stasi, this activity was a way to stomp out
"political-ideological diversion" and "political underground" activity.[23]

Brauner was an unlikely leader. He was dismissed from school after
barely finishing the eighth grade; thereafter he went on to trade school
for locksmiths and was co-opted into joining the MfS's army at the age
of nineteen, in 1965. He came from a working class family and had a
positive political attitude toward the state, even though he did not join
the East German Communist Party (SED) until a year later, in 1966.
At the Stasi he moved from the guard regiment, to watchman duty, to
working as an archivist, where he filed informant card files. He longed for
another activity but was deemed unsuitable for operational work because
of speech difficulties. He completed ninth and tenth grade at night school
while he was working. The MfS liked him and always praised his "open,"
"helpful" character. The only criticism they had was that he was "often
too good-natured." He was considered an average worker who had no
problems but he was not destined to be on the fast track.[24]

Therefore it seems a surprise that he was suddenly assigned to the
coveted position of building a new department. The only clue is a passing reference that he took care of the service dogs while he was in the
army. Brauner's initial job in the new position was to use differentiation
dogs in solving threatening anonymous phone calls, but his area quickly
expanded into searching for "inflammatory writings by enemies of the
state." Brauner clearly loved the work, and his career blossomed with the
new responsibility. His solid yearly evaluations turned into glowing ones;
he was praised for his engagement, dedication, and success.[25]

To qualify for the new position, Brauner went to the Pretzsch Dog
Training School for a seven-week course on training differentiation dogs.
Derda, the head of the school, wrote that he was the "best participant
in the training course." Within ten months he had developed smell differentiation into a "fully functional and effective means for manhunts"
and had received two bonuses for "model achievements." With his help
a number of anonymous perpetrators were identified. One notable case
was the identification of an anonymous perpetrator who spent three years

calling in death threats to Stasi workers. He even helped the police identify
the murderer of a retired woman in a small town.[26]

The ministry strongly supported Brauner as he took steps to qualify for
his new position. One of his most amazing achievements given his tenth
grade education was the completion of a seventy-seven-page trade school
master's-style thesis at the MfS Law School in Potsdam in February 1982
on "The Application of a Criminalistic Method – Smell Differentiation –
to Solve the MfS's Political-Operational Tasks."[27]

Brauner displayed a solid understanding of the science of smell and basis
for smell differentiation. The ultimate goal of his work, of course, was
to show how the method could be applied to state security's "political-
operational' needs. The practical application of the method consisted of
selecting five operational files – primarily from church or university or
political underground surveillance (XX) – and showing how the method
worked there.[28]

Although a science of smell exists – odorology – no instrument had yet
been developed that could replace a dog. The specially trained differentiation dog served as a "living smell analyzer." Smell vacuum cleaners were
being developed that could secure smell traces within two minutes but
never seemed to have taken hold.[29]

Whereas the regular police could be fairly open about taking official
smell samples, the secret police also needed to take secret samples for
the smell conserves. Because there was a special protocol to follow, only
criminal technicians at the regular police or differentiation dog handlers
were allowed to take smell conserves from suspects.[30]

The MfS took open smell samples if they were working on a criminal
case. They stretched this official mode of operation by using a cover story
that they had, for example, stopped someone to test their blood alcohol
level. Official smell samples were taken the way instructed in the police
manual, but they gave themselves more license to approach intimate areas.
Brauner instructed his readers to lay the sterile dust cloth between the
suspect's shirt and undershirt and near the groin area.[31]

Acquiring secret smells posed problems because mistakes could be
made. Rubbing a suspect's clothes was a common way to acquire their
smell but care had to be taken that no one else wore the clothes. Not
surprisingly, more cover stories or "operational combinations" had to be
used. One method was to have an informant get the suspect to touch or
sit on an object, like the Ministry of Interior's specially outfitted chairs,
for at least ten minutes. Then they could leave a cloth on other parts of
the chair for the required thirty minutes.[32]

Scent differentiation was used and adopted in several other East Bloc countries, such as the Soviet Union, Czechoslovakia, and Hungary. Whereas smell differentiation could not be used as proof in court in East Germany, it could in Hungary. The Soviet Union only used short-term storage of smells and thus did not have to store the rows of jam jars filled with scents.[33]

In order to gain firsthand experience on the topic of scent differentiation dogs, and as a dog lover, I called the police station in Pretzsch to inquire if there were any courses I could take or people I could talk to in order to learn more about this method. The police officer told me that the school no longer offered this type of training and that I should call a police school in Nordrhein Westfalen in West Germany. When I provided him with three names of leading scent differentiation dog trainers, he roared like a lion: "They are all dead... they are lying under the earth with the worms." Because the topic had become associated with the perceived perverse methods of the Stasi, East Germans wanted to dissociate themselves from it.

Disappointed that I could not enroll for a scent differentiation class, I followed another lead. I had seen the name of a dog trainer, Bernd Marschall, in the files on perfumed scent differentiation method. He lived in the small, provincial town of Pößneck in the beautiful Thüringen countryside. I found his name and telephone number and discovered that he now owned and ran a taxi service. When I called he thought I was looking for a taxi. Marschall greeted me in a much friendlier way than the policeman from Pretzsch. He told me he could show me the method and that he still had three dogs.

When I arrived at the train station in Pößneck, casual in jeans, he greeted me at the station, also in jeans, so I thought we were both ready for some hands-on dog training. He introduced me to his German shepherd, to his Saint Bernard in a kennel in the courtyard to his house, and to a small, yappy mutt who served as the "guard dog" because of her shrill bark when strangers showed up. Marschall had trained dogs since he was a teenager and initially served at the border as a dog handler. Later he became the local MfS Gera district dog handler. He explained that he no longer had a scent differentiation dog, because the method had been abolished and DNA now served as a definitive way to identify criminals. He currently offered his services as a dog psychologist.

Instead of working with the dogs, we sat down at a table, and he drew diagrams explaining how the dogs were trained for scent differentiation. He started by saying that he never had any food with him because that would mix up the smells for the dogs. Dogs were rewarded with lots of praise and petting. Trainers usually worked in a medium-sized room with cans containing different smells. Dogs were trained to match smells with each other.

As I left the house, Marschall handed me a blue cloth and told me that the Ministry of Interior handed out the sterile dust cloths. They did not necessarily use yellow ones featured in the Stasi films.

APPLICATIONS OF SMELL DIFFERENTIATION

Murders, robberies, and sexual assault were all areas in which the regular East German police could apply smell differentiation after it had been introduced into police practice by the early 1970s. Fingerprinting was always a good way to identify a criminal, but if he or she wore gloves, they were hard to track down. Smells, on the other hand, could not be masked. Even if they could, most criminals did not know of the method, although the state secret became increasingly difficult to hide, as it was hard to surreptitiously collect smell samples.

East Germany prided itself on the fact that precious few murders occurred there in comparison to the capitalistic West Germany. Even so, there were a number of spectacular murder cases, many of which were solved using advanced criminalistic methods and sometimes smell differentiation.

Many criminalists, like Dr. Hans Girod, were enthused about smell differentiation and lamented the disrepute that came to be attached to it after the fall of the Berlin Wall because of the Stasi's application of the method. Girod relates a rape-murder case in which the woman's chest and bra were brushed with a yellow dust cloth to collect the smells of the perpetrator. The rapist-murderer was so impressed by the differentiation method when he saw the dog compare the smell traces from the bra to the smell conserve collected from his armpit that he confessed immediately.[34]

Before the ministry began to build up its own internal capacities for smell differentiation, it often worked on cases together with the police's criminal technology department. For example, during the mid-1970s the Halle district office investigated a case of massive distribution of inflammatory leaflets protesting the deportation of Wolf Biermann to West Germany in 1976. On 23 December protesters distributed five hundred inflammatory leaflets in mailboxes around Halle. The Stasi worked on the case feverishly over Christmas, drawing up plans. By 27 December they opened an operational file called "Invocation" and started pursuing traces. Within half a year they had contacted ten thousand (yes, ten thousand) people. The authors of the flyers were careful not to leave any traces behind. The Stasi only found fingerprints on two flyers. The perpetrators had used a child's plastic printer kit that used rubber stamps with ink to create letters. Whereas the focus of the investigation became this stamp kit, the Stasi also followed leads on the paper used.[35]

The Stasi visited one of their first suspects, Uli Jork, on the first day they heard about the flyer distribution. When the twenty-five-year old book dealer opened the door, the Stasi officer placed his foot in the door opening and let himself in. He took him to the local state security office, where he was fingerprinted and traces of smell were gathered from under his armpit with a dust cloth. After about twenty minutes, a Stasi staff member came back, removed the cloth with rubber gloves, and placed it in a jam jar. Uli Jork never knew what the dust cloth under the armpit meant, but he had an alibi and was let go. By 5 January, the Stasi had taken smell conserves and fingerprints from more than fifty-one people. When they compared them with smells from thirty-six flyers, they found no matches.[36]

The Stasi had better luck with matching smell traces to a suspect they had forced to become an informant because he had contacts with ministers and young people with "negative ideological attitudes." Although he claimed he was out of town at the time of the crime, the Stasi took some smell traces from him, and they matched those on some of the flyers.[37]

Whereas the police primarily used smell differentiation to assist their crime scene investigations for criminal acts, the MfS adopted the technique to use in other areas, like hunting for people who distributed "inflammatory" flyers or leaflets, destroyed state flags, created political graffiti, and participated in people-smuggling. They also used it in areas we traditionally associate with police work, like arson, threatening anonymous phone calls, and murder.[38]

Most people committing illegal acts try to cover up or destroy any visible traces or identifying features like fingerprints, saliva, and handwriting. Wearing gloves to avoid leaving fingerprints is the most common method for avoiding identification. People who wrote critical leaflets or letters against the German Democratic Republic (GDR) began to wear gloves and use water instead of saliva to moisten their stamps. They also used stamps or letters cut out from magazines to craft their writings. The "Invocation" case was fairly typical for Stasi cases involving distributing political flyers or leaflets. By 1979, however, the Leipzig office had its resources for securing and comparing suspects' smells. And as the rows of dissident smells found in 1989 indicate, they had likely become the most industrious of all units in the area of smell differentiation targeted at enemies of the state. By the early 1980s the Leipzig MfS office was helping the police solve crimes using its differentiation dogs. Brauner himself served on a murder investigation involving the case of a retired woman who had been robbed and murdered, and he received several bonuses because his smell differentiation work led to the capture of the murderer.[39]

HISTORY REDUX

The East German police were not the first to introduce the idea of storing smells in glass jars. Dr. Friedo Schmidt, author of numerous books on dogs and their history, describes how objects found at a crime scene should be saved and stored; his book *Criminal Traces and Police Dogs* was published in 1910! He suggested using glass containers to store crime scene objects, because they would not take on the odor of other materials, as would paper, wood, or cardboard. He suggested using "wide-necked sealable glass-receptacles equipped with a glass-stopper" because they were transparent and thus the object could be seen easily in the jar.[40] Unlike the East Germans, Schmidt does not describe storing scent cloths with suspect smells in jars, only crime scene objects.

The Dutch seem to be the most enthusiastic users of a form of smell differentiation. Their method parallels the East German method most closely. They not only developed methods for storing smells but used absorptive materials to collect smells from other objects and then placed them in jars. The Dutch version of smell differentiation was called "suspect discrimination" and involved developing "scent identification line-ups" in order to identify people based on their odor. The National Tracking Dog School was founded in 1919. Scent identification lineups began in 1920 and started with dogs comparing a smell preserved in a bottle to one of the suspects. Later they collected smells from suspects and placed them in a row for dogs to smell. By the 1960s aluminum tubes stuffed with scent cloths were lined up for dogs to smell. During the 1970s the aluminum tubes were replaced with stainless steel tubes. In the 1980s, the Dutch started using scent collection cloths. Unlike the East Germans, they originally used sterilized gauze pads to collect scents. Later they used "Kings cotton," a specially made cotton bandage processed by the Rotterdam police; once the oils were removed, the cloths were dried and placed separately in vacuum-packed plastic. Most of the cases described by Adee

Schoon and Ruud Haak in their book on the topic describe typical police cases and not cases from intelligence or surveillance work.[41]

The West Germans did not use a comparable method until 1987/88; this method was used in Nordrhein-Westfalen and was called "smell traces comparison." This method is now also used in several other police stations in Germany, such as Minden and Stuttgart. It is not clear whether the German security and intelligence agencies also use the method.[42]

Finding antecedents to, and current uses of, the East German police and Stasi's application of smell differentiation is not an endorsement of using police methods for national security or espionage purposes or for tracking down perceived "enemies of the state." It does serve to show how police methods can be transformed and used for security or espionage purposes. This was not simply a bizarre aberration developed by the Stasi to track down dissidents, no matter how visually bizarre the smell jars seemed. The fact that dissidents became main targets in the 1980s shows how targets had shifted over the four decades of the state's existence from enemy spies to enemies within, and how much power the Stasi had secured over the population.

13

Spy Dust

In East Berlin, a Stasi officer shoots a radioactive bullet at a diplomat's car tire with an air gun. An informant uses his handkerchief to dust two chairs in a hotel room in Zurich with a chemical substance that fluoresces under ultraviolet light. Another informant applies a liquid substance that sniffer dogs can identify to a suspect's clothes. An intelligence officer applies a radioactive substance to a West German five-mark bill. And an informant brushes a dissident's manuscript with the radioactive isotope barium, which emits gamma rays picked up by a vibrating radiation detection device.

All these scenarios illustrate the use of a chemical or radioactive substance to track objects or people. Such techniques have been used by the world's most powerful spy agencies, like the Soviet Committee for State Security (KGB) and the CIA. Secrecy still surrounds methods used by existing intelligence organizations, but the files of the former East German Ministry for State Security offer us the first detailed glimpse into how "spy dust" was used for surveillance and intelligence purposes.

Since the end of the Cold War, even more sophisticated technological devices have been developed to track new enemies of the state, such as terrorists. We seldom think about the possible dangers or weaknesses of these methods, even though history documents a long list of abuses in the name of state security. The Cold War spy dust story can offer us insight into the limits and possibilities of technology in security even as it is practiced today.

I first discovered the Stasi's use of spy dust as I was systematically sifting through the files of the Stasi's technical operations sector (OTS) in 1998. The phrase "marking material" came up frequently in planning documents. Most intriguing were mysterious references to the code word "Cloud."

WESTERN ORIGINS

The term "spy dust" first appeared publicly in a 15 February 1986 *New York Times* headline: "U.S. Says 'Spy Dust' Used by the Russians Is No Health Hazard." This started an uproar over allegations that the KGB had marked U.S. diplomats with a chemical substance known as "*metka.*" Defectors from the KGB, however, had told the CIA of this practice long before.[1]

In the police world, tracking materials are most often called tracers, detective dyes, and tagging, tracking, and trap substances. Although there is a direct connection between intelligence agencies' spy dust method and the police use of tracers, the public is unaware of the criminalistic origins of spy dust and its use in espionage.

Contrary to expectations, tracing materials actually originated in Western police science and not the KGB. The Stasi's secret literature makes clear that most of their marking techniques were adopted from, or similar to, criminalistic techniques discussed in the open literature of professional police work journals. Because the Stasi was in part a secret *police* in which foreign intelligence and counterintelligence units were under one roof, this should not be entirely surprising.

Although not known to the public, there was nothing officially secret about the West German police agencies' application of these "trap substances" – as they called the method – to track gasoline thieves and later to retrieve stolen money. Not only did the West Germans use the method quite extensively, but they also researched and wrote about different methods and substances to use and shared experiences catching thieves. A non-specialist merely needs to scan the main West German criminalistic journal, *Kriminalistik,* to find that it is full of articles on chemical trap substances from the early 1950s to the 1970s. German police liked to use fluorescing chemicals and dyes like eosin, fuchsin, rhodamine B, fluorescin, and silver nitrate.

New chemicals were introduced once the old ones became known. Some of the chemicals changed color when an acid was added, others simply dyed the skin, and the most popular chemicals were activated under ultraviolet light.[2] Silver nitrate was popular for a while because it was easy to use and did not require a UV light: once the thief touched the marked object, dark spots appeared on the hands. Problems are also discussed in the German literature, such as the transfer of trap substances to innocent people.[3]

In addition to adopting common chemical trap substances used internationally and by the West Germans, the East German police favored a fluorescing quinoline it called oxin. But oxin could be difficult to detect, and in 1961 the Criminal Technical Institute's new isotope lab began experimenting with radioactive isotopes to develop more sensitive detection methods.[4]

The West Germans and Austrians also experimented with radioactive isotopes as trap substances. The earliest example I have found in the Western German-speaking world occurred in 1966. Dr. Ernst Ronai, a senior police official from the criminal-technical services in Vienna, successfully used a gamma emitter trap substance in a case involving the repeated theft of clothes and wallets from a lecture cloakroom at the University of Vienna's pathological institute in 1965–66.[5]

Police officials worked together with the Academy of Sciences Institute for Radium Research and Nuclear Physics for expert scientific support.[6] Money marked with a radioactive gold wire was placed in a coat pocket. The radioactivity of the gold (c. 1 μ Ci Au ^{198}) had a half-life of 2.7 days, and Ronai reported that they selected this isotope because it would not endanger anyone's health. The criminal was captured when a Geiger counter picked up the radiation, causing an alarm to trip.[7]

It is not clear if radioactive isotopes had been used before this case, but Ronai's method became known among German-speaking police stations, and as late as 1975 radioactive isotopes were still used in West Germany. Senior Inspector Erich Schock, from the Munich criminal police (the "Kripo"), reported that low doses of a gold isotope used together with a powerful new radiation detector machine, only available in Munich, could be very useful when a suspect has been narrowed down to a small group of people. He concluded that Ronai's dosage of gold was "too high and dangerous."[8]

Marking objects to determine if someone has stolen them has occurred in a primitive way ever since time immemorial. Detectives in the mid-nineteenth century refer to "marking" money to determine if someone has stolen it.[9] The British police seem to be the first to have used marking in a scientific way. When British police began to use the substance in the 1930s, it coincided with an increasingly scientific approach to solving crimes. In fact, the term "forensic science" was coined in the 1930s.

The British also seemed to have pioneered the use of radioactive isotopes as tracers. In 1940, Professor F. G. Tryhorn, a founder of forensics science and later director of the Forensic Science Laboratory at Harrogate, experimented with identifying objects by radioactive labeling. Later, dyes were used for marking objects like documents for identification, but the method had shortcomings. For example, the dye would appear on the criminal's hands and could quickly be removed.[10]

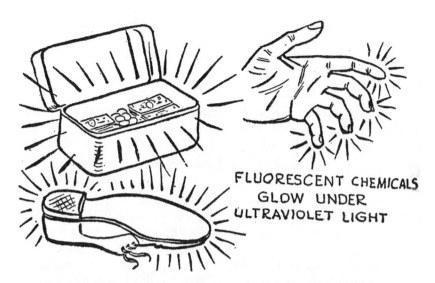

FLUORESCENT CHEMICALS
GLOW UNDER
ULTRAVIOLET LIGHT

28. Illustration of the uses of fluorescent chemicals. Tracking methods originated in Western police science; forensic scientists experimented with both fluorescing chemicals and radioactive isotopes. Marking money to trace the criminal was the most common use of the method. (From Lynn Poole. *Science, the Super Sleuth.*)

Tryhorn and his associates were not concerned about health hazards in their discussions of using radioactive labeling. This is not surprising, as no one knew about the harmful effect of radiation on the human organism at the time. Unlike the Germans in the sixties and seventies, they were not even concerned about which isotope was used. Instead, they were enthused about a new technology and how it could be used to solve crimes.[11]

In the United States, the FBI used chemical tracers to catch criminals stealing gasoline during World War II. Because they used different chemicals for detecting stolen gas, it is not clear if they knew of the British work in the area.[12] There is some evidence that the FBI also experimented with radioactive tracers in the 1940s.[13] The New York City Police Laboratory used detective dyes, fluorescent powders, and radioactive detectors in the 1940s and possibly earlier.[14] Like their European counterparts, Americans' most common marking objective was also money.

But the topic of tracers was not limited to that hidden world of police specialists. During the 1950s tracers were included in a lively book on popular science called *Science, the Super Sleuth*. Lynn Poole, producer of the Johns Hopkins science TV series, primarily shows how chemicals were used to "trace criminals," though he refers to the emergence of radioactive isotopes as a possible method. Poole also features the classic case of stealing money from the moneybox.[15]

"CLOUD"

In addition to adopting and transforming the traditional criminalistic marking techniques for spy work, the Stasi also developed its own super-secret methods. The in-house methods were so secret that they had a code name or number. Hidden behind the code name "Cloud" lies not only a method, but a large-scale program headed by Dr. Franz Leuteritz.

In 1967, the Stasi approached Leuteritz, a young, bespectacled nuclear physicist working on his dissertation on scintillation and proportional spectrometry at the Academy of Sciences Institute for Applied Radioactivity in Leipzig. Not yet a member of the East German Socialist Party, he had been fairly active in the Free German Youth (*Freie Deutsche Jugend*). He was recruited into Department 32 of the Stasi's Technical Operations Sector in the fall of 1967 and completed his dissertation at the Humboldt University in Berlin in 1969.[16]

At the time Leuteritz was recruited, Department 32 had been working on invisible ink and marking materials (the two techniques are related) – and, more recently, radioactivity. With his knowledge in the areas of nuclear measurement technology and X-ray fluorescent analysis, he was highly suitable for this job. In the course of his career, Leuteritz received many honors and medals, including, in 1983, the prestigious 1st Class Friedrich-Engels Prize.[17]

Leuteritz quickly gained a reputation as bright, hard working, and very knowledgeable, with few interests outside of science, apart from family. Although he was largely an apolitical scientist, paradoxically, working for the Ministry for State Security (MfS) was a political act. His evaluations were always positive, and he rose quickly in the ranks. Within four years he was the architect and leader of the "Cloud" program, and, within six years, he was the head of Department 34's unit for radioactivity.[18]

Leuteritz's appointment was timely. Bruno Beater, deputy to Minister of State Security Erich Mielke, asked the technical division to "develop and produce radioactive marking of objects and people for use in operational work in order to discover and prevent secretly transported people in border-crossing traffic."[19]

Completion of the project was aimed at the fiftieth anniversary, in 1973, of the founding of the Soviet Union. The technical division had already been working on operational uses of radioactive isotopes. By December

29. Dr. Franz Leuteritz. Leuteritz was the architect of the top secret "Cloud" program to develop the use of radioactive isotopes for tracking. The MfS recruited him shortly before he completed his Ph.D. in nuclear physics. (BStU)

1972, Leuteritz's group had developed three methods for marking people and objects: a self-sticking plastic foil carrying a radioactive isotope, radioactive needles to be secretly pinned on the clothes or personal objects of the marked person, and a radioactive liquid to be sprayed in small doses on the marked person's clothing (from a distance no greater than 30 cm).[20]

None of the methods were supposed to actually touch a person. The needles, for example, were placed on clothing, and agents were cautioned not to place them too close to the gonads. All three methods could be used on objects like wallets, briefcases, or cigarette cases.[21]

One drawback of the radioactive spraying method using Scandium-46 was that the liquid could not be removed from clothing; staff suggested cutting out the piece of clothing marked. That method was discontinued by the 1980s.[22]

TABLE 1. *Spy dust methods used in the "Cloud" program in the 1980s*[23]

Method	Isotope (Element)	Half-Life	"Cloud" Nr.
Plastic			
47100–010	Mn-54 (Manganese)	312.2 Days	101
47100–020	Sc-46 (Scandium)	83.81 Days	102
47100–030	Co-58 (Cobalt)	70.8 Days	103
47100–040	Ba-140 (Barium)	12.7 Days	104
Needles			
47100–310	Fe-59 (Iron)	44.5 Days	105
47100–320	Co-58 (Cobalt)	70.8 Days	106
47100–330	Ag-110m (Silver)	249.8 Days	107
Liquid Spray			
47100–650	Br-82 (Bromine)	1.4 Days	
47100–670	Co-58 (Cobalt)	70.8 Days	
47100–680	Cs-137 (Cesium)	30.2 Years	
Paper			
47101–310	Mn-54 (Manganese)	312.2 Days	112
47101–320*	Sc-46 (Scandium)	83.81 Days	113
47101–330	Ba-140 (Barium)	12.7 Days	114
47100–340	I-131 (Iodine)	8 Days	115
47100–350	Br-82 (Bromine)	1.4 Days	116
47100–360	Na-24 (Sodium)	14.96 Hours	117
47100–370	Co-58 (Cobalt)	70.8 Days	
47100–380	C-14 (Carbon)	5715 Years	
47100–390	Cs-137 (Cesium)	30.2 Years	
47100–400	H-3 (Hydrogen)	12.3 Years	
Pen Ink			
47101–610	S-35 (Sulfur)	87.2 Days	
47101–620	P-32 (Phosphorus)	14.3 Days	
47101–630	Pr-143 (Praseodymium)	13.57 Days	
Car Magnets			
47102–10	Sc-46 (Scandium)	83.8 Days	122
47102–20	Co-58 (Cobalt)	70.8 Days	123
47102–30	Nb-95 (Niobium)	34.97 Days	124
47102–40	Ba-140 (Barium)	12.7 Days	
Air Gun			
47101–010	Ag-110m (Silver)	249.8 Days	

* This method was the most popular.

Several other ways to mark items were developed later in the 1970s. A special projectile was made that could be shot into the treads of tires with a commercially available West German air gun. The projectile was a drilled-out lead bullet with an aluminum front containing radioactive silver 110 as a marking substance. When bounced off a tire, the bullet would separate from the front piece, leaving behind the marker. The instructions on using this method guaranteed that the car would still be safe to drive. They also manufactured radioactive magnets to be attached to bumpers.[24]

But the majority of tracers, both chemical and radioactive, were used to mark money or documents. Department 34 developed at least ten different types of radioactive markers for paper and at least six for vehicles.[25] The most common radioactive isotope used for tracking was scandium-46, which had a half-life of 83.81 days.

Although radioactive marking seems to have been used a little before 1972, 1973 marked the beginning of a large-scale program. Two departments – 26 (phone tapping and surveillance) and VIII (observation) – used "Cloud" fairly extensively in the 1970s and 1980s. One source states that radioactive marking was used one hundred times in 1975 alone. By the 1980s there seems to have been a sharp decrease; surviving notes indicate only about fifty-eight radioactive markings between 1982 and 1988. Scandium-46 was used forty-four times out of the fifty-eight listed. All but one of the scandium markings was used on paper.[26]

Although many of the operational files seem to have been destroyed, the remaining evidence documents the methods themselves – the isotopes used, marking techniques, objects marked, and so on.

The East German secret police were not greatly concerned about the health hazards of using radioactivity – they employed machines that emitted high doses of X-rays at border crossings to reveal would-be escapees hiding in vehicles. The next greatest use of radioactivity in operations appears to have been in the area of security technology and tracers.

The Stasi enthusiastically embraced radioactive tracers; it allowed them a kind of ghost surveillance. Marked objects could be detected several meters away and did not have to be retrieved. Unlike chemical marking, which had to be tested after the deed was done, radioactive tracers could provide immediate proof while the action took place. Moreover, if a person or car was under surveillance, it was easy to keep track of the subject or object, even if it was hidden or behind a wall. If a marked person was hidden in a car, X- and gamma rays were penetrating enough for the subject to be detected within the vehicle.

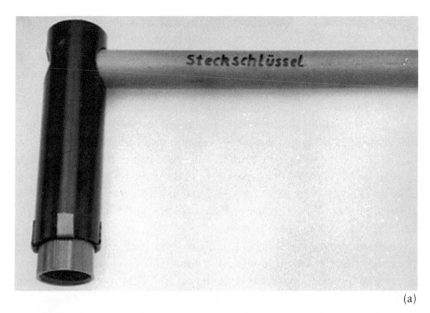

(a)

(b)

30. A vial for transporting radioactive isotopes and the magnet used to open it. Scandium-46 was the most popular radioactive isotope used in the 1980s. Isotopes were transported and stored in these vials from West Germany. A magnet (a) was used to open, close, and transport the vials (b) to and from the Rossendorf Nuclear Reactor Institute, the technical division's silent partner. (BStU)

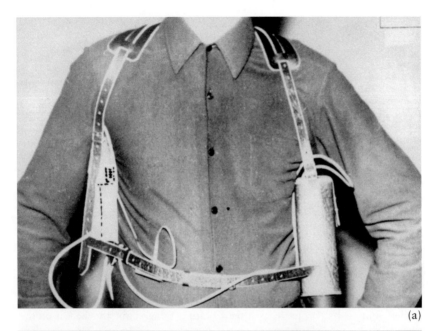

(a)

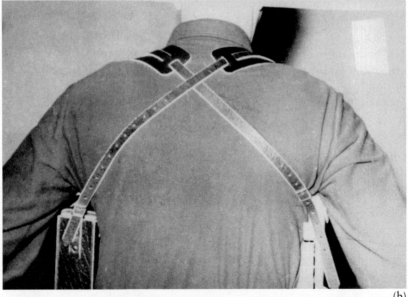

(b)

31. A special harness for carrying a nuclear detection device and its battery pack. A vibrator was placed under the operator's armpit and was used as an alarm signal when a radioactive isotope was detected. (BStU)

32. "Cloud 005" – a scintillator nuclear detection instrument. The device is on the left, and the battery pack, with the vibrating signal alarm attached, is on the right. (BStU)

The Stasi tended to use scintillator detection devices rather than Geiger-Müller counters. Aside from the fact that Leuteritz's specialty lay in that area, scintillator counters were thought to be more sensitive for measuring the ionizing particles that emanated from radioactive isotopes sprayed or placed on or in objects.

Five detection instruments were developed code-named "Cloud 001" through "Cloud 005." Whereas the first four models were somewhat better than commercial models available at the time, "Cloud 005" was ahead of its time. It vibrated – much as a mobile phone or pager does today. It was strapped to the torso to alert the operator that an isotope had been detected.

SILENT PARTNER

As a result of cooperative arrangements the Stasi maintained with industry and research institutes, the technical division had an unlimited supply of radioactive isotopes at its disposal. By 1971, OTS entered into a very secret arrangement with the Central Institute for Nuclear Research of the Academy of Sciences in Rossendorf, home of East Germany's major nuclear reactor, which made it possible for the scientists to obtain whatever they wanted within days. Their liaison there, Dr. Karl Jantsch, a Stasi informant and head of the section for radioactive preparations, was even available outside of business hours in case staff needed a radioactive isotope immediately. This state of affairs changed in 1987 when the Rossendorf reactor was out of service and the only radioactive isotope they could obtain was scandium-46.[27]

Secrecy and safety reigned when material was transported or disposed of. The Stasi used special vans with exchangeable license plates to transport radioactive materials. An envelope in each van was "to be opened in case of emergency or accident." The letter inside warned that the transported material should be returned immediately.

The Rossendorf facility not only supplied radioactive material, it prepared specialty items for the Stasi. For example, "Cloud 105," "106," and "107" involved radioactively activating commercial needles made in Czechoslovakia, which were coated with copper at Rossendorf. The ease of this method made it good for secret work, although returning the needles after use was a burden. By mid-February 1973, one hundred needles had been prepared at Rossendorf. It took forty hours to radiate them; six days later they were ready for use.[28]

SAFETY CONCERNS

There is no doubt that the technical staff thought about safety in conjunction with various operational scenarios. But safety concerns were differentially applied to staff and to those who were marked. As "Cloud" director Leuteritz explained, "it is necessary principally to maintain the legal regulations; however, some deviations are allowable if badly calculated operational conditions exist."[29]

Those whose work involved radiation could be exposed to no more than five REMs (Röntgen Equivalent in Man, a very low dosage still acceptable in 2006) per year, and there were elaborate tables describing the amount of exposure allowed for different parts of the body. But those perceived as possible criminals could be exposed to more radiation – "internal" standards were applied to them.

In an interview with the author, Paul Rossi, a health physicist at Michigan State University, said that he believes that the Stasi's victims would have been exposed to a dangerous amount of radiation: "I had a chance to get some calculations run for the money marking case that was mentioned in the paper. It appears with that isotope and that amount that a person would receive just under ten R per hour if the bill were a half centimeter away from the surface of the skin. It wouldn't take too terribly long before visible effects from the radiation could be noticed at these exposure rates."[30]

Additionally, it was difficult to keep track of and retrieve every marked object – meaning that people were often exposed for a longer time than intended. Potential damage to humans was rarely discussed in scientific papers, but one consumer did discuss the pros and cons of different marking materials, noting that radioactive marking could cause somatic damage.[31]

Radioactive isotopes were stored in a strong room shielded with lead in a basement room at the building of the technical division. In this room safe, the methods were often stored in items ranging from plastic soap containers to camera cases.[32]

USES OF SPY DUST

Tracking Diplomats

Espionage has been described as silent warfare. Technological artifacts often reflect this. To keep track of diplomats, the Stasi used magnets under car bumpers and the modified West German air guns to shoot isotope-laced bullets at car tires from as far as twenty-five meters away; when a bullet met its mark, the tire could be traced for some one hundred days. The OTS liked this method because the material remained on the object and did not spread when it hit. On the negative side, researchers wrote, it was not always possible to tell if the tire had been hit. Sometimes the "Cloud 003" detection device had to be used. If the bullet hit glass, the bullet had to be recovered. And if the bullet were to strike a person, it was to be removed quickly and returned to Department 34.[33]

Although this technique seems far-fetched, I have found some evidence that it was used: Department 34 recorded that the "Cloud" shotgun method was given to Department VIII.[34] However, I have yet to find any details of a specific case.

In addition to using air guns for marking tires, OTS developed a radioactive car tracking method that involved magnets. The magnets, developed in 1975, were used to observe Western diplomats' cars, for surveillance of military liaison vehicles, to observe people in small towns or out-of-the-way places, and to detect cases of people-smuggling.[35]

The observation department was the main user of the magnets. The ceramic material for the magnets came from an East German company in Hermsdorf, with PVC material purchased from a West German company. Special containers were developed to transport the magnets, which were coated with scandium-46. To avoid their detection, scientists recommended placing them underneath a bumper.[36]

Marking Money

Marking money continues to be the most common type of marking done by the police. The Stasi also marked money and other paper extensively. Even though intelligence, counterintelligence, and internal security were all under one roof at the Stasi, East Germany did have a separate criminal-technical branch within its police force. But the Stasi also investigated the theft of money. This may be explained by the fact that these cases often involved the government-owned post office and that the money often came from West Germany (across the border). Other cases seem misplaced and perhaps reveal the extent to which the agency had become a jack-of-all trades, or a "Gal Friday" (*Mädchen für alles*), as Erich Mielke put it.[37]

Although the Stasi stressed the necessity of returning marked material to the labs, clearly one could not keep track of the path of all marked objects or people. Between 9 and 16 May 1988, the MfS marked twenty West German five-mark bills with 60 μCi's of Sc-46 in order to prove that Western money was being stolen from letters. By the end of May only eight bills had been recovered. The remaining twelve were never found, and the thief was not caught.[38]

Guarding Secrets

Whereas the marking of money developed out of common police practice, the Stasi also used the technique for solving many other problems in secretive East German society. It seems that preventing the "unauthorized viewing of secret documents" was also a common marking objective. These secret documents could be nearly anywhere, including of course at Stasi offices. One of the reasons radioactive marking was preferred over the chemical kind was the efficiency of immediate results. Chemical marking could only be proved after a crime had occurred. In the case of marking secret documents, the "criminal" could be caught in action as they looked at or stole the documents.[39]

The Stasi targeted a scientist, Dr. Manfred Ludwig, who worked at the Carl Zeiss company in Jena, because they thought he was smuggling secret documents to the West. To collect proof, they planted a secret military document marked with a radioactive isotope on his desk. Luckily, he did not take the bait and put the file away.[40]

Marking was not limited to domestic surveillance. The foreign department adopted it also. If an agent suspected that his or her spy equipment was being looked at secretly, they used chemical marking. For observations in the West, tinkers developed a two-step chemical method to avoid UV-detection; the chemicals for the method were hidden in a West German deodorant bottle with the brand name "BAC."[41]

Even though radioactive markings were theoretically banned for use abroad, the technicians did develop a radioactive paper marking method for GDR-produced postcards sent to and from foreign countries. In this way, the post control department could keep track of these cards.[42]

Of course, radioactive marking had other operational disadvantages aside from health concerns. A radioactive detector needed to be set up in a room adjacent to the one in which the document was located. If the document were taken away, the decrease in the intensity of the radioactivity would be registered.[43]

It is not clear how often "Cloud" technology was used, or how often it was successful. An interesting example in which the Stasi reported success in the technical functioning of "Cloud" is a case in which hundreds of packages from West Germany were being stolen from a provincial post office in Gera. Initially, I found a reference in the OTS files in which "Cloud" was reported as a technical success in an operation codenamed "Bermuda" – but the operational file makes no direct reference to the method and material. Instead, there are only vague references to "operational-technical measures." Interestingly, the final evidence used to catch the thief came from an informant.[44] OTS may have been claiming success in order to cater to Mielke's desire for increased use of technology and to justify faith in the ability of science to solve problems.

Targeting Spies

Like the KGB, the MfS used spy dust to keep track of suspected spies. There is no evidence that the Stasi actually used radioactive substances on suspected enemy spies. In the mid-sixties they experimented with tagging dead letter drops with scandium to penetrate enemy communication, but no evidence has surfaced proving that they actually used the material in an operation.[45]

There is extensive material documenting the use of chemical substances to mark spies. In fact, chemical marking had been the main type of spy dust used until the "Cloud" program, and OTS had developed hundreds of different kinds of chemical marking. "Operation II," an operation targeting suspected British spies, is one major example of using chemical substances against possible enemy agents.

"Operation II"

In February 1986, OTS chemists sprayed two white handkerchiefs with hydrazine sulfate, a highly toxic, reactive, cancer-causing chemical often used in rocket fuel, photographic development, and dyes. They neatly refolded the handkerchief into its portable blue plastic tissue holder, cleaned the cover off, and passed it on to an agent with instructions on its use.[46]

Four years earlier, in the fall of 1982, the MfS's Q branch – OTS – had received a fairly routine request from economic counterintelligence: they needed a way to identify East German scientists who they thought might be working for, and meeting with, British intelligence in hotel rooms abroad. This operation was called "Operation II," to differentiate it from two other operations against the CIA and the West German intelligence agency (BND). The problem they posed for the technicians was that they needed a way to apply the substance in front of the spy runner surreptitiously and that it should not be transferable to other people, yet it should be long lasting enough to test for several days after return of the traveling scientist.[47]

There were hundreds of different types of chemical marking materials in the scientists' secret arsenal that they could chose from, but radioactive marking was forbidden abroad. OTS was quick to decide on using "contact marking material" to meet the spy catchers' request. Unlike simply marking an object for recognition, contact marking material was used to determine if one object came in contact with another object and was not used directly on people.[48]

Major Christa Sabisch, a Q-lab chemist who had earned her undergraduate degree in physical chemistry from Leningrad State University in 1965, was charged with developing a secret way for agents to apply the spy dust. As a subdepartment head in OTS's marking material group, she developed four clever marked concealments: a treated man's business suit, a glove, a handkerchief, and a plastic bag.[49]

Double agent "Richter" (Dr. Rolf Hillig), a leader in the field of microelectronics, had been working for the MfS since 1966 and was allowed to travel West. During one of these visits, British intelligence recruited him, he told his case officer, and then he became a Stasi controlled double agent for some twenty-five years.[50]

When "Richter" returned from his missions abroad at trade fairs, conferences, and symposia, his case officer debriefed him on his meetings with Leonhard F., his British handler, who was interested in research, development, and production of defense-related electronics. Ostensibly working for the Ministry of Defense, Leonhard F. employed all the hallmarks of espionage during his contact and meetings with his two agents – "Richter" and "Bach" (Alfred K.): he provided them with a cover address in England, secret writing, various containers to store money, instructions, and even integrated circuits.[51] The goal of using the substance was "to secure objective proof for the existence of enemy contact."[52]

Between 1983 and 1986, the OTS's Q lab armed double agents "Richter" and "Bach" with the treated business suits, handkerchiefs, gloves, deodorant spray cans, and conference plastic bags when they traveled West.[53] Unlike Q's admonishment to James Bond to return the technology in pristine condition, the double agents were instructed to destroy the spy dust after using it.

Richter's first mission began in the fall of 1983, when he was instructed to apply a scent marking onto his British handler's car seats and to the chair in his hotel room during the Productronica, a leading, annual microelectronic trade fair. Seven East German scientist suspects also attended the meeting, and, upon their return home, Stasi technicians broke into their apartments to test samples of their clothes. Two out of the seven samples, "Mikro" and "Diode," were positive when presented to a trained scent differentiation dog.[54]

A year later, at the same fall meeting, agent "Richter" tested out the prepared business suit impregnated with a fluorescing substance, and the MfS concluded that "Mikro" and "Diode" must have come into contact with the "enemy" in the car seat or hotel room. But the test was not conclusive, because this material easily transferred to other objects and had spread to the whole delegation; "Richter" tried again the next year, using an impregnated set of grey leather gloves that he surreptitiously rubbed on the seat of the British suspect at the meeting room in the hotel. Unlike the FBI, the MfS did not plan sting operations or use listening devices or hidden video cameras to tape the proof of treasonous activity.

Observers sent to the West for support photographed the British spy handler and the MfS double agents in their trench coats as they left the car. They traveled as far as Munich, Paris, Vienna, and even London to find the fictitious cover address and F.'s home.

In March 1986, "Richter" was sent to Zürich, Switzerland, armed with his treated handkerchief. He dutifully applied the substance to the chairs at the hotel meeting room on the occasion of Semicon, Europe's most important trade show for semiconductor equipment and a showcase for American technology. A trip to Italy followed in the fall with another prepared handkerchief, tubes of filter paper, and a detection substance in a vial to detect the hydrazine sulfate. If there was a positive reaction when the treated filter paper was applied to the marking, it turned a strong blue-violet color. In 1986 alone, chemists examined 211 samples from clothes, seats, and personal belongings to find out if there were any traces of marking material that "Richter" left behind, but they were all negative.[55]

By May 1987, case officers concluded that the results of the numerous markings were inconclusive and that there was no evidence of spy activity among the traveling scientists. General Major Alfred Kleine, who had requested technical support on this operation, did recommend developing methods to keep the marking material under control to prevent it from spreading, as it had in this case.[56]

By 1988 it seemed that everyone called upon to support catching the suspected spies was growing weary of the operation: the mail interceptors reported that they had run out of paper and could not help anymore, counterintelligence was still not sure which British intelligence agency F. worked for, and OTS deflected requests for developing a new, more suitable marking material. Nevertheless, officers persisted and found new agents to send abroad for marking missions, but to no avail. They never did catch the phantom spy.[57]

Murdering Dissidents?

As marking material became more common in the Stasi's arsenal of tools, the applications reflected the culture and society of the country: for example, secret documents, suspected spies, and even passports were marked at the border.

Dissidents had become a thorn in the side of the Stasi, and specialists developed a variety of methods to keep track of them. Slipping an informant into a dissident's circle of friends was probably the most common. Telephone taps and surveillance followed. It has been very difficult to find a clear-cut case in which chemical or radioactive marking was used on a dissident. The question becomes more acute because one prominent dissident, Jürgen Fuchs, had fears that the camera used to take his picture in prison emitted harmful X-rays. He died of cancer in 1997; several other dissidents also died of cancer.

There is no remaining evidence that would indicate that radioactive isotopes were used to deliberately harm or kill enemies of the state. Such "wet" operations were rarely preserved on paper. In November 2006 ex-KGB spy Alexander Litvinenko was poisoned and died of a lethal dose of polonium-210, an alpha emitter that would not have been useful as a marking method because it did not penetrate objects, as did the "Cloud" gamma emitters. This case gives us pause to wonder, however, whether the Stasi too might have used their supply of radioactive isotopes for murder.

There are only oblique references to marking a dissident or their belongings. An MfS dissertation refers to marking a three-hundred-page manuscript with "radioactive marking" so that the package could be recognized at the post office when sent to other dissidents. There is also a reference to a "marking order" made against Jürgen Fuchs in 1987, but the Stasi withdrew the informant from the job. As enemies of the state, dissidents too were seen as criminals who needed to be caught and punished. Marking often provided hidden proof in court cases.

A CULTURE OF SECRECY

The years of the Cold War saw the emergence of huge bureaucratic intelligence agencies caught up in the day-to-day work of running and recruiting agents and developing new techniques. This culture sometimes acted as a positive engine for technological advancement, leading, for example, to the development of spy planes and satellites in the United States and smaller, quieter, and more technically advanced cameras internationally. But this end-in-itself culture of secrecy presented many opportunities for abuse.

Science conducted in secret leads to dangerous temptations. At one extreme, the ordinary safeguards placed on the treatment of human subjects are frequently ignored. Scientists or intelligence professionals justified bypassing human decency in the name of freedom or socialism. Certainly, the use of spy dust or smell science cannot be compared in magnitude of harm to the evil of Nazi medical experiments, to the U.S. government's plutonium experiments on citizens during the 1940s, 1950s, and 1960s, and even to the CIA's experiments with LSD.[58]

The Stasi spy dust episode, and other stories featured in *Seduced by Secrets*, are similar to the Western science-based projects in other ways: they all blindly believed in the power of science or technology to solve social or intelligence problems. It is striking how similar the CIA's initial goals were to the Stasi's when they started experimenting with LSD.

Whereas the CIA attempted to use science to control agent's minds, the MfS sought to control dissidents, criminals, and spies by tracking them using scientific methods.

Even if spy dust seems relatively benign, still, by the time it debuted in Eastern Germany in the 1970s, the health hazards of radioactivity were well known. Given the operational return on radioactive spy dust, the risk appears to have been considerably greater than the result warranted. Whereas the health hazards were considered, safety was differentially applied to Stasi personnel and alleged spies or criminals.

All the Stasi spy techniques were used, and operations conducted, without accountability. And this is perhaps what differentiates East Bloc espionage from that in the West: some of the CIA's abuses conducted behind the cloak of secrecy were exposed through democratic oversight committees and open public discussion.

There was clearly a communist style to conducting and using espionage, but this approach did not create ideologically impregnated technology or methods. In fact, methods East and methods West were strikingly similar. It was the context in which the spy agency operated, and his or her license to spy without restraints, that led to widespread discontent and criticism. It was the context that dictated the personnel to recruit and appoint. And it was the communist context that created a friendly attitude to science and technology and the desire to acquire the best from the West.

The obsessive secrecy imbedded in all operations had grown out of the closed Soviet society and the communist conspirational zeal to create a new society. It is not only abuse that comes with secrecy, but the creation of a cultish, elitist secret society that holds the keys to power. Of course, secrecy is often a necessity. Imagine if this book had been published before the fall of the Berlin Wall! It would have paralyzed operations by revealing methods and operations that were central to East Bloc society and politics, many of which were similar to the West. In fact, much of this cat-and-mouse game involves keeping the secrets from the enemy.

If the leaders were the magi, then the scientists had been co-opted by a regime that knew how to use their expertise and apolitical attitudes for their own ends. In many of the secret programs the scientists seemed more interested in the technical workings than the societal effects of their specialized knowledge.

Faith in technology in the name of state security was not unique to the Stasi and has not disappeared from society. In fact, as technological developments have accelerated over the last half-century, our dependence on technology and faith in it have only increased.

Note on Archival Sources

Seduced by Secrets is primarily based on thousands of Ministry for State Security files now housed at the Federal File Authority. Contrary to popular belief, not all the files are available to the public or to scholars. Many have not been organized and catalogued, and others are closed.

When I was working at the File Authority, no finding aids existed. Researchers had to provide staff members with key words related to their project and then submit them for research.

The most important records at the Federal Commissioner for the Records of the State Security Service of the Former German Democratic Republic (BStU) for my research came from:

1. *The Technical Operations Sector (OTS).* I looked at most of the files numbered 1–2,424. Apparently, only a small fraction of this department's files are catalogued and ready to use. According to the 2004 BStU Activity Report, about ten thousand files exist. Fortunately, many of the files I examined include yearly reports that provide an overview of the sector's activities.

2. *Department XVIII for the "Protection of the Economy."* Because a large portion of the Sector for Science and Technology (SWT) files were destroyed, along with the other HV A (foreign intelligence arm of the Ministry for State Security) records, this department provided especially helpful information because of its cooperation with the SWT and its focus on computer technology. This department's files are very well catalogued and include some 15,000 files to choose from. I examined several thousand files, primarily from the subdepartments XVIII/5 and XVIII/8.

3. *The HV A Sector for Science and Technology.* Information from the SWT can be found in files, card files, and an electronic database.

Some actual files from the SWT remain at headquarters, including workbooks that detail requests from industry for information from the West and several files on Werner Stiller. The files Stiller brought with him to the West, including those on a number of agents, were also used. The Leipzig regional office has all of the HV A material, and I have seen this, as it related to the Sector for Science and Technology. The Gera regional office also provided some further information.

4. *System for Information, Research and Evaluation (SIRA), Rosenholz, and statistical datasheets*. The so-called SIRA database, which details the agent's spy material; *Rosenholz* data, which reveals both the cover name and real names of agents; and statistical datasheets provide the backbone for most of the material about the SWT.

5. *Department III for Electronic Intelligence and Counterintelligence*. This is a well-catalogued department with a good electronic index. I would like to thank Wolfgang Borkmann and Jürgen Tetzel for allowing me to examine the electronic index independently.

6. Many files of agents or informants including the files for "Gorbachev," Ronneberger, "Salle," "Jonny and Cornelia," "Messing," and "Baron."

7. The personnel index cards from all SWT staff members, as well as numerous index cards and the files themselves from OTS staff members.

8. The theses and dissertations from the Ministry for State Security's Law School in Potsdam. These documents proved enormously helpful, and I examined hundreds written by staff for most of the chapters in Part II.

Notes

Preface

1. See the website www.bstu.bund.de for more information on the creation and history of the Federal Commissioner.
2. Barbara Tuchman. *Practicing History*. New York: Ballantine Books, 1982, pp. 80–90.

Introduction

1. Cf. John Keegan. *Intelligence in War: Knowledge of the Enemy from Napoleon to Al-Qaeda*. New York: Alfred A. Knopf, 2003, pp. 3–4.
2. The BStU webpage offers an overview of current and past research on the Stasi: www.bstu.bund.de. In English, the most recent overview with a bibliography is Mike Dennis. *The Stasi: Myth and Reality*. London: Longman, 2003.

Chapter 1: Agent Gorbachev

1. This chapter is based on the "Gorbachev" file at the archives of the former Ministry for State Security (*Der Bundesbeauftragter für die Unterlagen des Staatssicherheitsdienstes der ehemaligen Deutschen Demokratischen Republik*, hereafter BStU). BStU, ZA, AIM 6731/85. Here 6731/85, I, vol. 2, fol. pp. 17–18. "Meeting Report." Pape. 6 September 1961.
2. Kristie Macrakis. "Does Effective Espionage Lead to Success in Science and Technology? Lessons from the East German Ministry for State Security." *Intelligence and National Security*, vol. 19, no. 1, Spring 2004, pp. 52–77, footnote 67.
3. Ibid.
4. BStU, Policy Documents. DA, 3/55/DSt 100938.
5. Ibid.
6. BStU, 6731/85, vol. 1, fol. 17–21. "Report," Bilke, 13 March 1957.
7. Ibid. vol. 2, fol. 19–22. "Information and Recruitment Report." 8 January 1958. Pape.

8. Ibid. fol. 21. See also fol. 215. File note by Pape, 17 January 1959. See Part I, vol. 2, fol. 100 for 4.5 to 5 million West German marks figure. "Evaluation of GM 'Gorbachev.'" 4 October 1961.

9. There is only one brief reference, which shows that the officers chose his code name in his wife's file: BStU, 12495/88, Part I, vol. 1, fol. 22, "Information and Recruitment Report on GM 'Maria.'" 14 September 1960.

10. BStU, 6731/85, Part II, vol. 1, fol. 118. Meeting. 19 April 1958. Fol. 125–27. Meeting. 28 April 1958. Also, Part I, vol. 1, fol. 198ff. File Notes. 20 May 1958.

11. Ibid. Part I, vol. 1, fol. 218. File Note on meeting with GM Maria and Gorbachev 19 September 1960. 4 October 1960. BStU, 12495/88, Part I, vol. 1.

12. BStU, 6731/85.

13. Ibid. fol. 250, "Report on company visit on 10/11.9. 1964 with GM 'Gorbachev' and his wife GM 'Maria.'" 6 October 1964.

14. BStU, 12495/88, I, vol. 1, fol. 91–94. Transcribed notes on business trip to West Berlin, 27 November 1985. Received by Lehman, 5 December 1985.

15. Ibid.

16. Interviews with the author.

17. BStU, 6731/85. Part I, vol. 2, 15 August 1962. Report on measures to secure agents in the aftermath of Thräne. Part I, vol. 1, 11 September 1961.

18. Ibid.

19. Ibid.

20. Maria Haendcke-Hoppe-Arndt. *Die Hauptabteilung XVIII: Volkswirtschaft.* MfS-Handbuch, Teil III/10. Berlin: BStU, 1997.

21. BStU, XVIII, 6660, and 6731/85, passim.

22. Ibid.

23. BStU, XVIII, 6660, "Evaluation of scientific-technical documents given to liaison officer of friendly service" 7 January 1969. Fol. 90.

24. Ibid. 1 August 1972, fol. 219.

25. Ibid. fol. 72.

26. Ibid.

27. BStU, 6731/85, fol. 177.

28. Ibid. vol. II, part 2.

29. Ibid.

30. Joachim Lampe. "Juristische Aufarbeitung der Westspionage des MfS: eine vorläufige Bilanz." Lecture held at conference in Tutzing, 1999. Reprinted by BStU. Berlin, 1999. – 35 S. – (BF informiert; 24)

Chapter 2: Stealing Secrets

1. Bicycle anecdote in Markus Wolf with Anne McElvoy. *Man Without a Face: The Autobiography of Communism's Greatest Spymaster.* New York: Random House, 1997, p. 180. This anecdote is not in the German version of Wolf's autobiography. Proletarian character and eating style, HV A officer interview with the author, Berlin, 1999.

2. "9 Anti-Reds Beheaded." *New York Times,* 30 December 1955, p. 2.

3. BStU, Heinrich Weiberg's cadre file.
4. Document IV-6 "HV A Meeting Chaired by [Markus] Wolf," 2 February 1953. Donald P. Steury, ed. *On the Front Lines of the Cold War: Documents on the Intelligence War in Berlin, 1946 to 1961.* Washington, DC: CIA History Staff, Center for the Study of Intelligence, 1999. Here pp. 288–95.
5. Ibid.
6. Dirk Dörrenberg. "Erkenntnisse des Verfassungsschutzes zur Westarbeit des MfS." In Georg Herbstritt and Helmut Müller-Engbers, eds. *Das Gesicht dem Westen zu...: DDR-Spionage gegen die Bundesrepublik Deutschland.* Bremen: Edition Temmen, 2003, pp. 72–111. Here p. 78.
7. The figure of four hundred staff members comes from an analysis of the SWT cadre card, and the figure of 40 percent of all agents comes from the *Rosenholz* materials.
8. Former SWT officer interview with author, December 1994.
9. Fred Bucy. "Technology Transfer and East-West Trade: A Reappraisal." *International Security*, Vol. 5, No. 3 (Winter, 1980–81), pp. 132–51. Hanns-D. Jacobsen. "Die Rolle der COCOM-Listen für die sowjetische Wirtschaft und Gesellschaft." *Osteuropa Wirtschaft.* 1989, pp. 93–117. Richard F. Staar "The High-Tech Transfer Offensive of the Soviet Union." *Strategic Review*, spring 198, pp. 32–39. John R. McIntyre and Richard T. Cupitt. "East-West Strategic Trade Control: Crumbling Consensus?" *Survey*, vol. 25, no. 1 (110), winter 1980, pp. 81–108. Tor Egil Forland, "An Act of Economic Warfare? The Dispute over NATO's Embargo Resolution, 1950–1951." *The International History Review*, vol. 12, no. 4, August 1990, pp. 490–513. Ian Jackson. *The Economic Cold War: America, Britain and East-West Trade, 1948–63.* New York: Palgrave, 2001.
10. Jay Tuck. *High-Tech Espionage.* New York: St. Martin's Press, 1986, ch. 13, pp. 180–206. Gerhardt Ronneberger. *Deckname "Saale:" High-Tech-Schmuggler unter Schalck-Golodkowski.* Berlin: Dietz, p. 94.
11. Werner Stiller interview with author, 3 September 1993. Werner Stiller. *Im Zentrum der Spionage.* Mainz: V. Hase & Koehler, 1986. *Beyond the Wall: Memoirs of an East and West German Spy.* Washington, DC: Brassey's, 1992.
12. SED Archive. Personnel File on Robert Rompe in the Central Party Commission.
13. Werner Stiller interview with author.
14. Christopher Andrew and Vasili Mitrokhin. *The Sword and the Shield: the Mitrokhin Archive and the Secret History of the KGB.* New York: Basic Books, 1999, p. 437.
15. BStU, Policy Documents, Commands.
16. Former officer interview with author, December 1994.
17. BStU, Policy Documents, "Instructions on the Installation of Directors for Cadre and Security Questions in the Office for Technology and Atomic Research and Technology." 28 February 1956.
18. *Protokoll der Verhandlungen der 3. Parteikonferenz der sozialistischen Einheitspartei Deutschlands, 24. März bis 30. März 1956.* Berlin: Dietz Verlag, 1956. BStU, Minister's Orders. Nr. 14/56. Creation of a Working Group for Scientific-Technical Evaluation, 8 June 1956.

19. BStU, MfS Paul Bilke's Cadre File. BStU, MfS, HA II/1408/1. Material from Walter Thräne's interrogation.
20. BStU, MfS, HA II, 1408/1. Fol. 112.
21. BStU, MfS, HA II/1408/1.
22. Ibid.
23. Ibid.
24. Ibid.
25. BStU, MfS, HA II/1408/1. Minutes of interrogation from 6–7 September 1962. p. 8. Fol. 184.
26. E-mail from Bernhard Priesemuth, 24 April 2005.
27. BStU, MfS, Paul Bilke's Cadre File.
28. BStU, "Guidelines for the Work of the Working Group for Scientific-Technical Evaluation," 19 December 1956, Signed by Major Last. Officer in evaluation unit interview with author, December 1994.
29. Ibid. p. 3.
30. BStU, MfS, Archive Nr. 8810/84, fol. 207, "Confirmation" from HV A/SWT/Abt. V about a scientist who could be used as an evaluator.
31. Ibid. pp. 3, 4.
32. Ibid. p. 6. For the figure of 150,000 marks see Stiller. *Beyond the Wall*. p. 126. For the figure of 32 percent see BStU, Lepizig Branch Office. Work Book Nr. 4106, Gerhard Jdaszek.
33. Peter Siebenmorgen. *"Staatssicherheit" der DDR: der Westen im Fadenkreuz der Stasi*. Bonn: Bouvier Verlag, 1993, p. 190.
34. BStU, Policy Commands, Council of Ministers, MfS, Office of the Director, 12 February and 9 July 1971. Other information pieced together from the cadre cards of SWT staff.
35. I have received 384 cadre cards from the BStU.
36. This data is based on the database I culled from the *Rosenholz* statistical sheets.
37. BStU, MfS, HA XVIII, Nr. 638, Nr. 4729, HV A, Nr. 678, fol. 142–43, XVIII, Nr. 9505.
38. BStU, Policy Documents, Commands, 2 April 1962, Order Nr. 172/62.
39. BStU, MfS, cadre card for Jauck and Lehe.
40. BStU, MfS, SIRA printout for AG 1.
41. Wolf. *Man Without a Face*. p. 290.
42. BStU, MfS, *Rosenholz*. F 16 Card: Konrad Grote, born 15 February 1941, Registration Number: XV/1967/64. F 22 Card: code name "Karen." In SIRA printouts, his code name transformed into "Koren." SWT Personnel Card, Cadre Department.
43. Ibid.
44. BStU, MfS, SIRA printouts for "Koren," 1980–85.
45. BStU, MfS, *Rosenholz* material. F 16, F 22 Cards: Hans-Joachim Zabel, born 9 July 1930, code name "Froebel." SWT Cadre Card. Printouts from SIRA "Froebel."
46. Craig R. Whitney. *Spy Trader: Germany's Devils Advocate and the Darkest Secrets of the Cold War*. New York: Times Books, 1993, pp. 204–17. Leslie Maitland Werner. "East German Held in Espionage Case." *New York Times*,

4 November 1983. "East German Enters Guilty Plea to Buying Secret U.S. Documents." *New York Times*, 22 February 1985.

47. Information from database I have developed based on *Rosenholz*.

48. This number is from a database I have developed based on the *Rosenholz* material.

49. "Spying at Peak in West Germany." *New York Times*, 15 October 1967, p. 26.

50. BStU, Order 23/69, 24. June 1969, on the coordination of measures for the procurement of prototypes of important military technology, signed by Mielke.

51. BStU, BV Gera, Abt. XV, 0367/7 "5. Kommentar zur Richtlinie 2/79 des Ministers" (VVS MfS 198 A 7/82). February 1982. p. 3.

52. BStU, Documents, Command, Order Nr. 23/69, 24 June 1969 and Order 29/69, 9 August 1969.

53. BStU. Orders: Order Nr. 23/Berlin, den 24. Juni 1969 and Nr. 9/84 Berlin, 13. April 1984. SIRA information.

54. See, for example, "Soviet Acquisition of Militarily Significant Western Technology," White Paper. Government Documents. "Transfer of United States High Technology to the Soviet Union and Soviet Bloc Nations." Report to Senate, no. 97–664. Printed 15 November 1982.

55. BStU, Minister's Secretary. 355. Heinrich Weiberg, "Short Report on Important Scientific-Technical Results." Bi-annual report. 12. August 1971.

56. Ibid. pp. 1–4.

57. Ibid. p. 8.

58. Ibid. pp. 4–9.

59. Ibid. p. 8.

60. Werner Stiller interview with author, 20 March 1994.

61. BStU, Card file on Horst Vogel, Interview, July 1995. Stiller Interview, March 1994.

62. Ibid.

63. See Markus Wolf. *Man Without a Face*. pp. 131–33. For Romeo spies see Marianne Quoirin. *Agentinnen aus Liebe*. Frankfurt: Eichborn, 1999 and Elisabeth Pfister. *Unternehmen Romeo*. Berlin: Aufbau Verlag, 1999.

64. Trial Judgement against Wolfgang R. Stuttgart Court, 7 October 1994. 4 Bjs 18/94. Information also from SIRA and *Rosenholz* materials. "Herzog" (Registration Number XV/2550/74).

65. Hans Pretterebner. *Der Fall Lucona: Ost-Spionage, Korruption und Mord im Dunstkreis der Regierunsspitze*. Wien: Knaur, 1989.

66. Ibid. p. 104.

67. Ibid. p. 113.

68. Ibid.

69. Stiller. *Beyond the Wall*. p. 165.

70. BStU, MfS AU 26/90, MfS/XV/6942/80.

71. Ibid. fols. 62–66. MfS IX/Tb/62/K 1–IX/Tb/63/K1 (Interrogation tape).

72. Ibid. fol. 62.

73. "Jack": SIRA and *Rosenholz* files.

74. BStU, MfS AU 26/90, MfS/XV/6942/80.

75. Ibid. MfS IX/Tb/62/K 1–IX/Tb/63/K1.
76. Ibid.
77. Ibid. BStU, MfS, AU 26/90.
78. Interview with Intelligence Officer, March 1994. BStU, Policy Documents, # 2/87, 12 March 1987. "On the Coordination of Tasks and Measures in order to Acquire Embargo Goods from Non-Socialist Countries and West Berlin."
79. Figure of 90 percent reported in *Der Spiegel*, 20/1991, p. 35. Amount given to SWT reported by a confidential source.
80. *Beschlussempfehlung und Bericht des 2. Untersuchungsausschusses nach Artikel 44 des Grundgesetzes. Drucksache 13/10900.* 1998, pp. 133–34, 261. Report of Schalck Commission.
81. Ibid.
82. BStU, Leipzig Branch, Work Book Nr. 4106, p. 31. Work Book Nr. 4133, p. 10.
83. Frank Weigelt interview with author, May 2004.
84. Markus Wolf, *Man Without a Face.* pp. 8–19 for description of CIA approach. Dirk Dörrenberg "Erkenntnisse des Verfassungsschutzes zur Westarbeit des MfS." *Rosenholz* files.
85. Trial Judgment, Bavarian High Provincial Court, 12 March 1992 against Wolf-Dieter Feuerstein, Kerstin F. , Kurt T., and Dr. Uwe Bodo Albrecht, pp. 84–85. Dieter Feurstein's version is in his autobiographical chapter: Klaus Eichner and Gotthold Schramm. *Kundschafter im Westen.* Berlin: Edition Ost, p. 225. Frank Weigelt's version communicated in interview with author, May 2004.
86. Georg Herbstritt. *Bundesbürger im Dienst der DDR-Spionage: eine analytische Studie.* Göttingen: Vandehoeck & Ruprecht, 2007, pp. 295–99.
87. Mark Franchetti. "Agent Reveals Young Putin's Spy Disaster." *Sunday Times* (London), 19 March 2000.
88. BStU, MfS, Matthias Warnig's SWT cadre card.
89. See Guy Chazon and David Crawford. "A Friendship Forged in Spying Pays Dividends in Russia Today." *Wall Street Journal*, 23 February 2005 (front page story).
90. "The Russians Are Coming." *Time*, 7 February 2005, retrieved from www.time.com archive for 7 February 2005. "Germany Seen Crawling with Russian Spies." *Deutsche Welle*, AP retrieved from www.dw-world.de, 29 January 2005.

Chapter 3: Hero, Traitor, Playboy, Spy

1. On 65 percent, Stiller interview with the author, March 1994. On memory, Herbert Hellenbroich interview with the author, 1995. On words, Helga Michnowski interview with the author, July 2002.
2. Interview with the author, September 1993. "Das Chaos war gewaltig." *Der Spiegel*, 46, Nr. 14/ 30 March 1992, p. 107 [Second part of three-part series on Werner Stiller].
3. Mrs. Fischer interview with the author, July 2003. Peter Fischer, curriculum vitae.

4. BStU, Werner Stiller, Cadre File.
5. Mrs. Fischer interview with author.
6. BStU, XV/2277/79. Vol. 2. IM-Analysis.
7. BStU, Werner Stiller, Personnel File, fol. 33–35. Enlistment Recommendation.
8. BStU, Cadre Card files on SWT staff.
9. BStU, Werner Stiller, Personnel File.
10. Stiller interview with the author, March 1994.
11. BStU, HV A, 402, SWT XIII. Yearly Report. 1978, 6.12.1977.
12. Ibid.
13. BStU, HV A, 863. Karl Hauffe File.
14. BStU, HV A, 402, SWT XIII. Yearly Report. 1978, 6.12.1977.
15. BStU, HV A, 854.
16. Interview with the author, March 1994.
17. Ibid.
18. Interview with the author, July 2002.
19. BStU, XV/2277/79. Major Schröder files on Stiller.
20. Ibid.
21. Ibid. Interrogation of Erzsebet Stiller by Major Schröder. Guido Knopp. *Top Spione: Verräter im Geheimen Krieg*. München: Goldmann Verlag, 1997, pp. 306–09. Interview with the author, March 1994.
22. Ibid.
23. "In der Ruhe liegt die Kraft." *Der Spiegel*, 46, Nr. 13, 1992, pp. 25–50 [First in three-part series]. Stiller interview with the author, March 1994. Interview with Kroß and Helga Mischnowski by Guido Knopp and Peter Adler, partly reproduced in Guido Knopp. *Top Spione*. pp. 308–09.
24. Helga interview with the author, 11 July 2002.
25. Stiller interview with the author, March 1994. Helga interview, July 2002. Werner Stiller. *Im Zentrum der Spionage*. Mainz: V. Hase & Koehler, 1986.
26. BStU, "Borste" (Registration Nrumber XV/5660/85). See also Knopp, *Top Spione*. pp. 312–16.
27. Ibid.
28. Ibid. 11–13 December 1978.
29. For information on the "Eagle Flight" method, see Wolfgang Jatzlau. "Research on the Historical Development of Department M during the 70s." *Diplomarbeit. JHS*, Nr. 313/89. pp. 16, 38.
30. BStU, XV/5660/85. "Borste" Report, 11.7.1978.
31. Ibid. 20 December 1978.
32. Ibid.
33. BStU, ZMA der HA II/2. Stiller to Erzsibe, 18 January 1979.
34. Interview with the author, March 1994.
35. Werner Stiller. *Im Zentrum der Spionage*.
36. BStU, XV/2277/79. Minutes on some information, 9 April 1982.
37. Ibid.
38. BStU, ZMA, II, report on radio messages from Hannover.
39. BStU, XV/5660/85. "Borste."
40. Markus Wolf with Anne McElvoy. *Man Without a Face: The Autobiography of Communism's Greatest Spymaster*. New York: Random House, 1997, pp. 176–78.

41. BStU, Stiller material, Abt. II.ZMA.
42. Ibid.
43. BStU, Stiller Material. "IM-Checking."
44. Stiller interview with the author, March 1994, Helga interview with the author, July 2002.
45. Stiller interview with the author, September 1993.
46. Cover story: "DDR-Geheimdienst enttarnt: die Spione des Markus Wolf." *Der Spiegel*, 33, Nr. 10, pp. 70–83. Here p. 70. March 1979.
47. "Jackal's betrayal" is mentioned in officer's workbooks and in the counter-intelligence files of departments II and XVIII.
48. *Kundschafter des Friedens*. Band I. Leipzig: Offizin Andersen Nexö, 1989. Chapter on Koppe, pp. 189–244. See also *Der Spiegel*. "DDR-Geheimdienst enttarnt." March 1979.
49. BStU, ZMA II, Stiller Material. Stiller interview with the author, March 1994.
50. Interview with the author, March 1994. See Hansjoachim Tiedge. *Der Überläufer: eine Lebensgeschichte*. Berlin: das neue Berlin, 1998, p. 145 for quote.
51. See Gabriele Gast's memoirs for reference to interest in Stiller: *Kundschafterin des Friedens: 17 Jahre Topspionin der DDR beim BND*. Frankfurt: Eichborn, 1999, pp. 239–42.
52. Helmut Wagner. *Schöne Grüße aus Pullach*. Berlin: Edition Ost, 2001, pp. 120–23. Stiller interview with the author.
53. Mrs. Fischer interview with the author, July 2003.
54. Ibid.
55. "Zwei Todfeinde an einem Tisch." *Stern*, 42, 1994, pp. 118–28. Horst Vogel and Markus Wolf interviews with the author 1999.
56. Hansjoachim Tiedge. *Der Überläufer*. p. 145.
57. Interview with the author, March 1994. Werner Stiller. *Im Zentrum der Spionage*.
58. Interview with the author, July 2002.
59. Werner Stiller. *Im Zentrum der Spionage*, p. 8.
60. Werner Stiller with Jefferson Adams. *Beyond the Wall: Memoirs of an East and West German Spy*. Washington, DC: Brassey's, 1992.

Chapter 4: The Crown Jewels

1. Walter Pincus. "Cold War Footnote: CIA Obtained East Germany's Foreign Spy Files." *The Washington Post*, 22 November 1998, p. A02.
2. Horst Vogel interview with the author, 1999. Robert Gerald Livingston and Georg Mascolo. "Das sind die Kronjuwelen." *Der Spiegel*, 59, Nr. 16, 18 April 2005; Josef Hufelschulte and U. Muenster. "Eine verhängnisvolle Affäre: Wie der US-Geheimdienst CIA in Moskau die komplette Agentendatei der DDR-Auslandsspionage erbeutete." *Focus*, 5, 1999, p. 32.
3. Interview with the author, 26 July 2006.
4. Milt Bearden and James Risen. *The Main Enemy: The Inside Story of the CIA's Final Showdown with the KGB*. New York: Random House, 2003, p. 420.

5. Ibid. pp. 439–40.

6. "Dumps" described by Robert Gerald Livingston in a lecture at the German Studies Association for a panel on the *Rosenholz* files. 8 October 2004.

7. Milt Bearden and James Risen. *The Main Enemy*, p. 438.

8. This version was first published by the German magazine *Focus*: "Eine verhängnisvolle Affäre."

9. Robert Gerald Livingston and Georg Mascolo. "Das sind die Kronjuwelen."

10. Milt Bearden and James Risen. *The Main Enemy*. p. 443.

11. Analysis of statistical sheets, which use the phrases "Situation I," "II," and "III." See Livingston and Mascolo ("Das sind die Kronjuwelen") for a brief discussion of the "war scare."

12. Milt Bearden discussion with the author, 18 May 2006.

13. Georg Mascolo, Heiner Schimmöller, and Schumacher. "Das Pharaonengrab der Stasi," *Der Spiegel*, 55, Nr. 3, 1999, pp. 32–38.

14. BStU, *Rosenholz* and SIRA material: "Irmgard Krüger" (Registration Number: XV/436/70). "Protokoll" (XV/4249/83), "Acker" (XV/5094/84), "Bauer" (XV/37/73).

15. BStU, *Rosenholz* and SIRA material. "Petermann" (XV/245/73) (Dieter Feuerstein), "Alfred" (Peter A.) (XV2189/72), "Schulze" (XV/28/79) (Peter Köhler). Court trial judgments from all three cases.

16. BStU, *Rosenholz* and SIRA: "Pfeiffer" (XV/18116/60) XIII/Ref. 1.

17. BStU, *Rosenholz* and SIRA; "Natur" (XV/7928/81) – Professor Gerhard P. "Test" (XV/623/86) – Professor Jürgen W. HV A/XV/2. "Ahrendt" (XV/6824/82) – Professor Otmar K. O. "Friese" (BLN XV/2101/74).

18. BStU, *Rosenholz* and SIRA: "Zelter" (Fritz H.) (XV/450/86). Department XV, Peter Grossmann, Case Officer. "Dora." (Peter Dölling) (XIV/2). Hubert Zwick, Case Officer.

19. Analysis of *Rosenholz* material.

20. BStU, *Rosenholz* and SIRA material on "Ilona" (XV/3980/63). SIRA databases 11 and 12: 280 pieces of information with a large share of Is and IIs.

21. Friedrich-Wilhelm Schlomann. *Operationsgebiet Bundesrepublik*. Munich: Universitas, 1984, pp. 235–36.

22. Trial information.

23. BStU, SIRA: MBB. Of these nineteen sources, eight come from SWT head-quarter departments, five from district offices, and six from other HV A departments.

24. BStU, *Rosenholz* and SIRA material on "Birke" (XV/841/83) and "Stein" (XII/1416/85). See also trial judgment on Lutz Rodig.

25. This is based on an analysis of *Rosenholz* SWT data. See also Kristie Macrakis. "Does Effective Espionage Lead to Success in Science and Technology? Lessons from the East German Ministry for State Security." *Intelligence and National Security*, 19, No. 1, Spring 2004, pp. 51–75 for discussion of Siemens SIRA data results.

26. *Rosenholz* agent card files on "Günter," Indictment against Eckard Schlobohm, 27 March 1995, Bavarian Court. Trial Judgement, 19 October 1995.

27. Adam Pertman. "Why They Spy." *The Boston Globe*, 25 February 2001, p. E1.
28. Peter Köhler Conviction. Bavarian Highest Court. Trial Judgement. 3 St 14/93. 30 November 1993.
29. Klaus Eichner and Gotthold Schramm, eds. *Kundschafter im Westen*. Berlin: Edition Ost, 2003, frontispiece.
30. An analysis of the *Rosenholz* statistical sheets for the SWT show that about 103 IMs worked for the MfS for "material" reasons and about 124 for ideological reasons.
31. H. Keith Melton. *The Ultimate Spy Book*. London: DK Publishing, 1996, pp. 8–9.
32. Quote from "Ich war 'Alfred'" (I was Alfred). In Klaus Eichner and Gotthold Schramm. *Kundschafter im Westen*. p. 291. See also trial material: *Indictment of Dr. Peter A. Der Generalbundesanwalt beim Bundesgerichtshof*. 29 November 1997. Trial Judgment: Hanseatisches Oberlandesgericht. 23 April 1998.
33. Interview with the author, June 2005.
34. Thomas Powers' 1988 introduction to John Marks. *The Search for the "Manchurian Candidate." The CIA and Mind Control*. New York: W.W. Norton, 1979, Norton paperback, 1991, p. vii.
35. See www.bstu.de on *Rosenholz* and Andreas Förster. "Rosenholz: Schatz oder Schätzen." *Berliner Zeitung*, 20 March 2004, p. 6.
36. BStU, *Rosenholz* and SIRA: "Weißkopf" (Manfred Wittig) (XV/4466/61), Department XV/3. See also August B.'s indictment, 3 OJ's 67/94. Düsseldorf, Germany.
37. Instructor definitions in Helmut Müller-Enbergs, ed. *Inoffizielle Mitarbeiter des Ministeriums für Staatssicherheit. Teil 2: Anleitungen für die Arbeit mit Agenten, Kundschaftern und Spionen in der Bundesrepublik Deutschland*. Berlin: Ch. Links Verlag, 1998.
38. Information on Wolfgang Holle from Eckard Schlobohm's indictment, 27 March 1995, ObJs I29/94, p. 4. Bavarian Highest Court.
39. This is based on an analysis of the *Rosenholz* statistical sheets. BStU.
40. Trial Judgment, 10 October 1996. Kurt Blaschke and Horst Lang. Stuttgart Court.
41. Ibid.
42. Ibid. See also *Rosenholz* card files and statistical sheet as corroboration.

Chapter 5: "Kid" and "Paul"

1. BStU, SIRA, "Optik" (Registration Number XV/2110/67).
2. James Hall visit, 5 March 2006.
3. Field Station Berlin Veterans Group website: www.fsbvg.org.
4. Ibid. Also www.lostplaces.de/berlinsigint.html.
5. BStU, MfS III/14,455. Hartmut Heiliger. "The Enemy's Potential in Radio/Electronic Intelligence in West Berlin." JHS, Potsdam, Trade School Thesis, 1986.
6. Interview with the author, October 2003.

7. BStU, SIRA, "Kid." Two registration numbers: XV/2325/79 and XV/2047/84.
8. BStU, SIRA, TDB 12. 47 from registration number XV/2352/79.
9. Ibid. XV/2047/84.
10. Klaus Eichner and Andreas Dobbert. *Headquarters Germany: Die USA-Geheimdienste in Deutschland.* Berlin: Edition Ost, 1997 and Markus Wolf. *Man Without a Face.* New York: Random House, 1997, p. 297.
11. Markus Wolf. *Man Without a Face.* p. 297.
12. Jeffrey M. Carney's domestic file.
13. Interview with the author, October 2003.
14. Ibid.
15. Josef Hufelschulte and Uwe Münster. "Sechs Cowboys gegen Kid." *Focus,* 16 June 1997, p. 34 and Carney's domestic file.
16. Carney interview with author.
17. Markus Wolf. *Man Without a Face.* p. 297.
18. Cf. John Koehler. *The Stasi.* Boulder, CO: Westview Press, 1999, p. 227.
19. Josef Hufelschulte and Uwe Münster. "Sechs Cowboys gegen Kid." p. 34.
20. Jeffrey Carney interview with the author, October 2003.
21. Stuart A. Herrington. *Traitors Among Us: Inside the Spy Catcher's World.* Novato, CA: Presidio, 1999, pp. 260–61.
22. Ibid. p. 342. BStU, SIRA. "Blitz" (XV/471/80).
23. Klaus Eichner and Andreas Dobbert. *Headquarters Germany.* p. 229.
24. Stuart Herrington. *Traitors Among Us* and John Koehler. *The Stasi.*
25. Koehler (ibid. p. 227) seems to think that Mielke and Wolf were present at the meeting, but neither Wolf or Hall recall this.
26. Herrington. *Traitors Among Us.* pp. 319–20 and Koehler. *The Stasi,* who also relies on Herrington's account.
27. James Hall conversation, 5 March 2006.
28. Eichner and Dobbert. *Headquarters Germany.* p. 229.
29. Herrington. *Traitors Among Us;* Wolf. *Man Without a Face;* and Koehler. *The Stasi.*
30. Confidential source.
31. Koehler. *The Stasi.* p. 227.
32. Confidential source.
33. Eichner and Dobbert. *Headquarters Germany.* pp. 240–42.
34. Wolf. *Man Without a Face.* p. 296.
35. Eichner and Dobbert. *Headquarters Germany.* p. 241.
36. Stephen Engelberg and Michael Wines. "U.S. Says Soldier Crippled Spy Post Set Up in Berlin." *New York Times,* 7 May 1989, p. 1 (cover story).
37. Paul Limbach and Heiner Emde. *Quick,* May 1990. Eichner and Dobbert. *Headquarters Germany.* pp. 243–45.
38. Eichner and Dobbert. *Headquarters Germany.* p. 244.
39. See Stephen Engelberg and Michael Wines. "U.S. Says Soldier Crippled Spy Post" for warrant officer salary. Wolf. *Man Without a Face* and Herrington. *Traitors Among Us* for espionage wages.
40. Herrington. *Traitors Among Us.* pp. 252–53.
41. Ibid. pp. 254–57.

42. Ibid.
43. Ibid.
44. Stephen Engelberg. "Jury Hears Tale of Spy Who Did it Out of Greed." *New York Times*, 19 July 1989, p. A 10. Also quoted in Koehler. *The Stasi*. p. 232.
45. Arrest description in Herrington. *Traitors Among Us*. Amount of money paid to Canna Clay in Eichner and Dobbert. *Headquarters Germany*. p. 239.
46. See, for example, Stephen Engelberg. "Spy Trial Opens Today with Facts Like Fiction." *New York Times*, 17 July 1989, p. A 12.
47. Confidential source.
48. Ibid.
49. Herrington. *Traitors Among Us*. p. 252.
50. Ibid. p. 333. Also Paul Limbach and Heiner Emde *Quick* article.
51. Herrington. *Traitors Among Us*. p. 334.

Chapter 6: The Computer Fiasco

1. The description is based on a picture in his cadre file: BStU, 4418/90. Gerhardt Ronneberger. *Deckname "Saale": High-Tech-Smuggler unter Schalck-Golodkowski*. Berlin: Dietz Verlag, 1999, pp. 7–8, 344.
2. Wenzel worked for Department XVIII/8. BStU. Artur Wenzel, Cadre File. 4418/90. Cf. Reinhard Buthmann. *Hochtechnologie und Staatssicherheit*. Analysis and Report. BStU, 2000.
3. Jay Tuck. *High-Tech Espionage*. New York: St. Martin's Press, 1986.
4. Ibid.
5. BStU, XVIII, 13,321, "Die Bundesrepublik Deutschland als Ziel des Ostblocks für den Erwerb von High Technology." May 1984, 38 pages. Fol. 112–50.
6. Ibid. Schütt letter, 10 July 1986. Fol. 110–11.
7. Interview with the author, 1994. BStU. XVIII, 13,321.
8. Jay Tuck. *High-Tech Espionage*. p. 149.
9. SED Archive, J IV 2/2 – various files from 1964 to 1989 in the Central Committee's minutes.
10. BStU, ZAIG, Nr. 2666.
11. Ibid.
12. Ibid.
13. Christopher Andrew and Vasili Mitrokhin. *The Sword and the Shield: The Mitrokhin Archive and the Secret History of the KGB*. New York: Basic Books, 1999, pp. 187–88 for reference on KGB source "Alvar." East German sources: BStU SIRA search under the keyword IBM and IBM 360. "Bill" (Registration Number XV/2185/64). "Sturm" (MfS/4981/60). "Ring" (XIV/1754/68). "Zentrum" (XIV/78/71). "Rabe" (XIV/342/70). Because the SIRA database begins in 1971, previous information is not documented in this request.
14. For more see Kristie Macrakis. "Espionage and Technology Transfer." In Kristie Macrakis and Dieter Hoffmann, eds. *Science under Socialism: East Germany in Comparative Perspective*. Cambridge: Harvard University Press,

1999 and idem. "The Case of Agent Gorbachev." *American Scientist*, 2000, p. 541. BStU, XVIII/13,336.

15. Friedrich Naumann. "Computerindustrie und Informatik im 'Schrittmaß' der Sozialismus." In Dieter Hoffmann and Kristie Macrakis, hrsg. *Naturwissenschaft und Technik in der DDR*. Berlin: Akademie Verlag, pp. 261–82. Here pp. 273–74.
16. See BStU, XVIII, 13,337.
17. Ibid. fol. 5. 17 June 1968. XVIII/2. "Kampfprogramm – I. Etappe."
18. Ibid.
19. Detlef Borchers. "Aktion 'Weltspitze.'" *Die Zeit*, 2002, pp. 64–65. I would like to thank Jerry Livingston for sending me this article.
20. Ibid.
21. BStU, XVIII/13,337. Fol. 34
22. Interview with the author, March 1994.
23. BStU, XVIII 10,207. Karl Nendel interview with the author, 1999.
24. BStU, SIRA: "Dora" (XV/129/78), HV A/XIV; "Zelter" (XV/450/86); "Seemann" (XV/2768/76). Names from BStU, *Rosenholz*.
25. BStU, XVIII. AIM "Leo" (7862/91).
26. BStU, XVIII, 9553. HA XVIII/8 to Alfred Kleine, 11.5. 1987 for *Aktuelle Kamera* story. XVIII/5807 for Schalck's letter to Mielke, 14.08.1987.
27. BStU, Ast. Erfurt, XVIII, 13, fol. 83.
28. BStU, XVIII/8, Nr. 4705. Fol. 53.
29. Wolfgang Biermann. "Mikroelektronik in der Volkswirtschaft der DDR." *Die Einheit*, 1989, pp. 27–32. Here p. 28. BStU, MfS, XVIII/8, Nr. 4705. 20 February 1986, p. 28. "Hohe Gewinne, kleines Risiko." *Der Spiegel*, 2/1996, pp. 74–82.
30. BStU, Dept. XVIII/8. Nr. 4705. 21 February, p. 19 of file, p. 2 of report.
31. BStU/AIM, 10823/91, Part I, Vol. 1. 29.4.66, pp. 102–05.
32. BStU, XVIII/4705. Fol. 43–45. "Jeder an seinem Platz das Beste für unseren sozialistischen Friedenstaat." *Neues Deutschland*, 7 January 1986, vol. 41, front page.
33. BStU, XVIII/4705. Fols. 18–20. 21 February 1986. Fols. 30–32, 20 February 1986. Fols. 21–29.
34. Ibid. fol. 82–93 pagination. Schalck to Nendel, 10 December 1985.
35. Ibid. pp. 3–5 of archive pagination. "Information on the state of and suggestions for the further development of the project 256 k bit chip," 6 March 1986. "Hohe Gewinne, kleines Risiko." pp. 74–82.
36. Ronneberger to Schalck and Nendel, 10 February 1988. Letter reprinted in Rainer O. M. Engberding. *Spionageziel Wirtschaft: Technologie zum Nulltarif*. Düsseldorf: VDI Verlag, 1993, pp. 101–02.
37. "The Toshiba Scandal Has Exporters Running for Cover." *Business Week*, 20 July 1987, pp. 86–87. "Legislation to Prohibit the Importation of Products Made by Toshiba Corp. and Kongsberg Vaapenfabrik Co." *Hearing before the Subcommittee on Ways and Means. House of Representatives*. Washington: U.S. Government Printing Office, 14 July 1987.
38. "Republicans Say Toshiba Broke COCOM Rules Often." *MDN* [?], 12 November 1987. I found this clipping in the Stasi file BKK 1172. "Pentagon:

Illegale Geschäfte Toshiba – DDR nicht bewiesen." *ADN-Information* in BStU, BKK 1172, p. 13.

39. BStU, BKK 1172. "Note on meeting with Toshiba on 26 November 1987." 26 November 1987.

40. Ronneberger to Schalck and Nendel, 10 February 1988. SED Archive, J IV 2/2 – various files from 1964 to 1989 in the Central Committee's minutes.

41. Ibid.

42. SED-Archive, IV 2/1/709. Quoted in Charles Maier "Vom Plan zur Pleite. Der Verfall des Sozialismus in Deutschland." In Jürgen Kocka and Martin Sabrow. *Die DDR als Geschichte: Fragen – Hypotheses – Perspektiven.* Berlin: Akademie Verlag, 1994, p. 113. "Toshiba beginnt mit Megabit-Chips." *Frankfurter Allgemeine Zeitung*, 7 January 1986 and "Hier kommt der 1-Megabit DRAM: Toshiba bereitet Massenproduktuion des ersten 1-Megabit DRAM vor." *Toshiba*, October 1985.

43. BStU, XVIII/8, Nr. 4705. 20 February 1986, supplementary information p. 28.

44. Party Archive, J IV 2/2A/3155. Biermann to Honecker, 12 September 1988. Party Archives, Vorl. SED 41668, Büro Honecker. Meeting notes. 28/29 September 1988. Former MfS officer in SWT interview with the author, summer 1995.

45. For Biermann's application see BstU, HV A 679, fol. 169–70. SIRA, Teildatenbank 11.

46. Court Judgement. Bayerisches Oberstes Landesgericht, gegen Peter Kurt K. and Hans-Joachim B.1993.

47. BStU, SIRA.

48. BStU, XVIII/10,974: Fol. 8.

49. BStU, XVIII/11,886, fol. 10. Memo, XVIII/8. 16 May 1986.

50. See www.leybold.com.

51. Ronneberger. *Deckname "Saale."* footnote 1, p. 205. XVIII files on Leybold.

52. BStU, XVIII/11,527.

53. Ronneberger. *Deckname "Saale."* p. 219.

54. Ibid. p. 220.

55. Ibid. pp. 309–19.

56. BStU, "Leo" AIM, 7862/91, vol. 2. Fol. 182, 213–14.

57. Ronneberger, *Deckname "Saale."* p. 317.

58. BStU, MfS, HV A, 677. References to the implanter on fols. 16, 25, 29, 30, 416, 418, 421.

59. Press Release, 11 April 1997. Der Generalbundesanwalt beim Bundesgerichtshof. IM "Rhein" is also mentioned in BStU, HV A 677.

60. *Beschlussempfehlung und Bericht des 2. Untersuchungsausschusses nach Artikel 44 des Grundgesetzes. Drucksache 13/10900.* 1998, pp. 221–23. Report of Schalck Commission. See also Andreas Förster. *Auf der Spur der Stasi-Millionen: Die Wien-Connection.* Berlin: Argon, 1998, pp. 98–107.

61. Ibid.

62. Ibid. especially Förster, p. 99.

63. Ibid. Förster, p. 102.

64. Ibid. Schalck commission, p. 222.

65. Ronneberger. *Deckname "Saale."*
66. BStU, "Operation II" Archive Nr. 16170/91.
67. Ibid.
68. Ibid. Paul Maddrell has written a book on the earlier years, 1945–61, focusing on Western "spying on science," but there is ample evidence that this activity continued after 1961. Paul Maddrell. *Spying on Science: Western Intelligence in Divided Germany, 1945–1961.* Oxford: Oxford University Press, 2006.
69. *Beschlussempfehlung und Bericht des 2. Untersuchungsausschusses nach Artikel 44 des Grundgesetzes. Drucksache 13/10900.* 1998, p. 159. Report of Schalck Commission.
70. BStU, XVIII/11,887.
71. BStU, XVIII/11,887. Fol. 44–124, 162.
72. Ibid. fol. 49–50. Kleine to Mielke, 16 March 1987.
73. Ibid. fol. 79. 8 October 1987. Fol. 82. 15 May 1987.
74. Ibid.
75. Thomas Reed. *At the Abyss: An Insider History of the Cold War.* New York: Presidio Press, 2004. Gus W. Weiss. "Duping the Soviets: The Farewell Dossier." *Studies in Intelligence,* vol. 39, no. 5, 1996. Also available on the Internet: www.cia.gov/csi/kent_csi/pdf/v39i5a14p.pdf.
76. Information on double agents from interviews and statements made at the *Teufelsberg* Conference, Berlin 1999.
77. BStU, XVIII, 13,321, "Die Bundesrepublik Deutschland als Ziel des Ostblocks für den Erwerb von High Technology." May 1984. Fol. 112–50.
78. Ibid. fol. 116.
79. Ibid. fol. 142 and Ronneberger IM file at the MfS and his memoirs passim.
80. Ibid.
81. BStU, XVIII, 13,321, fol. 20–25 and fol. 23–24 for figures. "Information." HA XVIII. 25.11.88.
82. "Volker Kempe." In Jochen Cerny, ed. *Wer war Wer – DDR: Ein biographisches Lexikon.* Berlin: Ch. Links Verlag, 1992, p. 225. BStU. MfS, Archive Number 562/89. Registration Number XV/3574/67. AIM "Norbert." vol. 1. Fol. 166–67. HA XVIII/8. Nr. 4706, p. 21.
83. Ibid. pp. 38–40.
84. Ibid.
85. BStU, XVIII/12,148. Fol. 19. "Copy of an IM Report." HV A/SWT/Department V. 29 October 1986.
86. Ibid.
87. Kristie Macrakis. "The Case of Agent Gorbachev." p. 541 and "Espionage and Technology Transfer."

Chapter 7: James Bond, Communist-Style

1. BStU, OTS 822, fol. 65. 7 February 1989.
2. BStU, MfS, Hauptverwaltung Aufklärung, Nr. 866.
3. MfS-BdL/Dok. Nr. 000652. 25 July 1960. MS-BdL/Dok. Nr. 002777, 25.1.1958.

4. Ibid.
5. BStU, Cadre File and officer short biographies.
6. MfS-BdL/Dok. Nr. 000652. 25 July 1960.
7. MfS-BdL/Dok (find) 6 January 1961, 3 August 1962.
8. Derek de Solla Price. *Little Science, Big Science.* New York: Columbia University Press, 1963. Passim.
9. BStU, MfS/JHS, MF 214, Genosse Oberst Hentschke, "Effective Planning and Meeting Operational Technological Needs at the MfS According to the Demands of Increased Work against the Enemy." 15 May 1968.
10. Ibid.
11. Ibid. pp. 2, 13.
12. Ibid.
13. Ibid.
14. Ibid.
15. Ibid.
16. BStU, MfS, 21970/90, Günter Schmidt Cadre File.
17. Ibid. 1 September 1960. Fol. 63.
18. Ibid. Justification for Resolution papers.
19. Ibid.
20. Ibid.
21. BStU, JHS, MfS 160 GVS 62/70. Oberst Günter Schmidt, Major Claus Hillenmaier. "Die Gestaltung der analytisch-prognostischen Arbeit als Bestandteil der Führungs- und Leitungstätigkeit im OTS." October 1970.
22. Ibid. BStU, OTS, 1806, fol. 2.
23. This description of departments is based on the chart in OTS 778, fol. 6 and the BStU's handbook on all MfS departments.
24. BStU, OTS 1918, fol. 87–90. Electronics and instruments building area (107), chemists (43), physicists (22), and criminalists (22). A large portion of the 211 trade school graduates also worked as: electricians (46); chemical engineers, lab technicians, or biologists (26); or economists (25); or worked in "fine work technology" or instrument building (21).
25. BStU, OTS 1806.
26. BStU, OTS, 1808, Delivered material for 1973.
27. Ibid.
28. Ibid.
29. Ibid. See OTS 2 for listening device in an ashtray.
30. Ibid.
31. BStU, MfS, Cadre File for Gerhard Müller. 25059/90.
32. Ibid.
33. BStU, MfS-BDL Nr. 002519. 1 June 1959.
34. Ibid. Pieced together from the yearly plans in BStU, OTS 1756.
35. BStU, OTS, 1756. "Analysis" 12 December 1968.
36. Ibid.
37. Ibid.
38. Ibid. and yearly report for 1969. 2 January 1970.
39. Ibid. Yearly Report for 1974. 23 January 1975. Yearly Report for 1975. January 1976.

40. Ibid. Yearly Report for 1980. 5 December 1980. Fol. 304.
41. Ibid. Yearly Report for 1973. 14 January 1974.
42. BStU, OTS 2408. Results from Area C's (Departments 32, 34, 35, and the Central Photo Office) technical work from 1979 to 1983.
43. Ibid. fol. 88.
44. Ibid. Sections on fingerprinting in yearly reports between 1979 and 1983. AIDA: "Automatische Interpretation daktyloskopische Abdrücke."
45. A staff member at the secret service technical division in Washington, DC, showed me their copy of the MfS fingerprint system on a microfilm reader. Information on the FBI fingerprint system can be found on their website: www.fbi.gov.
46. BStU, JHS, 395/75. Wolfgang Reimann. "Problems Implementing Hidden OTS Cooperation with Economic and Scientific Institutions to Guarantee Secrecy." *Diplomarbeit*, 30 December 1975.
47. BStU, OTS, 1535. Schmidt to Minister Mielke, 4 March 1969.
48. BStU, OTS 361.
49. Ibid.
50. David Gill and Ulrich Schröter. *Das Ministerium für Staatssicherheit: Anatomie des Mielke-Imperiums*. Berlin: Rowohlt, 1991, p. 118.
51. Ibid. p. 36.
52. Ibid. p. 54.
53. BStU, OTS 1626, OTS 1628, fol. 112 on the dogs.
54. BStU, OTS 1328.
55. Christopher Andrew and Vasili Mitrokhin. *The World Was Going Our Way: the KGB and the Battle for the Third World*. New York: Basic Books, 2005, p. 39.
56. Markus Wolf. *Man Without a Face*. New York: Random House, 1997, p. 308.
57. Ibid.
58. BStU, OTS 1977, fol. 16–19.
59. BStU, OTS 1977.
60. Ibid.
61. BStU, OTS 1977. Lonely Planet Guides. *Cuba*. Melbourne, Oakland, London: Lonely Planet Publications, 2000, p. 219.
62. BStU, OTS 1977.
63. Ibid. fol. 23–24.
64. Ibid. fol. 97.
65. Ibid.
66. Ibid. references throughout the file.
67. Ibid.
68. OTS, 1978, fol. 102 and OTS 622.
69. BStU, OTS 1977. Fol . 62; OTS 2038, 19 February 1975.
70. "Dirección General de Inteligencia (DGI). General Intelligence Directorate Ministry of the Interior." FAS Intelligence Resource Program. www.fas.org/irp/world/cuba/dgi/index.html; also GlobalSecurity.org. p. 2. www.globalsecurity.org/intell/world/cuba/dgi.htm.
71. BStU, OTS, 1977.

72. See, for example: Gary Marx. "Cuba Arrests More Dissidents, Vows to Put Them on Trial." *Chicago Tribune*, 20 March 2003.

73. See John O. Koehler. *Stasi: The Untold Story of the East German Secret Police*. Boulder: Westview Press, 1999, pp. 297–310 for background information on the Stasi's support of the Nicaraguan Revolution. For specifics on spy technology see BStU, OTS, 1302.

74. Ibid. p. 302.

75. BStU, OTS 1302.

76. Ibid.

77. Ibid.

78. Ibid.

79. Ibid.

80. BStU, OTS 618.

81. BStU, MfS, XXII, 658/2, fol. 137–38.

82. BStU, XXII, 5836. Fol. 55. Fol. 97 for explosive socks.

83. Ibid. fol. 118.

84. BStU, AGM, 484, fol. 19 for quote. See Thomas Auerbach. *Einsatzkommandos an der unsichtbaren Front: Terror- and Sabotagevorbereitungen des MfS gegen die Bundesrepublik Deutschland*. Berlin: Ch. Links Verlag, 1999.

85. Ibid. BStU, XXII, 658/2, fol. 7.

86. Auerbach. *Einsatzkommandos an der unsichtbaren Front*. p. 15.

87. The author visited this site with David Crawford in the summer of 2000.

88. BStU, MfS, XXII, 5836. Whole file is on the training of the technical "service area 2."

89. Ibid. fol. 76.

90. "Oma im Altkader." *Der Spiegel*, 24/1990, pp. 86–89. James D. Denton and Peter Schweizer. "Murdering SDI." *National Review*, July 31, 1987, pp. 37–39. Jeremy Paxman and Robert Harris. *A Higher Form of Killing: The Secret Story of Chemical and Biological Warfare*. New York: Random House, 2002, pp. 200–02.

91. Wolfgang Welsch. *Ich war Staatsfeind Nr. 1*. Frankfurt: Eichborn, 2001, pp. 294–367.

92. "Interim Report: Alleged Assassination Plots Involving Foreign Leaders," 94–465. 1975, p. 72. Church Committee Report.

93. BStU, Arbeitsbereich Neiber, Nr. 250. "Final Report on Research Topic 'Studies on Chemical Substances with Criminal Relevance.'" 19 September 1988.

94. Langdon Winner. *The Whale and the Reactor: A Search for Limits in an Age of High Technology*. Chicago: University of Chicago Press, 1986, pp. 19–39.

Chapter 8: Communicating Secrets

1. Visit to BKA on 3 May 1999 and June 2000.

2. Federal Prosecutor, Karlsruhe, Germany. Trial Judgment on Joachim and Gisela Preuß, 1994.

3. Heinz Vielan and Manfred Schell. *Verrat in Bonn*. Berlin: Ullstein, 1978, pp. 185–253. *Die lautlose Macht: Geheimdienste nach dem Zweiten Weltkrieg*. Vol. 2. Stuttgart: Verlag das Beste, 1985, pp. 149–63.

4. Ibid.
5. Vielan and Schell. *Verrat in Bonn.* pp. 189–92, 198–204, 209–16, 223–29.
6. *Die lautlose Macht.* Vol. 1, pp. 123–47.
7. Gabriele Gast. *Kundschafterin des Friedens: 17 Jahre Topspionin der DDR beim BND.* Frankfurt: Eichborn, 1999, pp. 21, 260.
8. BStU, GVS MfS 008 – Nr. 1002/68, p. 29. Richtlinie 2/68 des Ministers für Staatssicherheit. Also reprinted in Helmut Müller-Engbers, ed. *Inoffizielle Mitarbeiter des Ministerium für Staatssicherheit.* Teil 2. Berlin: Ch. Links, 1998, pp. 373–74.
9. Ibid.
10. Ibid.
11. BStU, JHS, MF 286. Höferer. "Analysis of TBK's in the BND's Communication System with its Agents in the GDR and Some Political-Operational Tasks to Penetrate the Communication System." Bachelor's Thesis. 1966.
12. BStU, JHS, Microfilm Z 243/58 "Container." Lecture 1958, OTS 1476, fol. 73 and JHS, MfS 160, Nr. 23/70. Gerhard Müller. "The Place of Operational Technology in Communication between the Area of Operations and the Center." Bachelor's Thesis. 1970. p. 22.
13. Ibid. "Container."
14. BStU, OTM, 1979 VVS, MfS 19 A 4/79 p. 35 of text.
15. BStU, OTS 778, fol. 39. OTS 1756 and OTS 1808, p. 33.
16. Werner Stiller. *Im Zentrum der Spionage.* Mainz: V. Hase & Koehler, 1986, p. 241.
17. BStU, OTS 1476, p. 76.
18. Müller. "The Place of Operational Technology." p. 6.
19. Marianne Quoirin. *Agentinnen aus Liebe.* Frankfurt: Eichborn, 1999, p. 80. Klaus Wagner. Bearbeitet von Guido Korte. *Spionageprozesse. Spionagemethoden des MfS (HVA) und östlicher (u.a. KGB) sowie nahöstlicher Nachrichtendienste in den Jahren 1977–1990.* Bruhl bei Köln: Fachhochschule des Bundes für öffentliche Verwaltung, Fachbereich Öffentliche Sicherheit, 2000.
20. Gast. *Kundschafterin des Friedens.* p. 243.
21. BStU, OTS 1808, fol. 33. OTS 1587, p. 43.
22. BStU, BV Gera, Abt. XV/0277, OTM, pp. 47–60 of text.
23. BStU, OTS 1462–1464, 2151.
24. Gerhard Müller case. Judgement. Oberlandesgericht Stuttgart, Dr. Gerhard. M. 1993.
25. Ibid.
26. For example, Gerhard Müller describes this process.

Chapter 9: Secret Writing Revealed

1. Gabriele Gast. *Kundschafterin des Friedens: 17 Jahre Topspionin der DDR beim BND.* Frankfurt am Main: Eichborn, 1999, p. 23. Former colleague confidential interview with the author, 2000.
2. Friedrich W. Schlomann. *Die Maulwürfe.* Munich: Universitas, 1993, p. 139.
3. Gast. *Kundschafterin des Friedens.* p. 87.

4. Ibid.
5. Ibid. p. 88.
6. Mark S. Zaid, Director James Madison Project. Press Release. "U.S. District Court Rules that World War I German Invisible Ink Formulas Must Still Remain Hidden from the Public." 14 February 2002. www.jamesmadison.edu.
7. Benjamin B. Fischer. "The Central Intelligence Agency's Office of Technical Service, 1951–2001: Celebrating Fifty Years of Technical Support to US Foreign Intelligence Operations." Brochure, p. 20.
8. Dan Tyler Moore and Martha Waller. *Cloak and Cipher*. Indianapolis and New York: Bobbs-Merrill Company, 1962, p. 204.
9. Department 32.
10. BStU, MfS OTS, 788. Positions in Department 34. Fol. 58–61. Department 34/*Referat* 2 and 4 developed new secret writing, whereas *Referat* 1 and 5 analyzed enemy secret writing.
11. BStU. Roland Wiedmann. *Die Organisationsstruktur des Ministerium für Staatssicherheit 1989*. Berlin: BStU, 1996, pp. 334–35. Counterintelligence was Department II; investigations were in Department IX.
12. Benjamin B. Fischer. "Celebrating Fifty Years." p. 19.
13. BStU, OTS, 1808, "Distributed operational-technical means and methods." 1972. Schmidt to Scholz, 13 March 1973. Fol. 6.
14. See Kristie Macrakis, Ryan D. Sweeder, and Elizabeth K. Bell. "Invisible Ink Revealed: Concept, Context and Catalysis." Sigma Xi Meeting, Detroit, November 2006. Professor Ryan Sweeder is a chemist, and two honors students, Elizabeth Bell and Kevin Kalinowski, are experimenting with the project.
15. BStU, OTS 2271. "Rules on using the secret writing database." 28.12.1987. Although I ordered information on the actual secret writing database, I only received these instructions.
16. BStU, OTS 2428. Procedure 41601 – 002. MfS 218. Nr. B 38/77.
17. BStU, OTS 670. "Instructions for Substance Pulverization and Preparation." 29 December 1965. Fol. 2–3. "Production of Secret Writing Paper by Spraying Suspensions and Solutions." 20 December 1965. Fol. 4–5.
18. BStU, OTS 670. "Making copy paper by rubbing a substance." Fol. 7–8. "Making copy paper through rolling a substance." Fol. 10–11.
19. BStU, OTS 2428 has material archived in 1977.
20. BStU, OTS 314. "Method 438." Fol. 180–82.
21. BStU, OTS 670. "Secret Message Follow-up Treatment with Steam." Fol. 13–14.
22. BStU, MfS, JHS, MF, GVS 66/73. Hans-Jürgen Kastner. "Representation and Research on the Influence of Operational Tactical and Organizational Measures as well as the Quality of the Training of the IM to Maintain Secrecy when Passing on Operational Information with Secret Writing." BV Magdeburg, SR E. 31 December 1973.
23. Ibid. Data pieced together from appendix. See also pp. 6, 9.
24. Ibid. pp. 6–7
25. Ibid. pp. 12–14.
26. Ibid. Instruction in appendix, p. 129.

27. See H. O. Nolan. *The Production and Detection of Messages in Concealed Writing and Images*. Publication no. 50. Geneva, Ill.: Riverbank Laboratories, 1918, p. 5. The publication is copyright by George Fabyan, the benefactor and director of the lab. I would like to thank H. Keith Melton for providing me with a copy of this rare publication and David Kahn for providing me with the author's name, as it was not on the title page.

28. BStU, MfS, OTS, 2242.

29. David Kahn. *The Codebreakers: The Comprehensive History of Secret Communication from Ancient Times to the Internet*. New York: Scribner, 1967, 1996, pp. 370–74.

30. H. O. Nolan. *The Production and Detection of Messages in Concealed Writing and Images*.

31. BStU, OTS 1594 and 1597.

32. BStU, OTS, 1808, "Distributed Operational-Technical Means and Methods." 1972. Schmidt to Scholz, 13 March 1973. Fol. 73.

33. BStU, OTS 2408. Fol. 58.

34. BStU, OTS 975. Instructions on how to use the "Nyom" instrument prepared in 1981. MfS 218. Nr. B 49/81. In 1980 the machine was called "Kristall."

35. BStU, OTS 2408. Yearly reports on secret writing between 1979 and 1983.

36. BStU, OTS 310, 314, and 2428.

37. BStU, OTS 1297. Fol. 1–204. Here fol. 7. "Development of a Method for the Isolation, Preparations and Analysis of Organic Substances." 30 December 1976. This report was developed by Department 32.

38. BStU, OTS 2408. Fol. 58.

39. Erich Schmidt-Eenboom. *Schnüffler ohne Nase: Der BND – die unheimliche Macht im Staate*. Düsseldorf: Econ Verlag, 1993, pp. 260–61.

40. BStU, OTS 822. "Information on Results from the Uncovering of the US Secret Services Secret Writing Material." November 1988. Fol. 43–44.

41. David Kahn. *The Codebreakers*. pp. 515, 524.

42. Sylvia de Pasquale. "Ich hoffe, daß die Post auch ankommt." In Joachim Kallinich and Sylvia de Pasquale, eds. *Ein Offenes Geheimnis: Post- und Telephonkontrolle in der DDR*. Berlin: Museumsstiftung Post und Telekommunikation, 2002, p. 63 (catalogue to the exhibit).

43. BStU, JHS, Nr. 313/89. Wolfgang Jatzlau. "Examination of the Historical Development of Department M in the 70s." 3 March 1989. Fol. 45.

44. Ibid.

45. BStU, OTS 2038, fol. 57.

46. Wolfgang Jatzlau. "Examination of the Historical Development of Department M." fol. 46–47.

47. Ibid. OTS 2408. Fol. 59. Report on activities of the secret writing department.

48. BStU, OTS 1594, 1696, 2006 for samples of technical investigations.

49. Wolfgang Jatzlau. "Examination of the Historical Development of Department M." fol. 17–18.

50. Helmut Wagner. *Schöne Grüße aus Pullach: Operationen des BND gegen die DDR*. Berlin: Das Neue Berlin, 2001, pp. 127–28.

51. Ibid. pp. 128–29.

52. Ibid. fol. 19–20. See also Jaztlau, fol. 17–18.
53. Ibid. fol. 21. For OTS success at identifying the secret writing material see OTS 2408, fol. 96.
54. See Chapter 3. OTS 2408, fol. 58, 79.
55. Benjamin B. Fischer. "Celebrating Fifty Years."
56. Ibid. p. 20.

Chapter 10: Eye Spy

1. Michel Foucault. *Discipline and Punish*, trans. A. Sheridan. New York: Vintage, 1979, pp. 195ff., esp. p. 214. Robert Gellately. "Denunciation in Twentieth-Century Germany: Aspects of Self-Policing in the Third Reich and the German Democratic Republic." In Sheila Fitzpatrick and Robert Gellately, eds. *Accusatory Practices: Denunciation in Modern European History, 1789–1989*. Chicago: University of Chicago Press, 1997, pp. 185–221.
2. B. Gertig and R. Schädlich. *Lehrbuch für Kriminalisten*. Berlin: Verlag für Fachliteratur der Volkspolizei, 1956, pp. 437–38.
3. Ibid. pp. 438–64.
4. BStU, JHS, Z 46/52. "Department XII Lecture." 1.8.1952.
5. BStU, Roland Wiedmann. *Die Organisationsstruktur des Ministeriums für Staatssicherheit*, 1989. Berlin: BStU, 1995, p. 257.
6. www.bstu.de/mfs/werwar/cd.htm. Dissertation title from BStU, pamphlet with lists of dissertations at the MfS's Law School.
7. BStU, VIII, 6677, fol. 36. Karli Coburger and Peter Rauscher. "Operative Ermittlung und Beobachtung." In Reinhard Grimmer et al., eds. *Die Sicherheit: Zur Abwehrarbeit des MfS*. Band 1. Berlin: Edition Ost, 2002, p. 384.
8. BStU, Hochschule, *Wörterbuch der politische-operativen Arbeit*. Potsdam, 1985, "Beobachtung, operative," p. 53.
9. BStU, VIII, 6677, fol. 107.
10. Ibid.
11. Ibid.
12. Ibid.
13. Ibid.
14. Stasi Museum, Normannenstrasse.
15. http://www.robot-camera.de/ROBOT_Historie/body_robot_historie.html. Ivor Matanle. *Collecting and Using Classic Cameras*. London: Thames and Hudson, 1986, p. 18.
16. H. Keith Melton. *The Ultimate Spy Book*. London: DK Publishing, 1996, p. 64.
17. BStU, JHS, MF, GVS 121/81. Holger Natho. "The Qualified Use of Specific Photographic Means and Methods in Operational Observation and the Further Qualified Laboratory Process as an Essential Part of the Acquisition of Material for Photo-Documentation in the Process of Operational Observation of Line VIII." Trade School Thesis. 5 March 1981. p. 11.
18. Ibid. p. 62 and Michael Pritchard and Douglas St. Denny. *Spy Camera*. London: Classic Collection Publications, 1993, pp. 82–83.

19. BStU, JHS, D 770. Siegmar Grumbd. "The Acquisition of Recognition Information for Operationally Interesting People on the basis of the Political-operational use of Criminalistic Photography." BV Frankfurt. 15 July 1968, p. 25.
20. Michael Pritchard and Douglas St. Denny. *Spy Camera*. p. 83.
21. Ibid.
22. Holger Natho. "The Qualified Use of Specific Photographic Means and Methods." p. 26.
23. H. Keith Melton. *The Ultimate Spy Book*. p. 66.
24. BStU, JHS, D 770. Siegmar Grumbd. "The acquisition of recognition information." p. 25.
25. BStU, OTS 361, fol. 9.
26. Ibid.
27. Detlev Vreisleben. "Die Geräuscharme Spiegelreflexkamera (GSK)." *Photodeal*, II/2001, pp. 28–29.
28. BStU, VIII, 1691/3.
29. BStU, OTS 361.
30. BStU, OTS 918–919: Plans and Blueprints.
31. BStU, VIII/1691/3.
32. BStU, VIII/6022. "Innovators' Suggestion," pp. 2–3.
33. BStU, VIII/6347. File on photography training.
34. I would like to thank H. Keith Melton for sending me a picture of this concealment. See the second edition of his *The Ultimate Spy Book* for a photograph (p. 76).
35. This whole section is based on BStU, MfS, BV Suhl, Abteilung VIII, 415. Fol. 1–28.
36. The observation targets emerge through a reading of many files from Department VIII for observation and investigations. In particular, VIII, 6677 was useful. See also Karli Coburger and Peter Rauscher. "Operative Ermittlung und Beobachtung." pp. 384–413.
37. BStU, MfS, XV/3339/73. "Reiner Bergmann."
38. BStU, JHS, Grabs.
39. BStU, JHS 425, Kullik.
40. BStU, JHS, MF 286. Höferer. "Analysis of TBK's in the BND's Communication System with its Agents in the GDR and Some Political-Operational Tasks to Penetrate the Communication System." Bachelor's Thesis. 1966.
41. BStU, VIII, AKG 1729/1, fol. 387.
42. John A. Fahey. *Licensed to Spy*. Annapolis, Md.: Naval Institute Press, 2002, p. 2.
43. Ibid. p. 5.
44. This figure from Karin Hartewig. *Das Auge der Partei: Fotographie und Staatssicherheit*. Berlin: Ch. Links Verlag, 2004, p. 80.
45. Ibid. p. 83.
46. John A. Fahey. *Licensed to Spy*.
47. Former MfS officer responsible for military liaison missions in the Cottbus district office interview. Brochure produced by the Allied Museum in Berlin for an exhibit about the military missions, "Mission Accomplished:

the Military Liaison Missions of the Western Forces in Potsdam from 1946–1990." Berlin, 2004, p. 92.

48. BStU, VIII/6479. Picture Report, 5 November 1975. Fol. 1–30. Regional Office Rostock.

49. BStU, Roland Wiedmann. *Die Organisationsstruktur des Ministeriums für Staatssicherheit.*

50. For biographical information see Dieter Hoffmann. "Robert Havemann: Antifascist, Communist, Dissident." In Kristie Macrakis and Dieter Hoffmann, eds. *Science under Socialism: East Germany in Comparative Perspective.* Cambridge: Harvard University Press, 1999, pp. 269–85.

51. Karin Hartewig. *Das Auge der Partei.* pp. 100–01.

52. Ibid. pp. 127–29.

53. A cartoon of this kind is featured in "Liebe öffnet jeden Tresor." *Der Spiegel,* 9/1991, pp. 84–94.

54. Ibid. p. 90.

55. Ian Fleming. *From Russia with Love.* New York: Penguin Edition, 2003, p. 82.

56. Wilhelm Dietl. "Flotte Moni von der Stasi." *Focus,* 28, 1997, pp. 64–68.

57. BStU, BV Dresden, Nr. 2086, pp. 3–10.

58. "Hauptnahe Bezüge." *Der Spiegel,* 37/1989, p. 21. See also Uta Falck. *VEB Bordell: Geschichte der Prostitution in der DDR.* Berlin: Ch. Links Verlag, 1998, p. 113.

59. BStU, VIII/2026, fol. pp. 206–52. 23 November 1984 Report.

60. Ibid.

61. Ibid.

62. Personal visit. See also the Westin Grand Hotel website: www.westingrand.com.

63. BStU, VIII/2026, fol. 206–52.

64. Trade school papers written at the Law School in Potsdam. See especially, BStU, JHS, Gerhard Wresch. "Problems Applying Photography and Demands on Photographic Documentation in the Area of Official Searches from the View of One Department." 14 August 1974.

65. Ibid. p. 12.

66. Ibid. pp. 8–9.

67. Ibid. pp. 17–18.

68. Ibid. pp. 23–24.

69. This section is based on the educational film made by the Stasi "Revisor" 1985 and BStU, AOP 2687/85 (website www.bstu.de). For a facsimile of a page from the search see Jens Giesecke. *Die DDR-Staatssicherheit: Schild und Schwert der Partei.* Berlin: Bundeszentrale für politische Bildung, 2002, p. 74.

70. BStU, Ast. Gera, BV Gera, Abteilung 26 ZMA 0051.

71. Ibid.

72. This description is based on the made-for-TV documentary called *Spy vs. Spy,* narrated by Roger Moore and part of the SPY-TEK series shown on the Discovery Channel in 1999.

73. Ibid.

74. Hansjoachim Tiedge. *Der Überläufer.* Berlin: Das Neue Berlin, 1998, pp. 428–35.

75. Ibid.
76. Markus Wolf. *Man Without a Face: The Autobiography of Communism's Greatest Spymaster*. New York: Random House, 1997, pp. 198–203.

Chapter 11: Big Ears

1. Horst Männchen interview with the author, May 2003. BStU, JHS, Horst Männchen. "Problems Applying Specific Technical-Physical Means and Methods through the MfS in the Counterintelligence and Intelligence of Electronic Warfare in the Class Struggle between Imperialism and Socialism." 1974.
2. Benjamin B. Fischer. "'One of the Biggest Ears in the World': East German SIGINT Operations." *International Journal of Intelligence and Counterintelligence*, 11, 1998, no. 2, pp. 142–53.
3. John M. Carroll. *Secrets of Electronic Espionage*. New York: E. P. Dutton, 1966, pp. 15–16.
4. Ibid. p. 23.
5. BStU, Order, 1956.
6. BStU, ZAIG, 18,533, fol. 2.
7. BStU, OTS 763. Horst Männchen interview with the author, May 2003.
8. BStU, OTS 361, OTS 2166.
9. BStU, OTS 763. Horst Männchen. "Funkelektronische Abwehr und Aufklärung (HA III im MfS und Abt. III der BV)." In Reinhard Grimmer, Werner Irmler, Willi Opitz, and Wolfgang Schwanitz, eds. *Die Sicherheit: Zur Abwehrarbeit des MfS*. Band 1. Berlin: Edition Ost, 2002, pp. 559–79. Here p. 562.
10. BStU, OTS 763.
11. Andreas Schmidt. "'Aufklärung' das Funkverkehrs und der Telephongespräche in Westdeutschland – Die Hauptabteilung III." In Hubertus Knabbe, ed. *West-Arbeit des MfS*. Berlin: Ch. Links Verlag, 1999, pp. 207–44. Here p. 208 for personnel chart.
12. Horst Männchen. "Funkelektronische Abwehr und Aufklärung (HA III im MfS und Abt. III der BV)." p. 561.
13. BStU, OTS, 763.
14. Ibid. Fols. 91–92.
15. Ibid.
16. Männchen. "Funkelektronische Abwehr und Aufklärung (HA III im MfS und Abt. III der BV)." OTS, 763.
17. BStU, OTS, 763.
18. Ibid.
19. BStU, OTS 1474. "Strategy 2000" report on technology for radio counterintelligence. Fol. 59.
20. Ibid.
21. Erich Schmidt-Eenboom. "The Bundesnachrichtendienst, the Bundeswehr and Sigint in the Cold War and After." *Intelligence and National Security*, 16, no. 1, 2001, pp. 129–76. Here p. 132.
22. Ibid. p. 131.
23. Ibid. p. 132.

24. Ibid. p. 133.
25. Ibid. pp. 134–35.
26. James Bamford. *The Puzzle Palace*. New York: Penguin Books, 1982, pp. 105–06.
27. Erich Schmidt-Eenboom. "The Bundesnachrichtendienst."
28. BStU, III 15,220. 9 March 1967. First Acting Director to the Minister to Head of Department I. Fol. 3.
29. "Wolfgang Berg" is a fictitious, composite portrait. BStU, III/11,682. 24 October 1985.
30. BStU, III/7974. Handwritten notes on lecture on Dossier Work. 22 June 1982.
31. Ibid. and Jürgen Schreiber. "Belauschter Altkanzler." *Tagesspiegel*, 10 April 2000.
32. Wolfgang Krach and Georg Mascolo. "So viele leckere Sachen." *Der Spiegel*, 14/2000, pp. 22–25. Here p. 25.
33. In 1990 two *Quick* journalists obtained dossiers and other material from Department III and published them in a four-part series in *Quick*: Heiner Emde and Paul Limbach. "z.B. Wörner: Auch hörten sie mit . . ." *Quick*, vol. 19, 1990, pp. 12–16.
34. Heiner Emde and Paul Limbach. "Angst vor PDS: Wahlkampf mit den Stasi-Akten?" *Quick*, vol. 23, 1990, pp. 38–41.
35. BStU, III/7974.
36. Heiner Emde and Paul Limbach. "Stasi knackte sogar BND-Tresor." *Quick*, vol. 21, 1990, pp. 26–32.
37. Ibid. pp. 28–29.
38. Ibid.
39. Heiner Emde and Paul Limbach. "Rüstungsriese MBB abgehört." *Quick*, vol. 24, 1990, pp. 40–43, 46.
40. Ibid. pp. 43, 46.
41. Ibid. p. 46.
42. Horst Männchen interview with the author, 31 May 2003.
43. BStU, Horst Männchen Cadre File.
44. BStU, Horst Männchen Cadre File, fol. 23–24.
45. BStU, III 15,220.
46. BStU, IIII/11,788. "Order Nr. 1/83 on the creation of HA III."
47. Andreas Schmidt. "'Aufklärung' das Funkverkehrs und der Telephonge-spräche in Westdeutschland." p. 208 (table) for lower figure. Männchen. "Funkelektronische Abwehr und Aufklärung (HA III im MfS und Abt. III der BV)." p. 573.
48. BStU, MfS, III/10, 593.
49. BStU, MfS III/10, 593, Männchen to Department of Finance, 5 January 1972.
50. Andreas Kabus. *Auftrag Windrose: der militärische Geheimdienst der DDR*. Berlin: Verlag Neues Leben, 1993, p. 141. Bodo Wegmann. "Die Aufklärung der Nationalen Volksarmee." In Georg Herbstritt and Helmut Müller-Engbers, eds. *Das Gesicht dem Westen zu . . . DDR-Spionage gegen die Bundesrepublik*. Bremen: Edition Temmen, 2003, pp. 215–23.
51. BStU, III/10, 593. Fol. 96, 99.
52. BStU, JHS, Horst Männchen. "Problems Applying Specific Technical-Physical Means and Methods."

53. Thorsten Schmidt and Jürgen Korsch. *Der Brocken: Berg zwischen Natur und Technik*. Wernigorode: Schmidt-Buck-Verlag, 1992. Description based on a visit.
54. www.lostplaces.de/brocken.
55. BStU, OTS 1474. "Strategy 2000: Prognostic-Conceptual Statements for the Chief Area of Technology for Tasks of Special Information Gathering." 30 August 1988. Fol. 30–31.
56. Männchen interview with the author, May 2003.
57. BStU, III 15,220.
58. BStU, III/585, Fol. 1–61. See also Andreas Schmidt's excellent chapter: "'Aufklärung' das Funkverkehrs und der Telephongespräche in Westdeutschland – Die Hauptabteilung III."
59. Ibid.
60. Ibid.
61. Ibid.
62. Ibid.
63. BStU, MfS, III, 11,669. Männchen to Schwanitz, 22 January 1987. Fols. 71–73. The machine cost 540,000 DM.
64. BStU, III/13,732. Fol. 237 ff. Letters on Saphir A/2 project. MfS, XVIII/9524, 11, 888, 13, 602.
65. Ibid.
66. BStU, III/15, 166. Fols. 169 ff.
67. Cf. Andreas Schmidt. "'Aufklärung' das Funkverkehrs und der Telephongespräche in Westdeutschland – Die Hauptabteilung III." pp. 231–32. BStU, III/248, 13, 732, 11,788. Fol. 26, 248, fol. 308.
68. BStU, III/13, 732. vol. 1. Fol. 5–30 and III/248.
69. BStU, III/13,732, fol. 46–51.
70. Ibid.
71. Ibid. fol. 30–44.
72. BStU, III/13, 732, vol. 2. Fol. 71–77, 91–94.
73. BStU, III/11,682, fols. 36–39.
74. Ibid. Fol. 108–12.
75. BStU, MfS, HA III/13,725. Fol. 31ff.
76. Schmidt. "'Aufklärung' das Funkverkehrs und der Telephongespräche in Westdeutschland – Die Hauptabteilung III." p. 212.
77. BStU, III/14,455. Hartmut Heiliger. "The Enemy's Potential in Radio/Electronic Intelligence in West Berlin." JHS, Potsdam, Trade School Thesis, 1986.
78. Ibid.
79. Ibid. Fol. 12–13.
80. BStU, III/13,732. Markus Wolf to Neiber, 3 March 1985. Fol. 131–33.
81. Ibid.
82. Horst Männchen interview with the author, May 2003.
83. BStU, MfS, III/13, 732. 10 July 1985. Information on System "Bowling Pin." Fol. 173–77.
84. Milt Bearden and James Risen. *The Main Enemy*. New York: Random House, 2003, pp. 386–87. Horst Männchen interview with the author, May 2003.

85. Quoted in an unpublished working paper with no reference: Gerhard Ehlert, Jochen Staadt, and Tobias Voigt. "Die Zusammenarbeit zwischen dem Ministerium für Staatssichherheit der DDR (MfS) und dem Ministerium des Innern Kubas (MININT)." Arbeitspapiere des Forschungsverbundes SED-Staat. Nr. 32/2002. Berlin, June 2002, p. 5.

86. Mention of CIA agent communication method in BStU, III, 9, 10, 229, 319, 11,788, 13,730, 15,166 at least. For Mielke meeting see III/11,788, 2 February 1983 notes.

87. BStU, III/11,788, 9 February 1983.

88. Ibid.

89. Ibid.

90. BStU, III/229 and 319.

91. Ibid.

92. Ibid. and III/15,166.

93. BStU, III/15,166.

94. Ibid.

Chapter 12: Smell Science

1. Citizen's Movement Leipzig, ed. *STASI Intern: Macht und Banalität.* Leipzig: Forum Verlag, 2001, p. 147.

2. Adee Schoon and Ruud Haak. *Suspect Discrimination: Training and Practicing Scent Identification Line-Ups.* Calgary, Canada: Detselig Enterprises, 2002, pp. 11–15.

3. William G. Syrotuck. *Scent and the Scenting Dog.* New York: Arner, 1972, pp. 13–14.

4. "Spezialschule für Polizeischutzhunde." *Berliner Zeitung.* 2 July 1983. Found in BStU, HA VII, 3553. Fol. 44.

5. BStU, VII/426.

6. BStU, VII/426. 14 March 1989. "Conception for Service Dogs at the MfS."

7. Ibid. Fols. 12–13.

8. BStU, JHS/MF/VVS 235/75. Werner Wollarz. "Possibilities and Preconditions for Using Tracking Dogs in the Process of Operational Observation of People to Investigate Operationally Relevant Activities." 14 January 1975.

9. Ibid. passim.

10. Ibid. p. 6.

11. Ibid. p. 4.

12. Ibid. passim.

13. Ibid.

14. BStU, OTS 806, 21 May 1974. Business Trip Report. Department 34. Fol. 307–12.

15. BStU, JHS/MF/VVS 235/75. Werner Wollarz. "Possibilities and Preconditions for Using Tracking Dogs in the Process of Operational Observation of People to Investigate Operationally Relevant Activities." 14 January 1975.

16. BStU, BdL/Dok. Nr. 007785. "On Using Smell Differentiation to Fight Crime." Ministry of the Interior. 13 December 1973.

17. Walter Derda. "The Identification of Traces through the Method of Securing, Conserving and Differentiating Smell Traces. The Differentiation of Smell Conserves through Differentiation Dogs." *Hochschule der Deutschen Volkspolizei "Karl Liebknecht."* Bachelor's Thesis. Berlin. 1983.

18. BStU, BdL/Dok. Nr. 007785. "On Using Smell Differentiation for Fighting Crime." Ministry of the Interior. 13 December 1973. The sneaker analogy is my own.

19. Ibid. pp. 14–15.

20. Ibid. pp. 12–13.

21. Ibid. pp. 16–17.

22. Ibid. p. 23.

23. BStU, JHS-Nr. 780/81. Manfred Brauner. "Applying a Criminalistic Method – Smell Differentiation – to Solve the MfS's Political-Operational Tasks." BV Leipzig, Department XX. 3 February 1982.

24. BStU, Manfred Brauner Cadre File.

25. Ibid.

26. Ibid. 25 May 1980.

27. BStU, MfS, JHS-Nr. 780/81. Manfred Brauner. "Applying a Criminalistic Method."

28. Ibid.

29. Ibid. p. 7, 47.

30. Ibid. pp. 34–36.

31. Ibid. pp. 35–36.

32. Ibid. p. 37.

33. Ibid.

34. Hans Girod. *Das Ekel von Rahnsdorf und andere spektakuläre Mordfälle aus der DDR.* Munich: Knauer, 1999, pp. 82–100.

35. Udo Grashoff. *Erhöhter Vorkommnisanfall: Aktionen nach der Bierman-Ausbürgerung im Bezirk Halle. Eine Dokumentation.* Halle: Zeit-Geschichte e.V.- Verein für erlebte Geschichte, 2001.

36. Ibid. p. 37.

37. Ibid. p. 39.

38. Ibid. p. 11.

39. BStU, JHS-Nr. 780/81. Manfred Brauner. "Applying a Criminalistic Method." pp. 33–34. See also the cadre file for his bonuses relating to this case.

40. Friedo Schmidt. *Verbrecherspur und Polizeihund.* Augsburg: SV, 1910.

41. Adee Schoon and Ruud Haak. *Suspect Discrimination.* pp. 25–38.

42. See, for example: http://www.polizei-minden.de/hunde/gs_hund.htm and http://polizeistuttgart.de/index.php?option=com_content&task=view&id=129&Itemid=78&limit=1&limitstart=3.

Chapter 13: Spy Dust

1. Christopher Andrew and Vasili Mitrokhin. *The Sword and the Shield: The Mitrokhin Archive and the Secret History of the KGB.* New York: Basic Books, p. 185.

2. W. Stedry. "Chemische Fangstoffe." *Kriminalistik*, 1960, pp. 204–07.
3. For representative *Kriminalistik* articles see: KTI Berlin, "Farbstoffe zur Überführung von Dieben." *Kriminalistik*, 1940, p. 82; Wilhelm Gerdau. "Anwendung fluoreszierender Fangstoffe." *Kriminalistik*, 1957, *11*, pp. 441–42; Dr. Max Frei and R. Schönbächler. "Erfahrungen mit Diebesfallen bei der Entwendung von Treibstoffen." *Kriminalistik*, 1958, *12*, pp. 365–67; Dr. M. Frei and Dr. J. Meier. "Neue Fangstoff." *Kriminalistik*, 1959, *13*, pp. 514–15; Richard Götz. "Anwendung von Fangmitteln für Diebesfallen." *Kriminalistik*, 1959, *13*, pp. 194–98; W. Stedry. "Chemische Fangstoffe." *Kriminalistik*, 14, pp. 204–07, 1960; and Ernst Setzepfand. "Übertragung von Fangmitteln auf Unschuldige." *Kriminalistik*, 1961, *15*, p. 450.
4. Herbert Schicht and Josef Wichtill. "Radioaktive Isotope im Dienste der Kriminalistik." *Schriftenreihe der DVP*, 1961, pp. 392–400.
5. Ernst Ronai. "Gammastrahlen als Fangmittel bei Diebsfallen." *Kriminalistik*, 6, 1966.
6. Ibid.
7. Ibid.
8. Erich Schock. "Gammastrahlen – neue Möglichkeiten bei Diebesfallen." *Kriminalistik*, 1975, 29, pp. 220–21.
9. George S. McWatters, ed. *Detectives of Europe and America or Life in the Secret Service*. Hartford: J. B. Burr, 1877, p. 619.
10. F. G. Tryhorn and E. E. Widdowson. "Identification of Objects by Radioactive Labeling." *The Police Journal*, *13*, 1940, pp. 45–52. For the history of the Criminal Investigation Department and Tryhorn's "scientific aid" courses, see www.lincs.police.uk/history/history16.shtml.
11. Ibid.
12. "A Method for Tracing Stolen Gasoline." *FBI Law Enforcement Bulletin*, January 1945, vol. 14, no. 1, pp. 3–5. This article is reprinted from 1939.
13. See reference in Jennet Conant. *Tuxedo Park*. New York: Simon & Schuster, 2002, pp. 173–75.
14. See "Detective Dyes, Fluorescent Powders and Radioactive Detectors." In Charles E. O'Hara and James W. Osterburg, eds. *An Introduction to Criminalistics: The Application of the Physical Sciences to the Detection of Crime*, 1949 (reprinted 1963), pp. 373–83 (ch. 28).
15. Lynn Poole. *Science, the Super Sleuth*. New York: Whittlesey House, 1954.
16. BStU, MfS, Cadre File. Franz Leuteritz.
17. Ibid.
18. Ibid.
19. BStU, MfS, OTS 1535, 1 December 1972, fol. 143.
20. This information comes from reading about a dozen OTS files.
21. BStU, OTS 2242.
22. BStU, OTS 2278, fol. 38.
23. Based on a list in OTS 2346, fol. 108.
24. BStU, OTS 2277.
25. BStU, OTS 2349, 2241, 2278.
26. Ibid.
27. BStU, OTS 2241, fol. 3.

28. BStU, OTS 2242. Karl Jantsch file: 1169/90. Dresden.

29. BStU, OTS 2350, "Investigations on Extensive Use of Radiation Relays for Solving Political-Operational Problems." Dr. Leuteritz, 25 March 1974. Fol. 87.

30. Paul Rossi (health physicist, Michigan State University) interview with the author, 22 March 2001.

31. BStU, MfS, VIII/2026. Department VII for observation discussed the pros and cons.

32. BStU, OTS 2278, fol. 21.

33. BStU, OTS 2277.

34. BStU, OTS 2349, fol. 8.

35. BStU, OTS 2241, fol. 81.

36. BStU, OTS2278, fol. 161.

37. See Heribert Schwan. *Erich Mielke: Der Mann, der die Stasi war*. Munich: Knauer, 1997.

38. BStU, OTS 2245.

39. BStU, JHS, Nr. 176/84. Dieter Ganschow. "Using marking material to solve specific practical political-operational tasks in the MfS." October 1984. Fols. 25, 31.

40. BStU, Gera, AIM 180/85, I, 2, fol. 43.

41. BStU, JHS-Nr. 380/85. Gerd Isensee. "Basic operational demands and conditions for use of Marking Material for observations in the West." October 1985.

42. BStU, OTS 2242, fol. 150.

43. Ibid.

44. BStU, BV Gera, Archive Nr. 1014/88. OV "Bermuda." Also, OTS 927.

45. BStU, VIII/2131. "Report on Experiments at the Bornholmer Control Point using radioactive Marking Material." 26 July 1965. Fol. 2–14. Willi Pohl. "The Use of Radioactive Marking Material in Securing Known Dead Letter Drops in Traffic Between West Berlin and West Germany." Bachelor's Thesis. 1962. Fol. 15–48.

46. BStU, OTS 2342, fol. 32–33; 46–47. The hydrazine sulfate marking material was code-numbered 46401–022. For the chemical composition, use, and toxicity level of hydrazine sulfate see http://physchem.ox.ac.uk/MSDS/HY/hydrazine_sulfate.htm.

47. BStU, OTS 2390, fol. 20–21. 3 August 1982. General Major Kleine to General Major Schmidt.

48. BStU, JHS, MF 643. Günther Gräf. "On the Value of Marking Material as Scientific Proof when used Operationally." December 1967. p. 7.

49. BStU, Personnel Files Card for Christa Sabisch. OTS 2422. "Use of Contact Marking Material in the Central Operational File 'Operation II,'" fol. 342.

50. BStU, "ZOV Operation II." Archive Nr. 16170/9. Vol. 1.

51. Ibid.

52. Ibid. fol. 184 and 197.

53. Ibid.

54. Ibid.

55. BStU, Operation II. Archive Nr. 16170/91.

56. Ibid. Engelhardt Report 7 September 1987. XVIII, 7888, p. 2, Kleine to Schmidt, 23 August 1998.
57. Ibid.
58. See John Marks. *The Search for the "Manchurian Candidate": The CIA and Mind Control*. New York: W.W. Norton, 1991 (reprint of 1979 book) for the CIA's experimentation with mind control.

Index